P9-DDV-503

# GUATEMALA
# BELIZE

MICHELIN
Travel Publications

## Note to readers

To understand how the guide is organised, turn to the contents list on page 4.

Just one point here about the practical information. The chapters entitled "Practical Information" give general information to help you prepare your trip and get along once there. In the chapters "Exploring Guatemala" and "Exploring Belize", after each description of a town or tour itinerary there is a practical section (e.g. p 150 "Making the most of Antigua") giving all the information about the place in question: access, useful addresses, accommodation, eating out, other things to do, shopping guide, etc.

The tour itineraries described and shown on the maps give ideas for excursions off the beaten track; ■ indicates possible overnight halts. To organise your trip according to the number of days you have available, turn to the map of tour itineraries on p 110.

Hotels and restaurants are classed by price category (in US dollars) to help you plan your budget. However, we are obliged to point out that living costs vary constantly and opening hours may change, so that prices and practical information may have changed since publication.

Michelin Travel Publications
Published in 2000

# ◀N E⊙S▶

N ew – In the NEOS guides emphasis is placed on the discovery and enjoyment of a new destination through meeting the people, tasting the food and absorbing the exotic atmosphere. In addition to recommendations on which sights to see, we give details on the most suitable places to stay and eat, on what to look out for in traditional markets and where to go in search of the hidden character of the region, its crafts and its dancing rhythms. For those keen to explore places on foot, we provide guidelines and useful addresses in order to help organise walks to suit all tastes.

E xpert – The NEOS guides are written by people who have travelled in the country and researched the sites before recommending them by the allocation of stars. Accommodation and restaurants are similarly recommended by a 🏠 on the grounds of quality and value for money. Cartographers have drawn easy-to-use maps with clearly marked itineraries, as well as detailed plans of towns, archeological sites and large museums.

⊙ pen to all cultures, the NEOS guides provide an insight into the daily lives of the local people. In a world that is becoming ever more accessible, it is vital that religious practices, regional etiquette, traditional customs and languages be understood and respected by all travellers. Equipped with this knowledge, visitors can seek to share and enjoy with confidence the best of the local cuisine, musical harmonies and the skills involved in the production of arts and crafts.

S ensitive to the atmosphere and heritage of a foreign land, the NEOS guides encourage travellers to see, hear, smell and feel a country, through words and images. Take inspiration from the enthusiasm of our experienced travel writers and make this a journey full of discovery and enchantment.

# GUATEMALA

## Exploring Belize

# GUATEMALA

**Official name**: República de Guatemala
**Land area**: 108 890sqkm
**Population**: 12 000 000
**Capital**: Guatemala City
**Currency**: the quetzal

# Setting the scene

On the banks of
Lake Atitlán

# THE LAND AND ITS CLIMATE

The heart of the Maya region, Guatemala nestles like a piece of jigsaw puzzle between the Pacific Ocean and the Caribbean Sea. The meanders of the Río Usumacinta separate El Petén from Chiapas in Mexico while the Río Sarstún marks the border with Belize; to the southeast, beyond the mountains, is a wavering frontier with Honduras and El Salvador. To the north and east of El Petén, the country's borders are formed by disconcertingly straight lines joining at a right angle.

With its 108 890sqkm (83% of the surface area of England) and a population estimated at twelve million, this northernmost country of Central America is third in size after Nicaragua and Honduras. At its maximum it measures 540km north to south, and 430km east to west at its widest point. And yet this small land area embraces a wide variety of climates and landscapes, with a multitude of spectacular panoramic vistas. Because of the compact shape of the country, it is easy to discover its many facets by venturing out in different directions from a few large towns.

## A land of contrasts

Impetuous, moderate, violent, gentle, harsh and delicate, arid and luxuriant – Guatemala has many moods. Within a short distance, the cloud-flecked jungle of El Petén gives way to the rugged mountains of the Highlands, the near-desert valleys of Oriente to the Caribbean coastlands, Pacific plain to volcanic mountain range, and humid tropical heat to the cool of the mountain tops. Despite this diversity, however, the country can be roughly divided into two major zones, the Highlands and the Lowlands.

### The Highlands
*See map p 136.*
Nearly 60% of Guatemala consists of steep-sided mountains. In the middle, between the two great mountain ranges, are the **high plateaux**, ranging in altitude from 1 500m to 2 500m. This is Maya country, the most densely populated part of Guatemala, a succession of fertile valleys, arid, windswept plateaux, *barrancos* (ravines), forests, and hillsides divided into straight-edged fields. Most of the big towns – Guatemala City, Quetzaltenango, Huehuetenango and Antigua (the former capital) – are found in the Highlands, despite the risk of earthquakes and volcanic eruptions. For this is where the Pacific, Caribbean and North American tectonic plates meet, and the region is regularly shaken by **earthquakes** of varying severity. On some occasions a violent quake has changed the course of the country's history (*see p 138 "Antigua" and p 182 "Quetzaltenango"*). The most recent big one, in February 1976, caused 25 000 deaths and much material damage; Guatemala's recovery from it has been slow and painful.

The high plateaux are bounded to the south by a string of **volcanoes**, the continuation of the Sierra Madre in Mexico. Studded with some thirty cones, this range runs northwest to southeast across Guatemala, parallel with the Pacific coast. **Tajumulco** rears above the department of San Marcos in the west, at 4 220m the highest volcano in Central America. Next in height comes **Tacaná**

The land and its climate

(4 093m) on the Mexican border. The range stretches out, with peaks of 2 500m to 4 000m, in an uninterrupted succession of grandiose landscapes. Lake Atitlán offers some particularly striking views, with **Tolimán** (3 154m), **San Pedro** (3 020m) and **Atitlán** (3 537m). Most spectacular of all are the active volcanoes like **Santiaguito** (2 488m), which rises from the flanks of Santa María in the Quetzaltenango region. To the southwest of the capital rises the cone of **Pacaya** (2 552m), in continual eruption, with frequent explosions and impressive lava fountains when it is particularly active.

Another result of the region's volcanic activity lies in the many **hot springs** in the Highlands, such as the Fuentes Georginas, tucked away in enchanting surroundings near Quetzaltenango.

To the north, the highest **range of non-volcanic mountains** in Central America cuts across the country. This is the **Cuchumatanes range**, a continuation of Mexico's Meseta de Chiapas, peaking at 3 837m in the vicinity of Huehuetenango. Further east this range gradually loses height. As it approaches the corridor formed by the valley of the Río Polochic and Lake Izabal, the **Sierra de Chuacús** and **Sierra de las Minas** split off from the **Sierra de Santa Cruz**. On the northern side of the latter, in the karst country of Alta Verapaz, the limestone is riddled with caves and underground rivers, as where the Río Cahabón plunges underground beneath the "natural bridge" of **Semuc Champey**. To the north of this region begins the vast expanse of El Petén's jungles.

## The Lowlands
The rest of the country is divided between the coastal regions and the immense forests of El Petén.

Wheat fields in Totonicapán department

G. Sioen/RAPHO

**The northern Lowlands** – *(See map p 228)*. The lowlands of **El Petén** in the north make up a third of the country's land area and spread over into Mexico and Belize. In the depths of this inhospitable jungle, where a mere 10% of Guatemala's population lives, nestle the ruins of the largest of the ancient Maya cities. El Petén is a limestone table land that never rises more than 200m above sea-level. Across it flow many small streams and two major rivers, the **Río de la Pasíon** and the **Río Usumacinta**, which forms the frontier with Mexico. Here and there, the karst limestone has collapsed to form lakes and cenotes (sink-holes).

**The Pacific plain** – *(See map p 216)*. On the southern side of the volcanic range, the coffee-growing country of the foothills *(boca costa)* rolls down to the alluvial plain, a fertile strip some fifty kilometres wide with soils rich in volcanic ash. Here sugar cane, cotton and tropical fruits are grown in abundance. Short rivers flow down from the Highlands and across this coastal strip to merge with the violent rollers of the Pacific. The littoral extends from Mexico to El Salvador in 300km of long **beaches** of black sand derived from volcanic rock, interspersed here and there with **mangrove swamps**.

**Oriente** – *(See map p 254)*. The east of the country from the Highlands to the Atlantic coast reveals yet another kind of landscape. The valleys of the Río Polochic and the 400km **Río Motagua**, the country's longest river, run between parallel mountain ranges, following the lines of geological faults. A semi-desert area where cacti grow gives way to a tropical climate the closer you get to Amatique Bay. This is ideal country for banana growing. Framed by the Santa Cruz and Las Minas mountain ranges lies **Lake Izabal**, the country's largest lake (590sqkm); from it, the **Río Dulce** flows down to the Ocean. The narrow **Caribbean coast** seems squeezed, hemmed in, between Belize and Honduras.

## "Land of eternal spring"

Guatemala's nickname derives from the nuances and variations of a climate that is affected more by altitude, relief and exposure than by the rhythm of the seasons. The steamy **climate** of the **hotlands** (tierras calientes), up to 800m above sea-level, turns milder as you climb up through the **temperate lands** (tierras templadas). At around 1800m this mild and pleasant climate gives way to the harsher temperatures of the **cold lands** (tierras frías), where the thermometer often falls to around 0°C in winter.

A broad distinction can be made between summer *(verano)* and winter *(invierno)*, or rather between the **dry season**, from October to April, and the **rainy season** that lasts the rest of the year. The Lowlands, however, receive more rain than the rest of the country and very often stay muffled all year round in a humid, sweltering heat. The Pacific coast, for example, receives abundant rain-fall because the clouds are halted by the chain of volcanoes. El Petén gets a respite from January to April, although the air remains heavy with moisture all year round. The Atlantic coast enjoys a tropical climate, hot and humid with a risk of hurricanes in September and October, as in Belize *(see p 287)*. The mountains around Cobán, barring the way to the trade winds that blow in from the Caribbean, have some rain all year round. The Highlands, by contrast, enjoy a very pleasant temperate climate, though nights can be chilly and the winter is severe at higher altitudes.

# NATURE ON REPRIEVE

Despite the Amerindians' deep respect for nature, forest clearance and slash-and-burn farming are causing serious soil erosion and may rob the country of some of its rare trees and animals. Urbanisation and the spread of farmland are driving nature into a last defensive corner; plant and animal habitats are constantly shrinking as human habitat advances.

## "Land of trees"

Among various possible origins of the name "Guatemala", the commonest etymological theory relates it to *Quauhtemallan*, which means "land of trees" in the Nahuatl language. Although this was a valid description of the country in the days of the conquest, farming and extensive logging of tropical timber species have now considerably changed the country's profile. According to one alarming report published in 1990 by the Guatemalan Environment Commission, 40% of the country's forest had disappeared in the preceding thirty years.

### Endangered forest

Types of forest vary with altitude, exposure and rainfall. In the Highlands, which is the most densely populated part of the country, the former **montane forests** of **oak** and **conifers** have been logged and cleared for new *milpas* (crop fields). Large expanses of original forest are becoming scarce. The one tree that is still to be found everywhere, in town and countryside alike, is the **ceiba** (silk cotton or kapok tree), saved by its status as national tree of Guatemala and sacred tree of the Maya. Its imposing silhouette can quite often be seen standing alone, the sole survivor in a field or village square. In some hamlets the market is held under the wide span of its protective branches.

The areas with the greatest abundance of fauna and flora are in regions with plentiful rain but a sparser human population.

The mountains of Alta Verapaz and Baja Verapaz, south of El Petén, are clad in **tropical rainforest**, its luxuriant vegetation sustained by the frequent rains that come in with the trade winds from the Caribbean. Particularly abundant in this type of ecosystem are tree ferns, lichens and epiphytes (plants that grow on other plants but which, unlike parasites, do not draw their nutrients from them) including some magnificent **orchids**. One such orchid, in flower from November to January, is Guatemala's national flower, the **monja blanca** (white nun).

The tropical forest of El Petén, which until recently was still almost virgin forest, is now in danger from an influx of landless farmers and the inconsiderate destruction of its natural resources, much coveted for their economic value. One of the precious assets of El Petén is the **sapodilla**

H. Choimet

The white nun orchid

(zapote) tree, sought out by the *chicleros* (tappers) who cut grooves in the trunk to gather the *chicle*, a milky gum used to make chewing-gum. Its hard wood was used to make lintels for the region's Mayan temples. Other precious woods much coveted by loggers are **mahogany**, palm, rosewood and ebony. In the north of the department, 1.5 million hectares of dense jungle were at last declared a **Maya Biosphere Reserve** in 1990.

## Preserving the littoral

The savannah, marshland and mangrove swamps of the Pacific littoral began to give way to banana plantations in the late 19C. Since then, taking advantage of the fertile soils and humid climate, ranchers and crop farmers have also moved in at the expense of the natural ecosystem.

The disappearance of the **mangrove swamps** is likely to cause serious problems. The mangroves form a fringe along the coast, anchored directly in the ocean or the bordering swamp, their aerial roots dangling; they act as a protective barrier for the littoral and provide refuge for many animal species. The **Monterrico Nature Reserve** has set up a programme to protect this ecosystem with the help of local communities. The inhabitants are allowed to cut **mangroves** provided they help to replant.

# Land of the quetzal

Animals forced out of their home areas by farmers and hunters are now mostly restricted to the border areas. Thus the north of the country still harbours a fauna which can be discovered in all its diversity in and around the archeological sites of El Petén.

## One vast aviary

Birds are especially abundant in Guatemala, with over 700 species including 160 migratory birds. A dawn trip along the Río Dulce, in El Petén or in the mangrove swamps of the Pacific coast is a fascinating experience for bird lovers.

The **quetzal** has its picture on the Guatemalan flag and the country's monetary unit is named after it, but in its wild state this national mascot is becoming rare. Hunted for its beautiful tail feathers since the days of the ancient Maya, the quetzal keeps well away from human habitations. Even in its biotope reserve in Baja Verapaz you would be very lucky to see one (*see illustration and sidebar p 210 "Cobán"*).

H. Choimet

Far more visible with its big multicoloured beak, the **toucan** lives in the tropical forests of both Guatemala and Belize, of which it is the national bird. It shares its habitat with other bright and noisy birds such as **parrots** and **parakeets**. More discreet, the hummingbird or **colibri**, the smallest bird in the world, beats its wings at such an extraordinary rate that it can hover, seemingly motionless, above a flower.

The toucan, national bird of Belize

The **ocellated turkey** or wild turkey (pavo petenero) is only to be found in the Cerro Cahuí biotope reserve on the shores of Lake Petén Itzá. Among the waterfowl that nest in the mangrove swamps, a multitude of ibises, ducks, kingfishers and pelicans can be seen, as well as the slender silhouettes of herons perching on the mangrove roots.

## Discretion is the better part of survival

Of the 250 species of mammal in Guatemala, the easiest to find are the **spider monkeys** (monos araña) with their strident calls, the **howler monkeys** (saraguatos) with their harsh roaring and the **coatis** (pizotes), rodents that are quick to dive into a visitor's bag in Tikal to snatch food. Other small mammals that haunt the Guatemalan forests include opossums, armadillos in their suits of tough armour, ant-eaters, agoutis, pacas and honey bears. **Jaguars** (known as *"tigres"*), **pumas** and **ocelots** lurk in the forest, as invisible as the quetzal.

Reptiles and amphibians also abound in El Petén. Inoffensive iguanas, lizards, frogs and toads people the humid regions, along with snakes, some of which are venomous such as the **barba amarilla** (fer-de-lance). Despite its imposing size, the boa constrictor is harmless to humans.

Of the insects, the Lowlands mosquitoes are voracious. More agreeable company are the beautiful **butterflies** of the Guatemalan countryside, particularly in the Cerro Cahuí biotope reserve.

## Protecting sea creatures

Although the marine fauna is less impressive here than in Belize, Guatemala nonetheless harbours a few endangered species.

**Manatees** (manatís), also called sea cows, are thought to be the source of legends about mermaids and sirens owing to their fishlike bodies. They frequent the estuaries, where freshwater and seawater meet and mingle, and can be found particularly in the Río Dulce.

The Monterrico nature reserve safeguards the reproduction of endangered species of cayman, iguana and **turtle**. It also runs drives to raise public awareness (see p 219 "The Pacific Coast").

**Land of the quetzal**

| Dates | Events | Sites |
|---|---|---|
| **Pre-Classic** | (2000 BC-250 AD) | |
| **Early** | (2000-900 BC) | |
| | Apogee of the Olmec civilisation. | |
| 1200 BC | First Mayan ceramics. | *Cuello (Belize)* |
| **Middle** | (900-300 BC) | |
| | First tombs in Copán valley. | *Copán* |
| **Late** | (300 BC-250 AD) | |
| | Influence of Teotihuacan. | *El Mirador* |
| | First buildings at Tikal. | *Kaminaljuyú,* |
| | | *Uaxactún, Tikal* |
| **36 BC** | | |
| **219 AD** | (300 BC-250 AD) | |
| | Earliest known written Mayan date. | *Chiapa de Corzo* |
| | | *(Mex.)* |
| | Founding of the Tikal dynasty. | |
| **Early Classic** | (250-550 AD) | |
| | First monuments, founding of Copán dynasty. | |
| 292 | First dated monument of the Classic period | *Tikal, Río Azul,* |
| | (Stela 29, Tikal). | *Caracol* |
| 378 | Tikal conquest of Uaxactún. | |
| 562 | Tikal conquered by Caracol. | |
| **Late Classic** | (550-900 AD) | |
| | Golden age of the Maya. | |
| 682 | Ah Cacao accedes to the throne. | *Tikal* |
| 695 | 18 Rabbit accedes to the throne. | *Copán* |
| 738 | 18 Rabbit captured and sacrificed by | |
| | Cauac Sky of Quiriguá. | |
| **Post-Classic** | (900 AD to Conquest) | |
| | Cities of El Petén abandoned. | *K'umarkaaj, Iximché,* |
| | | *Mixco Viejo* |
| | Apogee in Yucatán. | |
| | Founding of Highland kingdoms. | |
| 909 | Last dated Mayan monument. | *Toniná (Mex.)* |
| **Colonial period** | (1524-1821) | |
| 1524 | Conquest by Pedro de Alvarado. | |
| 1527 | Founding of the capital Santiago (Antigua). | |
| 1697 | Fall of the Itzás, last Mayan kingdom. | |
| 1773 | Santiago destroyed by earthquake. | |
| 1821 | Independence of New Spain and Guatemala. | |
| **Republican period (1839 to today)** | | |
| 1839 | Creation of the Republic of Guatemala. | |
| 1873-1885 | Justo Rufino Barrios dictatorship. | |
| 1954 | Jacobo Arbenz comes to power. | |
| 1976 | 4 February, earthquake. | |
| 1981 | British Honduras achieves independence | |
| | and takes the name of Belize. | |
| 1982 | Coup d'état by General Ríos Montt. | |
| 1986 | Election of a civilian President, Vinicio Cerezo. | |
| 1992 | Rigoberta Menchú receives Nobel Prize. | |
| 1996 | Election of President Alvaro Arzú | |
| | 29 December, signing of peace treaty between | |
| | government and guerrillas. | |
| 1998 | The URNG becomes a political party. | |

# THE ANCIENT MAYA

The culture of the Maya, once regarded as a minor expression of indigenous American civilization, is now recognised as one of the greatest ancient cultures alongside those of the Persians, Greeks and Egyptians. Their astonishing knowledge of astronomy, the complexity of their writing system and the gigantic scale of their architecture have fascinated generations of archeologists and are now open to the admiration of the public at large. Our knowledge of the ancient Maya has made spectacular progress since the mid-20C. Their inscriptions are being deciphered with ever greater precision. Every tomb discovered, every city dug out from its shroud of jungle vegetation, sheds fresh light on the refinement of their arts and the sophistication of their thinking. Many preconceived ideas have now been corrected: the Maya were not the peaceful people described a few decades ago, and they did not "disappear"; rather, they abandoned their great cities while still conserving the essence of their beliefs right down to the present day.

## The main periods of Mayan civilization

Mayan civilization is divided into three major periods. The oldest vestiges discovered date from around 2000 BC, and the civilization retained its original character until the arrival of the Spanish in the 16C. It is still alive among the modern Mayans.

**The Pre-Classic period** runs from 2000 BC-250 AD. The key feature of the Late Pre-Classic (300 BC-250 AD) was the building of the first temples. **El Mirador**, **Tikal** and **Uaxactún** are the most important towns from that period in what is now Guatemala.

**The Classic period** can be divided into Early Classic from 250-550 AD and Late Classic from 550-900 AD, which was the period when **Tikal**, **Copán** (Honduras) and **Palenque** (Mexico) reached their peak and then declined.

**The Post-Classic period**, after 900, was the time when **Chichén Itzá** and **Uxmal**, in Mexico, were thriving cities.

Mayan civilization developed in Central America, in an area that today covers parts of Mexico, Guatemala, Belize, Honduras and El Salvador.

**The Mayan area**, defined as the area that shared common technologies and beliefs, falls into three distinct geographical zones.

The **Highlands** or cold lands are an extremely mountainous region (Los Altos) consisting mainly of a range of volcanoes running parallel to the Pacific coast. This zone was at its most dynamic in the Pre-Classic (Kaminaljuyú) and Post-Classic periods. Today this is the most densely populated part of the Mayan territory and is home to the majority of Guatemalan and Chiapas indigenous people.

The **Lowlands** consist of a low-lying plain (about 300m above sea level) covered in dense tropical vegetation. It was on this plain, today called **El Petén**, that the major cities of the Classic period were built.

The **hotlands** lie on a vast limestone plateau that extends into the **Yucatán peninsula** (Mexico). This ancient seabed is now karst country devoid of surface rivers.

**The ancient Maya**

## First buds of a civilization (1200 BC-250 AD)

Although recent discoveries have confirmed the presence of prehistoric communities on the American continent, the hypothesis that they first arrived as migrants is still the most commonly accepted among historians; nomadic tribes from Asia are thought to have crossed the Bering Strait some 20 000 years ago before gradually moving southwards. The earliest sedentary farming settlements in the Mayan region probably date back to 12 000 BC. The peoples that preceded the rise of the Mayan culture proper were the **Olmecs**, mother of all Mesoamerican cultures, and the Mixe-Xoqueans who lived on the Pacific coast of Chiapas. The oldest pottery of indisputably Mayan style, found at the Cuello site in Belize, dates from 1200 BC.

## The golden age of the builder kings (250-800 AD)

Around 250 AD, the founding of the first royal dynasties accelerated urban concentration and great building works were begun. In the heart of El Petén's virgin forest, temples and palaces were built around large squares, each forming the centre of a **large city-state**. Tikal, Uaxactún, Caracol, Yaxchilán, Calakmul and many other cities on either bank of the Usumacinta river fought fiercely for territorial control. Military victories and religious devotion strengthened the power of these sovereigns who strove constantly to embellish their capitals.

The 7C and 8C were the **heyday** of classic Mayan culture. Numerous **stelae** were erected on the ceremonial plazas, glorifying the sovereigns or marking events in the calendar cycles. Walls were covered with **glyphs** and paintings on the orders of the *ahau*, chiefs by divine right whose charisma or authority stimulated creativity. Thus **18 Rabbit** in Copán, **Ah Cacao** in Tikal and **Kin Pakal** in Palenque became architects of their people's greatness. Alliances were forged between tribes, creating a dynamic of exchange that produced a homogeneous civilization across a wide area.

## Twilight of the gods (800-950 AD)

In the 9C Mayan civilization began to **decline**. Stelae became scarcer, no more major building works were undertaken and, little by little, the big cities were abandoned. This end of a golden age has puzzled many historians and given rise to some wildly fantastic theories. Epidemics and invasions have now been excluded from the likely hypotheses, in favour of a combination of internal causes with inexorably destructive effects. As a result of the concentration of power in cities, the population became increasingly urbanised, which doubtless created serious supply problems. The farmers, having to feed an increasing urban population using age-old techniques, deforested ever larger areas. The result was **drought** and **famine**; the most recent skeletons found in Copán show obvious signs of malnutrition. Tensions within the ruling class and rivalry between neighbouring kingdoms, sharpened by unrest in underfed populations, probably caused the power structure to break up and the community to split into rebel groups which then scattered.

## Mountain kingdoms (950-1524 AD)

Around 1000 AD, while in the hotlands the jungle was creeping back to cover eight centuries of splendour, Mayan history, lacking the chronicler scribes of yore, slipped back into oblivion. Foreign incursions from Mexico shifted the focus of settlement to **Los Altos**. Such invasions may have incited the Maya of the Post-Classic period to form powerful kingdoms that were soon competing

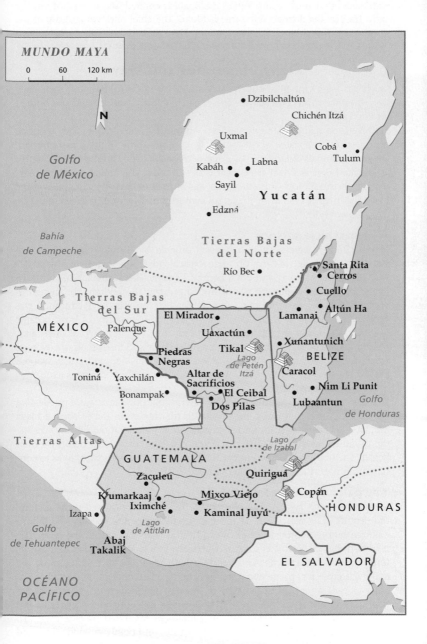

MUNDO MAYA

0    60    120 km

N

Golfo
de México

Bahía
de Campeche

• Dzibilchaltún

Chichén Itzá

Uxmal

Cobá •
Tulum •

Kabáh •    • Labna

Sayil

Y u c a t á n

• Edzná

T i e r r a s   B a j a s
d e l   N o r t e

Río Bec •

• Santa Rita
• Cerros

• Cuello

T i e r r a s   B a j a s
d e l   S u r

• El Mirador

Uaxactún •

Lamanai    • Altún Ha

MÉXICO    Palenque

Tikal •    • Xunantunich

Piedras
Negras

Lago
de Petén
Itzá

Caracol    BELIZE

Toniná •    Yaxchilán •    Altar de
Sacrificios

Bonampak •    • El Ceibal

• Nim Li Punit

Dos Pilas    Lubaantun •

Golfo
de Honduras

T i e r r a s   A l t a s    Lago
de Izabal

GUATEMALA

Zaculeu •    Quiriguá •

K'umarkaaj •    Mixco Viejo •    • Copán

Izapa •    Iximché •    • Kaminal Juyú    HONDURAS

Lago
de Atitlán

Golfo
de Tehuantepec

Abaj
Takalik

EL SALVADOR

OCÉANO
PACÍFICO

**21**

with each other once again. When the Spanish entered Mayan territory in the early 16C, it was divided into large fiefdoms, the chief ones being those of the **Quiché** and **Cakchiquel**. By that time the Mexican tribes of Toltec origin, such as the Pipil, were already well integrated into Mayan culture.

# Daily life among the Maya

Much has been written about the customs of the ancient Maya and their daily lives, from the royal court to the *milpa* (a patch of forest land, cleared and burned for cultivation).

However, too many writers forget to point out that the lifestyles they describe are those of the Yucatec Maya of the 16C and not those of the Classic period. **Diego de Landa's** *Relación de las Cosas de Yucatán* (1566, published in English as *Yucatán Before and After the Conquest*) is still today the main source of information on the subject. But since this was a tradition-based society, it is quite likely that their Mayan ancestors eight centuries earlier lived in much the same way.

## A hierarchical society

Mayan children were born into a world ordered by cosmic rules and a caste system. A child's day of birth (in the *tzolkin* calendar) was interpreted by priests well versed in astrology, and often became its name (hence the famous King 18 Rabbit of Copán). From the age of five to puberty all children wore a sign of virginity: a white pearl for boys and a red seashell for girls. Boys' education was very soon dictated by their social status. The great majority of boys became farmers, going daily to their *milpas* and producing, with the help of their families, the staples of life. While the men built the home and made tools, the women wove clothes and made pots for domestic use. Craftsmen and artists worked exclusively for the ruling class, which included scribes, shamans (sorcerer-priests), officers and traders.

Marriage was carefully arranged by the parents, but polygamy was a privilege of the nobility. At the end of a life attuned to the rhythm of the seasons, a Maya prepared his or her descent into the underworld – not without anxiety, despite the promise that their descendants would continue to perform rituals on their behalf. The dead were buried under the floors of their own homes, so as to continue to protect their families after death.

## The painful badge of nobility

Membership of a ruling caste chosen by the gods necessitated some distinctive features. To match up to the canons of aristocratic beauty, high-born children had to submit to a series of physical trials right from the start. The new-born baby's head was squeezed between two wooden boards to make its forehead slope backwards. To identify it with its protector god **Itzamná**, the child was given a permanent squint by hanging a ball of resin between its eyes. Later its ears were pierced in order to insert a ring-shaped ornament (the ear flare). The nobles dyed their hair red and wore it in a ponytail brought forward over the head and completed by small forelocks separated by jade rings. To enhance their beauty the women filed their teeth into points or had them inlaid with jade. Astonishingly, even today many indigenous people have their **teeth**

The ancient Maya

inlaid; this has become a visible sign of "wealth". A recent women's fashion is to have gold stars inset in the incisors, while the men prefer to have a tooth filed on three sides, then rimmed with a gold or silver wire.

## The ball game

This was not a specifically Mayan invention, but it certainly played an important role in the ritual and daily life of the elite. It was played by all the peoples of Mesoamerica, although the size of the court and the rules of the game varied considerably. It was not played just for fun but was linked to an underlying **cosmic philosophy** that was always just beneath the surface. The court was divided into two T-shaped camps (*ik*, the wind or "breath of life" in Yucatec Maya, was written as a T-shaped glyph), and the ball arcing through the air from east to west represented the course of the sun. The players passed the **rubber ball** (*hule*) to each other, preventing it from touching the ground within their own camp; if it did, the opposing team scored a point. Players could not use hands or feet, so they had to contort their bodies in perilous and spectacular ways; having to throw themselves to the ground and play with buttocks and hips, they wore protective trappings worthy of American football players.

R. Marca

Ball player

After the match there might be a **human sacrifice** ceremony. There has been much speculation about this gruesome epilogue, carved with great realism in the Chichén Itzá ball court, and it has even been suggested that the captain of the winning team was beheaded! More recent interpretations of this ritual are much more moderate. Among the Maya, human sacrifice was not practised on anything like the same scale as the massacres often carried out, later on, by the Aztecs. However, an enemy sovereign might be put to death in this ceremony, in circumstances worthy of his rank. Before dying, he identified with the gods of *Xibalbá*, who according to mythology were the first ball game enthusiasts. This may have been the fate of King 18 Rabbit of Copán, captured and put to death by his governor of Quiriguá in 738.

# Kings and gods

## Cosmic balance

In Mayan cosmology the world is a vast quadrilateral held up by four bearer-gods (the *bacabs*) at the cardinal points. In the middle, the *axis mundi* is a huge, smooth-trunked silk cotton tree (*Ceiba pentandra*, also called the kapok tree). The branches of this "tree of life" vanish into a heaven peopled by restless gods (represented by the movements of the stars); its roots plunge down into a terrifying underworld from which no-one has ever returned. It is in the super-position of these three levels that cosmic equilibrium, the harmony of the Mayan universe, is created, thanks to the omnipotence of the king and the benevolence of the gods.

The **heavens**, divided into thirteen levels, are marked out by the course of the sun, the star supreme and "great fertiliser", passing tirelessly through the three levels of the universe. The bird (muan) symbolises the upper world and can often be seen perched on the "tree of life" or on the head of a god. At night, the vault of the heavens becomes the playground of the gods, their presence manifested in the movements of moon and stars.

The **underworld** is the most terrifying, the only invisible one. Its very name, **Xibalbá**, evokes the fear (xib) it inspires. It is divided into nine levels, each one the domain of a fearsome god. This nether world, cold and wet, is represented by water symbols (seashell, water lily, fish) and unappealing skeletal creatures. The way into this last abode of common mortals is through a cave, a body of water or the mouth of a monster. The king merely passes through, identified in so doing with the sun at night, before rejoining his ancestors in the firmament above.

The **middle world** is like a hanging garden at the centre of the universe, peopled by human beings who cultivate maize, which according to mythology is their own flesh. They place their destiny in the hands of the king, sole guarantor of the common weal. For this reason, the king was sometimes represented as the axis of the world in place of the "tree of life".

## The king, axis of the world

Life was not all pleasure for a Mayan ruler during the Classic period. The privileges of the title went hand in hand with a crushing responsibility and some painful duties. One of the most characteristic rituals incumbent on the king was **self-mutilation**. This meant piercing the ear or penis with an obsidian point or sting-ray spine, thus inflicting pain proportionate to the value of the act. The royal blood, regarded as the supreme offering, was collected in a bowl then burnt or poured on the ground; this vital fluid fertilised the middle world and proved the king's inherited divine right. There was a form of royal suffering for women too: a carved panel in Yaxchilán (Mexico) shows a queen piercing her tongue to run a thorn-studded string through it. Through self-mutilation accompanied by hallucinations, the king could also communicate with his ancestors and the gods. These supernatural visions, ensuring the smooth running of the kingdom, are depicted on the stelae by "floating" figures that protect the ruler from above in the heavens (Stela 31 at Tikal).

The importance of the king's warfaring is well illustrated in the numerous scenes of battle or bound prisoners carved or painted on stelae, frescoes and stucco designs on buildings and on

Polychrome vase
discovered at Tikal

J.-P. Courau/EXPLORER

pottery. All these images are evidence against the reputedly peaceful character of the Maya, thought for many years to contrast with the warlike tendencies of the peoples of central Mexico.

## Gods at the service of kingly power

Unlike the Toltec and Aztec cultures of the Mexican Altiplano, the gods in Mayan iconography, however numerous they may be, accompany the king as indispensable accessories to legitimise his power and prove his worth. Their presence is generally associated with sovereignty, except in the codices, whose function was that of a liturgical guide something like a missal. The Dresden Codex, for example, is a virtual catalogue of gods.

There were gods of the elements, of crops, of the cardinal points, even of numbers: **Mayan polytheism** knew no bounds. However, three key figures stand out from this spiritual throng.

The god **Itzamná** is the creator of all things. He is shown in many forms, including, in the Classic period, as lord of the pantheon. As Sun God (Kinich Ahau) he takes the form of a mask, a snake, a monster, a bird or just a red hand, symbol of creation. In human form he is an old man with a face that is easy to recognise from its square, squinting pupils and the filed tooth showing below the upper lip.

**Kauil** (more commonly called God K) can be seen everywhere as he always accompanies the king: in the form of a sceptre held by the sovereign, nestling in his imposing head-dress, or emerging from the jaws of a two-headed snake which the sovereign holds against his chest. Kauil, protector of royal power, has a long nose, a smoking axe buried in his forehead, and one leg in the form of a snake.

The maize god **Yum Kaax** will perhaps soon be re-baptised, like many of his peers and royal subjects, since progress in deciphering the syllables of glyphs is changing the pronunciation of names at a confusingly fast pace. He takes the form of a young man with an aristocratic face (Copán); sometimes his head replaces the cob on a maize plant.

## Animals as metaphors of the divine

Going round a Mayan site is often like going round a petrified zoo peopled with fantastic creatures: two-headed dragon-snakes, tortoise-jaguars, monsters with fleshless jaws and so on. These strange animals represent the supernatural dimension of the gods and reflect the animistic spirit of the Maya. Among the most emblematic is that universal symbol, the **serpent**, representing both the heavens and the fertility of the earth. Clinging to the "tree of life" it is the sky, the Milky Way; swirling around the head of the king it is the "vision" of the ancestors; rigid and with two heads, in the arms of the sovereign, it is the rod that marks royal authority.

The **jaguar** in all its majesty symbolises royal power. As a direct result of the respect in which it was held, the jaguar was sacrificed in major ceremonies. Its skin then became part of the king's attire or covered the throne.

The **monkey**, guardian of the arts, wisdom and writing, was also protector of the scribes.

The heavenly **bird** (called *muan*), the sky emblem, perches in the king's head-dress or on the "tree of life".

**King and gods**

The **rabbit**, as in ancient China, represents the Moon, the female aspect, fecundity (if you look carefully you can see the rabbit with his two ears, looking leftward, in the shadows on the face of the moon).

The **seashell** symbolises the female aspect, the watery world of *Xibalbá* (world of the dead), and fertility.

The **fish** and the **bat** (*tzotz*) are figures of the underworld.

# The time lords

## Star watchers

**Astronomy** was the science the Maya devoted most energy to, for in their thought system the heavens were inseparably linked with religious beliefs. The movements of the stars were observed from natural observation points like Copán, artificial ones as at Uaxactún, or observatories like the one at Chichén Itzá. Mayan art includes many representations of the sky, highlighting its symbolic importance: Sun, Moon and planets (Venus, Mars), constellations (Orion, Pleiades), the Milky Way. They are often portrayed as a "celestial ribbon" around the sovereign. The world's boundaries are marked by the **cardinal points** that frame the course of the sun. The ordering of the world depends on strict observance of these confines: the ball court and the image of the sovereign both on an east-west axis, tombs on a north-south axis, etc. **Venus** was the focus of special attention, for in both its guises – as morning star and evening star – it symbolised the course of time, as did the Sun, and was also associated with the art of war. While **equinoxes** and **solstices** measured out the farming seasons and determined the orientation of certain buildings, unusual phenomena such as **eclipses** and **conjunctions of planets** were interpreted by learned astrologer-priests. Using sky maps, these priests fixed the most propitious dates for the great ceremonies. The **Dresden Codex**, a veritable ritual almanac, is a magnificent illustration of their astonishing astronomical knowledge.

## The number system

The Mayan vigesimal counting system (on a base of 20) probably originated from the practice of counting on fingers and toes. Its notation used only three symbols: a stylised **shell** for zero, a **dot** for one, a **bar** for 5. The invention of zero and vertical reading enabled them to establish a system of **multiplication by position**. The numbers (0 to 19) were "stacked" on different levels of a column, and at each higher level they moved up a further power of 20. With this mathematical convention, it was possible to use just three signs to express the huge numbers that were indispensable for the Long Count (*see below*). Numbers could also be represented by heads or figures shown in profile, an esthetic variant that was to enrich Mayan sculpture with new motifs.

## The Mayan calendar

The **tzolkin** (ritual calendar) was of 260 days, representing the intermeshing of a sequence of numbers (1-13) with 20 name days. Each day therefore had a name with its corresponding glyph (Imix, Ik, Akbal, Kan, Chicchan, Cimi, Manik, Lamat, Muluc, Oc, Chuen, Eb, Ben, Ix, Men, Cib, Caban, Etznab, Cauac,

**The ancient Maya**

Ahau), combined with a number between 1 and 13. Every day the day-name series moved on and the number increased by one, returning to 1 on the fourteenth day (for example 1 Imix, 2 Ik, 3 Akbal, 4 Kan etc., up to 13 Ben, then 1 Ix, 2 Men, 3 Cib etc). The entire sequence thus lasted 260 days (13 x 20), then began over again. This was the calendar used for the farming year (to time sowing and harvesting) and for great events in kingly life (enthronement, military campaigns etc).

The **haab** (solar calendar), also called the **Vague Year**, was of 365 days, divided into eighteen 20-day months plus a period of 5 days at the end considered to be unlucky *(Uayeb)*. The months were named and the days in the month were numbered from 0 to 19 (e.g. 0 Pop, 1 Pop, 2 Pop, 3 Pop etc, up to 19 Pop, then 0 Uo, 1 Uo, 2 Uo, 3 Uo, up to 19 Uo etc). After 365 days the same sequence began again.

*Tzolkin* and *haab* rolled simultaneously, their combined cycle repeating itself **every 52 years** (18 980 days, this being the lowest common multiple of 260 and 365; the ritual calendar round revolved 73 times in the course of 52 solar cycles).

A date in the Mayan calendar indicates first the date in the ritual calendar and then the date in the solar calendar. Thus a cycle might begin 1 Imix 0 Pop, 2 Ik 1 Pop, 3 Akbal 2 Pop, and might finish with 11 Etznab 2 Uayeb, 12 Cauac 3 Uayeb, 13 Ahau 4 Uayeb. As the same date was repeated every 52 years, the Long Count system was devised in order to designate each single day in Mayan chronology.

The **Initial Series**, or **Long Count**, is a day count starting from a mythical date, Day 0, which corresponds to 13 August 3114 BC in our Gregorian calendar. Mayan civilization did not yet exist at that date, so we do not know why that day was chosen. The vast number of days that had gone by before the Classic period were divided into time units that might be compared to our months, years, centuries and millennia.

In the Long Count, periods are divided into **tuns** (18 20-day months). A day is a **kin** (the name of the Sun God), a month of 20 *kin* is an *uinal* and 18 *uinals* make a *tun*. Thus we have, from the bottom up, *kins* (days), *uinals* (multiples of 20 days), *tuns* (multiples of 360 days), *katuns* (multiples of 20 *tuns* or 7 200 days) and *baktuns* (multiples of 20 *katuns* or 144 000 days). This superposition known as the Initial Series enables today's archeologists to date stelae and monuments with great precision and so reconstitute a chronology. The Maya world reached the peak of its glory in *Baktun* 9; we are now reaching the end of *Baktun* 12. In the Initial Series, 1 January 2000 reads 12.19.6.15.0, or 12 *baktuns*, 19 *katuns*, 6 *tuns*, 15 *uinals* and 0 *kins*.

The "kin" glyph

The Initial Series is completed by the so-called **Lunar Series**, which places the Long Count in its astral context. This indicates the length of the moon cycle, the number of days since the new moon, as well as also sometimes referring to the Venus cycle of 584 days.

R. Marca

# Writing, a privilege of the elite

## Alchemy of the glyphs

Starting in the Pre-Classic period, perhaps under the influence of the Olmec or Zapotec cultures, a written language developed that came to be used, with a few local variants, throughout the Mayan area. This hieroglyphic writing is made up of image blocks stacked in parallel vertical columns and read two by two, from left to right and from top to bottom. Many of the blocks are composed of a main motif (human head or zoomorph in profile, hand etc) along with small additional motifs (symbols) that act as affixes or complete the syllabic composition.

Three types of glyph can be distinguished: **logograms** that represent a whole word (e.g. a jaguar head for a jaguar), **phonetic** glyphs indicating the sound of a syllable (e.g. the syllables ba-la-ma = jaguar), and **semantic** glyphs which specify one of several possible meanings for a glyph. These three types of signs can be combined in one text, and a combination of glyphs can also be intended to be read syllabically, like a **rebus**.

The scribes *(ah dzib)*, who had a wonderful command of this very complex writing with its symbiosis of science and art, ranked very high in the social hierarchy. Only the elite could read their texts, the historical or religious content of which was far more symbolic than narrative.

## Codices and books carved in stone

The **Mayan codices** (manuscripts) are strips of fig bark with a smooth white gypsum coating and screen-folded. They can be several metres long. Complete with illustrations and colour, they contain religious and divinatory texts and astronomical almanacs, perhaps intended as manuals for priests. The four Mayan codices that have come down to us all date from the Post-Classic period or the early days of the Conquest. The oldest; the **Grolier Codex**, dates from the 13C, but not all authorities acknowledge it as authentic. The **Dresden Codex** is the most remarkable, for its calligraphy and its astronomical and calendrical content. The **Paris** and **Madrid Codices**, though more crudely executed, provide valuable information about the ancient writing system. Codices from the Classic period have been found in tombs, but so severely damaged by damp that they have proved to be illegible. Four surviving codices seems meager fare compared to the hundreds that existed when the Spaniards arrived. Many of these were destroyed in the famous auto da fé carried out on the orders of **Diego de Landa**, bishop of Yucatán, in 1562. By an irony of fate, a few years later it was Diego de Landa himself who first tried to decipher the glyphs.

### Breaking the code

These mysterious signs with their hidden meanings have stimulated the European imagination ever since the Renaissance. The first "alphabet", by Diego de Landa, was found by Abbott Brasseur de Bourbourg in 1864, arousing keen interest at a time when Champollion's work on Egyptian hieroglyphics was fresh in people's minds. A hundred years and some expert amateur epigraphists later, Eric Thompson, Yuri Knorosov and Tatiana Proskouriakoff advanced theories that were sometimes in sharp contradiction but nonetheless made a major contribution to decipherment. The next generation (Peter Mathews, Karl Taube), with the benefit of computers, resolved more of the semantic enigmas of this sophisticated writing system. Today, we know the meaning of more than 60% of the glyphs, but enthusiasm for the task is as strong as ever.

Extract from the Dresden Codex

J.-P. Courau/EXPLORER

The ancient Maya

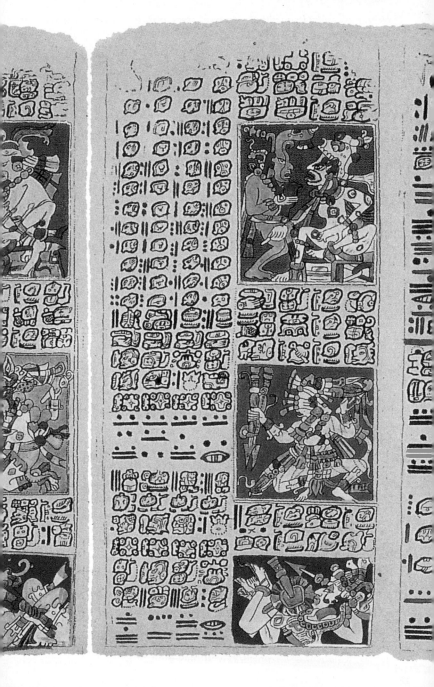

Writing was also frequently inscribed – modelled in stucco or carved – on stelae, panels, lintels and stairways. These inscriptions record historical events, to the greater glory of the sovereign. Heroic deeds in battle, the dynastic lineage and the close links uniting the king with the gods were artistically portrayed on the city's monuments. The purpose, apart from honouring the king, was to assert irrefutably his legitimacy as part of a symbolic chronology. That is why most of the inscriptions consist of dates (often a whole double column!) and the names of cities and kings. The rest is a succession of titles and ritual acts which together make somewhat indigestible reading for the layman.

## The Popol Vuh

The Popol Vuh was the sacred book of the Quiché Maya. The name means "book of wisdom" or "book of the community" and it contains ancient myths, along the lines of the Hindu *Mahabharata*. It is a highly poetic text, full of the names of divine creatures, which first tells of the creation of the world, beginning with the first fruitless attempts by the Creators to make a man capable of worshipping them. Neither with clay nor wood did they manage to give the gods' future servant the right qualities. Then come the adventures of demigods, the heroic twins Hunahpu and Xbalanque, battling against the malevolent Lords of *Xibalbá (see sidebar p 122 "Guatemala City")*. The book ends with the origins of the Quiché people – the first of whom was a man made of maize dough – and the tribe's dynastic history.

Generations of scribes must have copied the *Popol Vuh* onto codices before these were systematically destroyed at the time of the Conquest. But its content, passed down in the oral tradition, was retranscribed in 1688 by **Francisco Jimenez**, a Dominican friar in Chichicastenango. This precious record was then lost in some library before being dug out again in the Archive of the Indies in Seville by the Dominican **Abbot Brasseur de Bourbourg**, who translated it into French and published it for the first time, in 1861. The similarity of some passages of the *Popol Vuh* with the Old Testament (the first man made of clay, the flood) has been attributed to the abbot's transcription. However, several of the episodes have also been found depicted on stelae at the pre-Mayan site of Izapa, showing the remarkable continuity of the region's myths. The *Popol Vuh* has made it possible to interpret many painted or sculpted scenes.

# Mayan architecture

Untiringly, unceasingly, the Maya cut huge blocks from the soft limestone and piled them up to build new pyramids and ever greater palaces. It is hard to imagine the skill and labour it took to build such gigantic monuments, given that the Maya did not use the wheel, were not familiar with the true arch and had no draft animals or beasts of burden.

## Building techniques

Only buildings intended for the elite were built of stone ; these are the ones you can see today at the Mayan archeological sites. Ordinary folk lived in **chozas**, windowless, chimneyless oval huts built of poles daubed with cob under a palm frond roof. This traditional type of housing is still used by the Maya of the hotlands today. All stone buildings rose from a **base** – a platform for a palace and a stepped pyramid for a temple. This was climbed by a vast staircase that often ran its entire width. The space inside was created by a **corbelled vault** (or false vault) in which the upper courses of the parallel supporting walls are progressively stepped inwards. They were built from solid mortar mixed with stones, only the facing stones being dressed. Roofs had slightly inclined sides, sometimes referred to as "mansard roofs" because of their odd resemblance to the 17C French roof style of that name. Ignorance of the true arch technique had some serious drawbacks, as more volume is taken up by the masonry than by the space inside. Mayan architects had to use great ingenuity to mask the inevitable heaviness of the construction with luxuriant ornamentation. The **cresteria** (roofcomb) was a wall built on top of the roof, sometimes of stone openwork, giving the building greater height and lightness and providing further decoration.

## A stone acropolis

Mayan architecture is based on a few building archetypes that are the same in all the ancient cities.

The **chambered palace**, residence of the nobility, consists of an alignment of narrow chambers, each opening to the outside through a single door. The wings of the building form quadrilaterals around **inner courtyards** (patios). The Spanish often compared these chambers to monks' cells. In some cases the whole room is virtually taken up by a stone bench acting as a bed.

The **corridor palace**, a less common structure, was intended more for ceremonial uses and the rituals of royal life. It has two long, parallel, covered corridors separated by a central wall, one opening onto the outside and one onto inner courtyards.

The **high temple** includes a rectangular entrance hall with one or three doors, taking up the whole width of the building and leading into the small, square **sanctuary**. It is built on a **stepped pyramid base** which can be as much as 50m high. The reason for building so high was to get closer to the gods, the temple being a gateway to the celestial world. At Tikal, the stairway leading up to the temple is continued in a stepped *cresteria*, accentuating the "Jacob's ladder" effect. This kind of temple has been compared to a petrified "tree of life" emerging like a silk cotton tree from the leafy canopy of the surrounding forest.

The **ball court** was always built near the palace or the main temple. The spectators, probably a very select group, occupied the tops of the twin stands (without seats), which also provided both an ornamental façade and the boundary of the central part of the I-shaped court. Below them, two low taluses sloped inward to provide a further area for the ball to bounce. The *marcadores*, carved stones, either round (representing the sun) or in the shape of a macaw's head as at Copán, marked the edges of the court. The ball courts in the Mayan area are generally fairly small, between 16m and 35m long, and do not have the rings that were introduced into Yucatán by the Toltecs around the year 1000.

# MAYAN ARCHITECTURE

## THE CEREMONIAL CENTRE

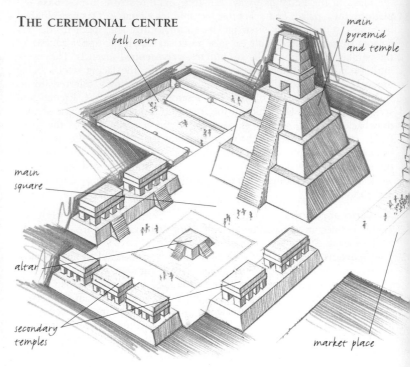

main pyramid and temple

ball court

main square

altar

secondary temples

market place

## VAULTS

STEPPED
OR CORBEL VAULT

CLASSIC VAULT
WITH COPPERED FACING

ARCHAIC VAULT
OF LARGE BLOCKS

TREFOIL (OR TRILOBED)
VAULT

CONCAVE VAULT

BOTTLE VAULT

H. Choimet

## THE TEMPLE

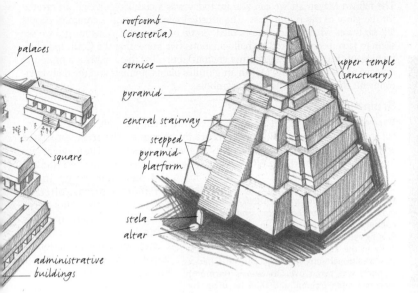

palaces

roofcomb
(cresteria)

cornice

pyramid

central stairway

stepped
pyramid-
platform

upper temple
(sanctuary)

square

stela

altar

administrative
buildings

## THE BALL COURT

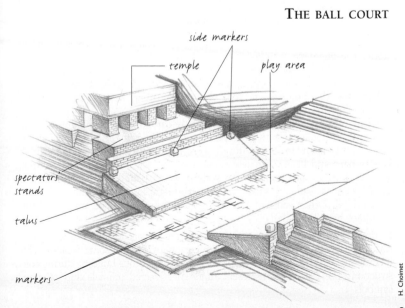

side markers

temple

play area

spectators'
stands

talus

markers

H. Choimet

# A race of artists

The refined Mayan art we can admire today was a codified "official" art created for the glory of the ruling class. The artistic expressions of the common people left no traces when their creators died. Some of the multifarious images we see seem to have been inspired by hallucinations (we know that the Court took hallucinogenic mushrooms and datura enemas); but all of them express a profound homage to Mother Nature. Mayan art glorifies plants, animals and the daily environment, transforming them into symbols.

## Sculpture

**Bas-relief** was the Mayan sculptors' favourite technique, although some local styles (7C Copán) included sculpture in the round. The **stela**, associated with the **altar**, gave this method its highest expression. These stelae are monoliths carved with the effigy of the king; some were as much as 10m tall and they were set up in the ceremonial plazas, often in connection with events in the Long Count calendar. They usually commemorated a change of *katun* (a period of about 20 years); less often, a change of *hotun* (period of about 5 years), as in Quiriguá. On the stela, which was sometimes carved front and back, the date of the calendar event was nearly always inscribed on the sides. Most sites have an alignment of stelae, looking like a forest of "trees of life" in stone. The dignitary, weighed down with symbolic ornaments from head to toe, carries the ceremonial bar that is the insignia of his power. The finest stelae are to be seen at Tikal, Quiriguá and Copán. A tip for recognising the oldest ones: the king has one foot behind the other, whereas on later ones they are turned out at 180°.

### Jungle tomb raiders

Because of its beauty and sensitivity, Mayan art is much coveted by collectors and the tomb robbers who supply them. In the 1970s the looting reached astonishing proportions, especially in the remote jungle of El Petén. First, this traditional activity of the *chicleros* (latex tappers) was taken over by *peones* (farmers) who had been trained, and then let drop, by archeology teams. But then the treasure trade modernised, adopting chain saws and helicopters, so that local authorities were obliged to take drastic protection measures. For a while, experts on Mayan culture were making their best finds not in the tombs but in the sale rooms!

Door **jambs** and **lintels** were also brilliantly carved by these sculptors, who played a particular role in creating the splendour of the cities of Piedras Negras and Yaxchilán. Some lintels were carved in sapodilla wood, which is very hard and heavy, but few examples have withstood the test of time, weather, insects and theft. Some superb wood panels that decorated the Tikal temples can be seen in the ethnographical museum in Basel, Switzerland. Other gems of the carver's art were produced on jade, flint, obsidian, bone and shell.

During the 7C, **tenon sculpture**, also known as engaged sculpture, was introduced, producing a strikingly three-dimensional effect on some façades. This method involves setting stone sculptures into the walls of a building during construction. These carvings represent dignitaries, sacred animals and religious symbols.

**Sculpture in the round and stucco modelling** were also used to decorate buildings. Stucco (a mixture of lime, gypsum, sand and resin or honey) was modelled to decorate door jambs, ramps and roofs. From the 3C on the most common motif was the giant **mask** of a jaguar or a terrifying god. In addition, the entire building was coated in plaster and painted in bright colours.

**The Mayan artist's palette**
To paint the superb decorations that covered their monuments, the Maya used a wide variety of vegetable and mineral pigments. The two predominant colours were red (hematite and cinnabar) and the famous Mayan blue (indigo, azurite). They used many other colours too, including green (malachite), black (soot) and white (kaolin or calcite).

## Painting

Tales of the powerful and their divine protectors painted on bark, stucco or clay give us another perspective on Mayan cultural excellence. The painters, often accorded as much prestige as the scribes, were skilful at handling colour in a symbolic way to illustrate the lives of kings and gods. The polychrome painting that covered all the stone buildings is the "hidden face" of a colour esthetic that has now disappeared, and which probably used garish colours that would shock our modern taste in the matter of ancient stone. **Frescoes**, omnipresent in Mayan architecture, incorporated a multitude of polychrome designs, flowered medallions, battle scenes or court scenes. There are now only a few traces to be seen in Guatemala.

## Ceramics

The quantity of funerary vessels found in the tombs is a good indication of the **sacred nature** of ceramics. At first containers for offerings, they became offerings in their own right. The god Itzamná in person set the example: on the Madrid Codex he is shown making a pot. For archeologists, ceramics are of prime importance for their **information value**, in several respects. In the first place, they make it possible to work out a chronology from the development of pottery techniques and styles. Secondly, they identify settlement areas and reveal patterns of trade. Further, the pictures and writing on pottery ware that has survived to our time reveal many details of royal life. Among the subjects most frequently portrayed on funerary vessels are audiences with the king (who sits on a throne facing a high-ranking visitor), scenes from court life (ritual ceremonies, festivals, etc), and representations of the underworld (gods, aquatic plants or animals, etc).

J. Gabanou/DIAF

Sculpture in the round at Copán

**A race of artists**

In its harmony of form, pattern and colour Mayan pottery reached a peak of refinement. Its **appearance** greatly depends on how the clay has been fired. Always carried out in the open and carefully controlled, the firing determined the colour of the finished piece. The more air that circulates, the more the iron in the clay oxidises and the lighter the colour of the piece. Pots can often be dated by their **form**. In the Early Classic, the Teotihuacán style tripod had a big influence on Mayan ceramics. Dishes were decorated on the outside. In the golden age of the Late Classic, two archetypes predominated: the footless cylindrical vase, used most often for offerings of chocolate, and dishes decorated on the inside. Local styles can be recognised from the **decoration**. The most typical of the Classic period are the codex style (black line design on pale cream ground), the Holmul style (red and orange design on pale cream) and the Altun Ha style (polychrome design on black).

Along with the funerary vessels, many figurines and large **incense burners** have been found; the latter held the *pom* (copal resin) which was the main offering to the gods, its purifying smoke rising heavenwards. Their bases or lids are often decorated with a rich baroque profusion of dignitaries or religious symbols. The finest collection of these objects is in the Popol Vuh museum.

Y. Keller

Sacred incense burner

The ancient Maya

# THE NEW WORLD

## From Conquistadors to colonial society

The arrival of the Spanish in the 16C was an extraordinary encounter between two civilizations, two continents. This land which the Spanish called the New World already possessed a history dating back more than a thousand years. But, since might is right, the Old World was to change the fate of the Mayan nation irreversibly.

## Spanish colonisation

### Military conquest

Three years after the fall of the Aztec capital, Hernán Cortés sent his faithful lieutenant **Pedro de Alvarado** to subdue the native populations further south. The expedition was a family affair, with Alvarado taking three brothers and two cousins with him. Within two years it was crowned with success, but involved much greed and cruelty. 420 conquistadors, 120 of them on horseback, accompanied by a thousand Amerindians from allied or newly conquered nations, entered Mayan territory on **13 February 1524**. In the first clash with the **Quiché**, the valiant warrior **Tecún Umán** achieved legendary status. Although killed by the invaders, he remains the symbol of Indigenous resistance and today his portrait can be seen on the 50-centavos banknote. Thanks to rivalries between the main tribes they encountered, the Spaniards gained control of the entire territory in less than four months. Pedro de Álvarado, whom the Mexicans nicknamed *Tonatiuh* ("bloodthirsty sun"), massacred pitilessly at the least sign of resistance. His reputation ran before him, so that very often he did not even have to

**El Dorado: Alvarado's myth**

Pedro de Alvarado was born in 1485, the same year as the famous Hernán Cortés whom he accompanied during the conquest of Mexico. However, his subsequent exactions against the indigenous people did not earn him as great a place in the history books. After his conquest of Guatemala he was appointed governor of the province. Still searching for El Dorado, he led a series of not very creditable expeditions as far south as Peru, and finally died in Mexico in 1541 after falling from his horse.

fight. At the Quiché capital of K'umarkaaj (Utatlán), he had the kingdom's two main **caciques** (natural chiefs) tortured and burned alive, as an example. The terrified **Cakchiquels** opted for allegiance and offered to help Alvarado fight the **Tzutuhils**. Far from being mollified by this attempt at conciliation, Alvarado was convinced the Cakchiquels were hiding some imaginary treasure from him and harassed them so hard that he provoked them into rebellion – a revolt that lasted several years.

### Spiritual conquest

Evangelisation was the great pretext for Spanish imperialism, whose real aspirations were far less pious. It was in the name of the "true faith" that the native peoples were "reduced", with two priests even accompanying Pedro de Alvarado on his military campaign. A significant figure in the conversion of Guatemala's indigenous people was **Bartolomé de Las Casas** (1474-1566), a Dominican friar but also a repentant former *encomendero* (holder of a concession of Indians). This famous "defender of the Indians" initiated a method of gentle, non-violent evangelisation in a part of highland Guatemala referred to at the time as the Land of War. In 1537 he obtained official backing to restrict access to this region to

When Conquistadors met Maya

Dominican missionaries; ten years later, the region acquired the name of **La Verapaz** ("true peace"), a name it has retained to this day. Bartolomé de Las Casas, Bishop of Chiapas and architect of the "New Laws" of 1542 designed to improve the lot of the native population, thus inaugurated a Dominican tradition of protecting the indigenous peoples of Central America. At the same time, **Santiago** quickly became a major centre for the Catholic faith. Churches and religious institutions mushroomed there, founded by the Franciscans and many orders of nuns from Spain and Mexico. Today, it is the ruins of these buildings that give Antigua its charm.

## The Captaincy General of Guatemala

**Santiago de Los Caballeros de Guatemala** was founded as early as 1524 – an "itinerant" capital for this new territory of the Spanish Crown, since the site changed several times before it could be permanently established at the foot of the Agua volcano *(see p 138 "Antigua")*. It was named in honour of St James, patron saint of Spanish knights ever since the Reconquest of Spain from the Moors. Guatemala was a Spanish colony which became a **captaincy general** in 1544. This autonomous province stretching from Yucatán to Panama was placed under the authority of the Viceroyalty of New Spain with its capital in Mexico City. Pedro de Alvarado was the first of a long succession of captains general lasting until 1821. The social hierarchy established in this period, with the Spanish at the top followed by the Creoles (people of Spanish stock born in the New World), has scarcely changed since. Once the **Catholic Church** had completed its work of evangelisation, it became a major centre of power through its secular clergy and the many religious orders that controlled education and public health.

# Colonial architecture

## The missal and the mason's trowel

The New World of the 16C was one vast building site. Colonial architecture was essentially **religious** and **urban**, reflecting the needs of a power structure representing the Crown, the influx of immigrants from Spain avid for a new life, and above all the religious orders keen to spread their evangelical work throughout the country. Santiago (modern Antigua) with its dozens of churches, religious institutions and oratories, became the spiritual capital of Guatemala. The palace of the captaincy general, the municipal palace and the luxurious residences in the town centre form the backdrop to a swarm of sanctuaries. In the countryside, a Franciscan or Dominican monastery would be built, preferably on the site of a former pre-Hispanic place of worship, to form the hub of a new village. Reproducing the esthetic canons of Renaissance Spain, the **Plateresque** style, with its finely-worked ornamentation (named for its resemblance to the silver filigree of the jeweller, the *platero*), stands side by side with the geometrical tracery of the Hispano-Moorish **Mudéjar** style. The increasingly resplendent religious architecture of the next century adopted the **Baroque** style. When fashion turned to the drawings in Italian architect Antonio Serlio's books, façades were lavishly covered in leafy scrollwork and lyrate columns modelled in plaster; the **Serlian style** was born. Traced at first with an entirely Spanish elegance, these motifs were later worked by native craftsmen, since the monks saw this as a highly educational activity. Over the centuries such "practical exercises" for novice Christians were to produce some subtle syncretic interpretations, a delight to the modern eye. Particularly worth seeing is the church of **San Andrés Xecul**, a marvel of variegated naive art with rampant jaguars crowning the façade.

## Gilded ardour

Gold does not stand up well to the combined action of earthquakes and volcanic eruptions, so few of the original **Baroque altarpieces** can be seen *in situ*. These carved and stuccoed wood altarpieces were gilded with gold foil to give a grand theatrical effect and exalt the grandeur of the Church. The style varied between the 17C and 18C and can be most easily recognised from the columns. Spirally fluted (or barley-sugar) columns are a sign of the 17C **Solomonic** style, the Temple of Solomon in Jerusalem supposedly having included columns of this kind. The inverted pilaster column (*estípite*) is the signature of the **Churrigueresque** style from the first half of the 18C, named after architect José de Churriguera and regarded as the most lavish expression of Spanish Baroque. From 1750, the **neoclassical** style brought architecture back to a forgotten sobriety.

**The captaincies general**
The Spanish colonies were divided into viceroyalties – covering vast expanses of territory – and four captaincies general, namely Guatemala (1544), Venezuela (1773), Chile (1778) and Cuba (1778).

## Religious institutions

Monasteries and convents were generally of a compact, rectangular plan with the longest side built along the length of the church. They needed protection against possibly hostile tribes and also had to withstand recurrent earthquakes. So bell-towers are squat, only just protruding above the roof, and walls are strengthened with buttresses. The monastery or **convent church** has just one nave. In the villages vaults were usually built of wood but few of the originals have lasted until now, most having been replaced to varying degrees of effect.

From the **coro alto**, a wide gallery sometimes stretching across two bays, monks or nuns could attend holy office without having to mix with parishioners. A door opened straight from it onto the upper gallery of the cloister, from which the cells led off. The **atrium** is wide with high walls emphasising its square plan. It had to accommodate a large crowd of native catechumens, who generally received instruction in the open air. In some cloisters the **fountains** with their laundry slabs are of daring design, like the star-shaped one at La Merced convent in Antigua. The religious communities' water engineering works were of a very high standard, and it was fairly common for a religious institution to be supplied by several kilometres of aqueduct.

## The town house
Like its Spanish model, the Creole residence was a microcosm cut off from the outside world. The building surrounded inner **courtyards** filled with flowers, where most domestic life took place. Huge, dark rooms, the setting for conventional colonial society life, were connected by numerous corridors. On the street side, high **iron-latticed windows** added a Hispanic-Moorish touch, giving a view out without a view in. The kitchen had a cooking area entirely covered by a big **chimney-hood**; the turreted pyramid shapes of these can be seen on any stroll through the streets of Antigua.

San Carlos University, Antigua

B. Brillion/MICHELIN

# FROM INDEPENDENCE TO PEACE

It is no easy thing to create a national identity in a country where colonisation has firmly established a white oligarchy. Independence, far from meeting the expectations of the essentially rural population, merely confirmed the inequality between two parallel societies. Power scarcely changed hands after the abolition of the captaincy general, and the traditional authoritarianism of the ruling class reached its apogee in military dictatorship. After the horrors of repression and its tragic results, only very recently has a young democracy ended decades of political violence.

## Independence

### A conservative national identity

In the Mexican thrust towards independence, which began in 1810, Central America's Creole oligarchy began its fight for independence, for reasons that were more economic than political. Why should they continue to fill the royal coffers of Ferdinand VII after the creation of an independent United States and the French Revolution? On **15 September 1821**, Mexico, Yucatán, Chiapas and Guatemala proclaimed their independence. In Mexico, General Iturbide dreamed of a new Mexican empire and succeeded in uniting the entire region in this short-lived adventure. In 1823 Guatemala became the political centre of the **United Provinces of Central America**. In 1839, following ferocious nationalist struggles between liberals and conservatives, Central America split up into several countries whose borders remained the subject of dispute until very recent times. Under the presidency of the conservative General **Rafael Carrera** (1851-1865), the Church and the landowners regained their property and privileges.

### The time of the reforms

The **revolution of 1871** led by General Granados brought **Justo Rufino Barrios** to power. He undertook numerous political, economic and social reforms as well as opening his country to technological progress with telegraph, telephone and railways etc. His great aspiration was to reunite Central America once more, by force of arms if necessary. He died on the battlefield in El Salvador in 1885, shortly after deciding to put his project into practice.

## The army in control

### Banana republic

Barrios was determined to bring the Guatemalan economy into the mainstream of modern capitalism, which logically entailed giving a warm welcome to North American investors. In 1880, a Boston firm began to take a keen interest in the hot, well-watered valley of the Río Motagua. This was the future **United Fruit Company**, which established banana plantations in several Central American countries and imposed United States economic and political domination over countries that were ill equipped to defend their own interests. United Fruit very soon became owner of the country's railways and the main port at Puerto Barrios. For a hundred years it ran approximately 100 000ha of banana plantations, which also constituted a decisive political weapon. For several decades the country was ruled by one dictator after another – a succession of generals who might have walked straight out of the pages of a García Márquez novel. None were inclined to resist pressure from Washington. The most radical, the tyrannical and violent General **Jorge Ubico** (1931-1944), was to crystallise opposition within the ranks of his own supporters, leading to the **revolution of 1944**. His life's work was the building of the National Palace in Guatemala City.

## A brief moment of reform

President **Juan José Arévalo** (1945-1951) inaugurated a period of social progress including, in particular, a new labour code and the right to strike. Then **Jacobo Arbenz**, who had actively participated in the armed insurrection of 1944, continued his predecessor's progressive policies and went down in history for his **Decree 900**. This was an agrarian reform law which forced the United Fruit Company to hand over a fair part of its uncultivated lands to the State. News of this hit the United States, then in the throes of McCarthyism, like a bombshell. Arbenz was a threat, and to overthrow him the CIA soon organised a military coup with the help of some Guatemalan army officers. Before leaving government in 1954, Arbenz managed to distribute more land in the space of two years than succeeding governments' agrarian reforms did in thirty.

## Dictators and guerrillas

The strong-arm military take-over soon re-established "order" and government by military junta. The Communist party was banned, the rich could sleep easy again. However, a number of young left-wing militants, deprived of free speech and encouraged by the success of the Cuban revolution, went underground. In 1960 they were joined by young rebel officers, quick to offer these ideologists a less pacific means of expression. During the **1960s**, a deeply divided guerrilla force developed, conducting sporadic actions that intensified over the 1970s. In 1972, the Guerrilla Army of the Poor or EGP (Ejército Guerillero de los Pobres) was founded, an organisation that directly involved some Quiché, who soon became the target of army repression. This took a tragic turn under the dictatorship of Lucas García. On 30 January 1980, García ordered an assault on the Spanish embassy where the representatives of various peasant movements had taken refuge. Thirty-nine people died in the fire. The following year, the first large-scale massacres of villagers in the north of the country were perpetrated.

## "Rifles and beans"

The coup d'état by General **Ríos Montt** in 1982 heralded the darkest period of modern history in Guatemala. Repression reached a peak; its main victims were still the indigenous farmers, drawn into a conflict in which they were spectators as much as participants. Obliged to feed and hide guerrilla fighters on their lands, they were accused by the army in power of collaborating with the public enemy. Many families were divided, their sons recruited into the army or heading for the hills. Four hundred and forty villages were razed, 100 000 people were massacred or disappeared, 40 000 fled to Mexico. Ríos Montt set up the famous **Civil Defence Patrols** (PACs), peasant militias armed and fed by the government (as the "rifles and beans" slogan emphasised) and forced to fight against the guerrillas in the villages. This initiative further worsened a conflict that was beginning to look like real civil war. The guerrilla reacted by uniting its scattered forces to form a single armed movement, the **URNG** (Guatemalan National Revolutionary Unity).

**Rigoberta Menchú, Nobel Peace Prize winner**
Rigoberta Menchú, a Quiché born in 1959, shared the fate of many poor indigenous girls in her province. At a very early age she went to work in the plantations with her parents, then as a housemaid in town. Her father, one of the leaders of the CUC farmers' movement (Comité de Unidad Campesina) was killed in the assault on the Spanish embassy in 1980. Shortly afterwards, the army executed her brother and mother in their village. Rigoberta fled to Mexico, where she began a campaign to focus attention on the tragedy being played out in her country and the suffering of the indigenous people. In 1992, at the age of 33, she was rewarded for her commitment with that year's Nobel peace prize. She tells the story of her life in the book I, "Rigoberta Menchú".

Rigoberta Menchú

## Peace and democracy

In 1986 civilian rule was re-established with the election of **Vinicio Cerezo**. The government made the first contacts with the guerrillas, who began to wind down their armed struggle. Cerezo's successor was **Jorge Serrano Elias**, who tried to protect his position by fomenting a civilian coup d'état but was removed from office and replaced by **Ramiro de León Carpio**, formerly government Solicitor for Human Rights.

Under his mandate, in 1994, the UN set up MINUGUA, a mission to monitor respect for human rights and oversee the peace process. It appointed Frenchman Jean Arnault as mediator in the peace negotiations, which were held in Oslo, Stockholm and Mexico City and were punctuated by several preliminary accords. On **29 December 1996**, the new President **Alvaro Arzú Irigoyen** and the URNG signed a historic peace agreement. A few weeks later the rebel troops handed in their arms and the paramilitary militias were disbanded. In 1998 the URNG became a fully-fledged political party. This was the start of a new era for Guatemala, which seems to be set for lasting peace.

# Political and administrative organisation

## Political institutions

Guatemala has a presidential system. The President of the Republic, elected by universal suffrage for a four-year mandate, is Head of State and leader of the government. The legislature is the **Congress of the Republic** with 80 seats, also renewable every four years.

## Administrative divisions

The country is divided into **22 departments**, each one administered by a governor appointed by the President of the Republic. The departments are divided in turn into municipalities (*municipios*). The mayor (*alcalde*) and his municipal councillors are appointed by the department governor. In municipalities with a big indigenous population there is also a *municipalidad indígena* representing each community (*see p 175 "Chichicastenango"*).

## Chronicle of a promised reform

The peace agreement of December 1996 signed under the mandate of President Arzú was intended to lead to a major constitutional reform including, among other things, recognition of the identity and customs of the indigenous peoples.

It was to be ushered in through a general referendum. But in the voting on 16 May 1999, in which more than 80 % of the population abstained, the unexpected result was 50.6 % of votes cast against the project. This "no" in the run-up to the end-1999 elections spread confusion in most of the major political parties.

# The economy

For Guatemala and the other countries of Central America hit by **Hurricane Mitch** in October 1998, that disaster had a significant impact on the national economy. Many roads and great expanses of banana and coffee plantations in the path of the hurricane were devastated. Growth, which had reached 4.8 % in 1998, is therefore likely to experience a slowdown. Several countries decided to cancel part of Guatemala's non-commercial bilateral debts to them, and to set up an aid fund for the Central American countries.

## A top-heavy primary sector

Guatemala is a country with a strong **farming** tradition. More than half the country's inhabitants live off the land, which accounts for a quarter of GNP and two thirds of exports.

In the Highlands, people grow mainly **maize**, their staple food for thousands of years, **frijoles** (beans) and squash. However, because of chronic land shortage and soil erosion they are having to carve out their *milpas* (fields) on ever steeper hillsides *(see p 53)*. On the fertile land in the valleys, market garden and horticultural crops are grown for sale on local markets or for export. On the Pacific coast, a dynamic economy is based on big cattle ranches and plantations of **sugar cane**, cotton and citrus fruit. From August to November the peasants generally move down from the Highlands to work as seasonal workers in these *fincas*. The forelands of the mountain ranges with their humid climates are particularly good for growing **coffee**, which is the country's primary source of foreign currency. In the Cobán region coffee is grown alongside **cardamom**, another export crop. The hot regions in the east of Guatemala grow tropical fruit and bananas on immense **plantations** near the Caribbean coast.

Near the big towns, a few small **industries** can be found involving sugar, textiles, food and pharmaceuticals.

## Foreign investment

Natural resource utilisation is mainly in the hands of foreign companies. This is the case for **nickel**, Guatemala's foremost mineral resource, and above all **oil**, which comes from wells in southern El Petén and is taken by pipeline to the Atlantic coast.

**Tourism** is a source of income that should increase steadily thanks to the 1996 peace agreement. Since hostilities ceased, Guatemala has also been attracting more foreign investors.

Following recent **privatisations**, the national electricity utility has been taken over by a Portuguese company, the telephone company TELGUA by a joint Guatemalan-Honduran group, the post office by Canadians and the railways by Americans.

Serena/HOA QUI

Coming home from market

# Meeting the people

In a village
of the Altiplano

# PEOPLES OF GUATEMALA

The population of Guatemala is astonishingly varied for a country of ten million people, but in fact there are two main population groups: the **Amerindians**, who live mainly in the highlands where population density, at nearly 500 per square kilometre, is highest; and the **Ladinos**, who although more urbanised are also to be found in the hot Petén region (population density 35 per square kilometre). The two groups live side by side, without any real mutual understanding. The Ladinos consider themselves worthy heirs to the colonial era. They hold State power and control the country's economy and politics to the almost total exclusion of the indigenous population; a mere handful of Amerindian members of parliament try to defend the interests of their community. Without openly admitting it, the Ladinos continue the exploitative relationship that the Spanish conquistadors established with the Maya. And yet the indigenous people have always been in the majority, accounting for nearly 60% of the total population, the highest proportion in any Latin American country. They are much more faithful to ancestral values, a feature that is both their strength and their weakness.

The Spanish word *indio* has pejorative connotations so *indígena* is preferred. Many well-meaning Europeans use the term *indio*, not realising that to the people themselves it communicates the opposite of respect!

## The Maya

There is no doubt that today's Maya are descended from the Maya of the Classic period of AD 250-900. Many seem to live virtually the same way Diego de Landa described in the 16C, and at that time their customs probably had not changed much since the 8C. Some Guatemalan Quiché still use the 260-day *tzolkin* calendar, while the motifs still woven in Chiapas today can be seen decorating royal tunics on relief-carved stelae.

Nonetheless, the traditional way of life has been changing in the past few years, since television was introduced – in areas with an electricity supply, at least – and especially with the influence of North American Protestant churches (*see p 67*) and of people returning from the United States after going to find work.

### The seven main Mayan families

The ethnic groups that make up today's very diverse indigenous population are the same as those encountered in 1524 by Pedro de Alvarado at the head of his troops.

**The Quiché** – From the *Popol Vuh* to Rigoberta Menchú, the Quiché have made a big contribution to Mayan culture, even giving their name, Mexicanised and then Hispanicised, to the country. Their powerful capital was **K'umarkaaj** (later called **Utatlán**). They are the biggest ethnic group and occupy the largest land area.

**From Quiché to Guatemala**
Kiché means "place of many trees" (ki = many, che = tree). The Mexican ethnic groups translated this word into Nahuatl as Quauhtemallan, which the Spanish then modified to Guatemala.

**The Cakchiquel** – The people of the "red tree" originally established their capital at **Iximché**, where the first Spanish town, named Guatemala, was rather hastily built. The Cakchiquel now live around Lake Atitlán, where the main town is **Solol**á.

F. Cavazzana/EXPLORER

Quiché colours

The Mam – Their pre-Hispanic capital was **Zaculeu**. Settled in the northern-most Highlands, they were the first victims of Pedro de Alvarado's conquering onslaught. Today they live around **Huehuetenango**.

The Tzutuhil – Their village of **Santiago Atitlán** is in almost the same place as the old Tzutuhil capital on the southern shore of Lake Atitlán, though no trace is left of the old settlement.

The Pokomam – These are the descendants of a warlike kingdom of the Post-Classic period that established its fortified city on the site of today's **Mixco Viejo**.

The Kekchi – The Kekchi held out until last and the Captain General left them to the sympathetic care of Fray Bartolomé de Las Casas; they are now scattered around the **Verapaces** region as far as Lake Izabal.

The Chorti – The territory of these sedentary farming people straddles the Guatemala-Honduras border. The focal centre of their culture is around the villages of **Camotán** and **Jocotán**.

# The Ladinos

Colonial society had an almost obsessive concern for racial distinction and *pureza de sangre* (purity of blood). In this context, the term *Ladino* originally referred to Amerindians who had learned to speak Spanish and at least partly abandoned their traditional customs. The term now covers all **non-Amerindians** in the very broadest sense: whites, including both Europeans and **Creoles** (whites of European origin born on the American continent), **Mestizos** of mixed race, and also those Amerindians who abandoned their native language and dress to adopt a Western lifestyle. The Ladino identity is very complex, straddling two worlds and two races. Ladinos are proud of their pre-Hispanic origins, which they think of as their "noble roots", yet despise today's Mayans; they criticise the Spanish colonisation of their land but envy the privileges the whites acquired through that same colonisation process.

**German immigration**
From 1850 to the early 20C, large numbers of German immigrants settled in Guatemala, especially around Cobán in the Verapaces. This was the only foreign colony to get established in that period. There were many similar projects after independence, such as an English colony in 1831 and a Belgian one in 1842, but none came to fruition. The German immigrants lived mainly from intensive farming and are now well integrated into Ladino society.

# The Garifunas

The smallest ethnic group in Guatemala, making up less than 1% of the country's population, are the Garifunas, a racial mix between Arawaks of St Vincent Island and African slaves brought by the Spanish in the 16C. Their resistance to the English occupation led to the **Caribbean War** of 1795. The following year, all the Black Caribs were deported to Roatan Island off the Honduras coast, and the few thousand survivors subsequently scattered along the coast of Central America from Honduras to Belize, where they are also called **Garinagus**. Their dialect is a mixture of Arawak, English, French Creole and African languages. They are settled around the village of **Lívingston**, accessible only by boat, and live off fishing and tourism. Many Garifunas used to work in the Puerto Barrios shipyards and when these closed in the 1960s large numbers emigrated to the United States while maintaining their families at home in Belize. The recent revival of interest in Garifuna music and dance, the famous *punta (see p 299 "The Belizean mosaic")*, has encouraged them to reassert their cultural identity.

# DAILY LIFE

In such a divided society as Guatemala, where the middle class is still a minority, lifestyles continue to differ widely. Members of each social class find a source of pride and equilibrium within their own community, rather than feeling they belong to a united national entity. And yet contacts and exchanges are everyday occurrences. People move and travel a lot, to sell at a neighbouring market or visit family members in the provinces. The multi-coloured buses that come and go along the Pan-American Highway, weighed down with bags and bundles, provide the link between town and country.

## Life in the countryside

Although most country folk in this predominantly rural land live the hardy lives of traditional peasants, it is the latifundia that dominate Guatemala's farming economy. In the **Highlands**, where settlement is at its most dense, even the steepest hillsides are cultivated, the Mayan farmers working their tiny fields individually or collectively. But from 1500m down to the coast, the land is given over to big **plantations** of coffee, sugar and bananas owned by Ladinos, who hire Amerindian labour for the harvest.

Family role division is very firmly fixed. Very early in the morning, the farmer sets off for the *milpa* (maize field) that constitutes his daily world. There he works with the most basic of tools: a digging hoe to prepare and maintain the soil, a machete for cutting wood, a dibble stick *(coa)* for sowing seed. In the afternoon, before sundown, he goes home with enough wood to cook supper. Then he does any maintenance required on the house he built with his own hands. Distractions in the evening are rare; as yet, TV has not taken over from conversation among the men in the village square. Meanwhile, the farmer's wife has been busy about her daily chores. She has been to the wash-place to do the laundry, to the market to buy or sell, she has fetched water – very few houses have running water, though they may have electricity – and sometimes wood. She has also made the *tortillas*, the flat maize pancakes that are the family's staple. The maize meal dough is soaked in quick-lime water and lemon juice then shaped by lightly slapping it in the palm of the hand, a gesture that soon becomes familiar to visitors. These activities mean frequent foot journeys by road and, especially noticeable, the use of the **mecapal** (tumpline), a leather band across the forehead which people use to carry heavy loads on their backs – including the wardrobes you see in the markets!

Terrace cultivation

F. Le Diascorn/RAPHO

Daily life

Daily life

Herculean prowess with a little help from the "mecapal"

## Housing

Using a minimum of manufactured materials, Guatemalan building styles adapt to the climate and natural resources of each region. In fact this choice is made for economic reasons, for as soon as there is enough money, breezeblocks are the quickest way to a

**El Mecapal**

| Para | For |
|------|-----|
| nosostros | we |
| los indios | Indians, |
| el cielo termina | the heavens end |
| donde comienza | where |
| el mecapal | the mecapal begins. |

(Poem by Humberto Ak'abal)

comfortable home. Wood, palm fronds or clay can be used in many different ways, providing effective protection from cold in the hills or the ventilation so essential in hot climates. Alas, this natural regulation is increasingly giving way to corrugated iron.

In the **Highlands,** houses are built of **adobe (large bricks of unbaked clay mixed with straw),** sometimes covered with a limewashed rendering. On the shores of Lake Atitlán, bamboos are used as a framework for cob walls. The roofs are tiled and have no chimney; smoke escapes through the cracks. In Quiché country all the roofs have a front overhang supported by posts, beneath which maize cobs can be seen drying. Many houses have a **temazcal** close by, a small, clay-built, igloo-shaped sweat-house for the traditional steam bath. The cleanliness and hygienic lifestyle of the Amerindians impressed (and shocked!) the Spanish, who forbade the use of the *temazcal* for fear that it would weaken their labourers' blood. Inside the house, furnishings are sparse and simple: a few items of pinewood furniture on the beaten earth floor, a hanging cradle, a small altar with pictures of saints. The few decorative items are often Western kitsch bought in the markets. Mattresses, stuffed with wheat straw, are changed yearly; sometimes people sleep on a simple straw mat.

In the **Lowlands** people live in rectangular wooden huts or cabins built of close-fitted boards or a lattice of branches, sometimes covered with cob. Inside is just one room, with one or more hammocks strung across it; cooking is usually done outside. Roofs are of palm fronds. Many Chortis living near the Honduran border still build their homes entirely of fan-palm fronds.

In El Petén, in the days of the counter-guerrilla resettlement operations of the early 1980s, more than 400 villages were razed and their populations relocated to new villages laid out by bulldozers in the jungle. Other villages have been created more recently to gradually repatriate thousands of refugees from Mexico; these are made up of sad corrugated-iron shacks lined up along streets cut straight as a die. In the Flores region, a Spanish development scheme that began in 1992 has provided several hundred such huts with rainwater collecting systems and tanks.

On the **Atlantic coast** there are examples of the famous Carib architecture with its wooden houses on stilts in attractive pastel colours.

## The milpa

This little field, lauded by the poet Miguel Ángel Asturias, is the daily world of the Maya farmer. After centuries of competition with the forest, farming has now won over the land – at the price of a worrying degree of deforestation. **Maize growing** is still practised by slash-and-burn methods in El Petén; in the hills you more often see perfectly ploughed fields. Terraces are rare, despite the steep hillsides; in their place are diagonal undulations to prevent landslides.

The Mayan peasant is tied to his land by an almost symbiotic bond. The *Popol Vuh* tells how man was created from maize dough; this communion between man and the fruit of his labour is the source of a philosophy far removed from any notion of exploiting the land. The life of the *milpa* is shaped by the seasons, the **rituals** of sowing and harvesting and the supernatural magic of germination. Adding chemical fertiliser or weedkiller does nothing to alter this unchanging harmony that keeps the Mayan people outside "our" time.

## The market

The market is an indispensable meeting place for economic and social life in country areas, and market day is the big event in rural life. The **women** play a decisive part. It is they who do the selling, bargaining in low voices. In the village of Almolonga, tons of flowers and vegetables are traded every day for delivery to the towns. Strolling between lines of saleswomen in gay *huipiles* are solemn-faced Ladino merchants, while multicoloured pyramids of vegetables pass by on the heads of hurrying women; the inattentive visitor is likely to get shoved unceremoniously aside! Everywhere else the market takes place once or twice a week and offers a much wider choice than the jumble of goods in the village *tienda* (shop). The market is the great weekly get-together where the community renews its ties and when the municipal council holds its meeting.

Once used to the dizzy swirl of colour and the silent jostling, it becomes evident that in fact the goods are neatly laid out, with textiles, poultry, fruit and vegetables each displayed in their own section of the market. There is an incongruous medley of hardware: cheap Asian imports alongside local craft work, local *huipil* soap balls of pork fat and ash alongside Made in China umbrellas. The **small street trades** add to the market's charm: the bird man who makes his canary choose an envelope to predict your future, the vendor grating a big block of ice to make "syrup snow" (*nieve de sabor*) or the bilingual barker with a loudspeaker on his van, offering a miracle remedy to get your cattle fit.

*Life in the countryside*

**Daily life**

## The washing-place

As in Europe in the days before the washing machine, the women and girls of the village do their laundry together; the washing-place is where they meet and work, commenting on the latest village news, for the better part of the morning. In the volcanic Highlands, washing-places are often located to take advantage of one of the hot and slightly sulphurous springs that abound there. Sometimes there are public baths alongside the washing-place. It may be the riverside as in Zunil, or a pond as in Cuatro Caminos, where the women, up to their waists in water, wash themselves and the laundry on the bank. Huge tench slip between their legs, quite undisturbed by the warm soapy water. More elaborate washing facilities, like those in Antigua, have retained their colonial form with a half-moon section jutting out above the main pool.

# Guatemala City: dream and nightmare

Guatemala City is the country's only big city. Although Quetzaltenango, Huehuetenango and Antigua have quite large populations, they have a very provincial atmosphere, far removed from the vicissitudes of a metropolis. The capital, by contrast, seems to concentrate all the ills of development: pollution, social inequality and violence create a world at the opposite pole to life in the countryside, which may be tough but is nourished by tradition.

Washday on the banks of Lake Atitlán

R. Marca

## The urban landscape

Housing in the towns is as diverse as the people. Repeated earthquakes have made rubble of all architectural conventions, and the resulting towns, rebuilt again and again, are a disparate mixture of styles. The dream of the successful Guatemalan is a concrete box with smoked glass windows, as far away as possible from the city's noisy commercial centre, left to the destitute once the steel shop shutters are pulled down in the evening. In any of the many ravines (*barrancos*) that ring the capital, a shanty town can spring up overnight. Several families get together and, evading police patrols, offload sandbags to build a platform on the sloping ground. A few planks and corrugated iron sheets by way of a roof and their shack is in place; the authorities may vainly evict the occupants over the following days, they will settle in anyway, as best they can.

## The frightened rich

It is quite possible to be very rich in Guatemala, which has the most vigorous economy in Central America. Some of the big family fortunes were built up in the early 20C in the plantations, others more recently when industry got off the ground or by laundering drug money, a practice long facilitated by a generous tax system. Blocks of luxury flats began to mushroom in the 1970s and '80s, closely followed by American-style shopping malls. For those who want to display their wealthy lifestyle, it is the done thing to have a luxury villa on the shores of Lake Atitlán and a "hut" with a private landing-stage on the Río Dulce. This apparently free and easy life has a serious downside, however: the rich live in fear of kidnapping, which is almost a national sport among the criminal classes. Credentials must be shown to get into the smart La Cañada district of Guatemala City with its impressive array of electrified barbed wire. Shopkeepers, too, are afraid and are gradually turning their shops into strongholds, serving customers through the bars. The fight against crime is the cornerstone of every electoral campaign and security firms are thriving. After the peace accord of December 1996, when many guerrillas and militiamen were "laid off", joining a criminal gang was the obvious way to a new livelihood for some of them.

## The urban poor

The life that awaits country people moving into town is very different. Most settle into the crowded shanty towns of Avenida del Ferrocarril (the disused railway that runs through the city), on the hillsides under constant threat from seismic faults or on the Mezquital waste tip, where they begin a life of crushing poverty. Here the Mayans turn Ladino, joining the many other poor Ladinos trying to make a living from small trades. The best jobs available are as **domestic servants**, for every well-off family has at least a housekeeper living in and taking care of the children and the house. More than a few also have a chauffeur-cum-gardener, who often in fact does all the odd jobs needed. Employers and servants may be very fond of each other, but the relationship always keeps to a strict social code. There are many social outcasts, especially children and old people fleeing family violence bred of poverty. Young children creeping under cardboard boxes to keep from the cold and escape police harassment are a common sight at nightfall near the bus station.

# Children of Guatemala

## An Amerindian childhood: from milpa to school

Roles are divided between the sexes from a very early age. A boy goes with his father to the fields, trotting proudly behind carrying the machete. Girls help their mothers in the house and with the laundry, and learn to weave. The state education system has been adapted to fit in with these activities, giving children the choice between morning or afternoon classes. But fewer girls than boys go to school: they have more work to do in the home than the boys have in the fields. They look after the smaller children, do their share of household chores, watch over the animals. If there are tourists in the area they are also formidable little saleswomen, tirelessly putting on their charming smiles to soften the hardest of hearts. Few children will ask you for money, but all will have something to sell you! The government is aware of this problem and a few years ago launched a major consciousness-raising campaign to get the girls into school, with the slogan *"Niña educada, Madre del desarollo"* ("Educated daughter, mother of development").

## A Ladino childhood: selection based on wealth

For those who have the means, the North American lifestyle is the model that shapes the broad lines of a city childhood. Guatemala is a paradise for private education. When enrolment time comes round, a host of schools with high-sounding names and innovative teaching methods splash out on advertising, competing fiercely for pupils. This is no accident: it would never enter the heads of a middle-class family, let alone the rich, to send their children to a state school alongside children of the lower social classes. Many parents send their children away to be educated; at lunch-time Antigua's central park is invaded by swarms of cheerful secondary school children in impeccable uniforms coming to nibble their lunches. Antigua, not far from the capital, but much less exposed to the perils of the big city, has a great many private schools and institutes, nearly all of them Church-run.

## Worlds apart

**Alvaro** is twelve and lives in a pretty villa in Guatemala City's Zone 9. He goes to Lenhsen College and enjoys only-child status at home as his eighteen-year-old brother is in the USA for a year to perfect his English. Alvaro's father is a doctor at the Roosevelt hospital, his mother works in a travel agency. He loves ecology and wants to be a vulcanologist. His grandparents, originally from Germany, have a country house in Cobán; on holiday there, he spends long days in the wild. It is always Concepción, his *"muchacha"*, who fetches him from school but he would rather ride home by bike. Concepción is Quiché, has lived in the house since Alvaro was born and is virtually one of the family. Alvaro's father has promised his son that for his fourteenth birthday he can go to Concepción's home village with her.

**Andrea** is eleven and lives in Santa Catarina Palopó, a Cakchiquel village on the shores of Lake Atitlán. An enchanting place, but a hard life when you are the oldest child of the family. Her mother weaves at home for a cooperative; her father has found work on a coffee plantation in San Lucas on the opposite shore and does not get home often. Every morning Andrea walks with her little sister past the brand new school being built beside the village's tourist hotel; then they take a boat to Panajachel, where she sells bracelets woven by her five brothers and sisters and pink fruit called *pitahayas*, when they are in season. She loves the effervescent life of "Pana" and takes her street seller's role very seriously. Around 2pm they have to think about getting back, as she still has three hours of school ahead of her, water to fetch and her little brother to wash. She dreams of finding a job in a Panajachel hotel when she grows up.

Children of Guatemala

Under the arcades of Antigua

J.-L. Dugast/HOA QUI

# TRADITIONAL DRESS

Traditional Amerindian clothing is unique for its vivid colours. In the markets, where all your senses are wide-awake, the medley of bright fabrics is the first thing to draw your attention: a real feast for the eyes! The variety is impressive, with a multitude of religious symbols and motifs illustrating ancestral myths. Every upland village has its own costume, worn like a uniform by every member of the community. It is above all a sign of belonging to a particular group and a mark of the people's respect for their forebears. Whether hand- or machine-woven, these elaborate fabrics embody all the vitality of Mayan culture and the magnificence of its two-thousand-year-old tradition.

## A changing tradition

Weaving is the quintessential feminine activity, formerly under the protection of the **goddess Ixchel**; it is a daily activity for almost all Mayan women. The beauty and diversity of their fabrics, mainly produced for family use, is enchanting. New techniques and new materials have been adopted without any loss of identity; the way of weaving and the form of the women's costume have scarcely varied since their beginnings. The old stelae show long tunics like those worn in modern Yucatán, and clay figurines show women weaving in a posture that has not changed since. But colonisation and the novelties of the modern world have been put to use to renew a lively textile art that also has its fashions.

## Uses and symbolism of the costume

### Women's dress

The women's dress is made up from rectangles of cloth as they come from the loom, sewn together in the simplest way. It looks almost exactly as it did in the pre-Hispanic era.

The most decorative item is the **huipil** (a Cakchiquel word), a tunic or blouse made from two rectangles of cloth. These are sewn together down one long side, leaving a gap in the middle for the neck. The new rectangle is then folded in two widthways and the sides sewn together, the seams stopping short of the shoulder fold to leave holes for the arms to go through. The neck hole may be further decorated to form a square or circle. The patiently woven *huipil* is made to last a lifetime. When a mother makes a *huipil* for her daughter, she puts tucks in either side of the neck opening so it can be let out as the child grows. When the girl reaches the age of motherhood, she inserts a zip in the side seam at breast height, so she can breast-feed. Now that the natural dyes have been gradually abandoned, *huipiles* fade more quickly and must be replaced more often.

The **corte** (skirt) is a long piece of cloth sewn together at the ends to form a tube. The woman steps into it, winds it around and adjusts it at the waist with the help of a wide woven belt, the **faja**.

The front of the skirt is covered by an **apron**, woven with an ikat pattern and gathered at the waist. Worn mainly to keep clean during the day's work, it is an integral part of the costume in many villages.

The **tzut** is a multi-purpose piece of cloth like a wide scarf. Folded and placed on the head, it protects from the sun and serves as a pad for carrying. Unfolded, it becomes a shawl to wrap up in during cold weather, or for carrying a child or goods.

The **hair and head-dress** add greatly to the charm of the costume. All Mayan women wear their hair long, often with a woven ribbon (*cinta de pelo*) wound around the head. This **cinta** (which can also be a narrow scarf) some-times ends in pom-poms,

R. Mattes

Like mother, like daughter

or is wound into the form of a disc, as in Santiago Atitlán (*see p 165*); it is then known as a **tocoyal**. The resemblance between the *tocoyal* and the royal head-dress shown on the Copán stelae is remarkable. Elderly women typically wear their hair in two plaits bound together by a *cinta* wound into each plait in turn.

**Jewellery**, though very important to Mayan women, is not as valuable as it once was. For everyday use plastic necklaces have replaced the old silver coins and glass beads, which have been sold off little by little to collectors.

## Men's dress

Only in a few villages is the traditional men's costume still worn on a day-to-day basis, but it is still widely adopted for festive occasions. It consists of a pair of simple, tubular **trousers** held at the waist by a woven belt. The **shirt** and **jacket** are imitations of the European varieties. The **ponchito**, generally worn over the trousers, is a short woollen blanket wound around the waist.

On their feet men wear **sandals** (*huaraches*), which are simple leather (or rubber tyre) soles laced around the ankles. Their headgear is a *tzut*, just like the women's version, but covering the forehead and with flaps down the back. But the men's *tzut* is only worn on festive occasions, or is worn turban-style by the *cofrades*, members of religious brotherhoods called *cofradías*.

Traditional dress

A group of "muchachos" from Todos Santos

The only accessory is the square woven **bag** *(morral)*, carried slung across the chest. This is used only by the men, who keep their lunch, string and knife in it when they go out to the fields.

The **cofradías' costumes** are of particularly high quality, requiring a major financial sacrifice by their owners. The one worn in Chichicastenango has short trousers *(sash)*, an embroidered black wool jacket and a multi-coloured *tzut*.

## Motifs

These reflect animist beliefs and ancient Mayan **myths**. The most characteristic design is found in the village of San Mateo Ixtatán; it represents the Sun and Moon, with the wearer's head at the centre of the universe. Geometric patterns and animal designs can also relate to episodes from the *Popol Vuh*, which has a veritable bestiary of characters from macaws to hummingbirds. Paper models of the designs are sold in the markets, but more experienced weavers do not hesitate to innovate, sometimes inspired by their dreams.

**Animals** are a favourite theme, more or less stylised and sometimes in curious combinations. In the village of Nahuala, for example, the two-headed bird symbolising duality is paired with an unexpected alter ego: the two-headed Habsburg eagle!

**Plants** are also a frequent theme, especially maize plants and trees (remember the words "Quiché" and "Guatemala" both mean "many trees").

**Lightning bolts** and **zigzags** represent the sky god Huracán.

**Diamonds** represent the universe and its cardinal points. This motif is found most frequently on *huipiles* from the Chiapas, but can also be seen in Guatemala. On the *huipil* of Santa María de Jesús it is the only symbol.

## A key to traditional dress

Learning to recognise the costumes of the biggest villages takes you to the heart of Mayan culture. If you turn to a woman at a bus stop and name her village while pointing at her *huipil*, she is sure to give you a big knowing smile in return. Costumes are also a key to understanding the trading relations between ethnic groups, by recognising, for example, the Cakchiquels who come to sell their vegetables in the Quiché market at Chichicastenango. Here are a few distinctive signs to help identify them.

**Cakchiquel**

| | |
|---|---|
| San Antonio Aguas Calientes | Double-sided quetzal design. |
| San Antonio Palopó | Men wear woollen skirts and no trousers. The men's shirt and the *huipil* are almost identical. Glass bead necklaces for women. |
| Santa Catarina Palopó | Greenish-blue acrylic dyes and metallic thread in the *huipil*. Scarf wound into the hair. |
| San Juan Sacatepéquez | Predominantly yellow *huipil*. Mythical bird (*muan*) or young cock motifs. |
| Sololá | Men wear a brown and cream woollen skirt over predominantly pink trousers. |

**Ixil**

| | |
|---|---|
| Chajul | Simple embroidered motifs on a plain background (hummingbirds, two-headed animals, human figures). |
| Nebaj | Plaited hairstyle with big pom-poms. Curled motif around the neck, mosaic pattern based on stylised birds. |

**Mam**

| | |
|---|---|
| Todos Santos Cuchumat n | The men's shirt has a wide embroidered collar. Hats worn by men and women. |

**Quiché**

| | |
|---|---|
| Almolonga and Zunil | Woven ribbon with motifs and small pom-poms in the hair. Geometrical star motifs. |
| Chichicastenango | Round neckline with sun rays all around. Large flower motifs or "W" pattern. |
| Quetzaltenango | Large machine-embroidered flowers sewn onto the *huipil*. Ikat skirt. |

**Tzutuhil**

| | |
|---|---|
| Santiago Atitlán | Wine-red or multi-coloured stylised animals embroidered onto a red-striped fabric (the "flame-red" *huipiles* offered for sale are specially dyed to please tourists). On Sundays and feast days the men wear trousers embroidered with birds. |

**Symbolism of the costume**

# Weaving

Spanish influence is reflected in the introduction of **wool** and **silk**, unknown to the Maya before the conquest. The conquistadors never banned the wearing of traditional costume; on the contrary, they encouraged it because it helped them control population movements. The introduction of the **foot loom** enabled weavers to increase their output; this was the beginning of the cloth trade. Renaissance Spanish dress styles also inspired the Mayan weavers, who began to incorporate **velvet** into the *huipil* (for collar and sleeves), and sometimes **lace**. Male dress too changed under the influence of European styles, with trousers replacing the loincloth, and shirt and jacket taking over from the cape.

Since the 19C modern influence has brought in **synthetic fibres** and with them a new range of colours, industrial weaving (for skirts, utility cloths and export fabrics) and the **sewing machine**.

## Fibres

The traditional fibre is **cotton**, which comes in two natural colours, white and light brown. It is less and less often spun with distaff and spindle and dyed as it used to be. Most of the balls or skeins you see in the markets are imported; the mercerised cotton preferred for embroidery, and which is also the dearest, is made by a major French brand!

**Silk** is used for ceremonial *huipiles*. Few Mayans can afford such a luxury and replace it with a silky corded cotton. Other plant fibres such as agave or sisal (*ixtle*) are also used in weaving, though only for making items for the home.

**Wool** is particularly suitable for the cold climate of the uplands. It is used for skirts, or mixed with cotton to make *huipiles*.

**Synthetic fibres** are very popular, especially in view of their price and the new colour range they have introduced. The most popular are acrylic (which is used, for example, to weave the very lovely *huipiles* of San Antonio Palopó) and gold or silver thread, which give fabrics a glitter that is much appreciated by the Cakchiquels.

## Looms

The Mayans use two types of loom. The **hip-strap loom** (telar de cintura or de palitos) is of pre-Columbian origin and is used only by women. It is made up of seven wooden parts that hold the warp and weft threads. Having no fixed frame, it is easy to carry; one end is attached to a tree or door, the other to a strap around the weaver's lower back (hence the name).

The **foot loom** (telar de pie) was introduced in the 17C and is traditionally worked by men. It makes wider cloth for skirts, utility cloths etc. In some villages, such as Patzún, it is used for the ground cloth of the *huipil*, which is then embroidered by the women.

The **sewing machine** is not a loom but it now plays an important part in making clothes. Running a sewing machine is something of a male preserve, and it is also used to embroider large flowers or collars sewn onto some *huipiles*. Although foreigners in search of authentic folk art despise the technique, it takes a high degree of skill and deserves attention.

Woman weaving on a hip-strap loom

R. Marca

Weaving

## Techniques

Combining the warp and weft threads is a rich and varied art in Guatemala. The simplest base is a **plain weave** with the weft thread taking one warp thread at a time. In **serge**, the floating threads create a diagonal texture. The basic decoration technique is single or double-sided **brocade**, in which the motif is created by weaving in an additional swivel weft thread. The village of San Antonio Aguas Calientes is famous for its quetzal design, identical on both sides of the cloth. **Embroidery** allows great freedom in the motif, and several fabrics can be superposed in **appliqué**. **Jaspe** (ikat or jaspé fabric) is an ancestral thread dyeing technique also found in Asia; it involves knotting the skein at calculated intervals before dyeing, leaving the thread with undyed parts that form a pattern on the woven cloth.

**Profession: farmer and embroiderer**

José Pop Pacach is a young Tzutuhil who lives in Santiago Atitlán. Breaking with tradition, at a very early age he showed as keen an interest in the needle as in the spade, and took up embroidery under the attentive eye of his grandmother. Every day around 3pm, when he gets in from his "milpa", José the farmer sits down to embroider exquisitely delicate birds. A friend gave him a book illustrated with pictures of Guatemalan birds, and ever since he has been faithfully reproducing the different species on ceremonial trousers, working with immense patience: thirty birds on each leg, a year's work. The trousers cost too much for villagers to buy, so they may never be worn, but they are nonetheless the quintessence of a lively and creative textile tradition.

# What future for the traje?

In weaving, as in many other fields, women are the guardians of tradition. The same cannot be said of the men, most of whom have given up their traditional dress (*traje*) for European wear. One reason for this vestimentary acculturation is **military service**, when many Mayans put off their *traje* for the first time to put on army fatigues. There is an economic factor, too: embroidery thread is expensive and it is very tempting to dress more cheaply in the **second-hand clothes** that come in from North America by the container-load and flood the markets. Used clothes regurgitated by Western consumer society thus end up on the backs of these artists of the handloom. In addition, girls who continue their education beyond primary school are very likely to find themselves wearing the plain-coloured blouse and pleated skirt uniform of some Church school in the nearest town.

Aware of the artistic heritage the Mayan costume represents, the **Ixchel Museum** in Guatemala City displays old *huipiles* with colours and motifs or patterns that are no longer used. For anyone interested in textiles, this museum is a must (*see p 121*). To end on an optimistic note, traditional culture has such a capacity for digesting outside contributions without losing its soul, that the costume still has a future. In fact tourism has encouraged a number of villages to revive craft techniques that were dying out.

Traditional dress

New colours from synthetic fibres

Béatrice Brillion/MICHELIN

# RELIGION

The diversity of religions is truly surprising for such a small country. It reflects the profound religious ardour of the indigenous people, who have kept all their polytheistic or **animistic beliefs** while adapting to most of the religious persuasions that have come to colonise this land of "sorcerers". But this strong spirituality is mainly expressed in a sense of oneness with nature, with the Earth that provides food for the body and, through the richly imaginative Mayan iconography, the mind. Passed down through the generations are many daily or seasonal rites honouring the generosity of the spirits that protect the land's fertility; they take the form of communal prayers in the *milpas* (maize fields) or around the houses. **Nahualism**, or belief in a supernatural animal double, is another example of the indigenous people's close bond with their environment. Only the community's leaders have such an alter ego or *nahual*: formerly the kings, now the shamans.

## Roman Catholicism

Roman Catholicism has been the official religion since the Spanish conquest, but its five hundred year supremacy is now endangered by an influx of North American Protestant churches (*see below*). The internal hierarchy of the **Roman Catholic Church** is itself deeply divided between the prelates of the secular clergy, who are close to the governing class, and the young **country priests** sent out by the religious orders, who are more sensitive to the indigenous people's cause. Many have learned to speak Quiché or Cakchiquel and are invited by their flock to attend pre-Hispanic rites; some have paid with their lives for their support of the peasants. With its colouring of local tradition, from All Souls' Day to the Holy Week processions (*see p 72 "Festivals and ceremonies"*), Roman Catholicism nevertheless remains the ferment of Guatemalan culture. Near the border with El Salvador and Honduras is a place of pilgrimage that cements the country's Catholic faith: **Esquipulas**, where the black statue of Jesus carved by Quirio Cataño in 1595 is kept. This holy image is credited with innumerable miracles; since 1759 it has been housed in an imposing four-towered Baroque basilica that is the flagship of Central American Catholicism, drawing over a million faithful a year, especially around 15 January (*see p 256*).

**Hermano Pedro: a strange kind of devotion**
Brother Pedro de Bethancourt, a Franciscan monk born in the Canary Islands in 1626, is widely venerated. He founded the first hospital for the poor in the capital and was beatified in 1981. His tomb is in the church of San Francisco in Antigua. But far from resting in peace, he is said to answer prayers for health or success; pilgrims come in their thousands and do not hesitate to knock on his tombstone to arouse his good will. Hundreds of dusty votive offerings are there to witness that faith really does work miracles – especially as the "Hermano" (Brother) recently moved out, his remains having been transferred to a side chapel where few visitors venture. After their prayers the faithful burn candles, each colour symbolising a specific request: white for the protection of children, green for business, black for jealousy or enemies etc. For a modest sum the temple merchants sell multicoloured candles to suit any and every circumstance.

# Amerindian syncretism

Most indigenous people are Catholics but have kept many of the religious customs of their forebears. Rural life is punctuated by the superstitions and supernatural beliefs passed on from generation to generation, with their corresponding occult practices. To ensure good harvests and protect their families, the Mayans regularly invoke divinities from the beyond or nature spirits (such as the *Pascual Abaj* of Chichicastenango), in caves, on hilltops, on the ruins of ancient pyramids – or even in church. Some of the offering rites seen in churches are patent proof that the priests have given up any attempt to impose orthodoxy. **Shamans**, intercessors, seers or healers (*curanderos*) officiate; only they know the rituals and the interminable litanies in indigenous languages mixed with Spanish. Incense (*pom*) purifies, the colour of the candle spells out the purpose of the request, the idol is honoured with flowers and aguardiente. In Quiché culture, a chicken is sacrificed in a rite to ensure fertility for a woman and prosperity for the household.

Along the wayside you are bound to notice the *costumbre* **altars**, blackened stone hearths spattered with melted wax and sprinkled with flowers. A burnt offering is the quintessential syncretic ritual. The gift goes up in smoke, materialising the spirit rising to meet the gods and ancestors. **Soothsaying** is another of the shaman's prerogatives. To read the omens they use quartz pebbles or *tzite* seeds (the fruit of the *pito* tree, *Erythrina Corallodendron*). The maize god **Yum Kaax** is still worshipped by some ethnic groups; his image can be seen carved on the bishop's seat in the church of Santiago Atitlán!

R. Marca

The "costumbre" altar, a place for offerings and prayer

## The cofradías

The indigenous people never having really accepted monotheism, the **saint worship** encouraged by the earliest Spanish evangelists naturally took over from the abundant Mayan pantheon. The saints' statues lined up along each side of the church naves are carefully dressed and treated with great veneration. They are piously looked after by the **cofrades**, members of the religious brotherhoods (*cofradías*) responsible for them. In some villages these take turns to house a holy statue in their own homes for a year; that way the faithful can call on their favourite saint at home.

Religion

In Chichicastenango, where there are no less than fourteen religious brotherhoods, their members can be recognised by the brightly coloured outfits they wear on Sundays and for religious celebrations. During Mass they sit in the choir on either side of the priest. For settling village disputes they wield more authority in the community than do the civil authorities. The **cofradía** directs the ceremony for its patron saint's festivities. The statue is dressed up and paraded round the village on a float decked with feathers and enveloped in a cloud of smoke from the incense and firecrackers. After being honoured this way for several days running, the saint is then settled into the new home.

**Amerindian syncretism**

**Prayer to San Simón**

"O powerful St Simon, I offer you this cigar, this "tortilla", this "aguardiente" and these little candles, if you will protect me from all dangers that threaten me. If I am sued for debts I cannot pay, make the judge decide in my favour (...) I ask you in the name of the One you sold for thirty pieces of silver that were given to those in greatest need."

**San Simón, patron saint of traders** – A village child guides curious tourists through a labyrinth of alleyways until rising smoke indicates their destination. In the yard, candles, bundles of cigars, eggs and resin are burning, all copiously sprinkled with aguardiente. In a dark room, saturated with the smell of incense and with Christmas music playing in the background, sits the hatted idol, a lighted cigar between its lips, surrounded by half-drunken *cofrades*. The atmosphere is not exactly contemplative and visitors are asked for a financial contribution, so it is excusable to think at first that the whole scene has been devised for their benefit. But no. A woman sits in front of the idol. The shaman earnestly addresses this figure, explaining that this woman's neighbour has cast a spell on her. Then he takes several mouthfuls of aguardiente and spits it out all over the woman's face and body.

The cult of St Simon, also called **Maximón** in Santiago Atitlán, began in the 19C. He is both *Mam*, benevolent grandfather-god of the ancient Maya, and Judas Iscariot, called Simon after his father to avoid confusion with St Judas Thaddeus. His European looks vary from place to place; he may be made of wood or plastic and in the village of Zunil he even wears sunglasses! Formerly protector of the traders who came down from the Highlands to the capital, he is now venerated in a handful of villages by anyone seeking relief from suffering or escape from vendettas. The Ladinos also have their St Simon, in the village of San Andrés Itzapa.

## Protestantism

You will not meet any Lutherans or Calvinists in Guatemala. South American Protestants are mostly evangelists and are simply known as **cristianos**. Forty per cent of Guatemalan Christians are now Protestants, belonging to a whole host of Methodist, Pentecostal or Presbyterian churches with such evocative names as "Fountain of life", "Heavenly abode", "Light of the world" or "Complete Gospel".

In 1982 **General Ríos Montt**, himself a Protestant, came to power and encouraged many sects from the United States to come and glean followers in Guatemala. This was not simply out of religious conviction, for these churches encourage an austere lifestyle with no alcohol or ostentation, and incite the poor to accept their fate.

The **evangelical churches** quickly became established, even in the most remote parts of the country. Their churches and chapels rarely go unnoticed: they are sometimes the only concrete-and-corrugated-iron building in the village. Some practise an aggressive form of proselytising, going even so far as to preach by loudspeaker or organise evangelical rock concerts in the market place. The Ladinos were the first to be won over but oddly enough the Amerindians, despite their more reserved character, have quite readily assimilated a form of religion whose rhythmic hymns sometimes take them to the very edge of trance. Following the trend, Mormons and Jehovah's Witnesses have also found many new souls to convert in Guatemala.

Religion

Worshipping St Simon in Zunil

L. Girard/EXPLORER

# FESTIVALS AND CEREMONIES

The Mayans seize every occasion to express their love of celebrating. Festival follows ceremony all year round, almost all of them connected with Roman Catholicism and some with pre-Hispanic traditions. The recent Protestant converts have had to give up a great many of them, including All Souls' Day, the Feast of the Dead. The Ladinos take an active part in the big festivals of the liturgical calendar, although in a less exuberant way. Music is an integral part of all festivities, be they sacred or profane; more often instrumental than vocal, their often repetitive themes invite people alternately to dance and to uplift their souls. Although all the instruments except the drum are of European origin, the stamping and more especially the wearing of masks for many traditional dances are ancestral customs. Here the mask is far more than a theatrical prop; it is a veritable "double" to which the wearer gives life. No festivity is complete without firecrackers, whose purpose is to awaken the Spirits and welcome them.

## Music, dance and drama

### The marimba

This instrument is the Latin American equivalent of Black Africa's wooden xylophone, the balaphon; it was introduced by black slaves in the 16C. Played by Amerindians and Ladinos alike, the marimba has become Guatemala's national instrument. It takes three to five musicians together to play its long row of **wooden slats**, and in processions, which often involve pentatonic melodies, the musicians must also be able to play as they walk. The marimba's sound box is made of **calabashes** and a vibrating tongue adds a special edge to the low notes. The Ladinos have produced a more sophisticated model, replacing the gourds by wooden tubes with pointed ends. Adding drums and double bass, they have created a repertoire of 19C waltzes and Latin rhythms of the 1930s.

### Ameridian ritual music

Amerindian music with its insistent melodies can induce a mystical melancholy at village celebrations. A type of **shawm** (of the oboe family) is accompanied by a roughly crafted guitar and violin and a square tambourine (*tupe*). These instruments can be seen and heard at the **Casa K'ojom** in Antigua. At syncretist rites the shaman's declamations have gradually replaced the true ritual chants still sung in Yucatán.

### Local bands

The popular bands are Ladino in origin but in rural areas they traditionally accompany the dead to their last resting-place – whence their solemn, rather lugubrious repertoire. Bands play an important part in the Holy Week processions, when their melodies are no livelier than usual.

### The Conquest dance

This dance is performed in Mexico and Guatemala, and although it is a very popular tourist attraction, its meaning should not be forgotten. Its origin lies in ancestral Mayan dances, adopted and perverted by the Spanish priests to relate landmarks in the history of Christendom (the *baile de los Moros y Cristianos* tells the tale of the Reconquest of Spain from the Muslim Moors) and the "glorious" deeds of the conquistadors (Cortés versus the Aztec Emperor Moctezuma). However, the Mayans have transformed the *baile de la Conquista* in their turn, transforming it into a malicious caricature of the white invaders, while in the *baile del Torito* they make fun of the corrida and mime a drunken bullfighter made to look a fool. The **mask** worn for this dance is quite unambiguous: fair hair and a very pink face above a velvet costume sparkling with mirrors, brocade and feathers. A character in a black mask and gold-braided costume is a reminder that the *encomenderos* (beneficiaries of concessions of Indians) used to appoint black supervisors to intimidate the Mayans. Other dances such as the *baile del Venado* (stag dance) derive more directly from the Mayan tradition, telling ancient myths in which the animals are the main characters. The dancers can keep stamping for hours to the sound of the marimba or saxophone. A ring of leaping dancers outlines a central area where sketches are played out. Chichicastenango celebrates St Thomas on 21 December in a trance: four dance troupes dancing side by side outside the church, each with its own band, in a grand cacophony.

P. Brosson

The characters in the "baile de la Conquista"

## The Rabinal Achí

Guatemala's biggest theatrical dance festival takes place in Rabinal (Baja Verapaz) on St Paul's day, with the only surviving **pre-Hispanic play** on the programme. What has mainly kept this tradition alive is the location of the village – where the people speak *Achí*, a derivative of **Quiché** – in a very isolated valley. In 1850 **Abbott Brasseur de Bourbourg**, to whom we owe the first bilingual edition of the *Popol Vuh* and the discovery of Diego de Landa's manuscript, was appointed village priest of Rabinal. He transcribed the words and music of the work despite the reticence of the villagers, who were well aware of its pagan content. The *Rabinal Achí* tells the tale of the trial of a Quiché warrior by the Rabinal court. The warrior, accused of territorial ambitions and designs on the wife and favourite of the *Achí* prince, is sacrificed at the end of the play. Among the many characters that appear are warrior eagles and jaguars. This region, which suffered many massacres during the civil war, still puts on its musical show as best it can with the support of the local clergy, despite competition from travelling players. Paradoxically, it may be the development of tourism that will in the future put new life into this magnificent Mayan play.

Serena/HOA QUI

Carpet of coloured sawdust during Holy Week

# Liturgical festivals

## The Feast of the Dead

The saints are worshipped so intensely that All Saints' Day is one of the main festivals of the liturgical year. And the festive atmosphere carries over to All Souls' the following day, which does not have the studied solemnity it has in the Old World. Here death is thought to close a natural cycle and is accepted with serenity – which does not prevent demonstrations of grief and indignation by a people who have suffered so many abuses in recent decades. The week before All Souls' Day, families begin by preparing the graves of their loved ones, repainting or reshaping them, decking them with flowers. The graves reflect the social status of their occupants: neat vaults for the Ladinos, lime-covered mounds for the Amerindians. On **2 November** towns and villages empty as the cemeteries fill with people in a cheerful, festive atmosphere. Outside, hawkers sell their wares and there is sometimes a merry-go-round! Inside, more than just a moment's silent communion, people have come to share a little of the joy of living with those who no longer have that chance. Transistors play, playing cards snap and families picnic among the tombs. The most typically Guatemalan tradition is flying **barriletes**, paper kites on bamboo frames that symbolise both the souls of the dead rising to heaven and the thoughts of the living going to meet them (sometimes messages to the dead are written on the kites). In the villages of **Sumpango** and **Santiago Sacatepéquez**, this practice has turned into a competition between the brotherhoods (*cofradías*), each trying to fly kites that can be as much as 8m across. The ritual has become a festival and draws so many people that it will soon have to move out of the graveyard to the local football ground. Flying *barriletes* is a great hit with the children. Throughout the All Saints' period, as the long school holidays approach, they play with small kites which can be seen by the hundred caught on the electricity wires. In **Todos Santos Cuchumatán**, in Mam country, an impressive horse race takes place on All Souls' Day, which is also the village's patron saint festival. The traditional dish throughout the country on that day is **fiambre**, a kind of stew containing a very varied mix of meats, vegetables, fish and spices, depending on the cook's resources.

## Holy Week

All the villages bring out their statues and follow the **Via Crucis** during Lent and Holy Week, but it is the Ladinos of Antigua that celebrate it on the grandest scale. This great demonstration of faith, an imitation of the Seville festivities, integrates perfectly into the magical surroundings of the city's narrow cobbled streets. Starting out from the many parish churches in outlying districts, the processions move around the colonial checkerboard without ever running into each other. As they go, they trample carpets of coloured sawdust, laid using stencils and decorated with flowers – masterpieces of ephemeral art. Statues of the Virgin and of Christ carrying the cross, on heavy wooden bases, sway in time to the bearers' rhythmic steps. The men carry Christ (up to 110 bearers!), the women carry the Virgin, relaying each other every other *cuadra* (block). Members of the **religious brotherhoods**, wearing purple or dressed up Roman style, supervise the procession as it moves into the central square and stops in front of the cathedral. After a tour of the decorated pavings in the afternoon, the night-time part of the festival with its illuminated floats is not to be missed either.

# THE TRAVELLER'S ART OF LIVING

When first approached, the Amerindians are rather timid or even mistrustful of Europeans – which is easy to understand in the light of five painful centuries of history, in addition, very often, to a language barrier. Nonetheless, a smile is the universal language for reaching out to local people.

## Mixing with the local population

Markets and above all local transport are good places for meeting Guatemalans.

**Travelling by bus –** The *camionetas*, old school buses that criss-cross the country, are generally crowded to the gunwales and only the first to get on board will enjoy any semblance of comfort. You are far more likely to end up riding the whole way on an upturned bucket between two squawking chickens, and do not be surprised if the driver suddenly tells everyone to get their heads down: he has probably just seen a police checkpoint up ahead. It is an uncomfortably close crush, but the inconvenience is a small price to pay for the chance to engage your neighbour in conversation and find out something about the local tradespeople.

### On the buses

The bus stopped near the banana capital of Morales, in Oriente. Peddlers selling miracle medicines climbed aboard straight away to reel off their sales pitch. The first was selling a treatment for nervous exhaustion, depression, sleeplessness, memory loss and impotence. He was unsuccessfully offering ten capsules of this wonder drug for five quetzals. The second, a fat woman in tight leggings, extolled in a hoarse voice the amazing properties of Xmill, a product that kills all protozoa and metazoa starting with the tapeworm that gives children the urge to eat earth. Above her head she brandished a picture of the well-known worm. Smarter than her fellow vendor, she was selling the pills two at a time for the modest sum of one quetzal. Everyone on the bus wanted some and she stepped triumphantly down again, a wad of banknotes in her hand.

Waiting for the "camionetas" to leave

B. Perousse/HOA QUI

73

**Eating in the comedor** – In every market there is a section set aside for the *comedores* where the Guatemalans come to eat at any time of day *(see p 76)*. Here they serve copious platefuls of *tortillas* (maize pancakes) and *frijoles* (black beans) with rice or *tamales* (baked or steamed maize and meat cakes). It is an excellent opportunity to tuck into a square meal alongside the local people – for peanuts!

**Language institutes** – An ideal way to combine learning Spanish with discovering Guatemalan culture; the language institutes offer individual lessons with teachers who are real mines of information about Guatemala. They can also provide courses with accommodation with Guatemalan families, sharing their daily lives *(see p 151 "Antigua" and p 192 "Quetzaltenango")*.

## Rules to bear in mind

– Guatemalans only use *Usted*, the formal word for "you", even at home. Informal forms of address should be avoided.

– To ask for anything in a shop or office, always start with a polite *"Con permiso"*, equivalent to "Excuse me, please".

– Do not get into serious political debates anywhere. Politics is a thorny subject and it is best to avoid quarrels that might turn nasty.

– Do not be impatient. Our sense of time is quite different to that of Latin Americans, who are not known for their punctuality. So do not be offended if they are late.

– Guatemalans have an irritating habit of getting on a bus without letting people get off first. To get off the bus against the incoming crush, use your bag as a shield or retreat to the nearest rear door.

– Do not take photographs without permission. Most indigenous women turn away when they see a camera pointing their way. If you ask their permission politely they may refuse, or they may honour you with their most charming smile.

– Respect plants and animals. The Amerindians live in total communion with nature and honour every component of the plant and animal world. So before chopping down a tree, an Amerindian greets it and asks its permission to cut it down.

– The Mayans practise animistic rites before altars, usually hidden in the mountains. Apart from two or three that have become veritable tourist attractions, these places are kept secret. If you are ever invited to attend one of these events, do not take photographs and do not disturb the ceremony.

# GUATEMALAN COOKING

Guatemala is not an especially favoured stop on the gourmet's world tour. Most tourist places have a wide range of Mexican, Italian, French, Chinese and American restaurants, but only the bare bones of Guatemala's culinary arts are represented.

## Chapín food

Off the beaten track, travellers who want to go *chapín* (Guatemalan) will eat in the *comedores* (small local restaurants), which generally offer good but not too varied traditional cookery.

**The classic formula** – No meal is without its accompaniment of **tortillas** (maize pancakes), served hot in a basket. They are eaten like bread and are used like a spoon to scoop up the food on the plate.

The basic ingredients of Guatemalan cooking appear at every meal, starting with the *desayuno chapín* (typical breakfast) that consists of eggs, **frijoles** (black beans), **plátanos** (plantain bananas) and cheese. Lunch is very much like breakfast, although with the addition of rice and chicken, sausages or meat. And supper is disturbingly similar to lunch.

Most Guatemalan restaurants offer Mexican-inspired dishes: **enchiladas**, a mixture of meat, vegetables and sometimes cheese, served on a thin crispy maize pancake; **guacamole**, puréed avocado; or **chiles rellenos**, sweet peppers stuffed with meat and vegetables and served with a spicy sauce. Meat or poultry can be tasty cooked with *pepián* (a brown sauce seasoned with pumpkin seeds) or *jocón* (a sauce of mixed herbs).

To taste **tamales** – maize dough mixed with meat or vegetables and wrapped in banana leaves – you will have to wait for a Saturday or feast day. Some traders hang a red lamp at the door of their shop by way of a sign to mark the event.

**A one-day special – fiambre**, a cold salad of vegetables, meat, fish and cheese, is prepared once a year. This traditional Feast of the Dead dish is eaten throughout the country on that day alone.

## Regional specialities

For those visiting the Cobán region, **kak-ik** is a delicious stew of spicy turkey with plantain bananas and vegetables.

Lívingston, on the Caribbean coast, gives a foretaste of Belize with its loaves of *pan de coco* (coconut bread) and its **tapado**, a stew made of lobster, prawns, fish, crab, coconut, plantain bananas and coriander. This region also offers excellent **ceviches**, fish, crustaceans or shellfish marinated in lemon juice.

## Fruit salad

Bananas were the country's chief product for many years and they still occupy a prominent place, alongside other tropical fruit such as pineapples, papayas, mangoes, apples, oranges, breadfruit (*ramón*) and coconuts.

Another essential part of the great fruit market are the women vendors who descend on the buses with piercing cries of "joooo...coooo...te". The *jocote*, fruit of the *marañon* tree, looks like a plum but is the ideal thirst-quencher on a long journey.

## Drinks

Most of the **coffee** produced in Guatemala is exported. Guatemalan tastes favour fairly weak coffee (by continental European standards), although in Antigua they serve a good Italian-style *expresso*. Cocoa, which was already cultivated in the days of the ancient Maya, is drunk strong; a cup of hot **chocolate** in the chilly evenings of Quetzaltenango is especially welcome.

Local beers like **Gallo** (lager type) or **Moza** (darker) are good thirst quenchers. Guatemala also produces rum *(ron)* and low-quality distilled alcohol *(aguardiente)*; the latter should be treated with great caution, as it is rot-gut of the fiercest kind. Many are those who can scarcely stagger out of the *cantinas* (taverns) before crumpling to the ground a few paces on, clutching a bottle of *Quetzalteca*, and staying put until morning.

To keep up with local fashions, try **atol de elote**, a thick drink made from maize, sugar and cinnamon. For a more refreshing drink, there are canned drinks and delicious *limonadas* (lemonade) and *naranjadas* (orangeade), served in glasses that get bigger and bigger the closer you get to the sweltering lowlands. The same applies to the **licuados** (fruit nectars) *con agua* (with water) or *con leche* (milk-shakes). Make sure they have been made with purified water.

Guatemalan cooking

Lunch in a "comedor"

R. Marca

# LANGUAGES

## Spanish

The **official language** of Guatemala is Spanish, introduced by the conquistadors in the 16C and adopted by the Ladino government upon independence. From a Ladino viewpoint, fluent Spanish is a way of asserting social status. Whether self-taught or learned at school, Spanish is also the **common language** for all indigenous peoples communicating with neighbouring ethnic groups. On the shores of Lake Atitlán, three different languages are spoken but Quiché, Cakchiquel and Tzutuhil speakers use Spanish when they meet in the tourist resort of Panajachel. Like all Latin American variants, Guatemalan Spanish differs significantly from the *castellano* of peninsular Spain; it also has specific features that distinguish it from the Spanish of neighbouring countries.

## A multiplicity of Mayan tongues

There still exist today **28 indigenous languages**, all derived from pre-Columbian Mayan tongues. The six million indigenous Guatemalans living mainly in the Highlands speak 22 of these. In fact anthropologists do not agree on the exact number of languages. It is also practically impossible to say how many people speak each language, and statistics can vary by 100%. Some Mayan languages like *Itzá* and *Mopán* are used by very small groups and are almost certain to die out. The six most commonly spoken indigenous languages, in order of importance, are *Quiché*, *Cakchiquel*, *Mam*, *Tzutuhil*, *Kekchi* and *Chorti*.

So many different languages in such a small area is largely due to the very mountainous terrain, which kept ethnic groups isolated from each other for so long. Language therefore played an important **endogamic** role: quite logically, people preferred to marry someone who spoke the same language.

The pre-Columbian hieroglyphic writing, practised by a handful of men of letters, died out with the kingdoms of the Classic era. Today's indigenous languages are mainly transmitted orally, as most of those who speak them can neither read nor write. But manuscripts in Latin characters began to be produced right from the Spanish conquest, and some of these, like the *Mémorial de Sololá* and *Títulos Indígenas*, have come down to us. Many Mayan words have two different spellings, a Ladino or colonial spelling and a phonetic Mayan or "decolonised" spelling used by the indigenous peoples. The word Quiché, for example, is often written K'iche', the apostrophe signifying the characteristic Mayan glottal stop.

### The Mayan tower of Babel

Although all the languages stem from a common source, some differ so widely that the groups that speak them cannot understand each other. Below are just three examples in Quiché, Cakchiquel and Tzutuhil, written phonetically (the "j" is pronounced as a guttural "ch" as in the Scottish "loch").

| | | | |
|---|---|---|---|
| Yes | jè | uts | jaèn |
| No | n'jè taj | mannè | majohon |
| What's your name? | su abé | ach(i)ca abi | na abi |

Practical Information

On the steps
of Santo Tomás'
church in "Chichi"

# BEFORE GOING

**Before going**

## • Time difference

Same time zone as Mexico, Belize and US Central Time. Guatemala is 1hr behind New York, Montreal and Toronto, 6hr behind London, 16hr behind Sydney and 18hr behind Auckland (with reference to GMT/UTC).

## • International dialling

To call Guatemala from abroad, dial the international service code + 502 (country code for Guatemala) + the 7 digits of the number you are calling.

## • When to go

The "land of eternal spring" is a misleading nickname, for each region has its own climate, varying according to altitude and relief. If you mean to travel around the country, try to go in the **dry season** from October to April (the latter being the hottest month of the year). In the hills, the dry season means temperatures that are high during the day but drop sharply at night. The coastal areas and El Petén, although hot and humid all year round, get less rain over this period. During the **wet season** from May to September you can generally expect clear skies in the morning followed by banks of cloud announcing storms in the afternoon. You should do your visiting during the first half of the day. During this season, especially in June and September, some unsurfaced roads in El Petén and the Altiplano become impassable.

Fate is a great provider, for the pleasantest time of year to visit Guatemala coincides with the period when most festivities are held! **Easter** is celebrated all over the country; do not miss the superb Holy Week processions (Palm Sunday to Easter Sunday), particularly in Antigua. This period is, of course, the highlight of the tourist season, closely followed by the **All Saints'** period and **Christmas**, which are also interesting for their religious celebrations. Book air tickets and hotel rooms well in advance.

Sunrise and sunset times vary very little in the course of the year. Whatever the season, you should get up early to make the most of the day.

|  | **Sunrise** | **Sunset** |
|---|---|---|
| 21 December | 6.23am | 5.38pm |
| 21 March | 6.06am | 6.13pm |
| 21 June | 5.34am | 6.34pm |
| 21 September | 5.51am | 5.59pm |

## • Packing list

### Clothing

Depending on itinerary and season, your luggage should contain a careful selection of outfits for summer and winter, sun and rain! Whatever the time of year, take light cotton clothing for hot, damp regions such as El Petén and the Caribbean and Pacific coasts. In tourist places wearing shorts goes unnoticed, but take more decent clothing for visiting the villages. A jumper (or two) plus a windcheater will be extremely useful for climbing volcanoes or spending nights in the mountains (temperatures can go down to freezing). Take a good pair of high-cut, non-slip, waterproof hiking shoes for walking in the mountains and the jungle and visiting archeological sites. Swimwear, sunglasses, a hat and a raincoat complete this all-weather wardrobe.

*Accessories*

A torch is useful for visiting certain caves, getting to an archeological site before daybreak or climbing back down a volcano after nightfall. 220V electrical appliances (such as razors) will only work with a 220V-110V transformer and an adaptor for flat-pronged sockets.

*Gifts to take with you*

You are very unlikely to be invited to any Guatemalan home, so the question of gifts only arises in the street. Take pens or small gadgets to hand out to children, rather than giving them money, which they ask for in the major tourist centres (around Lake Atitlán, in Chichicastenango and Antigua).

## • Travel for everyone

*Travelling with children*

Everything depends on the type of trip you envisage. Do not forget that children feel the heat more than adults, so remember to protect them well from the sun and to give something to drink at regular intervals. Some bus journeys are gruelling, so hire an air-conditioned vehicle for long trips.

*Single women*

Travelling alone does not pose any special problems so long as you take the usual safety precautions. Avoid wearing any clothing that may be judged provocative (low-cut tops and bare legs), going to places frequented only by men, and being on deserted streets, particularly at night, or mountain roads. Some of this advice is just as valid for men travelling alone. Some women travellers complain of the insistent and meaningful stares they get from certain Guatemalan men, particularly when the latter's inhibitions are relaxed by a few glasses of *aguardiente*. Just as in any Latin country, the simplest thing to do is to ignore them. If one addresses you, remain polite but firm and take your leave as quickly as possible. When requesting information (particularly if asking your way), it is always better to ask women or old people.

*Senior travellers*

If you travel by comfortable, air-conditioned minibuses, travelling in Guatemala will be no more wearing than anywhere else. However, it is best to be fit and healthy to withstand the frequent changes in temperature and altitude between the Lowlands and the Highlands. It is advisable to get into condition if you intend to go walking in the mountains. Visiting some of the big archeological sites, such as Tikal, is also quite a strenuous (but exceedingly rewarding) affair, particularly when it is hot and damp.

*Disabled travellers*

Amenities for disabled travellers are virtually non-existent. In addition, the cobbled streets in places such as Chichicastenango and Antigua make it difficult to get around.

## • Address book

*Embassies and consulates*

**United Kingdom** – Guatemalan Embassy, 13 Fawcett Street, London SW10 9HN, ☎ (0171)351 3042, Fax (0171)376 5708.

**USA** – Guatemalan Embassy, 2220 R Street NW, Washington DC, ☎ (202)745 4952, Fax (202)745 1908.

There are also around 20 Guatemalan Consulates in the USA.

**Before going**

**Canada –** Guatemalan Embassy, 130 Albert Street, Suite 1010, Ottawa, Ontario, K1P 5G4, ☎ (613)233 7237 / 7188, Fax (613)233 0135.

Consulate, 777 Hornby Street, Suite 760, Vancouver, BC, V6Z 1S4, ☎ (604)688 5209 / 689 5210, Fax (604)688 5210.

*Tourist information*

**United Kingdom –** contact the Guatemalan Embassy above.

**USA –** Coventry Group, 3200 N Military Trail, Suite 400, Boca Raton, FL 33431, ☎ (800)464 8281, Fax (51)241 7687.

In other countries contact the embassies and consulates listed above or the head office of INGUAT (Instituto Guatemalteco de Turismo), 7a Avenida 1-17, Zone 4, Centro Cívico, Guatemala City, ☎ (331) 1333.

*Web sites*

A few sites to check out before going:

www.travel-guatemala.org.gt

www.infovia.com.gt/inguat

www.guatesoft.com/inguat

www.guatemalaweb.com *(created by the owner of the Posada Belén, see p 130 "Making the most of Guatemala City").*

To locate a Guatemala telephone number from abroad, dial international enquiries + 502.

## ● Documents required

*ID, visas*

A **passport** valid six months after your return date and a **return ticket** (or a ticket continuing on to another country) are sufficient to stay in Guatemala for up to three months. If you wish to prolong your visit, you must go personally to the Dirección General de Migración, 41a Calle 17-36, Zone 8, Guatemala City, ☎ 475 1390 / 1302.

*Customs*

You can take with you up to three litres of alcohol and two cartons of cigarettes.

*Vaccinations*

No vaccinations are required by the Guatemalan authorities to enter the country. If travelling outside of tourist centres, it is advisable to have yourself vaccinated against A and B hepatitis and typhoid, and to have a DT Polio booster if need be.

A course of anti-malaria treatment is recommended if staying for long periods in rural areas less than 1500m above sea level (particularly the El Petén jungle), or less than 400m above sea level in Belize.

*Driving licence*

A national driving licence is sufficient to rent a car for up to a month. If you intend to keep the vehicle longer, you will need an international driving licence.

## ● Local currency

*Cash*

Guatemala's currency unit is the **quetzal** (Q), named after the national bird. Notes: 100, 50, 20, 10, 5, 1 and 0.5 quetzals. Take a supply of small change when heading away from tourist centres. Coins: 1, 5, 10 and 25 **centavos** (1 quetzal = 100 centavos). Hotels, travel agencies and car rental firms often show their prices in US dollars. These places frequently accept both currencies for cash payments. If you pay in local currency the dollar price is simply converted at the dollar rate; the same goes for credit card payments.

*Exchange*

**1Q = US$0.15** (approx). Buy **US dollars** before leaving as virtually no Guatemalan bank will change any other foreign currency. Check the state of the banknotes you are sold, as shopkeepers and banks systematically refuse dollar notes in poor condition. On the other hand, they are not as fussy about quetzal banknotes, as proven by the extremely tatty state of some small denomination notes in circulation – virtually all the 5Q, 1Q and 0.5Q notes are worn, torn, stuck back together and often scribbled on.

The black-market moneychangers who offer their services in the vicinity of the main Post Office in Guatemala City do not offer a good enough exchange rate to risk doing business in the street with strangers. It is much better to take your money out away from prying eyes, in a bank for example.

*Travellers' cheques*

Travellers' cheques should be in **US dollars**. Most banks will change them if they are issued by **Visa** or **American Express**, up to a limit of US$200-400 per transaction. Thomas Cook travellers' cheques should not be taken, as virtually no place will accept them, apart from the Banco del Café in Guatemala City and Antigua and the Banco de Occidente in Quetzaltenango.

*Credit cards*

**International Visa** cards are the most widely accepted in Guatemala, more so than MasterCard, American Express or Diner's Club. At some banks cash can be obtained over the counter with a credit card. There are also some cashpoints *(cajeros automáticos)* in the big towns *(see the practical information in the sections devoted to each town)*. NB, shopkeepers add a 2-8% commission for payment of goods or services (hotel rooms) by credit card.

● **Spending money**

Guatemala is still a cheap place to visit. For **under US$20** a day, budget travellers will have no difficulty finding accommodation in modest guest houses or with local people, eating in markets or small local eateries and travelling around by bus. For more comfortable accommodation in attractive middle category hotels plus meals in restaurants, you should allow **US$30-50** a day. Renting a car (approx US$50 a day) can double this budget. In major tourist centres such as Guatemala City, Antigua, Panajachel, Chichicastenango and Flores, if you decide to give in to your taste for luxury, your daily budget can easily jump to **US$130**. These budgets are for one person in a double room, excluding going out, shopping and entry fees to museums.

● **Booking in advance**

From November to April Guatemala celebrates a succession of festivals which attract increasing numbers of tourists. Book your air tickets and hotel rooms in advance during the high season, and consult the calendar of local celebrations to assess how full accommodation in a town may be. In Antigua the good hotels are booked up several months ahead for Holy Week, all hotels in Todos Santos Cuchumatán and Huehuetenango are likely to be full over the All Saints' period, and those in Cobán during the month of August. The number of hire vehicles available is not enough to fulfil all needs in the high season, so it is advisable to book a rental vehicle before arriving.

**Before going**

## • Travel / Health Insurance

Before buying insurance, make sure you are not already covered by assistance/repatriation insurance included in the cost of your ticket (this is often the case if you book through a tour operator). Holders of some bank cards get automatic insurance cover abroad, so check with your bank. If necessary, you can take out standard insurance covering the costs of cancelling your trip, falling ill once there and repatriation.

Ask your insurance broker or travel agent for information.

# GETTING THERE

## • By air

If flying from Europe to Guatemala you will have at least one stopover or change of plane in (depending on airline) either Madrid (Iberia), Amsterdam (KLM) or the USA (Air France, American Airlines, Continental Airlines, United Airlines). The full journey takes approximately 14-18hr.

Travel agents and tour operators negotiate special rates with most airline companies, which makes return flights cheaper.

### Airports

All flights from Europe and the United States land at the **Aeropuerto Internacional La Aurora** in Guatemala City (see p 127 "Making the most of Guatemala City"). The country does have another international airport, at Santa Elena (near Flores), for a few flights to/from Mexico and Belize.

### Confirmation

Remember to confirm your return flight 72hr before departure, at your airline company's office (see p 129 "Making the most of Guatemala City").

### Airport tax

On leaving Guatemala you have to pay a US$20 departure tax. Payment can be made in US dollars or quetzals.

## • By bus

Several Guatemalan transport companies (contact details in the practical sections of each town) run daily services to/from border towns in Mexico, Belize, Honduras and El Salvador.

## • By car

Car rental firms only authorise their vehicles to cross borders under exceptional circumstances. It is therefore virtually impossible to travel throughout Central America in the same car, unless you own it.

## • By boat

There are three daily boat connections between Punta Gorda (Belize) and Puerto Barrios (see p 278 "Making the most of Puerto Barrios").

## • Crossing borders

National buses do not cross borders and neither can rental vehicles. You therefore have to cross the no man's land between two countries on foot. You have to show your passport to the customs authorities in both countries and pay first

Getting there

a departure tax and then an entry tax (*for more details see p 267 "Copán" and p 370 "San Ignacio" in Belize*). If you have no local currency you can pay in US dollars or obtain cash from the black-market moneychangers that are to be found at every border post. If travelling by boat, remember to pay the departure tax at the immigration office before boarding (*addresses in the practical sections of the port towns concerned*).

# THE BASICS

## ● Address book

### Tourist information

Only major tourist centres have **INGUAT** (*Instituto Guatemalteco de Turismo*) offices and Chichicastenango does not, even though it is one of the most visited places in Guatemala. In the practical sections of each town we indicate where tourist information can be obtained when there is no INGUAT.

Many tourist establishments (hotels, restaurants, bars, language schools) distribute copies of **Revue**, an English-language monthly, free of charge. This publishes useful addresses for travellers, articles, small ads and a calendar of cultural activities in the main towns – although half of the magazine is devoted to Antigua.

### Embassies and consulates

**United Kingdom –** The British Embassy, Avenida la Reforma 16-00, Zone 10, Edificio Torre Internacional, Floor 11, Guatemala City, ☎ 367 5425-9, Fax 367 5430.

**USA –** American Embassy, Avenida la Reforma 7-01, Zone 10, Guatemala City, ☎ 331 1541/55, Fax 331 8885.

**Canada –** Canadian Embassy,13a Calle 8-44, Zone 10, Edificio Plaza Edyma, Floor 6, Guatemala City, ☎ 333 6104/40.

## ● Opening and closing times

### Banks

In major towns: Monday-Friday, 9am-6pm (sometimes to 7pm) and Saturdays 9am-1pm. In smaller places: Monday-Friday 9am-3pm. In Chichicastenango the banks open on Sundays (market day).

### Post Offices

Opening hours vary from place to place. As a general rule, 8am-4pm, closed weekends. The main post office in Guatemala City is closed on Wednesday afternoons.

### Shops

Monday-Saturday 9am-6pm. Some shops close for lunch and on Saturday afternoons.

### Markets

These are busiest between 6am and 11am. In permanent markets some stalls stay open until around 6pm.

**Daily markets –** Antigua, Guatemala City, Cobán, Esquipulas, Huehuetenango, Panajachel, Quetzaltenango, San Juan Sacatepéquez, San Pedro Sacatepéquez, Santa Cruz del Quiché, Santiago Atitlán, Totonicapán.

The basics

**The basics**

**Weekly markets** – Listed here are the permanent markets which are particularly lively on certain days.

**Sunday:** Antigua, Chichicastenango, Comalapa, Momostenango, Nahualá, Nebaj, Patzún, San Cristóbal Totonicapán, San Cristóbal Verapaz, San Juan Atitán, San Juan Chamelco, San Lucas Tolimán, San Martín Jilotepeque, San Martín Sacatepéquez, San Mateo Ixtatán, San Sebastián, Santa María Chiquimula, Tecpán Guatemala, Tactic, Tamahú, Todos Santos Cuchumatán, Tucurú.

**Monday:** Antigua, Chimaltenango, Zunil.

**Tuesday:** Comalapa, Olintepeque, Patzún, San Martín Jilotepeque, Sololá, Totonicapán.

**Wednesday:** Chimaltenango, Patzicía, Santa Lucía La Reforma, Santiago Sacatepéquez.

**Thursday:** Antigua, Chichicastenango, Nahualá, Nebaj, Sacapulas, San Cristóbal Verapaz, San Juan Atitán, San Juan Chamelco, San Lucas Tolimán, San Martín Jilotepeque, San Mateo Ixtatán, San Sebastián, Tactic, Tamahú, Tecpán Guatemala, Todos Santos Cuchumatán, Tucurú.

**Friday:** Chimaltenango, Comalapa, Patzún, San Francisco El Alto, Santiago Atitlán, Santiago Sacatepéquez, Sololá.

**Saturday:** Antigua, Patzicía, Totonicapán.

*Restaurants*

Lunch served from 11.30am, last meals served around 9pm (11pm in big tourist centres). Restaurants close one day a week; the day varies depending on restaurant and town (most restaurants in Antigua are closed on Mondays).

*Offices*

9am-4.30pm, closed weekends and lunchtimes.

## ● Museums, monuments and archeological sites

*Opening times*

Generally speaking, monuments and archeological sites are open every day 9am-5pm. Museums have more or less the same opening hours and are closed one day a week.

*Fees*

Entrance fees to many museums and sites have gone up considerably over the last few years. Foreigners now have to pay entrance fees ranging from 10Q to 30Q (much less for Guatemalan nationals) depending on the place. The entrance fee charged at famous archeological sites such as Tikal is, of course, much higher.

## ● Mail

You will find a post office (*Correos*) in every town. Guatemalans themselves will advise you to use the postal service only for mail of no importance. A postcard takes about 3 weeks to reach Europe. Never send cash to Guatemala; if indeed the envelope ever reaches its destination, it is almost certain to have been emptied of its contents. For urgent mail or parcels it is better to use the services of private firms such as DHL. To collect Poste Restante mail (*Lista de Correos*) you must show your passport.

## • Telephone, fax and e-mail

**TELGUA** (formerly GUATEL), the recently privatised national telecommunications company, has offices in all major towns from which you can telephone or send faxes all over the world. Local and international calls can be made **"de teléfono a teléfono"**, the call being charged as soon as anyone answers, or you can ask for **"de persona a persona"** and give the exact name of the person you wish to speak to; in this case the call is only charged from the moment that the person requested answers. This is useful if you have to go through a switchboard or when there is an answering machine. Telephone kiosks, generally found near TELGUA premises, take 10 or 25 centavos coins and are for local calls only.

In the major tourist centres (Antigua, Panajachel, Flores), the small telecommunications companies *(see "Post office / Telephone" in the Making the most of ... section of each town)* charge much lower rates than TELGUA's - up to half as much for brief long-distance calls and sending faxes. **Cybercafés** are also easy to find in these places. You can create your own e-mail address on the spot and surf the Net (0.50-1Q a minute).

### International calls

**Codes –** To call out of Guatemala, dial 00 + the international code of the country you are calling + the national number you wish to reach (omitting any initial 0). UK: 00 + 44; USA: 00 + 1; Canada: 00 + 1; Australia: 00 + 61; New Zealand: 00 + 64.

**Tariffs –** It is expensive to call Europe – around 35Q for the first minute + 10Q for every subsequent minute. International calls *(larga distancia internacional)* via small telecommunications companies cost about 18Q a minute. The cost of sending a fax page is about the same as the first minute of a telephone call.

It is possible to make collect calls *(cobro revertido)* to some countries, ask at TELGUA or a private company.

### Local calls

Some numbers are followed by the words *"Abonado Comunitario"*. This means it is in fact a public telephone service to which people who do not have private lines subscribe; you will be asked to leave a message or to call back when the person you wish to contact has been fetched to the kiosk (if they are nearby). For example, calls to the villages around Lake Atitlán are centralised in the TELGUA office in Panajachel.

**Codes –** The disappearance of regional codes has considerably simplified local calls. To call someone in the same town or in another department, you now simply have to dial the 7-digit number.

**Tariffs –** Unlike international calls, local calls are very cheap: 10 centavos a minute within the same town.

### National enquiries

Dial 1524.

## • Public holidays

| | | |
|---|---|---|
| **1 January** | New Year's Day | Año Nuevo |
| **March-April** | Maundy Thursday | Jueves Santo |
| | Good Friday | Viernes Santo |
| **1 May** | Labour Day | Día del Trabajo |
| **30 June** | Army Day | Día del Ejército |
| **15 September** | Independence Day | Día de la Independencia |

**The basics**

| **20 October** | Revolution Day | Día de la Revolución |
| **1 November** | All Saints' Day | Todos Santos |
| **25 December** | Christmas Day | Navidad |
| **31 December** | New Year's Eve | Día del Año Viejo |

## • Local celebrations

Alongside the major religious festivals that are celebrated nation-wide (All Saints, Holy Week), each locality holds an annual festival in honour of its patron saint. This is a major event in local life. From low-key patron saint tributes through to major festivals attracting hundreds of visitors, you are sure to have the opportunity of taking part in one of these fiestas during your stay. For further details on the biggest celebrations, read the detailed descriptions in the "Exploring Guatemala" section.

# GETTING AROUND

A car is the best solution, particularly for short visits. You will save time and avoid the fatigue of long bus journeys. If you prefer to opt for local transport, think seriously about renting a car (or taxi) by the day to explore areas where there is little public transport.

## • By car

### Rental

**Self-drive rental –** Once outside Guatemala City you will have a very hard job finding a rental vehicle, as the local network is very limited except in some department capitals. All companies have their head offices in the capital (see p 127 "Making the most of Guatemala City"). To compare rates and conditions without walking miles, go to La Aurora airport, where all the rental agencies are lined up next to each other within 100m. Some international companies **(Avis, Hertz)** are to be found in Guatemala but have virtually no offices outside of Guatemala City. The Guatemalan company **Tabarini** has offices in all large towns. In the high season it is advisable to rent a vehicle before arriving, either directly with the rental company or through your travel agent. You must be at least 25 years old and when you sign the contract you will be asked to pay the full cost of rental plus a deposit by credit card. A cheap car costs at least US$50 a day (US$350 a week), with unlimited mileage, insurance and taxes included. Examine the vehicle very closely before leaving the rental office to avoid being penalised on your return for pre-existing damage. An excess of around US$850 is charged in the case of theft or accident; some rental agencies (Tabarini) reduce this to US$500 on payment of an additional daily charge.

**Chauffeur-driven rental –** If you are worried about driving in Guatemala (especially on mountain roads), allow an additional US$25 a day for a driver. Accommodation, meals and, of course, petrol are your responsibility. For a one-day trip it is sometimes better value to hire a taxi by the hour.

**Borders –** Rental cars are not authorised to cross borders, but some companies (Hertz, Tabarini) will issue an authorisation to go as far as the Copán archeological site in Honduras.

Getting around

*Highway code*

The mileages shown on your road map do not mean very much! You will learn to recalculate journey times depending on means of transport (car or bus), climate and the state of the roads.

The country has approx 3 000km of surfaced roads, although this figure is increasing due to surfacing work being carried out on many stretches. The main roads (national or departmental) are generally speaking in good repair, barring a few potholes here and there. One of the busiest major roads is the **CA1 (Pan-American Highway)**, which goes through Guatemala from La Mesilla (Mexico) to San Cristóbal Frontera (El Salvador) on its journey right down Central America. Two other roads are essential for visiting the country: the **CA2 (Carretera del Pacífico)**, which follows the Pacific coast from Ciudad Tecún Umán in Mexico to Ciudad de Pedro de Alvarado in El Salvador, and the **CA9 (Carretera al Atlántico)** that links Puerto San José on the Pacific with Puerto Barrios on the Atlantic. The latter road was much damaged when **Hurricane Mitch** blew through in October 1998.

Driving the tight hairpin bends in the mountains and the bumpy dirt tracks of the secondary roads is not so easy. Before driving off into a remote region, make a habit of asking the locals or other motorists about road conditions. Many stony tracks (*carreteras de terracería*) that are enveloped in clouds of dust during the dry season turn into torrents of mud after storms and are then impracticable, even in a jeep, particularly in El Petén and the Altiplano.

There is one – almost certain! – rule: Guatemala drives on the right. As far as everything else goes, in Guatemala it is the most forceful and intrepid driver who wins out. On the winding mountain roads, some drivers (particularly bus drivers) have the terrifying habit of driving at breakneck speed, rarely respecting safety distances and overtaking on bends where visibility is virtually zero. Be careful, you are not obliged to imitate them! It is wiser to pull over to let these "lords of the highway" pass. If you are travelling with one of them, all you can do is to adopt the same attitude as the other passengers: hold your breath and pray! The outskirts of built-up areas are usually indicated by a series of humps (*tumulos* or *vibradores*) obliging vehicles to slow down. You have to be quick off the mark driving in towns, especially in Guatemala City's traffic jams. Drivers brake and accelerate alternately and rapidly, hands permanently on the horn. Traffic lights are sometimes located on the opposite side of crossroads – but do not worry, the drivers behind you will let you know, in a chorus of horns, just as soon as the lights change to green!

**Driving at night is dangerous** on secondary roads because of lack of street lighting, unexpected obstacles and the risk of attack. To indicate you have broken down, do as the locals do: put some branches across the road.

*Fuel*

Petrol stations (*gasolineras*) can be found at regular intervals along main roads. When travelling on smaller roads it is advisable to fill up whenever you come to a petrol station, and to carry an emergency can of petrol when driving in isolated areas. Petrol is cheap, approx 2.60Q a litre for four-star (*súper*) and 2.50Q a litre for 2-star (*regular*). Prices are shown in American gallons (1 US gallon = 3.79 litres).

Getting around

### Parking in town

Use hotel car parks or paying town car parks (*parqueos*) to limit the risks of theft or break-ins and avoid fines for obstructive parking. The Guatemalan authorities use the clamp (*cepo*) and it will cost you US$120 to get your vehicle back.

### In emergencies

If you are involved in an accident, do not move your vehicle and call the police, ☎ 110 or 120. Minor accidents are usually settled privately.

## • By taxi

Department capitals have at least one taxi rank. Since in most towns tourist sights are often close together, taxis are not very useful – except in Guatemala City (*see p 127 "Making the most of Guatemala City"*) – but they offer a practical alternative for a day out exploring villages that are hard to get to by public transport. Plan your route in advance so as to negotiate an hourly or daily rate. As far as possible, tell the driver how long you intend to spend in each place, to avoid any possible misunderstandings when it comes to paying.

## • By train

The railway network is very limited, for obvious topographical reasons; only the Lowlands possess a railway line, running between Ciudad Tecún Umán (Mexico) and Puerto Barrios. Passenger services have been suspended for an indefinite period of time.

## • By bus

This is the most practical means of transport and for a good number of isolated hamlets it is their only link with the rest of the world. The *camionetas*, crowded and uncomfortable old buses, plunge you right into the heart of everyday Guatemala. What a lot of people you meet on their ageless seats creaking with the weight of large families! Three or four passengers on a seat intended for two – not counting the children and chickens – and a centre aisle packed out with the latest arrivals. A few tips for improving your travel conditions, although experience will teach you many other tricks: whenever possible, board at a bus station so that you get a seat, and sit near a door, front or back, to be able to get off easily. With a bit of luck and if you board very early, you can go for the window seat behind the driver, which means you can stretch your legs, an appreciable luxury on long journeys. And if you do have to travel standing up, duck down with the other passengers if you see a policeman (in theory the company risks a fine, but of course everyone knows what is really going on!). All major towns have a **bus station** that is easily accessible from the centre. If there are no direct buses to where you are going, it is easy to change on one of the major

**Profession: "ayudante"**

Poised on the bus steps, the "ayudante" (helper, assistant) reels off the destinations and blows the horn a last time to hurry up latecomers. As quick as lightning he grabs hold of a suitcase and then suddenly he is up on the roof, loading up the bulky bundles of a family on their way back from market. A foot poises briefly on the edge of a window before he enters discreetly by the emergency exit. Everything is in order, and with two sharp bangs on the bodywork he gives the starting signal. He spots the police up ahead on the road? At a shout from him everyone gets their heads down and as if by magic he empties the centre aisle of passengers. Now he just has to distribute tickets. By hanging onto the luggage rack he squeezes through the compact crowd, contorting himself into perilously acrobatic manoeuvres. This is the climax of his rubber-man cum spider-man show!

roads (at Los Encuentros, Cuatro Caminos or La Ruidosa, for example) and your journey will not necessarily take any longer as connections are frequent. Do not rely on timetables: drivers fix themselves a minimum number of passengers before setting off (which in fact means when the vehicle is crowded out), so they leave before or after the time given, depending on how full they are! To get to isolated villages – particularly for market days – travel early in the morning, as there are few buses in the afternoons and virtually none at night.

As well as these *camionetas* there are also **pullman** (first class) buses on long-distance routes (between Guatemala City and Cobán, for example). These are faster, incomparably more comfortable and very reasonably priced. Buy your ticket in advance at the transport company's offices (*contact details in the practical section of each town*).

### ● By pick-up

These take over for some destinations with no public transport. They are generally to be found around the bus station or on the main square of the village. This is the only means of transport from Zunil up to Fuentes Georginas, for example (*see p 190*).

### ● By private minibus (shuttle or minibus services)

Ten times more expensive than a journey by *camioneta* but a hundred times more comfortable! These minibuses, carrying about ten passengers, run regular services between major tourist centres (Antigua, Guatemala City, Panajachel, and Chichicastenango on market days). Book seats at a travel agent or through your hotel. From Antigua and Panajachel these vehicles can take you to any other part of Guatemala, a worthwhile solution if there are enough passengers.

### ● By boat

Some places are only accessible by boat. To get to Livingston, to which there are no roads, you can take a daily boat service across Amatique Bay from Puerto Barrios (*see p 278*), or travel down the Río Dulce by boat – a mini-cruise that is turning into one of the most "in" excursions in Oriente. Similarly, archeology fans have to travel by pirogue to discover some Mayan ruins deep in El Petén (Ceibal, Piedras Negras); these river expeditions can take anything from 2hr to several days depending on distance to the site. Information from travel agencies in Flores (*see p 237*).

There are other boat trips to be made for pure pleasure rather than necessity. Visiting the villages around Lake Atitlán by *lancha* (motor launch) is now a classic; less touristy but also very enjoyable is a trip around Lake Amatitlán or down the Chiquimulilla Canal at daybreak.

**Getting around**

### • Renting a bike

Rental agencies can be found in the major tourist centres *(see p 151 "Antigua" and p 169 "Panajachel")*. Allow about US$10 a day for a pushbike.

### • Hitch-hiking

To be avoided for safety reasons, particularly in remote regions or if you are alone. As soon as you arrive somewhere where public transport is infrequent, check out the timetable for buses going back so as not to find yourself stuck there.

### • Domestic flights

Several department capitals have small airfields served by the national airline company **INTER**, Aeropuerto La Aurora, Zone 13, Guatemala City, ☎ 361 2144. Also at 7a Avenida 14-35, Zone 9, ☎ 334 2574 or 331 6979. Distances between towns are never so great that you have to travel by plane. The only worthwhile domestic flight – and essential during the rainy season – is between Guatemala City and Flores (Tikal). There is just no choice between a 45min flight and a 12hr (minimum) journey over a gruelling road! Several companies fly between the capital and Flores *(see p 129 and p 236, the practical sections of these two towns)*. Travel agencies and tour operators outside of Guatemala can sometimes offer special rates for domestic flights. Ask when you book your flight to Guatemala.

### • Organised tours and excursions

**Travel agencies** – INGUAT publishes an annual list of travel agencies by region *(Guía de Agencias de Viajes)*; it can be useful outside of major tourist centres. In Antigua, Flores and Panajachel, on the other hand, there are many travel agencies, and a short walk around town will give you a good idea of their excursion programmes. From a day's visit of the surrounding area to a week-long expedition, anyone interested in archeology, ecology, ethnology or sport is bound to find what they are looking for. Some hotels also run à la carte or package tours.

**Guides** – In museums and on Antigua's Parque Central you will be accosted by numerous "guides" all proudly flaunting an official badge. Not all of them are competent. Without going so far as to test their capacities before accepting their services, at least ask them a couple of precise questions about the place to judge their knowledge. INGUAT also provides contact details for registered guides, but here again you take your chances!

# BED AND BOARD

### • Where to stay

All department capitals have at least one hotel, but when off the beaten track and once you have eliminated the unsavoury guest houses, the list of accommodation dwindles pitifully. In fact you will only find accommodation worthy of the name in tourist centres. However, the country is gradually improving its tourist infrastructure so as to cope with increasing numbers of visitors.

## • Price range

Hotel prices given in this guide are calculated on the basis of a double room without breakfast, and include **10% IVA** (VAT) and **10% hotel tax**. Make sure that prices displayed at reception are inclusive of all taxes. Payment in US dollars is accepted in most big hotels.

There is no blanket distinction to be made nation-wide between high and low seasons (dry and wet seasons); prices fluctuate more in relation to local festivities, religious celebrations and market days. So during Holy Week hotels in Antigua double their prices, whereas those in Guatemala City offer considerable reductions. It is possible to negotiate worthwhile discounts in the off-season.

## • Various categories

Beware of the word *"hotel"*, which in fact covers every type of accommodation from spartan rooms through ultramodern complexes to beautifully renovated colonial residences. Some hotels call themselves *posadas* (inns) to give a rustic feel.

### Hotels

Avoid spending the night in department capitals and places little frequented by tourists, for the hotels often leave a lot to be desired. Apart from the question of hygiene and cleanliness, these hotels are not very safe. You can get a general idea of accommodation in Guatemala from the prices, although a high price does not necessarily guarantee a good hotel, and vice versa.

At US$10-25 there are two categories of hotel depending on geographical location. In overnight halt towns – of no special interest but good for exploring around about – accommodation is often nondescript and **functional**. In this same price range a tourist locality is more likely to offer **hotels with character**. The modest rooms do not all have private bathrooms.

Allow US$25-50 for simple but relatively **comfortable** accommodation. This intermediate category covers old or modern hotels with varying degrees of character, in a wide variety of settings. Rooms all have private bathrooms, fans or air conditioning (in hot regions) and sometimes television.

US$50-100 means **very comfortable** hotels. Most of the rooms have modern amenities (comfortable bedding, toilet facilities in a good state of repair, television, mini-bar) even when they are in lovely, renovated colonial buildings.

Lastly, if you pay over US$100 you will be staying in **luxury** establishments providing personal service, or in big **international category** hotels.

Small, family-type guest houses are very common in the most touristy places. They are popular for their low prices but also because they allow guests to meet other travellers and exchange tips. Whether they are called *hospedaje*, *pensión*, *hostal* or even *hotel*, guest houses can be as good as they can be bad. You should not be too demanding as to comfort or, sometimes, unfortunately, even cleanliness. The rooms are usually very basic with nothing more than a bed between four walls, without bathrooms. Some owners nevertheless make considerable efforts to make them attractive. We include some addresses of guesthouses under US$10, when their quality makes them stand out or they offer the only accommodation in the locality.

### Camping

To be avoided for safety reasons. There are enough cheap guesthouses for you not to have to pitch your tent. It is, however, a good way of staying in Tikal cheaply.

**Bed and board**

**Bed and board**

### Self-catering

Networks of self-catering rental apartments are developing in towns where there are language schools (Antigua and Quetzaltenango). This economical solution is particularly suited to stays of one to several weeks. Consult the small ads in *Revue* magazine *(see p 85 "The basics")*, language schools and tourist establishments.

### Bed & Breakfast

Home-stay accommodation is usually combined with Spanish language classes, and is therefore found in the above-mentioned towns (Antigua and Quetzaltenango). Language schools all charge more or less the same price of around US$100 a week for 20hr of lessons plus accommodation and full board with a family. People taking part in aid programmes for Mayan communities (contact details through language schools) can lodge with Mayan families in the Altiplano.

## • Eating out

### In hotels

Most hotels serve food of some kind, from modest cafeterias through to chic restaurants depending on the category of hotel. In isolated places full board accommodation may be the only way to get a decent meal.

### In restaurants

Tourist towns have a wide range of eating places for anyone fond of Mexican, Asian, Italian, French or American cuisine. On the other hand, you will find very few restaurants serving good local cuisine. Typical dishes on restaurant menus are often only a feeble approximation of what you can eat in places frequented by Guatemalans.

### In comedores

As a rule, these cheap, modest restaurants are the best places for tasting local specialities. The menu gives a choice of two or three dishes of meat or chicken served with vegetables or rice and accompanied by *tortillas*. Some *comedores* serve a healthy meal, others are only for those with strong digestive systems.

### On the hoof

Many street traders set up stalls or move around the streets with little carts; among them, the ice-cream sellers can be identified by their little bells. At any and every hour of the day you can snack on fritters, *tortillas*, *tacos* or delicious slices of mango and pineapple. You can also sip fresh orange juice or milk shakes made from fresh fruit served, as are all take-away drinks, in plastic pouches with straws. When travelling by bus, illicit street vendors pop up in swarms at every halt selling refreshments, bags of peanuts or biscuits, and handfuls of fruit. An unexpected bonus when you have not had time to buy provisions before setting out on a long journey!

R. Marca

# SPORTS AND PASTIMES

Archeological sites, colourful markets and local festivities: the Mayan world of past and present can easily be combined with other leisure activities.

## ● Cross country

### Walking

This is an excellent way to discover the country and its inhabitants. Altiplano, nature reserves and tropical forest lend themselves to a fair number of walking excursions. Do not ever go off adventuring alone, however, and make sure you respect the safety precautions recommended by INGUAT and/or the police in certain high-risk areas. When going on long-distance walks or hikes, for safety's sake we advise you to work out your route beforehand with a specialised travel agent or to hire the services of professionals on the spot. In Guatemala City, **Ek Chuah**, 3a Calle 6-24, Zone 2, ☎ 232 0745, organises tours throughout the country.

Climbing volcanoes remains one of the great walking classics, despite repeated warnings by INGUAT about attacks on tourists. Agencies in Antigua propose excursions with armed escorts, which usually turn out to be empty promises as groups are accompanied by a guide only. Even for climbs considered to be easy, you should be in good physical shape. Specialised tourist agencies in your country of departure may be able to help you find a package walking tour to explore volcanoes.

### Mountain biking

The mountainous relief and altitude make it essential to be very fit. Never ride alone in the mountains. Some specialist agencies in Antigua *(see p 151)* organise bike excursions lasting one or several days.

### Horse riding

You can explore the area around Antigua or Lake Atitlán on horseback. Details from the San Jorge hotel (Antigua), the Atitlán hotel (Panajachel) or the Posada de Santiago (Santiago Atitlán) *(see the practical information sections of the places concerned)*.

### Tennis

Major hotel complexes generally have at least one tennis court.

### Golf

You can play on an 18-hole course at the **Guatemala Country Club**, 30 Avenida Final Z-11, Colonia Country, Guatemala City, ☎ 594 7488. In the Antigua area the Monte María Country Club now has a 9-hole course, ☎ 832 4422.

## ● The sea

The country has two ocean coastlines, several lakes and quite a number of rivers, but their tourism potential is still considerably under-exploited.

### Swimming

Most big hotels have a swimming-pool, and some are open to non-guests for an entry fee. Near Retalhuleu is the Parque Acuático Xocomil, a large complex comprising several pools and water activities *(see p 225)*.

### Rafting

A rafting expedition is a sporty way to explore the jungle and some of the isolated Mayan sites in El Petén. In Guatemala City you can obtain details from **Expediciones Maya**, 15a Calle 1-91, Zone 10, Floor 1, ☎ 337 4666.

### Scuba diving

Compared with Belize, Mexico and Honduras, Guatemala is the poor cousin when it comes to scuba diving. Addicts of this sport will have to be content with dips in Lake Atitlán (*information from the La Iguana Perdida guest house in Santa Cruz La Laguna, p 173*).

### Fishing

The waters of lakes Atitlán, Amatitlán and Izabal are stuffed with fish, but although providing a livelihood for local populations, fishing has not yet been promoted as a tourist activity. The same thing goes for sea fishing.

## • Night life

Except in places where a lot of tourists can be found, nightfall marks the end of all forms of activity, so this section is only relevant to Antigua, Panajachel, Quetzaltenango, Flores, Livingston and parts of Guatemala City.

### Cinema, theatre

Cinemas show the latest general-public American films, in English with Spanish subtitles. Some bars also have video rooms where travellers of all nationalities come to brush up their Spanish (or English!). A pleasant enough atmosphere for watching American or Spanish classics.

### Bars and nightclubs

Bars and nightclubs are international as far as ambience, music, staff and customers go. Only a very few wealthy Guatemalans mix with this "gringo" crowd. The rest of the population spends its last quetzals in the local *cantinas* (bars). You are advised to avoid these taverns, as the *guaro* (rough distilled alcohol) and beer rapidly get drinkers heated up.

### Concerts and live shows

Big hotels put on *marimba* concerts for tourists, which gives a vague idea of local folklore for those not lucky enough to attend a patron saint festival. Depending on time of year, some places put on extraordinary performances of dances handed down from pre-Hispanic and colonial times (*baile de la Conquista, baile del Venado, Palo Volador*).

# SHOPPING

## • What's on offer

See p 58 "Traditional dress"

### Arts and crafts

Among the piles of fruit and vegetables in the markets, everyday utensils in **leather**, **basketwork** and **pottery** can be spotted. This is where the locals come to buy kitchen ware, a new shopping basket, hanks of yarn for weaving or a *mecapal* (a leather strap worn around the forehead for carrying heavy loads). The water jars that the village women carry proudly on their heads have unfortunately been replaced by ordinary plastic containers. Alongside these everyday objects, you can now find handicrafts purpose-made for tourists, copying traditional shapes and motifs. Among other things you can buy reproductions of masks used in pre-Hispanic dances, small items of furniture, and painted **wood** boxes. But there is one type of handicraft that really stands out, for it has made Guatemala's reputation and is its pride and joy: textiles.

### Textiles

The outfits and accessories worn by the Mayans of the Altiplano are a real festival of shapes and colours. Some of these splendid **woven items** are to be found on the stalls of local markets. With *huipiles* (blouses), *tzutes* (multi-purpose lengths of cloth folded on the head), *tocoyales* (strips of cloth wound around the head), *cortes* (skirts), etc, buyers are simply spoilt for choice. If there is space left in your luggage, you could also buy a woollen **blanket** from Momostenango. Some of the richly embroidered costumes look much better worn than displayed in the shop, and you can always turn them into decorative objects once home – which is just what some shops already do, using traditional motifs on tablecloths, table mats, serviettes, scarves, belts, hammocks, purses and other objects. The indigenous people do not necessarily appreciate foreigners wearing their **traditional dress**, so it is better to wait until you get home before flaunting the red trousers with white stripes that you bought in Todos Santos market. While still on the spot, you are better off wearing garments made for tourists, which include local motifs and weaves used for trousers, dresses and Western-style shirts.

### Jewellery

In Panajachel and Antigua visitors are accosted by itinerant vendors laden with (often junky) necklaces, bracelets, earrings and rings. If your budget allows, you can also take home superb **jade** jewellery. This stone, an essential component of Mayan civilisation, varies in colour from an almost-white pale green through all shades of green to black. From pendants and earrings to reproductions of ancient masks, Antigua jewellers *(see p 156)* offer a very wide choice of items worked in gold or silver.

### Music

Apart from the flutes on sale at every Antigua street corner, you will find traditional musical instruments (maracas, drums) at Casa K'ojom *(see p 148)*, as well as tapes and CDs.

### Coffee

Guatemala produces excellent coffee, mainly for export. The most highly reputed of the country's coffee plantations are those around Antigua, so you should make your purchases in the specialist shops there *(see p 157)*, or directly from the *fincas* themselves.

### • Where to shop

#### What to buy where

The **Altiplano** is the favourite region for shopping as it is the heart of Maya country. Each village produces its own specific objects, but the place of origin does not necessarily offer the widest choice. Craftsmen are more likely to sell their products on the markets in big towns such as **Guatemala City**, **Antigua** and **Panajachel**, where handicrafts from all over Guatemala can be found.

#### Markets

In the local market, often located near the bus station and thereby named *mercado terminal*, you will find food, everyday utensils, clothes and accessories. The **San Francisco El Alto** market, one of the biggest and busiest in Guatemala, is a real "must". In tourist towns the number of stalls devoted to souvenirs is increasing all the time, to the detriment of other types of merchandise. In **Chichicastenango**,

**Shopping**

for example, masks, wooden objects and textiles produced for foreigners have taken over most of the market, whereas the goods and produce for locals have been relegated to the side streets. The ultimate (and most impersonal) form of this type of market is the **mercado de artesanías** now found in some towns (Guatemala City, Antigua, Panajachel). These places with their handicraft stalls lined up in rows lack authenticity but allow travellers in a hurry to get an overview of the country's craft products. Wherever you are, the golden rule is to bargain, always.

### Shops

Tourist towns are increasingly populated by souvenir shops *(tiendas)*. Some sell higher quality goods than those found on the markets *(see Colibrí and the Centro de textiles tradicionales Nim Po't in Antigua)*. Generally speaking, prices are fixed and it is difficult to bargain.

### • Bartering
*See p 100*

### • Duty
IVA *(Impuesto sobre el Valor Añadido)*, which is our VAT, stands at 10%.

### • Mailing things home
If it is not possible to take your purchases home in your luggage, use the services of a specialist firm such as DHL. Antigua, Flores and Panajachel all have several companies of this type *(see the practical section of each town)*.

# HEALTH AND SAFETY

### • Precautions
*See p 82 Vaccinations*

**Malaria** is a danger in some places less than 1500m above sea-level. So if you are likely to be staying for some time in El Petén or Belize it is best to take a course of preventive treatment and arm yourself with effective mosquito repellent *(repelente)*.

The most frequent cause of illness is the **heat**. To avoid sunburn and the risk of sunstroke, get your skin accustomed to the sun gradually, use a barrier cream and keep your head covered. Remember to drink water frequently when you are expending energy (walks, visits to archeological sites).

The local **cooking** is not particularly spicy but a change of diet can in itself cause digestive problems. Be extremely careful in restaurants, where hygiene is not always all it should be; food poisoning is mainly caused by seafood, insufficiently cooked meat or badly washed salads, raw vegetables and fruit (if in doubt, leave it out!) Do not eat fruit bought on markets until it has been peeled or washed. You are strongly advised against drinking tap **water**. Bottles of mineral water (*agua pura*) and pouches of ice (*hielo*) made from purified water can be bought almost everywhere. If you intend to stay in remote villages, take the precaution of carrying water purifying tablets with you.

Poisonous snakes, insects etc. are in fact quite rare. To avoid getting bitten when walking in the jungle, you should cover arms and legs and wear high-cut shoes.

### • Medical kit

Take essential medicines with you: aspirin, antiseptic cream, dressings, diarrhoea tablets, anti-mosquito lotion (containing 35-35 repellent or 50% DEET), sun barrier cream, water purifying tablets. If required, all major towns have chemists where you can buy these products without too much trouble, along with toiletries and other sundries.

### • Health

**First aid**

In an emergency call the Ambulance service, ☎ 128, or the Red Cross (*Cruz Roja*), ☎ 125.

**Hospitals**

The hospitals leave a lot to be desired. It is better to be treated in the medical establishments in Guatemala City, but if you have a serious health problem you should try to have yourself repatriated.

**Chemists / Pharmacies**

These can be found in all major towns. The list of duty chemists (*farmacias de turno*) is usually posted on their doors.

**Doctors / Dentists**

In tourist centres the hotels or INGUAT will supply contact details for doctors, many of whom speak English.

### • Emergencies

Police (*Policia Nacional*), ☎ 110 or 120.
Fire Brigade (*Bomberos*), ☎ 122 or 123.

# A TO Z

### • Addresses

13a C 7-20, Z-9 – how do these esoteric signs, halfway between Mayan glyph and mathematical formula, help you to find your way around the capital? The *avenidas* (avenues) run north-south and intersect at right angles with the *calles* (streets). The numbering system goes from west to east on *avenidas* and from north to south on *calles*. Addresses give the number or name of the *avenida* or *calle* first, followed by the number of the (lower) street or avenue crossing it, then the number of the building; this latter figure is in fact the distance from the intersection thus identified to the building itself. Last comes the number of the zone. So 13a C 7-20, Z-9 (which reads *trece calle, siete veinte, zona nueve*) tells you the place you are looking for is at no 20 on Street 13 between Avenues 7 and 8 in Zone 9. Likewise, 2a Ave 4-15, Z-1 (*segunda avenida, cuatro quince, zona uno*) is at no 15 on 2nd Avenue between Streets 4 and 5 in Zone 1. Only big towns are divided up into districts (*zonas*), within which the street and avenue numbering is repeated. It is therefore essential to know the zone in Guatemala City, since two places a good few kilometres apart may have identical addresses except for the zone.

## • Bartering
Buying handicrafts in a market without bargaining (*regatear*) is inconceivable. Do not hesitate to offer half price if the vendor's is obviously excessive. Little by little you will succeed in coming to an agreement on the value of the object. If need be, pretend to give up and leave – the vendor will come after you to offer his best price. You are quite likely to have to do some hard bargaining with taxi drivers who have no meter in their vehicle. It is also worth trying to negotiate the price of hotel rooms in the low season.

## • Drinking water
*See p 98 "Health and safety"*

Avoid drinking tap water even where it is treated, as in Guatemala City. Drink bottled drinks, without ice unless it is made from purified water. There is no risk involved in drinking the sterilised water that hotels and restaurants provide. In Guatemala, *agua mineral* means sparkling water; for non-sparkling ask for *agua pura*.

## • Electricity
110 volts and 60 hertz, with flat-pronged plugs as in the United States. A very few places have 220 volts.

## • Laundry
Big towns have several laundries (*lavanderías*), some of which are self-service. Most hotels have a laundry service, a more practical solution but also more expensive.

## • Newspapers
Apart from a few American newspapers to be had in tourist places, the main means of keeping up with the news is the national press – inexhaustible when it comes to murders and accidents within the country. Of the Guatemalan dailies, *Prensa Libre* and *Siglo Veintiuno* have a large readership. The survival of *Crónica*, an independent, high-quality weekly, seems increasingly threatened since it took a stand against the present government.

## • Radio and television
You will become familiar with the various music radio stations during your bus journeys! The BBC World Service can be found on the short wave band at 5975, 6175 and 15220.

Along with the 5 national channels, most hotel TV sets have cable, with programmes that come mainly from Mexico and the United States. Progress is reaching the countryside as well, as you will notice from the occasional gigantic satellite dish in some isolated hamlet.

## • Smoking

National and international brands are on sale in bars and grocer's shops, and on the streets. A packet of cigarettes costs approximately 8Q; in some places it is possible to buy cigarettes one at a time. Many high-class restaurants provide non-smoking dining-rooms.

## • Taking photographs

Guatemala offers a variety of landscape subjects (archeological sites, mountains, volcanoes, jungles) and interesting street scenes (markets, local celebrations). You will be expected to respect religious ceremonies, with the exception of the major ones such as Holy Week and All Saints. Sometimes the camera may be seen as intruding into locals' privacy, so be polite and ask for permission before taking photos – and be prepared for refusals! Sometimes a few words can work miracles and the people you are speaking to will spontaneously offer to pose for the camera.

Big towns have Fuji and Kodak shops selling a relatively varied selection of film at prices similar to those in Europe.

## • Thefts

Deserted streets and crowded places are where most theft takes place. Markets and public transport are the favourite hunting grounds for pickpockets, who take advantage of some pushing and shoving to filch a wallet in a couple of seconds. A bit of common sense and you will avoid a lot of problems. Keep your money in a pouch hidden under your clothes, but always keep a few quetzals to hand to avoid having to pull out a wad of notes when paying for purchases or bus tickets. Do not wear jewellery, it attracts attention even if it has no value. Keep a photocopy of your passport on you, and if possible leave the original with your air ticket in the safe of your hotel. If you travel by bus, remember that big bags are systematically carried on the roof, which means it is virtually impossible to keep an eye on your luggage once you have sat down.

## • Tipping / Gratuities

It is usual to leave a 10% tip (*propina*) in restaurants but more rarely in *comedores*. You can also give the hotel chambermaid a few quetzals; indeed, she may well leave an envelope on your bedside table to remind you.

## • Toilets

In all toilets you will find a basket for used toilet paper, since the poor quality of the plumbing means that waste water is not always evacuated efficiently. The habit is maintained in most places, even in recently-constructed buildings.

## • Units of Measurement

Officially Guatemala uses the metric system, but people sometimes still use old Spanish measurements such as the *vara* (0.84m) or *cuerda* (41.81m), the *manzana* (0.70ha) or *caballería* (46.5ha), the *libra* (0.46kg) or *arroba* (11.51kg). To make things even more complicated, some US units of measurement have been adopted, such as the American gallon (3.79 litres) for petrol, and feet (*pies*) and miles (*millas*) for distances.

Distances in this guide are given in kilometres. As a rule of thumb, one kilometre is five-eighths of a mile: 5 miles is therefore about 8 kilometres, 10 miles is about 16 kilometres and 20 miles is about 32 kilometres.

Consult the table below for other useful metric equivalents:

| Degrees Celsius | 35° | 30° | 25° | 20° | 15° | 10° | 5° | 0° | -5° | -10° |
|---|---|---|---|---|---|---|---|---|---|---|
| Degrees Fahrenheit | 95° | 86° | 77° | 68° | 59° | 50° | 41° | 32° | 23° | 15° |

I centimetre (cm) = 0.4 inch
I metre (m) = 3.3 feet
I metre (m) = 1.09 yards
I litre = 1.06 quart
I litre = 0.22 gallon
I kilogram (kg) = 2.2 pounds

## • Weather forecasts
On television and in the national press.

# LOOK AND LEARN

## • General works on Latin America
Ades, Dawn, **Art in Latin America: The Modern Era, 1820-1980,** Yale, 1993.
Beavers, Randall A., **The Birds of Tikal: An Annotated Checklist for Tikal National Park and Petén, Guatemala,** Texas A&M University Press, 1992.
Bethell, Leslie, **A Cultural History of Latin America: Literature, Music and the Visual Arts in the 19th and 20th Centuries (Cambridge History of Latin America),** Cambridge University Press, 1998.
Jones, Oakah L., **Guatemala in the Spanish Colonial Period,** University of Oklahoma Press, 1994.
Kelly, Joyce, **An Archaeological Guide to Northern Central America: Belize, Guatemala, Honduras, and El Salvador,** University of Oklahoma Press, 1996.
Williamson, Edwin, **The Penguin History of Latin America**, Penguin Books, 1993.

## • Mayan archeology and civilisation
Heptig, Vince, Tum, Roberta M. and Tum, Rigoberta, **A Mayan Struggle: Portrait of a Guatemalan People in Danger**, Mayamedia, 1997.
Miller, Arthur G., **Maya Rulers of Time: A Study of Architectural Sculpture at Tikal, Guatemala**, Books on Demand, 1993.
Pettersen, Carmen L., **The Maya of Guatemala: Life and Dress,** Ixchel Museum, 1977.
Proskouria, Tatian, **Album of Mayan Architecture**, University of Oklahoma Press, 1977.
Schele, Linda, et al., **The Code of Kings: The Language of Seven Sacred Maya Temples and Tombs**, Scribner, 1998.
Sexton, James D. et al., **Heart of Heaven, Heart of Earth, and Other Mayan Folktales**, Smithsonian Institution Press, 1999.
Sharer, Robert J., **The Ancient Maya**, Stanford University Press, 1994.
Stierlin, Henri, **The Maya,** Benedikt Taschen Verlag, 1997.
Vankirk, Jacques, **Remarkable Remains of the Ancient Peoples of Guatemala**, University of Oklahoma Press, 1996.

## • Holiday reading

Connely Benz, Stephen, **Guatemalan Journey**, University of Texas Press, 1996.
Handy, Jim, **Gift of the Devil: A History of Guatemala**, South End Press, 1985.
Menchu, Rigoberta, Wright, Ann (Translator), **Crossing Borders**, Verso, 1998.
Menchu, Rigoberta and Burgos-Debray, Elizabeth, **I, Rigoberta Menchu: An Indian Woman in Guatemala**, Verso, 1984.
Schweidel, David, **Confidence of the Heart**, Milkweed Editions, 1995.
Stoll, David, **Rigoberta Menchu and the Story of all Poor Guatemalans**, Westview Press, 1999.

## • Maps

Kevin Healey's Travel Map of **Guatemala**, 1:500 000. International Travel Maps.
Mapa Turístico de **Guatemala**, 1:1 000 000. Free from INGUAT.
Traveller's reference map of **Belize**, 1:350 000. International Travel Map Productions.

## • Music

Compilations of Marimba music are readily available.

# USEFUL WORDS AND EXPRESSIONS

To all intents and purposes, every letter is pronounced in Spanish. A few clarifications will nevertheless help you understand Guatemalans. The "ll" in *llave* is pronounced as if it were a "y" (*yavé*); the "ñ" in *señor* is pronounced "senyor"; "v" and "b" are almost indistinguishable (*vaca* and *baca* are pronounced virtually identically). The "j" (*jota*) is a guttural "ch" as in the Scottish "loch", and the rolled "r" is produced by vibrating the tip of the tongue against the roof of the mouth. Latin-Americanisms – words which do not exist in Castilian Spanish or are used in a different context – are in *italics* in this glossary.

**Numbers**

| | | | |
|---|---|---|---|
| one | uno | eleven | once |
| two | dos | twelve | doce |
| three | tres | thirteen | trece |
| four | cuatro | fourteen | catorce |
| five | cinco | fifteen | quince |
| six | seis | sixteen | dieciséis |
| seven | siete | twenty | veinte |
| eight | ocho | thirty | treinta |
| nine | nueve | hundred | cien |
| ten | diez | thousand | mil |

Composite numbers are then made up as follows: *diecisiete* (seventeen), *veintidós* (twenty-two), etc.

**Days**

| | | | |
|---|---|---|---|
| Monday | lunes | Friday | viernes |
| Tuesday | martes | Saturday | sábado |
| Wednesday | miércoles | Sunday | domingo |
| Thursday | jueves | | |

## Useful words and expressions

### Months and seasons

| | | | |
|---|---|---|---|
| January | enero | November | noviembre |
| February | febrero | December | diciembre |
| March | marzo | spring | primavera |
| April | abril | summer | verano (dry |
| May | mayo | | season in |
| June | junio | | Guatemala) |
| July | julio | autumn | otoño |
| August | agosto | winter | invierno (wet |
| September | septiembre | | season in |
| October | octubre | | Guatemala) |

### Common expressions

| | | | |
|---|---|---|---|
| yes, no | sí, no | don't mention it | *no tenga pena* |
| hello, good morning | buenos días | at your service | *para servirle* |
| good afternoon | buenas tardes | excuse me | con permiso |
| good evening, | buenas noches | my apologies | perdón, disculpe |
| good night | | I don't understand | no entiendo |
| goodbye | adiós, *que le vaya bien* ("have a good journey") | I don't speak Spanish | no hablo español |
| | | to chat | *platicar* |
| | | Sir, you | señor, Usted |
| see you later | hasta luego | Madam | señora |
| pleased to meet you | encantado(a), mucho gusto | | seño' (used in Guatemala to indi- |
| How are you? | ¿Qué tal? | | cate respect) |
| please | por favor | Miss | señorita |
| thank you (very much) | (muchas) gracias | | |

### The time

| | | | |
|---|---|---|---|
| When? | ¿Cuándo? | yesterday | ayer |
| What time is it? | ¿Qué hora es? | tomorrow morning | mañana por la |
| now | ahora | | mañana |
| at once | *ahorita* | tomorrow afternoon | mañana por la |
| date | fecha | | tarde |
| year | año | tomorrow evening | mañana por la |
| century | siglo | | noche |
| today | hoy | | |

### Directions

| | | | |
|---|---|---|---|
| Where is...? | ¿Dónde está...? | near to | cerca de |
| address | dirección | far from | lejos de |
| on/to the right | a la derecha | (street) corner | esquina |
| on/to the left | a la izquierda | map | mapa |
| straight ahead | recto | district (of a town) | *zona* |
| to turn | girar | | |

### Transport

| | | | |
|---|---|---|---|
| (plane, train) ticket | boleto (avión, tren) | bus station | terminal de bus |
| | | car | *carro* |
| return ticket | ida y vuelta | petrol station | *gasolinera* |
| ship | barco | puncture repair | *pinchazo* |
| boat | lancha | road hump | tumulo, vibrador |
| pirogue | *cayuco* | main road | carretera |
| river | río | unsurfaced road, | carretera de |
| jetty | muelle | track | terracería |
| bus, coach | *camioneta* | path | sendero, vereda |
| 1st class bus | *pullman* | street | calle |

| avenue | avenida | parking | parqueo |
|---|---|---|---|
| block of houses | *cuadra* | forbidden | prohibido |
| a fine | multa | wheel clamp | cepo |

## Hotels

| inn, small hotel | posada | bed | cama |
|---|---|---|---|
| reception | recepción | sheet | sábana |
| receptionist | recepcionista | blanket | *chamarra* |
| guest, client | huésped, cliente | toilets | servicios, baño |
| single room | habitación sencilla | air conditioning | aire acondicionado |
| double room | habitación doble | fan | ventilador |
| key | llave | heating | calefacción |
| bathroom | cuarto de baño | pay (the bill) | cancelar |

## Restaurant

| to eat | comer | dinner | cena |
|---|---|---|---|
| to drink | beber | meal | comida |
| I would like... | quisiera... | bill | cuenta |
| breakfast | desayuno | menu | menú, carta |
| lunch | almuerzo | tip | propina |

## The menu

| aguacate | avocado | langosta | spiny lobster |
|---|---|---|---|
| ajo | garlic | mantequilla | butter |
| arroz | rice | manzana | apple |
| azúcar | sugar | mariscos | seafood |
| banano | banana | pan | bread |
| bistec | steak | patata, papa | potato |
| camarón | prawn | pavo | turkey |
| cangrejo | crab | pie (pronounced "pié") | tart |
| carne asada | roast meat | | |
| cebolla | onion | plátano | plantain banana |
| ceviche | marinated fish or seafood | pollo frito | fried chicken |
| | | pimienta | pepper |
| cerdo | pork | postre | dessert |
| frijoles | beans | queso | cheese |
| guacamole | avocado purée | res | beef |
| helado | ice cream | tamal | maize dumpling |
| huevos revueltos | scrambled eggs | tortilla | maize pancake |
| jamón | ham | | |

## Drinks

| tea | té | fruit juice | *jugo de fruta* |
|---|---|---|---|
| black coffee | café solo | milk-shake | *licuado* |
| milk coffee | café con leche | | *(con leche)* |
| chocolate | chocolate | beer | cerveza |
| mineral water | *agua pura* | rum | ron |
| sparkling water | *agua mineral* | wine | vino |
| ice | hielo | spirits, "fire-water" | *aguardiente, guaro* |
| orangeade | naranjada | | |
| lemonade | limonada | | |

Useful words and expressions

105

## Purchasing

| How much is it? | ¿Cúanto es? | traveller's cheque | cheque de viaje |
| dear | caro | credit card | tarjeta de crédito |
| cheap | barato | market | mercado |
| to bargain | regatear | shop | tienda |
| cash | efectivo | weaving | tejido |

## Communications

| envelope | sobre | international call | llamada larga |
| stamp | sello | | distancia |
| letterbox | buzón | collect call | cobro revertido |
| post office | oficina de correos | | |

## Visiting

| guide | guía | window, counter | taquilla |
| entrance | entrada, ingreso | ticket | boleto |
| exit | salida | to wait | esperar |
| open | abierto | floor, storey | piso |
| closed | cerrado | staircase | escalera |

## Clothing and accessories

| huipil | blouse, shift, tunic | jaspe | ikat, jaspé fabric |
| corte | skirt | morral | bag |
| tzut | multi-purpose length of cloth worn folded on the head | mecapal | tumpline (leather forehead strap for carrying loads) |
| tocoyal | long strip of cloth worn as a head-dress | petate | mat, rug |
| | | metate | milling stone, quern |

## Maize vocabulary

| maíz | maize | nixtamal | container in which maize is cooked |
| milpa | maize field, cultivated plot | comal | earthenware disc on which tortillas are cooked |
| mazorca | cob | | |
| tuza | leaf | | |
| xilote | heart of the cob | atol | drink made of maize juice |
| elote | ripe heart | | |
| olote | the core after the grain has been stripped off | | |

## Some common words

| Altiplano | Highlands | comedor | small eatery |
| Ayuntamiento | town hall | cantina | tavern, pub |
| chapín | Guatemalan | nahual | guardian spirit, animal "double" |
| Ladino | Of mixed race, non-Amerindian in the widest sense | cofradía | brotherhood |
| | | copal, pom | resin incense |
| ladinizado | Amerindian who has adopted the Ladino way of life | chicle | gum-like sap used to make chewing-gum |
| gringo(a) | North American (by extension, any white foreigner) | chiclero | chicle tapper |

| | | | |
|---|---|---|---|
| ceiba | silk cotton or kapok tree, the Mayan tree of life | cordillera, sierra | mountain range |
| | | cerro | hill |
| | | barranco | ravine |
| finca | (coffee, etc) plantation, large farm | | |

# Exploring Guatemala

Tikal's temples,
surging up from
the El Petén Jungle

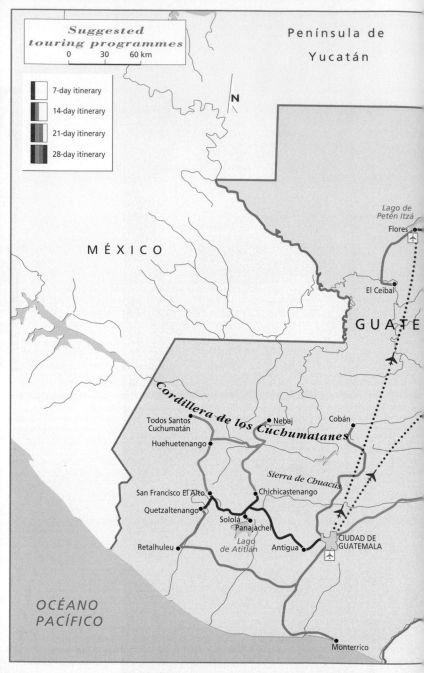

## GUATEMALA

**Suggested touring programmes**

0    30    60 km

- 7-day itinerary
- 14-day itinerary
- 21-day itinerary
- 28-day itinerary

Península de Yucatán

MÉXICO

Lago de Petén Itzá

Flores

El Ceibal

GUATE

Cordillera de los Cuchumatanes

Todos Santos Cuchumatán

Nebaj

Cobán

Huehuetenango

Sierra de Chuacús

San Francisco El Alto

Chichicastenango

Quetzaltenango

Sololá

Panajachel

CIUDAD DE GUATEMALA

Retalhuleu

Lago de Atitlán

Antigua

OCÉANO PACÍFICO

Monterrico

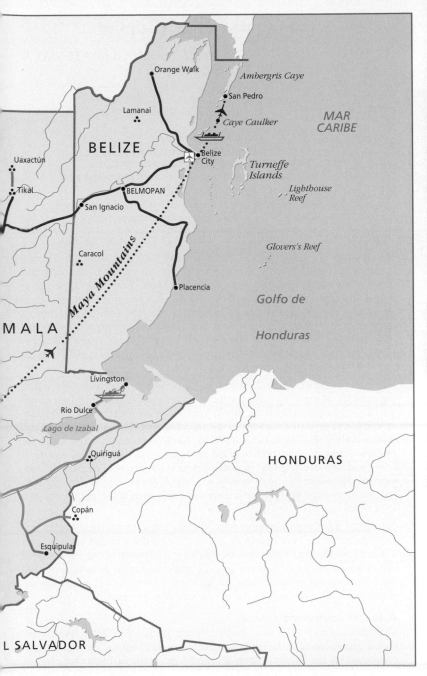

Guatemala City

# GUATEMALA CITY★
## (CIUDAD DE GUATEMALA / NUEVA GUATEMALA DE LA ASUNCIÓN)
Capital of the country and of Guatemala department
Pop approx 2 000 000 (inc suburbs) – Alt 1 500m
Temperate climate all year

### Not to be missed
Flying in over the town in daylight.
Visiting the museums in the residential district.
The All Saints' celebrations in the village of Santiago Sacatepéquez.

### And remember...
If you are not spending long in the country, go straight to Antigua.
Avoid being caught in traffic when offices close on Fridays.
At night take a taxi, particularly in Zone 1.

Seen from the sky, the panorama over Guatemala City is breathtaking. The city is spread out on a flat valley bottom with vertiginous ravines to the north and east that separate it from the surrounding mountain chains. The airport is so close to the centre that the main districts of the city can easily be picked out as the plane comes in to land, flying low over the old town with its small houses huddled close together and the wide avenues lined with gigantic Coca-Cola and McDonald's signs. The regular checkerboard layout of these Americanised districts, dotted with the occasional skyscraper, continues right up to the residential suburbs stretching away to the south and west.

Although smaller and more human than Mexico City, Guatemala City suffers the same ills as most big Latin American cities. The capital is regularly paralysed by traffic jams that leave drivers trapped in an interminable nightmare of horns and exhaust fumes. Beset by anarchic town planning, its slums are mushrooming, clinging to the sides of the *barrancos* (ravines), a last refuge for victims of rural outmigration, war and earthquakes. To combat the climate of crime and violence reigning in some districts, shopkeepers employ the services of intimidating security guards who stand guard, sub-machine guns at the ready, in front of most banks, jewellers and even some restaurants and food shops.

But despite its inhospitable appearance, the city has some interesting sights and the most important museums in the country. Given that any visit to Guatemala is more than likely to either start or end here, it is worth taking advantage of this to stop a day or so. Tourists generally prefer to stay in Antigua and make the 2hr round trip to visit "Guate". What sweet revenge for the former capital, dispossessed of its title and its riches over two centuries ago!

## A fourth turbulent capital
The earthquake of 1773 that shook Santiago de Los Caballeros, the former capital later renamed La Antigua Guatemala (*see p 139 "Antigua"*), forced the representatives of the Spanish crown to take refuge in the La Ermita valley. This

site protected by ravines was supposed to withstand the frequent tremors in the region. It was therefore decided to transfer all Antigua's wealth here, and on 2 January 1776 the new capital officially took over, under the name of **La Nueva Guatemala de La Asunción**.

The new capital was built on the usual colonial grid pattern, laid out around a central square lined with the town's most important buildings (now Zone 1). Antigua's Baroque architecture was abandoned in favour of a Neoclassical style. The new metropolis, which took about a century to become fully populated, seems to have been gradually threatened by the economic prosperity of Quetzaltenango, the second largest city in the country *(see p 184)*. But an earthquake was again to change the course of history, with the destruction of its rival in 1902 leaving the field free for the capital to develop.

However, bad luck was also to strike Guatemala City, in the shape of two devastating tremors during the course of the 20C. The violent **earthquake of 24 December 1917**, which shook the capital intermittently for over a month, destroyed a large number of buildings. Major construction works were immediately undertaken, which modernised the city's appearance. Over the years the residential districts rapidly extended south and west. The region again suffered severely from the **earthquake of 4 February 1976**, with this cataclysm completing destruction of most remaining vestiges of the colonial era. Those it has been possible to restore are nevertheless worth visiting.

*For finding your way around the capital's zones, see the district divisions in "Making the most of Guatemala City". The Spanish street names have been replaced by American-type numbering, with an address system that is initially puzzling to Europeans (see p 99 "A to Z").*

A busy street in the city centre

G. Boutin/HOA QUI

# The old town (Zone I)
*Allow half a day.*
*Most churches are open 8am-12noon and 3pm-6pm.*

Polluted, noisy and jammed with traffic, this district of exhaust-blackened frontages rapidly becomes suffocating. But this historic heart, the centre of political and religious power, is the best place for apprehending daily life in the capital and the events that are important to Guatemala. There is always something happening here: all major national events, be they of jubilation or protestation, converge on Plaza de la Constitución; hundreds of students fill its avenues with their floats and slogans during the Huelga de Dolores, a few days before the moving Holy Week processions set out from its various churches.

## Strikers in the streets!
For the past 100 years, the universities have gone on strike on the Friday preceding Holy Week, to commemorate the first edition of a student journal denouncing the dictatorship of Manuel Cabrera, which came out on St Dolores Day 1898. The "Huelga de Dolores" (Dolores Strike) parade proceeds through the streets of Zone I behind the "Chabela", the event's skeleton mascot. The students, disguised in penitents' hoods that evoke the Inquisition, denounce politicians in theatrical sketches, satires, songs and humorous – and often obscene – slogans. The "voice of those who have no voice", as one participant describes it, is a tremendous letting off of steam that ranges from serious demands to burlesque carnival, depending on the political and social climate.

## Plaza de la Constitución★ (Map I, C1 and Map II, B1)
Every Sunday this vast square is taken over by a colourful crowd that sets up stalls selling textiles and food. During national celebrations a sound system is set up on the esplanade, which is packed out with a surging, noisy crowd dotted with brightly-coloured *huipiles*. On ordinary days the majestic proportions of this square are visible, enhancing the imposing appearance of the buildings around it. Also known as **Parque Central**, this square has an unusual shape, being extended westward by a second esplanade, the **Parque Centenario**. The latter was created on the site of the former Palacio de los Capitanes Generales, which was built when the capital was transferred but destroyed in the 1917 earthquake and never rebuilt.

**The Palacio Nacional★** (Map II, B1) *(9am-5.30pm; weekends 9am-12noon / 1pm-4pm. No fee)* stretches along the north side of the square. Completed in 1943, a few months before the fall of Jorge Ubico, this building with its eclectic architecture stands out because of the strange greenish colour of its façade. The former presidential palace still houses a few ministries, whereas some ceremonial rooms are open to the public.

All the richly decorated corridors opening onto patios can be visited. Above the main staircase, a **fresco★** by Alfredo Gálvez Suárez relates the history of Guatemala, the conquest being symbolised by a meeting between the Popol Vuh and Don Quixote and the battle between Pedro de Alvarado and Tecún Umán *(see p 37)*. If asked, the attendants will open the **sala de banquetes★** on the 2nd floor, where official banquets are held. This hall has a superb marquetry parquet floor, composed of a variety of tropical woods, and a remarkable painted wood **ceiling★★**. The **stained glass** by Julio Urruela Vásquez depicts the

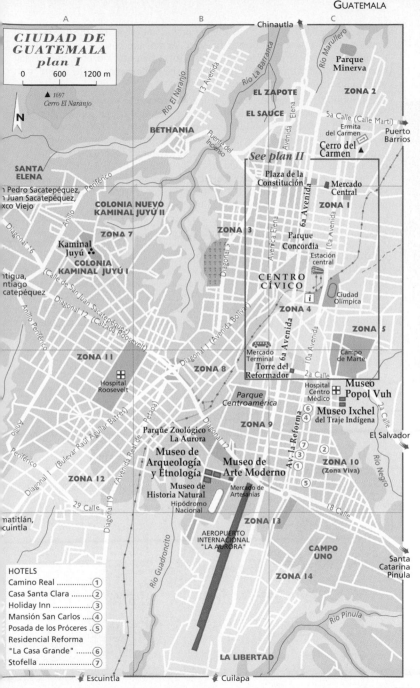

CIUDAD DE
GUATEMALA
plan I

0    600    1200 m

▲ 1697
Cerro El Naranjo

N

Chinautla

Río Marrullero

Parque
Minerva

ZONA 2

EL ZAPOTE

EL SAUCE

Río La Barranca

13 Avenida

Río El Naranjo

BÉTHANIA

Avenida Elena

5a Calle (Calle Martí)

Ermita
del Carmen

Puerto
Barrios

Puente del
Incienso

SANTA
ELENA

Periférico

Cerro del
Carmen

See plan II

n Pedro Sacatepéquez,
n Juan Sacatepéquez,
xco Viejo

COLONIA NUEVO
KAMINAL JUYÚ II

Plaza de la
Constitución

Mercado
Central

6a Avenida

ZONA 1

ZONA 7

ZONA 3

Avenida Elena

Parque
Concordia

10a Avenida

Anillo

Diagonal 16

Kaminal
Juyú

COLONIA
KAMINAL JUYÚ I

Estación
central

Diagonal 3

CENTRO
CÍVICO

ntigua,
ntiago
catepéquez

(Calle de San Juan Sacatepéquez)

Diagonal 12 (Calzada Roosevelt)

Ciudad
Olímpica

Diagonal 1 (Avenida Bolívar)

ZONA 4

i

Anillo Periférico

ZONA 5

ZONA 11

ZONA 8

Diagonal 1 (Avenida Bolívar)

6a Avenida

10a Avenida

Campo
de Marte

Hospital
Roosevelt

Mercado
Terminal

Torre del
Reformador

2a Calle

Museo
Popol Vuh

Periférico

Diagonal 35 de Pedapa

Parque
Centroamérica

Hospital
Centro
Médico

Museo Ixchel
del Traje Indígena

2a Calle

Diagonal 12

ZONA 9

⑥
④

El Salvador

Río Negro

Av. la Reforma

Parque Zoológico
La Aurora

Museo de
Arqueología
y Etnología

Museo de
Arte Moderno

⑦
③
①

②

ZONA 10
(Zona Viva)

ZONA 12

Diagonal 1 (Bulevar Raúl Aguilar Batres)

(Avenida Real de Pedapa)

Museo de
Historia Natural

Mercado de
Artesanías

⑤

29 Calle

Hipódromo
Nacional

ZONA 13

18 Calle

Diagonal 19

matitlán,
cuintla

Río Guadroncito

AEROPUERTO
INTERNACIONAL
"LA AURORA"

CAMPO
UNO

Santa
Catarina
Pinula

ZONA 14

Río Pinula

HOTELS
Camino Real ................①
Casa Santa Clara .........②
Holiday Inn ..................③
Mansión San Carlos ....④
Posada de los Próceres .⑤
Residencial Reforma
"La Casa Grande" .......⑥
Stofella ........................⑦

LA LIBERTAD

Escuintla

Cuilapa

ten civic virtues and at either end a white orchid and a quetzal, the two national symbols *(see p 15 and p 210)*, can be seen. Across the corridor is the **sala de recepciones**★, where distinguished guests meet beneath a bronze and crystal chandelier weighing 2t. The cupola is marked **kilometre 0**, the point from which all distances in the country are calculated.

The imposing Neoclassical façade of the **Catedral Metropolitana** (Map II, B1) *(8am-12noon / 3pm-5pm)* looks down over the east side of the square. Although inaugurated in 1815, the building was not finished until 1868 after the addition of two bell-towers. Among the religious works and furnishings brought from Antigua cathedral, the showpiece is the **Virgen del Socorro**; this statue, the oldest in the country, was brought from Spain by Pedro de Alvarado's expedition. But the **replica of the Black Christ of Esquipulas** *(see p 256)* in the left aisle steals the show; the faithful take it in turns to offer prayers to this sculpture, its feet worn by fervent caressing and kissing.

The modern building on the west side of Parque Centenario houses the **Biblioteca** and the **Archivos Generales de Centroamérica**.

## Around Plaza de la Constitución

Behind the cathedral, on 9a Avenida between 6a and 8a Calles, is the **Mercado Central** (Plan I, C1-C2 and Plan II, B1) *(see "Making the most of Guatemala City")*, now located below ground level underneath the public car park after the original structure was destroyed in the 1976 earthquake. Despite its austere architecture the place does not lack interest, with its maze of alleyways revealing pile after

Plaza de la Constitución on Sunday

pile of fruit, vegetables, meat, fish, spices, textiles, weaving yarns, basketry, wood, leather, etc. A big selection of Guatemalan handicrafts is to be found on the 1st floor, and the *comedores* section is a cheap place to eat.

*Continue down 8a Calle in the opposite direction to the cathedral, as far as 11a Ave. Turn left and walk 2 blocks up this avenue.*

On the corner of 5a Calle and 11a Avenida is a two-tone zigzag-patterned dome sitting on top of a building flanked by two massive towers. Although its architecture is similar to that of Antigua, the **church of La Merced*** (Map II, C1) is distinguished from its "elder" by its extremely sober façade. The building is interesting for its opulent interior decoration: a very lovely organ, paintings, sculptures, altars and Baroque altarpieces brought from La Merced in Antigua. Its **Jesús Nazareño**, carved by Mateo de Zúñiga in the middle of the 17C and a major Holy Week figure, is reputed for its miracles and was the centrepiece of an immense procession after the 1976 earthquake.

*Walk back to 10a Ave and turn south into it; continue 3 blocks.*

On the corner of 10a Avenida and 9a Calle, the **Museo Nacional de Historia** (Map II, B1) exhibits objects relating to the history of Guatemala as well as a large collection of old photographs. The building was seriously damaged in the last earthquake and has since undergone major restoration work.

One block south, on the corner of 10a Calle, is the **church of San Miguel de Capuchinas** (Map II, B1). The gilding on its Baroque altarpieces, which came from Antigua, is positively dazzling and there is a superb coffered **ceiling*** in Mudéjar style. This church houses the **Cristo de Las Palmas**, an unusual carving showing Jesus on a donkey.

*Leaving the church of San Miguel de Capuchinas, turn right into 10a Calle and walk along it for 2 blocks.*

On the corner of 12a Ave and 10a Calle, the imposing **church of Santo Domingo** (Map II, C1) – also known as the Basilica del Rosario – displays a number of Baroque works, in particular a lovely statue of **Nuestra Señora del Rosario**. The most spectacular Good Friday procession leaves from here.

## Towards Zone 2

*Go north back up 12a Ave to Diagonal 9, at the foot of the hill, just on the edge of Zone 2. Vehicles can drive up to the top by taking the road on the right of the Instituto Tecnológico de Computación.*

When mass is being held *(daily 7am, 8am; Sundays and public holidays 7.30am, 9.30am, 11.30am, 5pm)* it is worth joining the faithful climbing the **Cerro del Carmen*** (del Carmen hill) (Map I, C1). At the top, in a delightful cactus garden overlooking the city, stands a hermitage housing a statue of the **Virgen del Carmen**, patron saint of the capital. The previous church, dating from the 17C, unfortunately succumbed to the 1917 earthquake. NB, this hill and its neighbourhood have a bad reputation, so you are strongly advised to go there by taxi in a group.

*On 5a Ave, take a taxi or a bus to the north end of 6a Ave, Zone 2, 2km from Plaza de la Constitución. (NB, in Zone 2 the order of the "calles" is reversed, with 1a Calle to the south of 2a Calle, contrary to the other zones in the capital).*

**Parque Minerva** (Map I, C1) is much appreciated by the *capitalinos* (inhabitants of the capital), who come here for entertainment at weekends. At the entrance to this amusement park the *comedores* are in hot competition: eye-

### The Virgen del Carmen

The nuns of Ávila convent in Spain entrusted a Franciscan monk, Juan Corz, to take a sculpture of the Virgin Mary to the New World; he reached Guatemala in 1604. Having taken up quarters in a cavern, the hermit placed the statue in a neighbouring grotto. Local people decided to build a real chapel to honour the statue, which was reputed for its miracles. But they discovered that it mysteriously returned to its original grotto at nightfall. It was therefore decided to build a hermitage worthy of the name on the Cerro del Carmen, to satisfy the demands of this capricious Virgin Mary.

watering smoke from barbecues forms a thick cloud and radios blast forth at full volume to attract customers, all in a funfair ambience.

The modest park is not of much interest except for **El Mapa en Relieve★** (relief map) *(9am-5.30pm; closed Mondays. Fee)*. This model covering 1 800sqm was made in 1905 by engineer Francisco Vela. His use of different scales for the horizontal (1:10 000) and vertical (1:2 000) measurements accentuates the uneven relief of the country. From the viewing towers there is an excellent "aerial" view of Guatemala – and Belize – and it is easy to follow thanks to the little signs indicating the main places.

## Along 6a Avenida

Returning to Plaza de la Constitución, take 6a Ave, heading south. This thoroughfare is one of the city's main shopping areas, lined all the way down with modest shops, shopping arcades, cinemas and restaurants; its pavements are jam-packed with stalls selling clothes and shoes, the frontages are covered with advertising and the roadway is invisible under an uninterrupted stream of cars and buses.

On the corner of 13a Calle stands the **church of San Francisco** (Map II, B2) *(closed Mondays)*, a building in Neoclassical style begun in 1780 but which took several decades to complete because of the many earthquakes. Here there are paintings of martyrs as well as a fine sculpture of the **Virgen de la Inmaculada Concepción**.

Some fifty metres further on, the avenue leads into **Parque Concordia★** (Map I, C2 and Map II, B2), one of the liveliest and pleasantest squares in the capital. The public authorities have started renovating it and are taking advantage of this to rid its central garden of the small-time vendors.

The strange medieval-style castle in the northeast of the square is the **Palacio de la Policía**, the police headquarters.

Four blocks further south you come to **18a Calle**, where a dense crowd tries to weave its way between the close-packed stalls of an open-air market spilling out into the roadway. This permanent crush is a godsend for pickpockets and anyone up to no good, so if your curiosity wins out over repeated warnings from local people, make sure you have nothing of value on you. Once deserted around 8pm, this street is reputed to be one of the most dangerous in Zone 1. To be strictly avoided at night!

## The administrative district

*1hr is enough to see the various buildings.*

In the south of Zone 1 the avenues spew out their streams of vehicles onto a large roundabout with concrete posts sticking up amid the haphazard traffic. At some time or another everyone passes through the administrative district, on the border between the old town and the residential area. If visiting the tourist office there, it is worth taking the opportunity to have a quick look around the Civic Centre, a set of public buildings built during the 1950s and '60s.

*CIUDAD DE GUATEMALA*
*Centro - plan II*

0    250    500 m

**Parque Minerva**
**Cerro del Carmen**

5a Calle
6a Calle
4a Calle

**Palacio Nacional**
**La Merced**

Parque Centenario

**Catedral Metropolitana**

9 Calle

**Biblioteca y Archivos Generales** ⑤

N

**Hospital General San Juan de Dios**

**Mercado Central**

7a Calle

**Plaza de la Constitución**

**Museo Nacional de Historia**

10 Calle
11 Calle
12 Calle

La Medalla Milagrosa

**San Miguel de Capuchinas**

**Santo Domingo**

10 Calle

④ ⑨
⑩

**San Francisco**

**Instituto Normal Belén**

**Palacio de la Policía**

13 Calle
⑦⑧  13 Calle "A"

**Parque Concordia**  ① ②

ZONA I

15 Calle
15 Calle "A"
14 Calle

16 Calle

18 Calle
19 Calle

17 Calle

20 Calle

**Mercado Sur No. 2**

18 Calle

21 Calle

CENTRO CÍVICO

20 Calle

Teatro al Aire Libre
21 Calle

22 Calle

**Centro Cultural Miguel Ángel Asturias**

**Municipalidad**

**Banco de Guatemala**

24 Calle
25 Calle

**Teatro Nacional**

ZONA 5

**Crédito Hipotecario Nacional**

IGSS
ℹ INGUAT

26 Calle

**CIUDAD OLÍMPICA**

25 Calle

igua

26 Calle

ZONA 8

27 Calle

28 Calle
29 Calle

ZONA 4

30 Calle

Mercado Terminal

31 Calle

⑥

**Capilla de Yurrita**

1a Calle

**Torre del Reformador** ⑪

Zona
Militar

ZONA 9

③

ZONA 10

✈, Parque La Aurora

**Museo Popol Vuh, Museo Ixchel**

HOTELS
Chalet Suizo ...............①
Colonial ......................②
Cortijo Reforma .........③
Del Centro .................④
Pan American ...........⑤
Plaza ..........................⑥
Posada Belén .............⑦
Posada San Francisco ⑧
Royal Palace ..............⑨
Spring ........................⑩
Villa Española ...........⑪

## The Centro Cívico (Zones 1 and 4) (Map I, C2 and Map II, B3)

*The buildings are numbered clockwise from the east (on the left when coming from Zone 1).*

Along 7a Avenida, on the right of the Ministry of Finance and the High Court, the frontage of the **Banco de Guatemala** (depicted on the 1 quetzal banknote) displays a gigantic high-relief mural by González Goyri; the interior of the building is decorated with murals painted on enamel by Carlos Mérida.

The interior and exterior of the **Crédito Hipotecario Nacional**, located just behind the bank, have also been decorated by these two artists.

Behind the railway that separates Zones 1 and 4, the ground floor of a big blue building with white balconies houses **INGUAT** (Instituto Guatemalteco de Turismo) *(see "Making the most of Guatemala City")*.

On the other side of 7a Avenida, the **IGSS** (Instituto Guatemalteco de Seguridad Social) sports an immense wall sculpture by Roberto González Goyri.

Just in front of the Social Security headquarters, the **Municipalidad** has two façades sculpted by Guillermo Grajeda Mena; a big mosaic by Carlos Mérida decorates the entrance hall.

The hill overlooking 6a Avenida offers an opportunity to flee the city's agitation by taking a pleasant walk. The buildings forming the **Centro Cultural Miguel Ángel de Asturias**★ (Map II, A3) *(8am-5pm; Saturdays 8am-4pm; closed Sundays. No fee)*, set in a pleasant, well-kept park, stand on the site of the old San José fort. Completed in 1978, this architectural complex created by artist Efraín Recinos houses three theatres and a museum. Although inspired by the Mayan pyramids, the **Teatro Nacional** looks rather more like a great liner; it holds something over 2 000 people. Nearby are the **Teatro de Cámara** (chamber music auditorium) and the **Teatro al Aire Libre** (open-air theatre). This latter with its open-air stage and tiered seating is reminiscent of an ancient amphitheatre. Just behind, the **Museo del Ejército** (Army Museum) exhibits a collection of arms of little interest, although from the flag room there is a good view over the capital.

*Carry on down 7a Ave towards Zone 4, 1km south of the Centro Cívico.*

From among the buildings on Ruta 6, between Avenida la Reforma and 7a Avenida, the curious **church of Nuestra Señora de Las Angustias** *(8am-12noon / 2pm-4pm; closed Mondays)* appears as if by magic. Usually called the **Capilla de Yurrita**★ (chapel of Yurrita) (Map II, B4), it takes its name from the family that had it built to give thanks to the Virgin Mary for protecting them from the eruption of the Santa María volcano. Built between 1928 and 1941, the chapel's extravagant, Art Nouveau-influenced architecture juxtaposes Byzantine, Gothic, Baroque and Moorish styles. This unusual building has virtually become the emblem of the capital.

## The residential area

*Allow 1 day to visit all the museums without rushing.*
*Buses 82 and 101 run along Avenida la Reforma between Zones 1 and 13.*

With its grid pattern of spacious tree-lined avenues, this gringo district is made up of a few luxury residences jammed between office blocks. Here are most of the big hotels, bars, restaurants, night spots, airline companies, travel agencies, embassies and, above all, the country's most important museums, grouped in two different sectors around Francisco Marroquín University and in Parque La Aurora.

At the beginning of Zone 9, 300m south of the chapel of Yurrita, the traffic passes underneath the **Torre del Reformador** (tower of the reformer) (Map I, C3 and Map II, A4-B4), an excellent landmark in the district. This 72m-tall monument, strongly influenced by the Eiffel Tower, straddles 7a Avenida and 2a Calle. It was inaugurated on 19 July 1935 by Jorge Ubico Castañeda, to commemorate the centenary of the birth of General Justo Rufino Barrios, the "Great Reformer" *(see p 41)*.

## Around Avenida la Reforma (Zones 9 and 10)

This wide avenue, the continuation of 10a Avenida, divides Zones 9 and 10. The numerous restaurants and luxury hotels form a lively district bearing the name **Zona Viva**, in the vicinity of the Camino Real hotel, Zone 10.

*Take any bus going down Avenida la Reforma and get off at 6a Calle, Zone 10. Follow this street to the bottom of the hill (approx 500m on foot).*

The two museums in Francisco Marroquín University are fascinating to visit, either before or after your trip around the country.

The story of the **Museo Ixchel del Traje Indígena**\*\* (Map I, C3) *(8am-5.50pm; Saturdays 9am-12.50pm; closed Sundays. Fee)* began in 1973, the year a Textile Committee was founded, to perpetuate the memory of the Guatemalan **weaver's craft**. Converted into a museum, it quite naturally took the name of Ix Chel, goddess of fertility and weaving. Since 1993 the institution has been housed in a modern Mayan temple specially designed to conserve this superb collection of traditional fabrics and clothes in the best possible conditions.

The ground floor houses a gallery, bookshop and children's area. The exhibition as such starts at the access ramp to the upper floor. *Allow 90min to visit. Commentaries in English and Spanish.* On the walls of the ramp are hung paintings by **Andrés Curruchich** (1891-1969), depicting the rural Mayan world. Curruchich was a Cakchiquel artist from San Juan Comalapa, and the most outstanding primitive painter.

On the 1st floor, two documentary films on traditional Mayan clothing and the religious brotherhoods make a good introduction to the museum, which occupies four rooms. In the pre-Columbian section, the **history of Mayan dress** since 1000 BC is related through well-designed, informative texts, pictures of clothing from the Pre-Classic to the Post-Classic and a description of the natural dyes used, made from indigo, bark, cochineal and shells. The following rooms, covering the period from the Conquest to the present day, retrace the encounter between European fashions and Mayan clothing, as well as the influence of industrialisation on ancestral techniques – the introduction of the *telar a pie* (foot loom) and of synthetic materials, for example. Life-size tableaux give a glimpse of the indigenous people's everyday life, including a pilgrimage to the Esquipulas Basilica, a wedding ceremony and a weaving session. The beauty and diversity of the Lake Atitlán costumes should arouse your curiosity if you have not already visited that region.

The visit ends with a permanent exhibition of watercolours by **Carmen Pettersen**, the artist who launched this conservation project for Mayan textiles.

**The Museo Popul Vuh**\*\* (Map I, C3) *(9am-5pm; Saturdays 9am-1pm; closed Sundays. Fee)* explores Guatemalan civilization from the Pre-Classic period to the colonial era. *Allow at least 2hr. The labelling is in Spanish only.*

**The Residential Area**

This museum starts with a reference to the *Popul Vuh*, as the first room is devoted to the **juego de pelota** (ball game) through an essential chapter from that sacred book of the Quiché, declared the National Book of Guatemala in 1972 *(see p 30)*.

The next two rooms illustrate the Pre-Classic period (2000 BC-250 AD) through ceramics and basalt stelae from Kaminaljuyú. After a section on Amatitlán ceramics dating from the Early Classic, room 5 displays a **three-dimensional model of the North Acropolis in Tikal** and a collection of zoomorphic and anthropomorphic figures from the Late Classic, including a series of figures representative of that era (warriors, ball players, kings, musicians). The following section has some magnificent **polychrome ceramics★★** from the Lowlands; pottery from Copán (Honduras) has a characteristic dark red colour, while Chamá ware has zigzag edging.

> **"Let this noise above our heads cease"**
>
> The ball games played between Hun Hunahpu and Vucub Hunahpu disturbed the tranquillity of the Lords of Xibalbá, inhabitants of the underworld. Seriously annoyed by the racket, the Lords enticed the twins into their underground domain and submitted them to several ordeals culminating in the sacrifice of the two brothers. The head of Hun was hung from a tree, which at once began to bear fruit. Xquic, daughter of one of the Lords of the Night, approached it, and after speaking to her, the skull spat into the palm of her hand. From this saliva were born Hunahpu and Xbalanque, the two heroes of the "Popul Vuh". (The recurring twins theme does not figure in some translations, which consider the original manuscript to use several names for a single person, making Hunahpu and Xbalanque one and the same).

The objects in room 7 are some of the most interesting in the museum. Alongside a reproduction of the famous **Dresden Codex★★** *(see p 28)*, there are **funerary urns★★★** to be admired from the Ixil triangle, formed by the villages of Nebaj, Chajul and San Juan Cotzal in the Quiché region. In the centre of the showcase, the great urn with a jaguar head on the lid is one of the most important Late Classic pieces.

M. Troncy/HOA QUI

Funerary urn

The visit ends with two rooms of colonial art. Among all the liturgical exhibits, including some fine repoussé silver, is a Virgen de Dolores in wood and alabaster and a superb 18C **Baroque altarpiece★★** dedicated to the Virgen de la Asunción, remarkable because of its exuberant plant decoration.

### Parque La Aurora (Zone 13)
(Map I, B3)

The international airport, a racecourse, a zoo, a handicrafts market *(see "Making the most of Guatemala City")* and three national museums share Parque La Aurora, in the south of the city.

**The Museo Nacional de Arqueología y Etnología★★** (Map I, B3) *(9am-4pm; closed Saturdays 12noon-2pm and Mondays all day. Fee)* holds the most important pre-Columbian collection in Central America. *Allow at least 2hr. Labelling in*

*Spanish*. Sadly, the museum has not made the most of its collection: despite a chronological display, the poor lighting on the exhibits makes it look jumbled. And yet the rooms house veritable treasures, including stelae and sculptures from Kaminaljuyú, bas-reliefs from Piedras Negras, censers from Amatitlán, funerary urns and ceramics from Mixco Viejo and Chinautla. In its centre is a lovely circular patio with a fountain, the only source of natural light, where stelae from El Petén emerge from among its columns.

Near the immense model of Tikal is the **jade room**\*\* *(9am-4pm; closed weekends)* housing some very fine items including the famous jade and shell mask found in El Petén.

The visit ends with an ethnological section displaying everyday utensils, textiles and the different kinds of housing in the Highlands and Lowlands.

Opposite is a building housing the **Museo de Arte Moderno**\* (Map I, B3) *(Same opening hours. Fee)*. The majority of works on show date from the 20C although a small part is devoted to the end of the 19C. Among other works are frescoes by Carlos Mérida, the artist who decorated several buildings in the Centro Cívico, and Efraín Recinos, who worked on the Centro Cultural Miguel Ángel de Asturias.

Behind this building is the **Museo de Historia Natural** (Map I, B3) *(Same opening hours. No fee)*, looking pretty tatty. It nevertheless offers interesting information on local flora and fauna, some exhibits of dusty and worn stuffed birds and animals, a collection of butterflies and a selection of minerals.

The **Parque Zoológico** (Map I, B3) *(9am-5pm; closed Mondays. Fee and paying car park)* looks like any other zoo without adequate funding. Its few specimens of local fauna and reproductions of Mayan stelae scattered around the park are not enough to make the visit worthwhile.

## The Kaminaljuyú archeological site (Zone 7) (Map I, A2)

*9am-4pm. Fee. 4km west of the city centre, at the end of 23a Ave, Zone 7. Take a taxi or bus showing Kaminaljuyú on 4a Ave, Zone 1. The Museo Nacional de Arqueología y Etnología is a good follow-up to the visit.*

At the entrance to some wasteland with boys playing football is a sign indicating the archeological site of Kaminaljuyú (hill of the dead), whose unforthcoming attendants consider it sufficient to tell visitors it is "very old"! Once inside, there is not really a lot more to learn, the site being nothing more than a heavily urbanised landscape with a few mounds of earth and two or three excavated structures protected by tin roofs. It bears absolutely no resemblance to the majestic stone pyramids scattered throughout the tropical jungle. And yet Kaminaljuyú is one

AKG Paris

Jade mask in the Archeology Museum

of the oldest and most important **Pre-Classic** ceremonial centres in Guatemala, as attested by the 200 or so tumuli listed by archeologists. All that remains are the adobe platforms, the leaf-thatched wooden temples having succumbed to time and weather.

The history of this city is gradually being pieced together as excavations proceed. Its inhabitants lived off the **jade** and **obsidian** used to make the numerous items found in the tombs. Very beautiful ceramics from the Miraflores phase (200 BC) have been discovered, as well as interesting bas-reliefs that herald the Mayan **writing** and **counting** systems. At the start of the Christian era, this great centre came under strong influence from the city of **Teotihuacan** (central Mexico), particularly as concerns the architecture of its pyramids and the making of effigies similar to those of the god Tlaloc (the Mexican rain god, recognisable from his round "spectacles"). Kaminaljuyú flourished between the 4C and 6C AD, then went into decline at the same time as Teotihuacan.

# Around Guatemala City

*A vehicle is recommended for exploring the surrounding area.*

After the crowded streets of the capital, the country places around about induce an intoxicating feeling of provincial calm. The villages are particularly picturesque on Friday and Sunday mornings, when the markets are held.

## Northwest of the capital

*See map p 137.*

*Leave by 8a Calle, Zone 1. The ringroad ("anillo periférico") is after Ing. Martin Prado Vélez bridge (Puente del Incienso). 3km before the ringroad, turn right towards San Juan Sacatepéquez.*

Leaving the capital by the **Puente del Incienso** is impressive. All of a sudden the city comes to an abrupt end at the edge of the *barrancos* (ravines), a spectacular landscape when enveloped in a light veil of mist – which hides the slums! Then the road begins to climb slowly up, round hairpin bends and through wooded hills fragrant with shady pines. After 25km it goes through **San Pedro Sacatepéquez**, a peaceful Cakchiquel township that on market days becomes positively frantic.

Continue 7km along the same road to the village of **San Juan Sacatepéquez**, famous for its **flower market★**. Buyers flock under the arcades of Plaza de Cataluña, strewn with voluminous armfuls of gladioli, carnations and chrysanthemums that blend in with the predominantly yellow *huipiles* of the saleswomen.

*7km after San Juan, take the left fork (the Mixco Viejo sign is set slightly back from the road). Continue 5km and take the road to the left at the hamlet of Montúfar. You have another 16km to drive on a recently surfaced road. Allow 90min for the 60km journey between the capital and Mixco Viejo. As this site is poorly served by public transport, take a taxi or hire a car.*

**The ruins of Mixco Viejo★** *(8am-5pm. Fee)* are worth the detour, if only for the **mountain scenery★★**. In the 13C, to fend off attacks by their Quiché and Cakchiquel neighbours, the Pokomam established their capital on this plateau encircled by deep ravines. Despite its fortifications, this ceremonial and defensive centre was not able to withstand the assault by Pedro de Alvarado's army

The Pacaya volcano in eruption

in 1525. After a siege lasting several weeks, the Spanish learnt of a secret passage which enabled them to defeat the impregnable citadel. The town was burnt and its survivors deported to Mixco, in another province to the west of the present capital.

This great **Post-Classic city**, partially restored in 1954 by a team of archeologists from the Museum of Mankind in Paris, suffered serious damage in the 1976 earthquake. However, there are still some pyramids scattered around paved esplanades, forming a rectangular ensemble that contrasts with the jagged relief of the *barrancos*.

You enter the site by squeezing through a narrow opening in the rock. A look at the **model** is useful for finding your way around more easily. Three of the various groups of structures are of particular interest. The path leading off to the right of the model goes up to Group B. The **ball court** below has stone markers representing serpents holding a man's head in their open jaws – the originals are in the Museo Nacional de Arqueología y Etnología. To the north of this structure can be seen the outline of the **twin pyramids**, a Mexican-influenced construction. The path continues towards a piece of raised land where the structures of Group A stand, including a second ball court. Retrace your steps back past Group B to the vast esplanade of Group C, the highest point in Mixco Viejo. Amid its various buildings rises the site's **main pyramid**, considerably damaged by the 1976 earthquake.

*Mixco Viejo is an excellent place for a walk or picnic (only drinks are on sale at the site). Start the visit in the early morning or late afternoon, to take advantage of the beautiful light and avoid the midday heat.*

## South of the capital
*See map p 137.*

25km along the road to Escuintla, it is worth making a detour to **Lake Amatitlán**, a resort patronised by well-off *capitalinos*. This lovely stretch of water, now polluted and infested with mosquitoes, has nevertheless conserved a certain charm untouched by international tourism. The whitebait sizzling in enormous frying pans and the mariachi bands give the row of *comedores* a festive appearance at weekends. After lunching, families rent pedalos or go around the lake on one of the coloured boats. While on the lake, someone will certainly point out the hill to which every **3 May** a huge procession of *lanchas* bears El Niño (Infant Jesus), a holy image reputed for its miracles.

2km north of the village of Amatitlán, in Parque de las Naciones Unidas, a **cable-car** (weekends only) takes visitors up to admire a lovely bird's-eye view of the lake and its surroundings.

South of the lake stands the **Pacaya volcano** (2 552m), which is a popular climb. The 2.5hr climb from the village of San Francisco de Sales, about 40km southwest of Guatemala City, is not particularly difficult, but save some strength to struggle up the ash-covered final 300 metres of the steep cone. Tour groups reach the summit just before nightfall so as to watch an unforgettable spectacle, visible only in clear weather and when the volcano is very active: from the second crater, in permanent eruption as witness the frequent **explosions**, fountains of incandescent **lava** can be seen, spurting up and then pouring down the sides of the cone.

*NB, the Pacaya is doubly dangerous. It is an active volcano with a constant risk of eruption; in 1998 several villages had to be evacuated a number of times. But more particularly, climbing it is dangerous because of the thefts and attacks perpetrated against climbers over the last few years. Ask advice from INGUAT before taking part in one of these excursions, generally organised from Antigua (see p 155 "Making the most of Antigua").*

## West of the capital

*Take Calzada Roosevelt towards the Pan-American Highway (CA1). After Mixco (not to be confused with Mixco Viejo), continue on to San Lucas Sacatepéquez, 30km from Guatemala City. Fork right (the road left continues on to Antigua) and drive 3km to Santiago Sacatepéquez.*

The village of **Santiago Sacatepéquez**, seriously damaged in the 1976 earthquake, is not of any great interest. However, if you are travelling in Guatemala around All Saints' Day, you should not miss spending **1 November**\*\* here. As in the rest of the country, the inhabitants gather in the cemetery to pay homage to their dead. Here the cult of the dead takes on a special form, since to mark the occasion the villagers fly multitudes of **kites** (barriletes); these gigantic wicker structures covered in coloured paper can be up to 6m wide. For the indigenous people, this magnificent traditional ceremony is a way of communicating with their ancestors.

---

# Making the most of Guatemala City

### COMING AND GOING

**By air** – As you will realise during your stay in Guatemala City (the planes skim the rooftops on takeoff and landing!), the *Aeropuerto Internacional La Aurora* (Map I, B4) has been built within the city, in Zone 13 just 2km south of Zona Viva. International and domestic flights are run by numerous airline companies (see below "Airline companies" and p 84 "Getting there"). US$20 airport tax on leaving Guatemala. Town buses and taxis waiting at the terminal exit run between the airport and the city centre (the set fare is US$7). It is possible to pay for the taxi ride in advance at the counter behind the luggage reclaim area. Minibus transfers to Antigua.

**By bus** – Long lines of buses converge on the *Terminal de Bus* in Zone 4 (Map I, B2 and Map II, A4). Once there, look for the destinations on the windscreens (get the driver to confirm his destination when you get on). All buses for Puerto San José (2hr) via Amatitlán and Escuintla leave from this terminus. For other destinations it is simpler to go directly to the offices of the various transport companies – their contact details are available from the Guatemalan embassy in your home country or from INGUAT once you arrive. Here we give the main destinations in alphabetical order.

– Antigua (1hr): buses leave every 15min between 5am and 7pm, from the *Terminal de Bus* (Map II, A2) on the corner of 4a Ave and 18a Calle, Zone 1.

– Chichicastenango (3hr30min): *Masheñita*, 10a Calle 10-03, Zone 7, ☎ 473 4471. Every hour between 6am and 5pm.

– Chiquimula (3hr30min): *Rutas Orientales*, 19a Calle 8-18, Zone 1, ☎ 253 7282. Every 30min between 4.30am and 6.30pm.

– Cobán (4hr): *Escobar "Monja Blanca"*, 8a Ave 15-16, Zone 1, ☎ 251 1878. Every hour between 4am and 5pm.

– Escuintla (1hr): *Esmeralda*, 8a Ave 38-41, Zone 3, ☎ 471 0327. Every 15min from 5am to 6pm.

– Esquipulas (4hr): *Rutas Orientales*, 19a Calle 8-18, Zone 1, ☎ 253 7282. Every 30min from 3.30am to 6pm.

– Flores (min 10hr): **Fuente del Norte**, corner of 17a Calle and 9a Ave, Zone 1, ☎ 232 7041. 8 buses between 3am and 8pm. **Líneas Máxima de Petén**, 9a Ave 17-18, Zone 1, ☎ 238 4032. 4 departures between 4pm and 8pm. **La Petenera / Línea Dorada**, 16a Calle 10-43, Zone 1, ☎ 232 9658. 1 night bus at 7.30pm (deluxe service).

– Huehuetenango (5hr): **Los Halcones**, 7a Ave 15-27, Zone 1, ☎ 238 1979. 1 bus in the morning and 1 in the afternoon. **Rápidos Zaculeu**, 9a Calle 11-42, Zone 1, ☎ 232 2858. As above. **Velásquez**, 20a Calle 1-37, Zone 1, ☎ 221 1084. Every hour from 8am to 5pm.

– Panajachel (3hr): **Rébulli**, 21a Calle 1-34, Zone 1, ☎ 230 2748. Every hour from 7am to 4pm.

– Quetzaltenango (4hr): **Galgos**, 7a Ave 19-44, Zone 1, ☎ 253 4868. 6 buses a day between 5.30am and 7pm. **Líneas América**, 2a Ave 18-47, Zone 1, ☎ 232 1432. As above.

– Puerto Barrios (min 5hr): **Litegua**, 15a Calle 10-40, Zone 1, ☎ 232 7578. Every hour between 5.30am and 5pm.

– Retalhuleu (3hr30min): **Galgos**, 7a Ave 19-44, Zone 1, ☎ 253 4868. 4 buses between 5.30am and 4.30pm.

**By private minibus –** Frequent private minibus services between Guatemala City (airport and city centre) and Antigua or Panajachel. The reception at your hotel will make reservations for you.

## FINDING YOUR WAY
See p 99 "Addresses" (A to Z)
Guatemala City is very spread out and is divided into 21 zones. The numbers of the streets and avenues are identical in each zone, so it is essential to know the zone number in order to find an address. Basically, you are unlikely to stray beyond zones 1, 4, 10 and 9 (going from north to south). Most of the sights and the cheap tourist places are to be found in the old town, Zone 1. Zone 4 has the capital's administrative and institutional buildings, forming the Centro Cívico. Further south you come to a residential district frequented by tourists. To the left of Avenida la Reforma is Zone 10, known as Zona Viva. To the right is Zone 9, where you will find the better hotels, the best restaurants, the night clubs, travel agencies, airline offices, embassies etc.

## GETTING AROUND
No part of Guatemala City is spared the traffic jams (with total paralysis on Fridays when offices close). You will often resort to walking if you stay in one district. But how can you avoid the traffic if you are going between the old town and Zona Viva? Whether by bus or car, your patience will be sorely tried!

**By bus –** The dilapidated state of the buses, the dangerous driving of some drivers and the complexity of the bus routes led the authorities to undertake a total restructuring of the network in 1998: new vehicles, new routes, new bus numbering system, fixed bus stops every 400m and clearer destination signs. A plan of these new routes should be available to tourists on arrival at the airport.

**By taxi –** Taxis on every street corner are a recent phenomenon. New vehicles are now fitted with meters – which drivers try to avoid using – with a fare scale of 1 to 4 depending on type of route. In town tariffs 1 or 2 are normally applied (price according to number of kilometres), whereas tariff 4 is intended for journeys on the express way (price according to time and not distance covered). If you insist on the meter being used (pick-up charge 3-4 quetzals), be careful to check the tariff used in order to avoid nasty surprises; a tariff 4 when you are stuck in a traffic jam means an exorbitant fare. You can also negotiate the fare for a journey at the start, without using the meter, or agree on an hourly rate – around US$10 an hour, negotiable. **Taxis Amarillos**, ☎ 332 1515. **Mayataxi**, ☎ 335 5098.

**By tuk-tuk –** The motor-bike version of the rickshaw. A score or so of them have been driving around the streets of the capital since mid 1997, and it is difficult to spot them because of the dense traffic. ☎ 440 1430.

**By rental car –** All the rental agencies have offices at the airport. **Ahorrent**, Airport, ☎ 332 6491-5; Bd de la Liberación 4-83, Zone 9, ☎ 361 5661. **Avis**, Airport, ☎ 331 0017; 12a Calle 2-73, Zone 9, ☎ 331 2750. **Budget**, Airport, ☎ 331 0273; Ave la Reforma 14-90, ☎ 331 6546. **Hertz**, Airport, ☎ 331 5374; 7a Ave 14-76, Zone 9, ☎ 331 5374. **Tabarini**, Airport, ☎ 331 4755; 2a Calle A, Zone 10, ☎ 331 9814. **Tally**, Airport, ☎ 332 6063; 7a Ave 15-24, Zone 1, ☎ 232 9845.

## ADDRESS BOOK

**Tourist information – INGUAT**, (Map II, B3), 7a Ave 1-17, Zone 4, Centro Cívico, ☎ 331 1333. 8am-4pm; closed Saturday afternoons and Sundays. On the ground floor of the big blue building, just behind the railway line as you come from Zone 1. They provide a fair amount of information but not much in the way of leaflets (INGUAT also has an office at the airport). For detailed maps of Guatemala it is better to go to the **Instituto Geográfico Militar**, Ave las Américas 5-76, Zone 13, ☎ 332 2611. 9am-5.15pm; closed weekends.

**Bank / Currency Exchange –** On arrival you can change money at the **Banco del Quetzal** on level 2 of the airport. There are a lot of banks around Parque Centenario, Zone 1 and in Zone 9. **Banco Internacional**, 7a Ave 11-20, Zone 1. **Banco del Café**, 4a Ave 8-66, Zone 1, the only place in the capital that changes Thomas Cook travellers' cheques. **Banco Industrial**, 7a Ave 11-52, Zone 1. Cash machine for Visa cards. **Credomatic de Guatemala**, 7a Ave 6-26, Zone 9, near the Torre del Reformador, gives cash on Visa cards. **American Express**, Ave la Reforma 9-30, Edificio Torre del País, Zone 9.

**Post office / Telephone –** The main post office (Map II, B1) is in the yellow building at the foot of the arch, on the corner of 7a Ave and 12a Calle, Zone 1. 9am-5.30pm; closed Wednesday afternoons and weekends. Urgent mail and parcels can be sent through **DHL**, 7a Ave 2-42, Zone 9, ☎ 332 3004. To make international calls or send faxes, **TELGUA**, on the corner of 8a Ave and 12a Calle, Zone 1, one block from the post office. 7am-9.30pm; closed Sundays. Other offices in the capital at 7a Ave 3-44, Zone 4 and the airport. To send an e-mail or consult Internet, **Café Virtual**, Gran Centro Los Próceres, suite 117, Zone 10, ☎ 332 8027. **Café Internet**, corner of 5a Ave and 16a Calle, Zone 10, ☎ 337 4060.

**Speaking clock** (Hora nacional), ☎ 1526.

**Telegrams** (Telefonogramas), ☎ 1627.

**Medical service – Hospital Bella Aurora**, 10a Calle 2-31, Zone 14, ☎ 368 1951-5. **Hospital Nuestra Señora del Pilar**, 3a Calle 10-71, Zone 15, Colonia Tecún Umán, ☎ 365 6980. **Hospital Centro Médico**, 6a Ave 3-47, Zone 10, ☎ 332 3555. The **Farmacia Ejecutiva**, 7a Ave 15-13, Zone 1, is open 24hr a day. In an emergency, **Ambulance**, ☎ 128, or the **Red Cross** (Cruz Roja), ☎ 125.

**Embassies and consulates – British Embassy**, Ave la Reforma 16-00, Zone 10, Edificio Torre Internacional, Floor 11, ☎ 367 5425-9, Fax 367 5430.
**American Embassy**, Ave la Reforma 7-01, Zone 10, ☎ 331 1541/55, Fax 331 8885. Mon-Fri 8am-5pm.
**Canadian Embassy**, 13a Calle 8-44, Zone 10, Edificio Plaza Edyma, floor 6, ☎ 333 6104/40.
**Belizean Consulate**, Ave la Reforma 1-50, Zone 9, Edificio El Reformador, Office 803, ☎ 334 5531 / 331 1137.

**Airline companies – Air France**, Ave la Reforma 9-00, Zone 9, Plaza Panamericana, ☎ 334 0043-5.
**Aviateca**, Aeropuerto La Aurora, Zone 13, ☎ 361 5784 / 334 7722. Also 7a Ave 14-35, Zone 9, ☎ 334 2575 / 360 1709.
**American Airlines**, 7a Ave 15-45, Zone 9, ☎ 334 7379. Offices in Hotel Dorado.
**British Airways**, 1a Ave 10-81, Zone 10, Edificio Inexsa, Floor 6, ☎ 332 7402-4.

*Making the most of Guatemala City*

**Continental Airlines**, 18a Calle 5-56, Zone 10, Edificio Unicentro, Floors 3 and 7, ☎ 366 6425.

**Iberia**, Ave la Reforma 8-60, Zone 9, Edificio Galerías Reforma, Suite 204, ☎ 332 0911 / 331 1012.

**KLM**, 6a Ave 20-25, Zone 10, Edificio Plaza Marítima, ☎ 337 0222-6.

**Lufthansa**, Diagonal 6 10-65, Zone 10, Centro Gerencial Las Margaritas Torre II, ☎ 336 5526.

**Mexicana de Aviación**, 13a Calle 8-44, Zone 10, ☎ 333 6001.

**United Airlines**, Ave la Reforma 1-50, Zone 9, Edificio El Reformador, ☎ 332 2995.

Other companies fly domestic routes and to neighbouring countries.

**Aerovías**, Aeropuerto La Aurora, Zone 13, ☎ 332 7470 / 361 5703. Tikal and Belize.

**INTER (Grupo TACA)**, Aeropuerto La Aurora, Zone 13, ☎ 361 2144. Also 7a Ave 14-35, Zone 9, ☎ 334 2574 / 331 6979. Flights between Guatemala City and Cobán.

**TACA**, Airport, PH361 5784. Also 7a Ave 14-35, Zone 9, ☎ 334 2575 / 360 1709. Belize.

**Tapsa**, Aeropuerto La Aurora, Zone 13, ☎ 331 9180 / 332 6046. Tikal.

**Tikal Jets**, Aeropuerto La Aurora, Zone 13, ☎ 334 5631 / 334 5568. Tikal and Belize.

**Useful numbers – Police** (Policía Nacional), ☎ 110 or 120.

**Fire Brigade** (Bomberos), ☎ 122 or 123.

**Safety –** Pickpocketing is frequent, be particularly vigilant on the buses, in crowded streets and in the markets. Avoid walking at night in Zone 1, particularly around 18a Calle which has a reputation for being dangerous.

**Laundry –** Laundry services are very common in hotels – more practical although more expensive than launderettes. **Lavandería Super Wash**, 12a Ave 12-28, Zone 1.

## WHERE TO STAY

### • Zone 1

*Under US$20*

**Hotel Posada San Francisco**, 13a Calle A 10-40, ☎ 221 1837 – 7rm ⊺ᵥ This new guesthouse is next door to the Posada Belén hotel, in a very quiet street right in the middle of Zone 1. The rooms are big but basic. Only two of them do not have a private bathroom.

*Around US$40*

**Hotel Chalet Suizo**, 14a Calle 6-82, Zone 1, ☎ 251 3786, Fax 232 0429 – 51rm ⊼ Small, unpretentious but well-kept guesthouse. Cheap for the rooms without bathrooms.

**Hotel Spring**, 8a Ave 12-65, Zone 1, ☎ 230 2858/2958, Fax 232 0107 – 30rm ✗ cc̄ An immense residence set around 3 patios. Big rooms with or without bathrooms in the old building. Those in the annexe (a recent building) all have bathrooms and TV but the prices are higher. Pleasant reception.

**Hotel Colonial**, 7a Ave 14-19, Zone 1, ☎ 232 6722, Fax 232 8671, colonial@infovia.com.gt – 42rm ⋪ A building with colonial atmosphere that does not lack charm. The impeccably kept rooms are all decorated differently and those downstairs have TV.

*Around US$50*

**⊛ Hotel Posada Belén**, 13a Calle A 10-30, Zone 1, ☎ 253 4530 / 232 6278, Fax 251 3478, pbelen@guatemalaweb.com – 10rm ⋪ ⊼ ✗ cc̄ A delightful colonial house with prettily furnished rooms that combine comfort with taste and simplicity. Your hosts will provide you with all sorts of useful information for your trip and can help organise your excursions throughout the country. René Sanchinelli has also created a very complete Internet site on Guatemala (see p 82). Booking in advance strongly recommended.

*Around US$60*

**Hotel del Centro**, 13a Calle 4-55, Zone 1, ☎ 232 5547 / 232 5980, Fax 230 0208 – 55rm ⋪ ♪ ⊺ᵥ ✗ cc̄ Located in a very busy thoroughfare in Zone 1; avoid sleeping on the street side. Vast, carpeted rooms with every comfort but lacking character.

**Hotel Pan American**, 9a Calle 5-63, Zone 1, ☎ 232 6807-9, Fax 232 6402 – 60rm ⋪ ⊼ ♪ ⊺ᵥ ✗ cc̄ The immense and quite classy entrance hall suggests a higher standard of rooms. Nondescript decoration. Bathrooms with small bathtubs. A bit expensive for what is provided.

**Hotel Royal Palace**, 6a Ave 12-66, Zone 1, ☎ 232 5125-8, Fax 238 3715 – 85rm ♨ ⤫ ♪ TV ✗ CC The luxury of this recently renovated hotel clashes somewhat with the surrounding district. Unfortunately the street-side rooms are noisy, since 6a Ave is one of the liveliest thoroughfares in Zone 1. Those facing inwards are quieter, although darker.

• **Zone 4**

*Around US$60*

**Hotel Plaza**, Vía 7, 6-16, Zone 4, ☎ 331 6173 / 331 0396, Fax 331 6824 – 65rm ♨ ♪ TV ✗ ⌇ CC A pity this hotel is on one of the noisiest and most polluted avenues in the city. The rooms are uninspiring but the place has one undeniable advantage: a swimming-pool!

• **Zone 9**

*Around US$50*

**Hotel Villa Española**, 2a Calle 7-51, Zone 9, ☎ 339 0187, Fax 332 2515 – 66rm ♨ ⤫ ♪ TV ✗ CC Half-way between the Torre del Reformador and the Cortijo Reforma hotel, it offers reasonable prices for the district. The colonial-inspired building flanks a dead-end street where you can park your car. The rooms provide every convenience but lack charm.

*Around US$60*

**Hotel Cortijo Reforma**, Ave la Reforma 2-18, Zone 9, ☎ 332 0712, Fax 331 8876, hotelcortijoreforma@ telcom.net – 150rm ♨ ♪ TV ✗ CC This big hotel's 14 storeys rise high above the street; choose a room on an upper floor for the view over the city. All have a lounge with kitchenette but the somewhat dated furniture leaves something to be desired.

• **Zone 10**

*Around US$60*

**Hotel Posada de los Próceres**, 16a Calle 2-40, Zone 10, ☎ 368 1405 / 363 0744, Fax 363 0746 – 24rm ♨ ⤫ ♪ TV CC Vast carpeted rooms supposed to fulfil international criteria. Of limited attraction apart from its comfort and reasonable prices for the district.

**Hotel Residencial Reforma "La Casa Grande"**, Ave la Reforma 7-67, Zone 10, ☎ 332 0914 / 331 7893, Fax 360 1388 – 30rm ♨ ♪ TV ✗ CC 50m from the US embassy, a fine residence in Moorish architecture with rooms on 2 floors. Those on the upper floor near the terrace are preferable. The setting is pleasant and the birdsong quickly makes you forget the traffic on Ave la Reforma.

⌖ **Hotel Casa Santa Clara**, 12a Calle 4-51, Zone 10, ☎ 339 1811, Fax 332 0775 – 14rm ♨ ♪ TV ✗ CC Right in the heart of Zona Viva, this high-class hotel is a haven of tranquillity with its little green patio. The rooms are spacious and exceedingly clean (some have communicating doors). There is a relaxed holiday atmosphere which no other hotel in the district has.

*Around US$80*

**Hotel Stofella**, 2a Ave 12-28, Zone 10, ☎ 334 6191, Fax 331 0823 – 28rm ♨ ♪ TV CC A hushed ambience suited to contemplation and a clientele mainly of businessmen. The rooms have every modern comfort. There is no restaurant but meals prepared by nearby establishments can be delivered to your room. Breakfast included in the price.

**Holiday Inn**, 1a Ave 13-22, Zone 10, ☎ 332 2555 / 332 2570, Fax 332 2584 – 209rm ♨ ▤ ♪ ✗ ⌇ CC No surprises here: international-standard rooms and a multitude of services for clients. Choose an upper floor so as to look out over the city and go for the corner rooms with balconies.

**Mansión San Carlos**, Ave la Reforma 7-89, Zone 10, ☎ 332 6055 / 362 9076, Fax 331 6411 – 7rm ♨ ♪ TV ✗ CC The yellow walls of this colonial house hide a little garden. If you are going to stay here, you might as well take the suite with fireplace and jacuzzi. The standard rooms have less charm than those of the La Casa Grande hotel next door.

*Over US$140*

**Hotel Camino Real**, corner of Ave la Reforma and 14a Calle, Zone 10, ☎ 333 4633, Fax 337 4313 – 400rm ♨ ▤ ♪ TV ✗ ⌇ ※ CC The biggest hotel in the capital has just been reno-vated. This little town within a city offers a business clientele every comfort and ex-cellent service, at corresponding prices.

## EATING OUT

*Under US$10*
The **Mercado Central** in Zone 1 (Map I, C1-C2 and Map II, B1) has an entire area given over to *comedores*, where buyers and sellers rub shoulders at lunchtime. Here you can taste numerous typical dishes and observe the pulsating life of the market.

Several fast-food chains have outlets in the capital, as proven by the **McDon-ald's** and **Burger King** signs. **Pollo Campero**, a local fast-food chain spe-cialising in chicken, has won Guatemalan hearts. You will find at least one in every district (and throughout the country).

**Café De Imeri**, 6a Calle 3-34, Zone 1 (Map II, A1), ☎ 232 3722. 8am-7.30pm; closed Sundays. This big build-ing is packed out at lunchtimes. Set menu at a price that cannot be beaten, in one of the pleasantest restaurants in town (pretty patio and inside terrace).

*Under US$20*
**El Gran Pavo**, 13a Calle 4-41, Zone 1 (Map II, B2), ☎ 232 9912. [CC] 10am-12midnight. Very colourful rooms to put you in the mood for the Mexican specialities served in this restaurant. Mariachi bands on Friday and Saturday evenings.

**Restaurante Altuna**, 5a Ave 12-31, Zone 1 (Map II, B1), ☎ 232 0669. [CC] 12noon-10pm; closed Sunday evenings. A choice of decor depending on taste: a central area with a tavern atmosphere surrounded by tables with real table-cloths, or private dining rooms with more chic. Good fish and seafood spe-cialities served by an efficient and cour-teous staff.

**Mesón El Quijote**, 11a Calle 5-27, Zone 1 (Map II, B1), ☎ 232 1741. 11am-1am. In the subdued atmosphere of this big *bodega* both decoration and menu pay tribute to the Basque country. A convivial place to dine or have a drink while listening to music. From 9pm groups play on the small stage hiding behind its red velvet curtain.

**Tre Fratelli**, 2a Ave 13-25, Zone 10 (Map I, C3), ☎ 366 2678. 🚕 [CC] 12noon-12midnight / Sundays to 10pm. An endless ballet of pasta and pizza dances between the tables of this lively restaurant. One of the few places in town with a terrace on the street.

*Around US$25*
**Hacienda Real**, 13a Calle 1-10, Zone 10 (Map I, C3), ☎ 333 5408. CC 12noon-12midnight. Coming out of the Holiday Inn you just cross the street into this plush hacienda with its colourful walls. In the dry season its patio with central fountain is a delight. Good meat and Mexican specialities.

**Trattoria Veneta**, 13a Calle 1-55, Zone 10 (Map I, C3), ☎ 331 0612. CC 12noon-3pm / 7pm-11pm; closed Sun-day evenings. A big dining room look-ing like an impeccable Swiss chalet; rather stiff service. It serves excellent Italian specialities at high prices.

## GOING OUT, HAVING A DRINK
The capital quietens down around 8pm, except in some parts of Zone 1 and in Zona Viva, the tourist district where most night-time venues are to be found.

**Bars – La Bodeguita del Centro**, 12a Calle 3-55, Zone 1. 6.30pm-1am; closed Sundays and Mondays. Have a drink and listen to the concerts in the lively at-mosphere of this former warehouse. Cuban groups play here regularly.

**Carlos'n Charlie's**, 3a Ave 12-38, Zone 10. 12noon-12midnight; closed Sunday evenings. Mexican-style bar & restau-rant where young people do not hesitate to dance on the tables.

**Shakespeare's Pub**, 13a Calle 1-51, Zone 10. An often-lively English-style pub. Concerts at weekends.

**Concerts –** Classical music at the **Teatro Nacional** (see "Theatres" sec-tion). Some bars have concerts at week-ends.

**Discos –** Most night clubs are in Zona Viva. **Casbah**, 14a Calle 0-40, Zone 10. **Iguana Azul**, corner of 12a Calle and 4a Ave, Zone 10. **Kalhua**, 1a Ave 15-06, Zone 10.

Guatemala City

## OTHER THINGS TO DO

**Excursions** – Guatemala City is a departure point for excursions throughout the country. For package tours ask in the big hotels or one of the capital's numerous travel agencies. The latter are listed in the yellow pages of the telephone directory (Directorio Telefónico), and you can also obtain a complete list (Guía de Agencias de Viajes) from INGUAT.

**Theatres** – To obtain the programme for the Teatro Nacional or the Teatro al Aire Libre, contact the **Centro Cultural Miguel Ángel Asturias** (Map II, A3), 24a Calle 3-81, Zone 1, ☎ 232 4041-5.

**Cinemas** – Many cinemas in Zone 1 show films in Spanish or in English with sub-titles. The **Alliance Française**, 4a Ave 12-39, Zone 1, ☎ 232 4827, shows French films a few evenings a week.

## SHOPPING GUIDE

**Arts and crafts** – In Zone 1 the **Mercado Central** (behind the Catedral Metropolitana) (Map II, B1) gives an excellent overview of what you will find in the rest of Guatemala, mainly woven fabrics and basketry or leather items. The vendors are on the spot 6am-6pm except Sunday afternoons, but the handicraft shops open a little later, around 10am. The **Mercado Terminal** (Map I, B2 and Map II, A4) in Zone 4, near the bus station, is of less interest as far as handicrafts go since it is almost entirely devoted to food – colours, smells and crowds guaranteed (watch out for thieves!). On the other hand, the **Mercado de Artesanía** (Map I, B3) in Parque Aurora, Zone 13, although specially designed for tourists, lacks life and authenticity. Worth a glimpse out of interest if in the area. 8am-6pm; closed Sunday afternoons.

**Bookshops** – **Arnel**, 9a Calle 6-65, Zone 1. Excellent selection of books, including some in foreign languages. **Librería del Pensativo**, La Cupola, corner of 7a Ave and 13a Calle, Zone 9.

Making the most of Guatemala City

133

R. Mattes

"Cofradía" from Chichicastenango

# THE HIGHLANDS

The Altiplano, land of craggy contrasts, lives in symbiosis with its capricious relief of jagged peaks, volcanoes and grandiose landscapes: Atitlán, one of the world's loveliest lakes, the perfect cones of its volcanoes standing guard; vertiginous ravines, scoring the region like gaping wounds hundreds of metres deep; deserted mountain passes whipped by the winds; valleys patchworked with small fields. In the heart of one of these valleys, surrounded by volcanoes, lies charming Antigua, Guatemala's colonial gem. The Altiplano is a land of Amerindians, a land of traditions, where time is measured out by market days and ancestral customs, colourful interludes where you can discover all the cultural wealth and diversity of the Mayan people.

GUATEMALA

ALTIPLANO

0     8     16 km

Comitán de Dominguez

Bulej

Xoxlac

Yolhuitz

San Mateo Ixtatán

Barillas

Santa Eulalia

Grijalva

San Miguel Acatán

San Antonio Huista

San Rafael

Soloma

MÉXICO

Paso Hondo

CA 1

Selegua

Cordillera

de

San Juán Ixcoy

los

Parque Naciona los Cuchumatane

★★ Todos Santos Cuchumatán ●

▲ 3837

Cuchumatanes ★★

★

Santiago Chimaltenango ●

Cuilco

Colotenango

● San Juán Atitán ★

Cuilco

Chiantla

Motozintla ●

★ Zaculeu ∴

Aguacatán

Huehuetenango

Tacaná ●

Ojetenán ●

Concepción Tutuapa ●

Malacatancito ●

▲ 2650 Co. Boquerones

Chiquibal ●

Coatán

4093 Volcán Tacana

Comitancillo ●

V. Tajumulco 4220 ▲

★ Momostenango ●

El Carmen ●

San Marcos ●

★ San Francisco El Alto

Tapachula ●

Catarina ●

El Tumbador ●

Totonicapán ●

▲ 3403

CA 2

★★ Quetzaltenango ●

Suchiate

Coatepeque ●

V. Sta María 3772 ▲

Zunil ★

★ San Pedro La Laguná

Ciudad Tecún Umán

San Felipe ●

3020 V. San Pedro ▲

Abaj Takalik ★

Santo Tomás ●

★★ Santiago Atitlán

P. N Atitlá

Icán

3000 m
2000
1000
500
200
0

Retalhuleu ★

Mazatenango ●

San Lorenzo ●

Ocosito

Samalá

Nahualate

Champérico

Playa Grande
P. N. de Laguna Lachuá
Lachuá
Rubelsanto
Carolina
Sébol
Santo Domingo
R.F. Franja Transversal del Norte
Chisec
Xaclbal
Yiquiché
▲ 1118
Copón
Rogá
Pemech
Dolores
Sierra de Chamá
★ Grutas de Lanquín
▲ 1255
Cabí
Reserva Natural Cerro Bisís
Lancetillo
1904 ▲
★ Cobán
San Pedro Carchá
2703 ▲ Co. Bisís
Chajul
Cotzal
San Juan Chamelco
San Juan Cotzal
San Cristóbal Verapaz
Santa Cruz Verapaz
Nebaj
Cunén
Uspantán
Chixoy
Pozo Vivo
Tactic
▲ 2131
Sacapulas
Negro
Purulhá
▲ 2305
nta Lucía Reforma
San Bartolomé Socotenango
Canillá
Emb. Chixoy
▲ 1619
★ Biotopo Mario Dary Rivera
Sierra de Chuacús
Cubulco
Rabinal
Salamá
Santa Cruz del Quiché
Chiché
Joyabaj
El Progreso
San Jerónimo
umarkaaj
Chichicastenango★★★
Grande
Motagua
Granados
CA 1
Mixco Viejo ★
Chuarrancho
ololá★★
Tecpán
San Raimundo
Puerto Barrios
Panajachel
Iximché
Comalapa
San Juan Sacatepéquez
Chinautla
CA 9
ago de itlán★★★
Patzún
Chimaltenango
San Pedro Sacatepéquez
3158 ▲ V. Tolimán
Madre Vieja
Santiago Sacatepéquez
CIUDAD DE GUATEMALA ★
3537 V. Atitlán
★★★ Antigua
San José Pinula
Patulul
★San Antonio Aguas Calientes
3976 ▲ V. Acatenango
Ciudad Vieja
San Juan del Obispo ★
Sta María de Jesús
L. de Amatitlán
3763 V. Fuego
▲ 3766 V. Agua
Santa Lucía Cotzumalguapa ★
Escuintla
V. Pacaya ▲ 2552
Nueva Santa Rosa
CA 1
N

**137**

# ANTIGUA ★★★
## (LA ANTIGUA GUATEMALA)
Capital of Sacatepéquez department
45km west of Guatemala City – Pop 30 000
Alt 1 530m – Temperate climate all year round

### Not to be missed
Strolling around the town's colonial streets.
The view of Antigua and its surroundings from the Las Capuchinas convent.
Breakfast on the Café Condesa's patio.
The Holy Week processions (see p 72).

### And remember...
Allow at least 2 days to make the most of the town and its surroundings.
Avoid Mondays, when museums and restaurants close.
Book hotel rooms in advance for Christmas and Holy Week.
For safety's sake, contact the tourist office before climbing a volcano.

Antigua the "colonial beauty", sister to San Miguel de Allende in Mexico, Cuzco in Peru and Santa Fe in New Mexico, sits in a peaceful valley encircled by three volcanoes: the **Agua** (3 766m), the **Fuego** (3 763m) and the **Acatenango** (3 976m). Blessed with a rich architectural heritage, a magnificent location and a pleasant climate, the former capital is Guatemala's most attractive town.

From its prestigious past it has conserved the straight-as-a-die grid layout around Plaza Mayor, its town houses set around vast flower-filled patios and its Baroque churches, some of whose façades, still miraculously standing, seem to be suspended by invisible threads. Its streets and avenues, with their uneven cobbles, are lined with low, gaily-coloured houses decorated with wrought ironwork. Here a tuft of wild grass emerges from the roof tiles, over there a branch of bougainvillæa pushes its exploratory way between the stones of an abandoned cloister. Details like this, revealed in glimpses to the observant stroller, contribute to the poetry and melancholic gentleness of the place.

This outer appearance of a city frozen in the 18C in fact hides a lively town whose main activity is tourism. Indigenous women appear as soon as visitors arrive, offering their woven fabrics for sale, while pretty young girls resplendent in colourful *huipiles* try to charm you into buying their handicrafts. A multitude of luxury hotels, sophisticated restaurants, trendy bars and Internet cafés open their doors to an ever-increasing flow of travellers and expatriates. Antigua has, in fact, become a holiday – or even permanent – home for a large North-American community of retirees, intellectuals, artists, businessmen and, especially, directors of language schools, one of the town's "specialities".

## An earth-shaking history
Rarely has nature so governed the destiny of a town. The first **Santiago de Los Caballeros**, so named in honour of St James, patron saint of the conquistadors, was established in 1524 by the Spanish lieutenant **Pedro de Alvarado** on the orders of **Hernán Cortés** (*see p 37*). Founded near Iximché, the Cakchiquel capital, it became the theatre of violent struggles between colonists and natives. Jorge de Alvarado, in charge of governing the colony in the absence of his brother, therefore decided to move the capital to a more peaceful site.

**The conquistadors' buried hopes** – In 1527 he chose the peaceful Almolonga valley, on the site of either San Miguel Escobar or **Ciudad Vieja** (Old Town), 2km further west; the exact spot has still not been determined. But this second Santiago was to experience further setbacks. In 1541, in the space of a few weeks, the conquistadors lost their governor, Pedro de Alvarado, and then their capital, buried under torrents of mud.

**Two centuries of influence for Santiago** – The survivors, deprived of a capital for the second time, set out to find a safe site. This time they opted for the Panchoy valley, a fertile area sufficiently far from any volcanoes but protected by hills, with quarries and forests abounding in building materials for the new town; a choice site for the future capital and one which benefited from the first town planning on the American continent.

**The "Sin Ventura"**

On hearing of Pedro de Alvarado's death in Mexico, his wife, Doña Beatriz de La Cueva, immediately went into mourning. After spending long weeks shut away within the black-draped walls of her palace, the young widow reappeared and had herself proclaimed governor under the name of "Sin Ventura" (Unlucky One). This fateful title was to reveal its full meaning several hours later. Torrential rain had been beating down on the region for several days and now the earth began to quake and the Agua volcano released the water held captive in its crater. The mudslide swept the entire town away. Doña Beatriz, one of the many victims of the catastrophe, had held power for barely 48 hours.

The new Santiago, founded officially in 1543, became from 1549 the **seat of the Captaincy General** of the area stretching from Chiapas to Panama. In 1566 Phillip II of Spain conferred on it the title of *"La Muy Noble y Muy Leal Ciudad de Santiago de los Caballeros de Guatemala"* (The Very Noble and Very Loyal City of St James of the Knights of Guatemala). In the course of the 17C and 18C the town was prodigiously influential, both culturally and spiritually, throughout Latin America. The main religious orders – Franciscans, Dominicans, Jesuits, Carmelites, Capuchins and Recollects – founded over thirty churches, fifteen or so convents and monasteries, hospitals, and a university that rivalled those of Mexico and Lima. But more calamities were to befall this third Santiago.

**The waning of the capital** – Of the **earthquakes** that shook the region throughout the 18C, two were extremely violent. That of 29 September 1717 destroyed a fair amount of the town. Most of the buildings were immediately rebuilt, but when the earth began to tremble again on 29 July 1773, it was with such cataclysmic violence that nothing was left but a vast field of rubble. This time the acting governor decided to transfer Santiago to the present site of Guatemala City, in the Ermita valley 45km away.

The following year the town was renamed **La Antigua Guatemala** (Old Guatemala) to distinguish it from the new capital. The authorities set up a system of veritable collective pillaging, intended to transfer every item of its riches to the new seat of power. But despite an order to demolish the few buildings still standing, part of the population refused to move and set to rebuilding the town. During the 19C, thanks to cochineal and coffee growing, Antigua even succeeded in recovering a semblance of prosperity, although in no way comparable with its former brilliance.

**A heritage to protect** – In 1944 the government finally decided to take its fate in hand and declared it a **national monument**. Restoration work was undertaken but once again, in 1976, a severe earthquake shook the region violently

**Antigua**

and destroyed a good number of its buildings. Three years later Antigua was proclaimed a **UNESCO** World Heritage Site. Thanks to international aid and tourism, this "museum-town" is once again rising from its ashes, proudly sporting the scars of its tumultuous past.

## Visiting the town
*Allow a day taking your time.*

You can see the whole of Antigua in a few hours, but the best way to discover it is just to stroll through its colonial streets, leaving chance to reveal its monumental ruins and Baroque façades.

*For ease of visiting, we suggest the following 3 walks: around Plaza Mayor and then, starting from that square, the south of the town and then the north.*

### Plaza Mayor★★ (B3)

The town's historical and geographical centre starts pulsating from dawn. Under its arcades indigenous women prepare *tortillas*, street vendors slice into juicy mangoes, shoe-shiners and souvenir sellers impatiently await their first customers. Gradually, the central square and its shaded benches start to receive a constant flow of *Antigueños*, weary travellers, and foreign students come to revise their Spanish lessons; this tower of Babel rings with Cakchiquel, Spanish and English.

A meeting-place where Amerindians, Ladinos and *gringos* mingle, Plaza Mayor (Main Square) is still, four and a half centuries later, the geographical centre of the town and the place where festivities are held. Its layout, at the heart of a network of perpendicular streets and avenues, was established by the engineer **Juan Bautista Antonelli** in 1541. Framed by the main administrative buildings and the cathedral, it was the seat of political and religious power but also held a small daily market, served as a bullring for feast day bullfights and was sometimes the setting for military parades, from which it took its other name of **Plaza de Armas**. In 1739 its **Parque Central★** (central garden) acquired the delightful Baroque **fountain★**, sculpted by Diego de Porres, that still draws the visitor's eye. With its pool surmounted by mermaids (copies), it is said to have been inspired by the Neptune fountain in Bologna, Italy.

On the south side of the square, the **Palacio de Los Capitanes Generales★** (B3) offers an imposing frontage of two storeys of arcades that perfectly echoes the Town Hall. From the middle of the 16C the residence of the King of Spain's representative stood on this spot. For two centuries the building underwent a multitude of alterations which generated an incredible maze of rooms. In the middle of the 18C it housed not only the residences of the governor and some Crown officials, but also the chancellery offices, archives, Law Court, a chapel and even a prison. Later additions devoid of all logic, plus, of course, the earthquakes, so damaged the palace that the governor had to call on the services of architect **Luis Díez de Navarro** to redesign the plans. Completed in 1764, the new building had to be abandoned just ten years later following the 1773 earthquake. The arms of the Bourbons and of King Charles III of Spain, in the centre of the façade (the only original element), date from this period. The building now houses the police headquarters, the administrative offices of Sacatepéquez department and the tourist office.

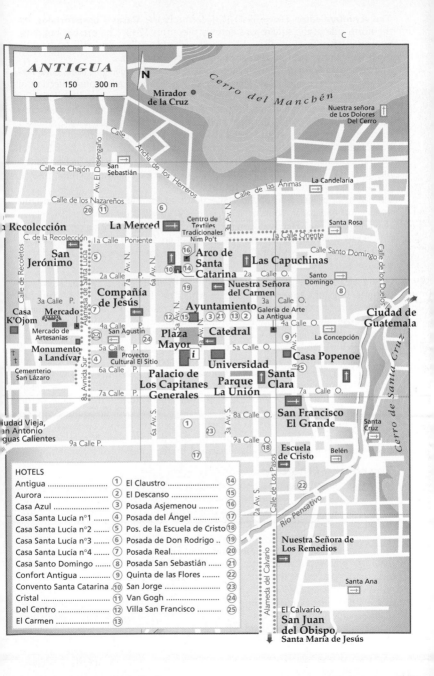

# ANTIGUA

0  150  300 m

**N**

Mirador
de la Cruz

*Cerro del Manchén*

Nuestra señora
de Los Dolores
Del Cerro

Calle de Chajón

Av. El Desengaño

Calle Ancha de los Herreros

San
Sebastián

La Candelaria

Calle de los Nazareños

Calle de las Ánimas

20  11  6

La Recolección

La Merced

Santa Rosa

C. de la Recolección

Centro de
Textiles
Tradicionales
Nim Po't

1a Calle Poniente

1a Calle Oriente

Calle Santo Domingo

Calle de Recoletos

San
Jerónimo

5

1a Av. N.

2a Av. N.

3a Av. N.

16

Arco de
Santa
Catarina

10  14

Las Capuchinas

Santo
Domingo

Calle de los Duelos

2a Calle P.

2a Calle O.

8

3a Calle P.

Compañía
de Jesús

19

Nuestra Señora
del Carmen

Casa
K'Ojom

Mercado

7

Ayuntamiento

Galería de Arte
La Antigua

3a Calle O.

Ciudad de
Guatemala

Mercado de
Artesanías

4a Calle P.

San Agustín

12  15

3  21  13  2

4a Calle O.

La Concepción

Monumento
a Landívar

24

Plaza
Mayor

i

Catedral

9

La Concepción

Cementerio
San Lázaro

5a Calle P.

Proyecto
Cultural El Sitio

5a Calle O.

Casa Popenoe

6a Calle P.

Universidad

25

Palacio de
Los Capitanes
Generales

Parque
La Unión

Santa
Clara

Ciudad Vieja,
San Antonio
Aguas Calientes

7a Calle P.

7a Calle O.

8a Avnida Sur

6a Av. S.

3a Av. S.

8a Calle O.

San Francisco
El Grande

Santa
Cruz

1

23

9a Calle P.

9a Calle O.

Escuela
de Cristo

Belén

17

18

22

Cerro de Santa Cruz

2a Av. S.

Calle de Los Pasos

Río Pensativo

Nuestra Señora de
Los Remedios

Alameda del Calvario

Santa Ana

El Calvario,
San Juan
del Obispo,
Santa María de Jesús

## HOTELS

| | | | |
|---|---|---|---|
| Antigua ........................ | (1) | El Claustro ...................... | (14) |
| Aurora .......................... | (2) | El Descanso .................... | (15) |
| Casa Azul ...................... | (3) | Posada Asjemenou ......... | (16) |
| Casa Santa Lucía n°1 ...... | (4) | Posada del Ángel ........... | (17) |
| Casa Santa Lucía n°2 ...... | (5) | Pos. de la Escuela de Cristo | (18) |
| Casa Santa Lucía n°3 ...... | (6) | Posada de Don Rodrigo .. | (19) |
| Casa Santa Lucía n°4 ...... | (7) | Posada Real..................... | (20) |
| Casa Santo Domingo ...... | (8) | Posada San Sebastián ...... | (21) |
| Confort Antigua ............. | (9) | Quinta de las Flores ....... | (22) |
| Convento Santa Catarina | (10) | San Jorge ....................... | (23) |
| Cristal ............................. | (11) | Van Gogh ....................... | (24) |
| Del Centro .................... | (12) | Villa San Francisco .......... | (25) |
| El Carmen ...................... | (13) | | |

141

**The Highlands**

The **Ayuntamiento**\* (Town Hall) (B3), formerly the **Casas Consistoriales**, on the north side of the square was entirely rebuilt in 1743. The present building, renovated after every earthquake, sports a double gallery and still houses the town hall, along with the tourist police and two museums.

The **Museo de Santiago**\*, also called Museo de Armas, *(9am-4pm; closed Saturdays and Sundays 12noon-2pm; closed Mondays. Fee)* houses a miscellaneous collection of items from the colonial period. On the ground floor there are 17C and 18C ceramics, craftsmen's tools and a portrait of Pedro de Alvarado. The visit continues across the patio, on one wall of which are the arms of the town representing St James on horseback above three volcanoes, one being the Fuego in eruption. There is also a striking map of Guatemala, created by the foliage of climbing plants, and a cell in which a superb silver tabernacle is kept. On the first floor is a collection of pre-Columbian weapons, along with swords, pistols, guns, canon and instruments of torture.

Once outside again, a second entrance leads to the **Museo del Libro Antiguo (Museum of Antiquarian Books)** *(9am-4pm; closed Saturdays and Sundays 12noon-2pm; closed Mondays. Fee)*. Here you can see a replica of the first working printing press in Central America, set up on this very spot in 1660. This museum exhibits some manuscripts, both originals and reproductions, retracing the history of printing since Gutenberg.

On the east side, the Baroque façade of the **cathedral**\* (B3) in fact masks a heap of ruins. Only the **sagrario** (chapel in which the Holy Sacrament is kept) has been restored so that the faithful can pay their respects. Known as the **church of San José**, this is the only part of the building accessible from Plaza Mayor. Access to the rest is on 5a Calle Oriente *(9am-5.30pm. Fee)*. There is practically nothing left of the building, rebuilt in 1680 under architect José de Porres. Of the many cupolas, aisles and chapels that covered an entire *manzana* (block of houses), only a few huge pillars stood up to the 1773 earthquake. The missing roof and dome have left a gaping hole in which sun and passing clouds sketch an ever-changing fresco. To the right, in front of a platform – the remains of the main altar – a stone bears the names of Bishop Francisco Marroquín, Pedro de Alvarado and his wife Beatriz de La Cueva. These three people, so closely linked with the history of Antigua, are buried beneath the cathedral. Nearby is a staircase leading to a **crypt**, its walls blackened by the candles left by worshippers.

## The south of the town

In 5a Calle Oriente, opposite the cathedral, a door opens onto the **patio**\*\* of the University of **San Carlos de Guatemala**\*\* (B3), framed by multifoil arches in Mudéjar style and adorned with a delightful fountain *(see p. 40)*. Founded in 1676, the first university in Central America – and the third on the continent after those in Mexico City and Lima – was initially located in the former St Thomas of Aquinas college near the Santo Domingo monastery. The study of theology, philosophy, medicine, canon law and indigenous languages was for a long time restricted to the sons of Spanish colonists before being opened up to those of mixed race. The university only occupied this building from 1763 to 1773. Unlike the other buildings in Antigua, this one stood up to the earthquake, thanks to the thickness of its columns and the "cement" used – a mixture of egg white, milk, honey, sand and water!

Ch. Lenars/EXPLORER

Good Friday procession

Once all the institutions had been transferred to the present capital, the building was used for a variety of purposes in turn: explosives factory, school, theatre and, since 1936, the **Museo de Arte Colonial**★ *(9am-4pm; closed Saturdays and Sundays 12noon-2pm; closed Mondays. Fee)*. Among the objects of religious art from the town's churches is a series of paintings by Tomás de Merlo relating the Passion of Christ. Some of these, including *The Crucifixion*, have been shamefully chopped up by previous owners to make them fit around doors! A series of paintings recounting the life of St Francis of Assisi, the work of Mexican painter Cristóbal de Villalpando, is also on show in this museum.

*On leaving the university, turn right and continue down 5a Calle to the corner of 1ra Avenida.*

**Casa Popenoe**★★ (C3) *(2-4pm; closed Sundays. Fee)* is a fine example of 17C architecture. In the 1930s an American couple, the Popenoes, undertook a meticulous restoration of their house, using old materials to restore the place to all its former charm. The building is laid out around a succession of flower-filled patios with several fountains and a washing place. The old floor tiles, lovely wooden ceilings and superb period furniture create a remarkable colonial atmosphere. *Part of the house is lived in, hence the limited visiting hours.*

*Go down 1ra Ave to the right on leaving Casa Popenoe, then turn right at the next junction into 6a Calle. Walk 1 block to a square.*

This is **Parque La Unión**★ (B3) one of the most picturesque squares in Antigua. On its rectangle of lawn planted with palm trees, vendors have taken to spreading their colourful textiles. In the midst of this little handicrafts market, women and their small daughters spread out the garments they have just washed at the **washing place**★.

On the east side of the square, a high wall protects the **Convent of Santa Clara**★★ (B3) *(9am-5pm. Fee)* from prying eyes. Founded in 1699 by an order originally from Puebla (Mexico), the building was designed to house 46 nuns but was destroyed by the 1717 earthquake. Rebuilt 17 years later, it was again damaged in 1773 and also in 1976. Now there is nothing left but a peaceful field of ruins enveloped in heavy bunches of purple and pink bougainvillea. Its majestic **cloister**★, framed by two storeys of arches and harbouring a delightful central **fountain**★, offers the most peaceful of strolls. On the left of the entrance is the church, with a **façade**★★ that is a masterpiece of Baroque art, abounding in geometrical and floral motifs.

Go one block east from the Santa Clara convent and you can see the superb dome of the church of the **Monastery of San Francisco El Grande**★ (C4) *(9am-5pm; closed Mondays. Fee)*. The Franciscans chose this site in the middle of the 16C and were constantly extending the building right up to the beginning of the 18C. At that time the complex housed a college that contributed greatly to Antigua's artistic and scientific influence. The new church, completed in 1702, did not survive the century's many earth tremors and it was not until 1960 that major reconstruction work was undertaken.

The **façade**★, heavily ornamented with wreathed columns and numerous statues, has conserved its 18C Baroque spirit. But these buildings are interesting, not so much for their architecture, as for the **tomb of Pedro de San José de Bethancourt** *(see sidebar p 65)*.

Antigua

The Baroque façade of Nuestra Señora del Carmen

Two hundred metres south of the church of San Francisco is a small parvis on which stands the **church of La Escuela de Cristo** (C4), built in 1730. The soberness of its undressed stone façade offers a stark contrast to the other religious buildings in Antigua. Not to be missed are the **Santo Cristo de Las Misericordias** and **Señor Sepultado**, both carved by Quirio Cataño at the end of the 16C, as well as the **Virgen de la Soledad**, attributed to Pedro de Mendoza. These figures play a particularly important role in the re-enactment of the crucifixion and the descent from the cross that takes place in front of the church during Holy Week.

*If you have time, continue south along Calle de los Pasos.*

On the left, after crossing the Río Pensativo, stands the delicate but cracked façade of the church of **Nuestra Señora de Los Remedios** (C5) (late 17C), where decapitated saints surround a central statue, forming a fragile equilibrium in a setting like an abandoned theatre.

All along the road from the church of San Francisco to the southern end of the Alameda del Calvario – also known as the **Via Crucis** (Way of the Cross) – there are **chapels** evoking the Passion of Christ. This tour ends in the **Calvario** (direction B5), built in the middle of the 17C then rebuilt in 1720 after a tremor. It contains paintings by Tomás de Merlo and some very lovely 17C carvings including a **Señor Sepultado** and a **Virgen de Dolores**. The faithful will lead visitors to the foot of an *esquisuchil*, a tree planted by "Hermano Pedro" whose flowers are reputed to have healing powers.

## The north of the town

3a Avenida Norte widens out in front of the **church of Nuestra Señora del Carmen** (B3), allowing passers-by to stand back and admire the extraordinary **façade\*\*** with its richly foliate designs inspired by the Mudéjar style. Apart from the columns in the upper part, with their plethora of motifs, the rest of the building, rebuilt for the third time in 1728, has not survived the earthquakes.

*Continue north along the same avenue, take the first right then immediately left into 2a Ave Norte.*

Some superb ruins, partly restored, hide behind the walls of **the convent of Las Capuchinas**★★ (B2) *(9am-5pm. Fee)*. This institution was founded by five Capuchin nuns from Madrid, and its construction, entrusted to architect Diego de Porres, was completed in 1736. First to strike the eye on entering the **cloister** is the profusion of bougainvillæa. A walk around this fine architectural ensemble unveils the lifestyle of these reclusive nuns, cut off from all contact with the outside world. The most striking building is the **Torre del Retiro**★★ (retreat tower), an open-roofed tower surrounded by 18 cells, each equipped with a toilet. From the top of the building there is a wonderful **view**★★ over the town and surrounding countryside.

*Retrace your steps to 2a Calle Oriente and continue 3 blocks to 5a Ave Norte.*

A landmark and symbol of the town, the **Arco de Santa Catarina**★ (B2) is by far the most photographed monument in Antigua. Built in 1693, this arch allowed the nuns of the **convent of Santa Catarina** (or Catalina) to cross from their cloister to the garden on the other side of the street. The church is now in ruins and the convent converted into a hotel *(see "Making the most of Antigua")*. Coming from the south, the arch almost appears to be part of the façade of the church of La Merced, but seen from the other side there is a wide **view**★ over 5a Avenida, with the orangey-yellow arch standing out against the dark cone of the Agua volcano.

**The Monastery of La Merced**★ (B2) *(8am-6.30pm. Fee)*, looking like nothing less than an enormous meringue, is the second symbol of the town. Completed in 1760, the church was deliberately built squat and solid in order to resist earth tremors. The overall impression is nevertheless one of surprising lightness, due to the white stucco filigree work covering the entire Churrigueresque **façade**★★ with its abundance of Baroque motifs and wreathed columns. The altars and holy images must have been transferred to the new capital after the 1773 earthquake, but in a chapel at the far end of the south aisle is the **Jesús Nazareño** carved by Alonso de La Paz in 1650; this statue, the most venerated in Antigua, forms the centrepiece of the impressive Good Friday procession. In the monastery ruins, at the centre of the cloister, stands the biggest fountain in Central America, the **Fuente de los Peces**★ (fountain of fishes).

*On leaving the church, continue 2 blocks down 1ra Calle to Alameda de Santa Lucía.*

**The Colegio de San Jerónimo**★ (A2) *(9am-5pm. Fee)* sits in a vast garden where townspeople come to picnic at weekends. The college, founded by the monks of the La Merced order, was opened in 1759 but had little success and closed down two years later. The solidity of the building saved it from demolition on the orders of Charles III' and the **Real Aduana** (Royal Customs) took possession of the premises from 1765.

At the end of 1ra Calle, the **Convento de La Recolección**★★ (direction A2) *(9am-5pm. Fee)* was built in the early 18C under the direction of architect Diego de Porres. Damaged by the tremor of 1717 (the year it was consecrated) then destroyed in 1773, it was left abandoned. Its spectacular ruins seem to have stepped right out of a historical epic film: an archway that has miraculously survived leads into the nave of the former church, strewn haphazardly with gigantic blocks of stone. *Ask the tourist police first about safety precautions when visiting this monument, as it is in an isolated part of town.*

The Highlands

R. Marca

The Santa Catarina arch against the Agua volcano

*Retrace your steps and turn into Calle de los Recoletos, the 1st street on the right.*

**The Casa K'ojom**★ (house of music) (A3) *(9.30am-12.30pm / 2pm-5pm; Saturdays to 4pm; closed Sundays. Fee)* devotes the major part of its rooms to traditional Guatemalan music through a large collection of instruments complemented by an audiovisual show. It also reveals various aspects of Mayan daily life and displays a reproduction of the effigy of **Maximón** in Santiago Atitlán *(see p 164)*.

*On leaving Casa K'ojom, turn right, then left into 5a Calle.*

On the corner of Alameda de Santa Lucía stands the **Monumento a Landívar** (A3), with its architecture reminiscent of the San Carlos University. This monument holds the remains of Rafael Landívar (1731-1793), the famous Guatemalan poet.

*Go north along Alameda de Santa Lucía to the market and turn into 4a Calle Poniente, heading towards Plaza Mayor.*

On the corner of 6a Avenida, the ruins of the **monastery of La Compañía de Jesús** (A3-B3) emerge from the souvenir and textile stalls ranged up against its walls. The Baroque façade of the **church** (late 17C) was originally covered with brightly-coloured motifs; some polychrome traces still subsist in the recesses and above the porch. When the Jesuits were expelled from the country in 1767, the building was abandoned. A century later it housed a textiles factory and then the town market, transferred near the bus station in 1976.

*Follow 1ra Ave Norte to the hill that rises to the north of Antigua.*

In clear weather the **Cerro del Manchén** (B1), more commonly known as **Cerro de la Cruz** (hill of the cross) offers a very lovely **view**★★ over the whole town, with the perfect cone of the Agua volcano as backdrop. *NB, because people have been attacked in this area you are strongly advised against going to this hill alone. The tourist police will provide a vehicle and escort free of charge!*

# The surrounding villages
*Hire a car or taxi to visit several places on the same day.*
*See map p 137.*

Antigua is an excellent base for excursions into the surrounding countryside. Sitting amid coffee plantations, in the shadow of the volcanoes' majestic outlines, the townships perpetuate their ancestral traditions.

## San Juan del Obispo★
*4km southeast of Antigua. Go down Alameda del Calvario towards Santa María de Jesús and Palín. About 2.5km after the Calvario, at the bridge before the hill, turn right and continue 500m to the village. Buses from Antigua every hour between 7am and 6pm.*

This little village nestling at the foot of the Agua volcano is worth a detour for its **Palacio del Obispo**★ (Bishop's Palace), the residence of Francisco Marroquín, first bishop of Guatemala. This house, built in the middle of the 16C, was considerably damaged by the 1773 earthquake. The nuns, who now occupy the restored building, act as guides, taking visitors through its superb **patios**★ and showing them the decorative items and furniture from the colonial era. It is worthwhile having a look at the adjoining **church**★, if open, which was built in the same period as the palace and has a remarkably well-preserved interior. This graceful structure, held up by wooden pillars, shelters a main altar in Baroque style, a magnificent **altarpiece**★ of paintings believed to date back to the 16C and a fine **ceiling** typical of Mudéjar art. From the parvis in front you can enjoy a panoramic **view**★ over the Panchoy valley and Antigua.

The Highlands

### Santa María de Jesús

*10km south-east of Antigua. Continue down the road to Palín, beyond the turn-off for San Juan del Obispo. Buses from Antigua every hour between 7am and 5pm.*

A pretty mountain road climbs up through coffee plantations to the highest village in the region, at an altitude of 2 050m. This modest township with its streets of trodden earth, bamboo fences and little cob cottages, is the departure point for climbing the Agua volcano *(see below)*. Non-sporty tourists will appreciate Santa María de Jesús for the variety in its traditional women's **costumes**. Despite the influence of neighbouring communities, many Cakchiquel women remain attached to their local *huipiles,* recognisable by the diamond motifs in predominantly blue, pink and purple hues.

### Ciudad Vieja

*6km southwest of Antigua by Alameda de Santa Lucía. Buses every 30min between 7am and 6pm.*

This place is of no great interest except that it was the capital before Antigua *(see introduction)*. It is, however, worth looking at the **church of Nuestra Señora de la Inmaculada Concepción** (early 18C), which stands on the site of a previous building erected in 1534. The dazzling whiteness of the church certainly does not belie its consecration to the Immaculate Conception. Its ornamented **façade**, decorated with pilasters and recesses, holding numerous statues of saints, compensates for the two ungainly bell towers.

### San Antonio Aguas Calientes★

*8km southwest of Antigua by Alameda de Santa Lucía. 3km after leaving the town, take the dirt track to the right. There is a longer route – approx 14km – via Ciudad Vieja: turn right at the cemetery after Ciudad Vieja, onto the road to San Miguel Dueñas. On entering this village, take the 1st turning on the right and follow the mountain road to San Antonio Aguas Calientes. Buses every 30min between 8am and 6pm.*

San Antonio owes its reputation to the quality of its **textiles** and its use of the *marcador* technique (double-sided brocade), which creates an identical motif on both sides of the fabric, with no distinction between right and wrong sides. As soon as you arrive in the village, the fabric stalls in the main square catch your eye and many of its inhabitants will try to sell you fabrics or weaving lessons. Just strolling around the streets you can see the weavers at work, the men working their *telares de pie* (foot looms) in their workshops, while the women kneeling in the courtyards of their houses work on their *telares de cintura* (hip-strap looms) attached to tree trunks.

## Climbing the volcanoes

Most travel agencies in Antigua run excursions to climb the three volcanoes in the Panchoy valley, from the summits of which there are spectacular panoramic views in clear weather. However, the most popular excursion is without a doubt up the **Pacaya**, an active volcano not far from the capital *(see p 126 "Guatemala City")*.

*NB, despite INGUAT's repeated warnings about the danger of these excursions – of getting lost or being attacked – the travel agencies continue to schedule this activity. Be it at your own risk! If despite everything you decide to venture up the volcanoes, hire the services of a professional guide (see "Making the most of Antigua"). For these climbs you need to be fit and to have a minimum of equipment: windcheater, warm clothing, non-slip shoes and torch are recommended. You should also take water and food.*

**Around Antigua**

The climb up the **Agua volcano** (3 766m) is a great classic. Despite the 1 700m altitude difference from Santa María de Jesús (*see above*) to the summit, the 5hr climb turns out to be relatively easy. As the refuge on top is often full, particularly at weekends, it is advisable to start out in the early morning so as to go there and back in one day. Weather permitting, the climb is amply rewarded by the **panorama**★★ stretching out over part of the Highlands and the Pacific Ocean.

The climb up **Acatenango** (3 976m) starts from the village of La Soledad, 15km west of Ciudad Vieja. This outing takes around ten hours and requires excellent physical condition. Experienced climbers can stop in the basic refuge at the top and the following morning set off to conquer the neighbouring volcano, the **Fuego** (3 763m). This second climb is very difficult and it can take a dozen hours to reach the crater, where a few wreaths of smoke give proof of dormant activity. It is also possible to climb up another, even tougher, side from Alotenango, 12km southwest of Antigua.

## Making the most of Antigua

### COMING AND GOING

**By bus** – The *Terminal de Buses* (A3) is located behind the market, on the east side of town at the end of 4a Calle Poniente. Buses every 15min from 6am to 6pm from Antigua to the capital (1hr), 1 connection a day to Panajachel (2hr30min) and 2 buses a day for Escuintla (2hr). As there are no direct services between Antigua and the rest of the country, change on the Pan-American Highway at Chimaltenango (1hr) or in Guatemala City.

**By private minibus** – The travel agencies run minibus services between Antigua and the other tourist centres, including several services a day to/from Guatemala City (45min) or Panajachel (2hr), as well as Chichicastenango on market days (3hr). If out of all the destinations on offer you do not find the one you want, get a group together to hire a minibus.

**By taxi** – Allow US$40 between Antigua and Guatemala City airport. Taxis wait on Parque Central and in front of the bus station. *Taxis Antigua*, ☎ 832 0479.

### FINDING YOUR WAY

The streets ("calles"), numbered 1 to 9 from north to south, intersect at right angles with the avenues ("avenidas"), numbered 1 to 8, from east to west. Addresses always indicate the direction from Parque Central: Norte (north), Sur (south), Poniente (west) and Oriente (east). The locals still use the old names for some streets, e.g. Calle del Arco for 5a Ave Norte.

### GETTING AROUND

Wherever you go, you will never be more than 5 blocks from Parque Central, which means Antigua can be visited on foot. The question of transport is therefore only relevant for the villages around about.

**By bus** – From the bus station; every 30min from 8am to 6pm for San Antonio Aguas Calientes and Ciudad Vieja; every hour for Santa María de Jesús and San Juan del Obispo.

**By taxi** – If you wish to visit several villages in a short time, a taxi may prove practical. The fare can be negotiated for your itinerary or by the hour. Allow approx US$10 an hour. Groups can hire a private minibus.

**By rental car** – *Tabarini*, 2a Calle Poniente #19 A, ☎ 832 3091. *Ahorrent*, 5a Calle Oriente #11B, ☎ 832 0787.

**By rental bike** – Several agencies rent out bicycles (approx US$2 an hour and US$12 a day). **Alquiler de Bicicletas**, 6a Ave Sur #6, ☎ 832 3311. Bicycle excursions with guide by **Mayan Bike Tours**, 1ra Ave Sur #15, ☎ 832 3383 or **Montaña Maya Bicycle Tours**, 6a Ave Sur #12B, ☎ 832 3316.

## ADDRESS BOOK

**Tourist information** – **INGUAT** (B3), 5a Calle Oriente, ☎ 832 0763, is located in part of the Palacio de los Capitanes Generales, on Parque Central. A pleasant and professional reception. Daily 8am-5pm. Town maps, information on cultural activities, language schools, accommodation and night-life. Information, brochures and small ads for tourists in the language schools, hotels and cafés (Doña Luisa, Delicias de Natura etc).

**Bank / Currency exchange** – Most of the banks are on Parque Central (B3) or nearby. **Banco de Occidente**, corner of 4a Calle Poniente and 5a Ave Norte. 8.30am-7pm; closed Saturday afternoons and Sundays. **Banco del Café**, 4a Calle Poniente #22. Takes Thomas Cook traveller's cheques. **Banco Industrial**, 5a Ave Sur #4. 8am-7pm; closed Sundays. 24hr cashpoint for Visa cards. **Lloyds Bank**, corner of 4a Ave and 4a Calle, on Parque Central. 9am-3pm; closed weekends.

**Post office / Telephone** – Post office (A3), corner of 4a Calle Poniente and Alameda de Santa Lucía (opposite the market), 8am-4pm; closed weekends. For express mailing, **DHL**, 6a Ave Sur #16, ☎ 832 3718. 8am-12noon / 2pm-6pm; closed Saturday afternoons and Sundays.

Antigua is at the cutting edge as far as telecommunications go, with no end of service providers offering telephone, fax, e-mail and Internet. **Conexión**, 4a Calle Oriente #14, inside La Fuente (see "Eating out"), ☎ 832 3768. 8.30am-7pm; weekends 9.30am-5.30pm. **Enlaces**, 6a Ave Norte #1, ☎ 832 0216. 8am-7.30pm; Sundays to 1pm. These firms offer better rates than the national company **TELGUA**

(B3), corner of 5a Calle Poniente and 5a Ave Sur. Telephone and fax only. 8am-8pm; Sundays 9am-4pm.

**Medical service** – **Hospital Nacional Pedro de Bethancourt**, 3a Ave Sur and 6a Calle Oriente, ☎ 832 0789 / 832 0301.

**Safety** – **Policía Municipal de Turismo**, 4a Ave Norte, on the right of the Ayuntamiento, ☎ 832 0532 / 832 4131. In charge of making sure your visit goes well: tourist escort to visit certain places reputed to be dangerous (such as the Cerro de la Cruz), assistance if documents are lost or stolen, surveillance of major cultural events.

**Language schools** – With around fifty schools in town you are simply spoilt for choice. A private teacher for 5hr a day (the most popular formula) costs around US$100 a week. Consult the list of schools recommended by the tourist office before enrolling. **Academia de Español Tecún Umán**, 6a Calle Poniente #34, ☎ 832 2792. **Proyecto Lingüístico Francisco Marroquín**, 7a Calle Poniente #31, ☎ 832 2886. **Academia de Español Sevilla**, Apartado Postal 380, 1ra Ave Sur #8, ☎ 832 5101.

**Laundry** – Many launderettes all over town. Allow approx US4 to wash and dry 5kg of washing. **Maysi's Express Laundry**, 6a Ave Sur #12B. 7am-6pm; Sundays 8am-12noon.

## WHERE TO STAY

Antigua offers innumerable accommodation possibilities: rooms in private houses through the language schools, charming guesthouses, luxury hotels. Prices are quoted inclusive of tax and for the low season. Practically all the hotels double their prices for Holy Week and Christmas.

### Under US$20

There are 4 Casa Santa Lucía hotels, identified by numbers. They all offer very well-kept rooms at extremely moderate rates.

**Casa Santa Lucía no1**, Alameda de Santa Lucía Sur #5 – 20rm ☎ The oldest of the Santa Lucías is the only one right on the street (there are no signs to indicate the others). The rooms are a bit dark but are still good value for money.

**Casa Santa Lucía no2**, Alameda de Santa Lucía Norte #21 – 12rm 🚿 A pleasant place with impeccable rooms. Alameda de Santa Lucía is a noisy street because of its proximity to the bus terminus, so take a room on the courtyard side.

**Casa Santa Lucía no3**, 6a Ave Norte #43A – 20rm 🚿 One of the best places in Antigua. This stone house with wrought-iron balconies and lamps is in a privileged location just by La Merced church. Very fine view over the town from the 3rd-floor windows and the terrace. Colonial atmosphere and irreproachably clean rooms at an unbeatable price.

**Casa Santa Lucía no4**, Alameda de Santa Lucía Norte #5 – 32rm 🚿 The latest in the series has more rooms. These lack light but, like its 3 sisters, this hotel is still very good value.

**Hotel Cristal,** Ave El Desegaño #25, ☎ 832 4177 – 11rm. Near the bus station, a hotel with small rooms, basic but clean, with or without private bathrooms. It is advisable to sleep on the courtyard side because of the frequent trucks and buses going by.

**Hotel Villa San Francisco**, 1ra Ave Sur #15, ☎ 832 3383, mayanbikel@guate.net – 8rm. Unpretentious guesthouse in the patio of the Mayan Bike Tours travel agency. Clean rooms with or without bathrooms. Telephone, fax and Internet services on-site.

*Under US$30*

**Hotel Van Gogh**, 6a Ave Norte #14, ☎ 832 0376 – 5rm ✗ 🆒 When the cool of the evening dissuades you from tarrying on the patio under the stars, settle comfortably down on the sofas by the fireplace in the lounge. This convivial hotel and restaurant offers 2 categories of rooms: the smallest (with shared shower) are moderately priced. The longer you stay, the less it costs per night.

**Hotel Confort Antigua**, 1ra Ave Norte, ☎ 832 0566 – 6rm 🆒 A family atmosphere in this peaceful hotel. Pleasant, clean accommodation with 1 bathroom for every 2 rooms. Breakfast included in the price.

**Hotel El Descanso**, 5a Ave Norte #9, ☎ 832 0142 – 5rm. You almost feel you are staying in a family home in this little house just by Parque Central. The rooms are on the 1st floor around a terrace where it is pleasant to relax. The 3 "dormitories" for 4 people (with shared bathroom) are better value for money than the 2 double rooms.

**Posada Asjemenou**, 5a Ave Norte #31, ☎ 832 2670 – 14rm 🚿 ✗ 🆒 North of Arco Santa Catarina, this pretty house is set around a patio occupied by the tables of the Expresso Café (see "Eating out"). Its modest rooms are somewhat dark, except for no1 (street side and no bathroom) or nos 11, 12 and 14 in the back courtyard.

*Around US$50*

**Hotel Posada Real**, Ave El Desengaño #24, ☎ 832 3396 – 8rm 🚿 📺 Recent rooms, very clean but with no special charm. Some have fireplaces. This comfortable hotel is good value for money in the low season.

**Hotel del Centro**, 4a Calle Poniente #22, ☎ 832 0657 – 10rm 🚿 📺 A pleasant little hotel near Parque Central. Quiet, comfortable rooms around a patio with a pretty fountain. Bathtubs in rooms 2 and 3.

**Hotel Posada de la Escuela de Cristo**, 9a Calle Oriente on the corner of Calle de los Pasos, ☎ 832 3255 – 21rm 🚿 🆒 All the atmosphere of this hotel comes from its succession of beautifully kept patios. A certain colonial charm but rather small, dark rooms.

**Hotel San Jorge**, 4a Ave Sur #13, ☎ 832 3132 – 14rm 🚿 📺 🐎 🆒 Impeccably maintained rooms with carpets, fireplaces and bathtubs. Breakfast is served free of charge. A pleasant welcome and numerous excursions organised. Despite its pretty garden, the place rather lacks character. Guests can use the Hotel Antigua's swimming-pool.

**Hotel Convento Santa Catarina**, 5a Ave Norte #28, under Arco Santa Catarina, ☎ 832 3080 – 11rm 🚿 ✗ You just have to see the flower-filled cloister of this former convent to fall under its spell. The rooms created out of the former cells are not perfect but they are tastefully decorated. For more comfort ask for the new rooms with kitchenettes, at the back of the building (to be avoided at weekends because of their proximity to La Casbah disco).

**Hotel Aurora**, 4a Calle Oriente #16, ☎ 832 0217 – 16rm ⌂ CC This big colonial residence houses one of the oldest hotels in Antigua and one of the loveliest patios in town. Its rooms with their yesteryear charm could nevertheless do with a bit of redecorating. Breakfast included.

**Posada San Sebastián**, 3a Ave Norte #4, ☎ 832 2621 – 8rm ⌂ TV CC A veritable antique shop (some items are for sale), this colonial house is littered with statues, old cast-iron irons, wooden chests and fabrics. A miscellaneous collection that gives the place all its character. Comfortable rooms.

**Hotel El Carmen**, 3a Ave Norte #9, ☎ 832 3850/47, hotelelcarmen@ quik.guate.com – 17rm ⌂ ⌂ TV ✗ CC The staff's warm welcome does not quite make up for the hotel's lack of soul. The rooms have all modern comforts but not enough windows. Lovely view over the roofs of Antigua from the terrace.

*Around US$80*

⊛ **Quinta de las Flores**, Calle del Hermano Pedro #26, ☎ 832 3721-5, Fax 832 3726 – 5 cottages and 9rm ⌂ ⌂ TV ✗ ⌂ CC The "estate of flowers" lives up to its name. You stay in a little park with a multitude of trees, flowers and fountains. Located 100m from the Belén church, in the southeast of the town, this hotel guarantees a restful stay beside the swimming-pool or in front of the fire, depending on season. Its cottages (sleeping 5), ideal for families or groups of friends, are very reasonably priced for accommodation of this quality. 20% reduction per additional week.

⊛ **El Claustro (The Cloister)**, 5a Ave Norte #23, ☎ 832 0712, cloister@mailzone.com – 7rm ⌂ Just opposite the Convento Santa Catarina, the ceramic "The Cloister" plaque is scarcely noticeable. And yet behind such discretion hides one of the loveliest hotels in Antigua. The setting and the rooms (all different) are the ultimate in comfort and

sophistication. No detail has been left to chance: soft sofas, loungers on the patio, rugs, fabrics, fireplaces, bookcases. Breakfast included.

**Hotel Posada de Don Rodrigo**, 5a Ave Norte #17, ☎ 832 0291 / 832 2664 – 34rm ⌂ ✗ CC The maze of staircases and patios in this superb 18C residence is a delight to the eye. All the rooms are differently decorated and possess a certain cachet, although of unequal quality. Those giving onto the patio are noisy during the restaurant opening hours (constant flow of tourists and marimba concerts). For Holy Week book rooms 300, 301, 302 or 303, which have some of the best views in Antigua of the processions down Calle del Arco.

**Hotel Casa Azul**, 4a Ave Norte #5, ☎ 832 0961/2, Fax 832 0944 – 10rm ⌂ ⌂ TV ⌂ CC The indisputable asset of this little luxury hotel is the view from the rooms on the 2nd floor (slightly more expensive than the others). Choose n° 8, with windows on 2 sides, or 12, smaller but looking out over the town on 3 sides. Sauna and jacuzzi for the use of guests. Breakfast included.

*Over US$80*

⊛ **Hotel Casa Santo Domingo**, 3a Calle Oriente #28, ☎ 832 0140, Fax 832 0102 – 92rm ⌂ ⌂ TV ✗ ⌂ ⌂ CC Have you ever slept in a museum? This former Dominican monastery combines top luxury with Antigua's historical heritage. Religious furniture in the entrance hall, computers sitting on antique capitals, 17C statues and paintings in the corridors, ruins harmoniously integrated into the fabric of the hotel. The various buildings, with comfortable rooms, are set in magnificent gardens where fountains and architectural remains peep out of their surroundings. A fairy-tale decor that is particularly appreciable in the evenings, when there are fewer tourist groups visiting.

**Posada del Ángel**, 4a Ave Sur #24A, ☎ 832 0260 – 4rm ⌂ ⌂ TV ⌂ CC One of the most select hotels in Antigua. Colonial setting and extremely attentive staff for those lucky enough to stay in one of the 4 luxury suites. Heated swimming-pool in the patio and fireplaces in the rooms.

*Hotel Antigua*, 8a Calle Poniente #1, ☎ 832 0288, Fax 832 0807 – 60rm ☂ ✐ TV ✗ ⏚ CC Big luxury hotel in a vast park with swimming-pool. The rooms with fireplaces have all the comforts expected in a hotel of this category, but you might miss Antigua's delightful colonial houses. Marimba concerts.

### EATING OUT

Many of Antigua's eating places are closed on Mondays, and a lot of them close quite early in the evening.

*Under US$10*

The stalls under the arcades or in the market serve local food to take away for a few quetzals.

*Delicias de Natura*, 7a Calle Poniente #11 (B3), ☎ 832 2949. 7.30am-3pm; closed Mondays. Fans of French loaves and croissants will be delighted to find this welcoming bakery run by a Frenchman and a Guatemalan woman. To take away or eat there in the adjoining little dining room.

*Café de las Empanadas*, corner of 4a Ave and 3a Calle (B3). 8am-5pm; closed Tuesdays. A tasty selection of sweet or savoury (tuna, chicken, meat) fritters for when you're feeling a little peckish. Rather limited choice at the end of the day.

*Rainbow Reading Room & Café*, corner 7a Ave Sur and 6a Calle Poniente (A3). 9am-11pm. A favourite place for travellers who want to swap experiences and books (the bookshop closes at 10pm). Sandwiches and vegetarian dishes to enjoy in a friendly atmosphere.

*Bagdad Café*, 1ra Calle Poniente #9 (B2). 8am-8pm. A pleasant little patio for having a drink or nibbling something after visiting the La Merced church. Telephone, fax and Internet available for use on-site.

*Expresso Café*, 5a Ave Norte #31 (B2), ☎ 832 2670. 7am-11pm. North of Arco Santa Catarina, this café that is part of the Posada Asjemenou serves good breakfasts as well as quick meals (sandwiches, pancakes, pizza). You can sit down to eat just as agreeably in its prettily decorated rooms or in the hotel patio.

*Cafetería y panadería Doña Luisa Xicotencatl*, 4a Calle Oriente #12 (B3). 7am-9pm. A delicious smell of hot bread wafts out of this baker's (the banana bread is a real treat). From the moment it opens the cafeteria patio swarms with customers enjoying the first rays of sunshine and pancakes, toast or appetising fruit salads. A pity the service is positively minimalist.

*La Fuente*, 4a Calle Oriente #14 (B3), ☎ 832 2676. 7am-7pm. The tables on the patio of this imposing colonial residence devoted to tourism make a pleasant halt for a drink or a snack. Take the opportunity to have a look in the souvenir shops around the patio or to use the telephone, fax or Internet services at Conexión (see "Post office / Telephone").

🍴 *Café La Condesa*, 5a Ave Norte #4, on Parque Central (B3), ☎ 832 0170. CC 7am-7pm. Go through the Casa del Conde bookshop to reach the two charming interconnecting patios. An ideal setting to enjoy brownies and muffins at tea-time or to start the day with a hearty breakfast. Do not miss brunch on Sundays (10am-2pm).

*Around US$10*

🍴 *La Genovesa*, 4a Ave Norte #27 (B2). 6pm-10pm; weekends 12noon-3pm; closed Mondays. You do not come to this little restaurant for the setting but quite simply for the pleasure of your taste buds. In an extremely friendly atmosphere you can enjoy the most succulent pasta. Don't miss the tiramisu for dessert.

🍴 *Café Flor*, 4a Ave Sur #1 (B3). 12noon-3pm / 6pm-10pm; closed Monday lunchtimes. A restaurant run by a very welcoming Salvadorian in a typical Antigua setting. The menu offers delicious Oriental specialities that combine Indian, Vietnamese, Indonesian and Thai dishes. No smoking in the main dining room.

🍴 *Beijing*, corner of 5a Calle and 6a Ave (B3). 12noon-10.30pm; closed Wednesdays. Chinese cuisine takes pride of place in this tastefully decorated restaurant where the atmosphere is accentuated by the warm tones characteristic of many Antigua establishments.

Friendly reception, pleasant surroundings and good food. An address to remember, particularly on Mondays when most of the town's restaurants are closed.

**Fridas**, 5a Ave Norte #29 (B2), ☎ 832 0504. **cc** 12.30pm-12midnight. This restaurant, serving Mexican specialities is much appreciated by tourists, especially as it closes late. It seems to be the trendy place to eat.

**Las Antorchas**, 3a Ave Sur #1 (B3), ☎ 832 0806. **cc** 8am-10pm; Sundays to 6pm. Run by a Frenchman in a large Antigua residence, this restaurant serves meat specialities. If you take breakfast here, try the delicious home-made jams.

**Asados de la calle del Arco**, 5a Ave Norte #1 (B3), a few metres from Parque Central. **cc** 7am-10pm. A place to dine in the evening when the candles on the tables give the patio a romantic air. Good quality Mexican specialities and Guatemalan dishes.

*US$10- US$20*

**Caffé Opera**, 6a Ave Norte #17 (B3), ☎ 832 0727. **cc** 9.30am-9pm; closed Wednesdays. Here they serve Italian specialities at rather high prices. Expresso lovers will enjoy the excellent Italian coffee, with opera music in the background.

**Posada de Don Rodrigo**, 5a Ave Norte #17 (B3), ☎ 832 0291. **cc** In the shade of an immense pine tree standing right in the middle of the patio, you can eat in one of the loveliest settings in Antigua. Good international cuisine although the servings are not very generous. Marimba concerts every day in the patio.

**Mesón Panza Verde**, 5a Ave Sur #19 (B4), ☎ 832 2925. **cc** 12noon-3pm / 7pm-10pm; closed Sunday evenings and Mondays. An elegant restaurant in a colonial decor around a patio almost hidden under cacti, ferns and laurels. The service – attentive and formal – is somewhat out-of-place compared to the quality of the cuisine, which is mainly Italian.

*Over US$20*

**El Sereno**, 4a Ave Sur #9 (B4), ☎ 832 3593. **cc** 12noon-3pm / 6.30pm-10pm. Extremely refined colo-

nial setting with fountains, fireplaces and candles. The varied menu of local and international specialities has earned it an excellent reputation with gourmets.

## GOING OUT, HAVING A DRINK

The monthly magazine **Revue**, in English, devotes a considerable number of its pages to Antigua, with lists of entertainment venues and a calendar of the month's cultural activities. Available free-of-charge from tourist establishments.

**Bars –** Most of the restaurants mentioned in the "Under US$10" section are very pleasant places to have a drink.

**Café La Escudilla**, 4a Ave Norte #4. 7am-1am. Behind this name there are in fact several bars located in the lounges of a colonial residence, around a patio (where you can also eat). **Riky's bar**, at the back of the house, is one of the liveliest places in Antigua in the evenings. American clientele and a background of jazz and rock music.

**Macondo**, 5a Ave Norte #28. 6.30pm-1am; closed Sundays. Just before Arco Santa Catarina on the way to La Merced, this big pub, with its video screens and music, is one of the places where people tend to meet up for a last drink when everywhere else is starting to close.

**Concerts –** Check the adverts posted regularly in the language schools and tourist establishments (Doña Luisa, Delicias de Natura, Casa Andinista etc) for details of live groups playing in bars. **Casa K'ojom** (see p 148) from time to time puts on performances of traditional music. Marimba concerts organised by the Posada de Don Rodrigo and Antigua hotels.

**Discos – La Casbah**, 5a Ave Norte #30. 7pm-2am. International music, mainly techno.

**La Chimenea**, corner of 7a Ave Norte and 2a Calle Poniente. Lively disco bar, 6pm-1am.

## OTHER THINGS TO DO

**Excursions –** The travel agencies offer absolutely every type of excursion imaginable, throughout the country, for those

**Making the most of Antigua**

interested in archeology, ecology, ethnology or sport. Where more or less the same services are offered, you can bring competition into play. The big classic is still climbing the volcanoes around Antigua. Although these excursions are strongly discouraged by the tourist police, they are included in most travel agencies' programmes. If you decide not to heed the warnings, one of the agencies recommended by INGUAT is **Gran Jaguar**, 4a Calle Poniente #30, ☎ 832 2712.

**Films** – A few places show videos on TV screens. The films are generally in English with Spanish subtitles or in Spanish with English subtitles. *Cinema Bistro*, 5a Ave Sur #14. *Rainbow Reading Room*, corner of 7a Ave Sur and 6a Calle Poniente. *El Sitio*, 5a Calle Poniente #15. The *Alliance Française*, 3a Calle Oriente #19A, ☎ 832 0223, shows French films.

**Outdoor pursuits** – Bicycle excursions with specialist agencies (see "Getting around").

The San Jorge hotel, 4a Ave Sur #13, ☎ 832 3132, organises pony trekking. You can use the swimming-pool of Hotel Antigua, even if you are not a guest there, by paying an entrance fee and buying a drink.

### SHOPPING GUIDE

Antigua has an impressive number of handicraft shops and markets, not counting the street vendors. Bags, jewellery, painted wood nicknacks, musical instruments, "huipiles", blankets and fabrics are to be had on every street corner.

**Textiles** – Souvenir and textile vendors set up every day under the arcades of Parque Central. The *mercado de artesanías* (A3), Alameda de Santa Lucía, next door to the bus station, has a wide range of handicrafts, but you can find similar articles in other places in town. In this delightful market the fabrics are laid out on the lawns of Parque La Unión, in front of the Santa Clara convent. There are also a few stands selling textiles and lots of souvenirs, backed up against the ruins of the church of La Compañía de Jesús. Do not forget to bargain.

Some shops sell more expensive but better quality articles. If you are not a connoisseur, these will give you a better chance of buying quality hand-woven fabrics. *Centro de textiles tradicionales Nim Po't*, 5a Ave Norte #29 (B2), ☎ 832 2681. 9am-5.30pm. No fee. North of Arco Santa Catarina, a shop-cum-museum of traditional Mayan costume. The collection of modern and old textiles, new or second-hand, is displayed in a huge warehouse. Interesting commentary on where the textiles come from, photos of costumes and weaving demonstrations. Non-negotiable prices. *Colibrí*, 4a Calle Oriente #3B. 9am-4pm. This shop stocks a wide choice of hand-made textiles in original colourways and with impeccable finishes.

**Jade** – Everything you ever wanted to know about the Mayan civilization's most precious stone. These specialist jewellers organise very informative visits to their workshops, where you can follow all the stages from cutting the stone through to finely chiselled finished jewellery.

*La Casa del Jade SA*, 4a Calle Oriente #3. Daily 9am-6pm.

*Jades SA*, 4a Calle Oriente #34. Daily 9am-9pm.

**Coffee** – Antigua is reputed for its excellent coffee. Tasting and sales at *Viejo Café*, corner of 6a Ave and 3a Calle, ☎ 832 1576. 8am-11pm; closed Tuesdays. Orders must be placed 48hr ahead. In the same street, *Tostaduría Antigua*, corner of 6a Ave and 6a Calle. 10am-12.30pm / 2.30pm-6pm; closed Saturdays and Sunday mornings.

**Art Galleries** – *Galería de Arte La Antigua*, 4a Calle Oriente #15, ☎ 832 2866. 10am-6pm; closed Mondays. Permanent and temporary exhibitions by contemporary painters, sculptors and photographers. A second gallery, *La Antigua*, is open every day, 2a Ave Sur #12, ☎ 832 6951.

*Proyecto Cultural El Sitio*, 5a Calle Poniente #15, ☎ 832 3037. 9am-7pm; closed Mondays. Apart from exhibitions, numerous cultural events are held in this colonial house (films, plays, concerts).

**Casa de la Cultura**, on the left of the cathedral. Cultural exhibitions and activities.

**Bookshops** – Antigua's bookshops offer a wide selection of novels, books on history and archeology, guides to the town and to Guatemala, in Spanish and English.

**Casa Andinista**, 4a Calle Oriente 5A. Opposite the Doña Luisa cafeteria; general books and a lot of guides to Central American countries (mainly in English). **La Casa del Conde**, 5a Ave Norte #4, on Parque Central. A large selection of books, from archeology to zoology, and a children's literature department. **Hamlin y White**, 4a Calle Oriente #12A, ☎ 832 2613. Reviews and magazines in Spanish or English. **Un Poco de Todo**, 5a Ave Norte #10A, on Parque Central, ☎ 832 0892. New and second-hand books. A few foreign language books. **Rainbow Reading Room & Café**, corner of 7a Ave Sur and 6a Calle Poniente. Large selection of second-hand books; browse while you drink your coffee (see "Eating out").

**Making the most of Antigua**

# LAKE ATITLÁN★★★

Sololá department
148km west of Guatemala City on CA1
Alt 1 560m – Temperate climate all year round
See map p 160

**Not to be missed**
A boat trip on the lake.
Sunset from Calle del Lago in Panajachel.
Holy Week in Santiago Atitlán.
The Friday market in Sololá.

**And remember...**
Lake visibility is best in the early morning, especially in December and January.
Take a guide when hiking or climbing the volcanoes.
Cross the lake early in the day so as to return before the wind rises.

Encircled by the perfect cones of three volcanoes, Lake Atitlán looks like one of those too-lovely-to-be-true colour prints. It exudes an impression of majesty but also of a peaceful way of life.

In the mornings the women meet up on the lakeside to do their washing when they are not off to one of the many markets in the region; young girls learn the arts of weaving and embroidery from their elders; peasants in the hills come home from their fields bearing enormous loads held in place by their *mecapal*, a leather strap around the forehead, while a few fishermen in *cayucos* (pirogues) glide gently over the azure mirror in which the volcanoes are reflected.

The apparent tranquillity of Lake Atitlán made it a favourite destination for hippies in the 1960s, then a resort for well-off Ladinos and one of the most visited locations in the country. This means that the tourist infrastructure has been developing constantly, in both Panajachel and the other villages around the lake. It is an ideal place to stop off for a few days and explore, on foot or by boat, the surrounding villages where the indigenous people continue to preserve their traditional lifestyle.

## A few facts and figures

The lake was apparently formed over 80 000 years ago by a volcanic eruption that created the caldera (vast crater) into which the watercourses poured. From this basin then rose the **Tolimán** (3 158m), **San Pedro** (3 020m) and **Atitlán** (3 535m) **volcanoes**, preventing the rivers from continuing on their way to the Pacific Ocean, except through underground passages. The lake covers approximately 130sqkm for a maximum measured depth of 324m, although it may reach 600m in parts.

---

**Market days**

To help plan visits, here are the market days in the various villages around the lake.

| | |
|---|---|
| Sunday | **San Pedro La Laguna**, Santiago Atitlán, San Lucas Tolimán |
| Tuesday | Sololá, Santiago Atitlán, San Lucas Tolimán. |
| Thursday | San Lucas Tolimán. |
| Friday | **Santiago Atitlán**, **Sololá**, San Lucas Tolimán. |

---

*The Highlands*

Its generous proportions mean Lake Atitlán is very well stocked with fish, but some species have disappeared from its waters over the last forty years because of the introduction of the *lubina negra* (black bass), a ferocious predator on smaller fish. The fishermen mainly haul in carp, mojarras and crabs in their nets.

*Turn left at Los Encuentros junction, 127km from the capital on the Pan-American Highway (CA1). At the next crossroads 1km further on, take the road left for 11km to Sololá. On leaving the village you start to drop very steeply for 9km in the direction of Panajachel. Halfway down, stop at San Jorge La Laguna mirador to admire the panoramic view over the lake.*

## Around the lake

*Allow 1 day by boat and 4 days on foot.*
*Some villages are not accessible by car.*

Whether on foot or by boat, it is worth discovering the dozen or so localities around the lake, divided between Cakchiqueles to the north and Tzutuhiles to the south. Going from village to village – and from one apostle's name to another – reveals a succession of spectacular views. If time is limited the simplest solution is to go round the lake by *lancha (see "Making the most of Lake Atitlán")*. Be warned that in the afternoons the lake waters turn choppy from the *xocomil* (pronounced shocomil) wind, from which many legends have derived: the soul of a young man desperately searching the surface of the water for his drowned loved one, or the imprisoned spirit of the lake crying out for vengeance. Whatever the explanation it makes the crossing a rough one!

*The villages are listed clockwise from east to west starting from Panajachel. Visits can be planned around market days, frequency of boat connections or, of course, personal desires.*

Fishermen in "cayucos" on Lake Atitlán

Serena/HOA QUI

**Lake Atitlán**

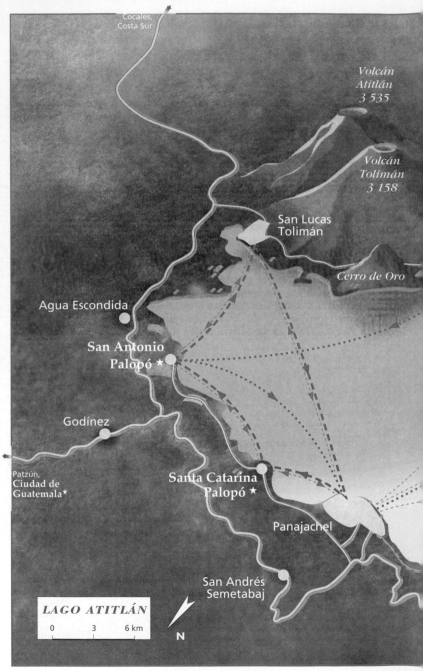

Cocales,
Costa Sur

*Volcán
Atitlán
3 535*

*Volcán
Tolimán
3 158*

San Lucas
Tolimán

*Cerro de Oro*

Agua Escondida

**San Antonio
Palopó** ★

Godínez

Patzún,
**Ciudad de
Guatemala**★

**Santa Catarina
Palopó** ★

Panajachel

San Andrés
Semetabaj

*LAGO ATITLÁN*

0    3    6 km

N

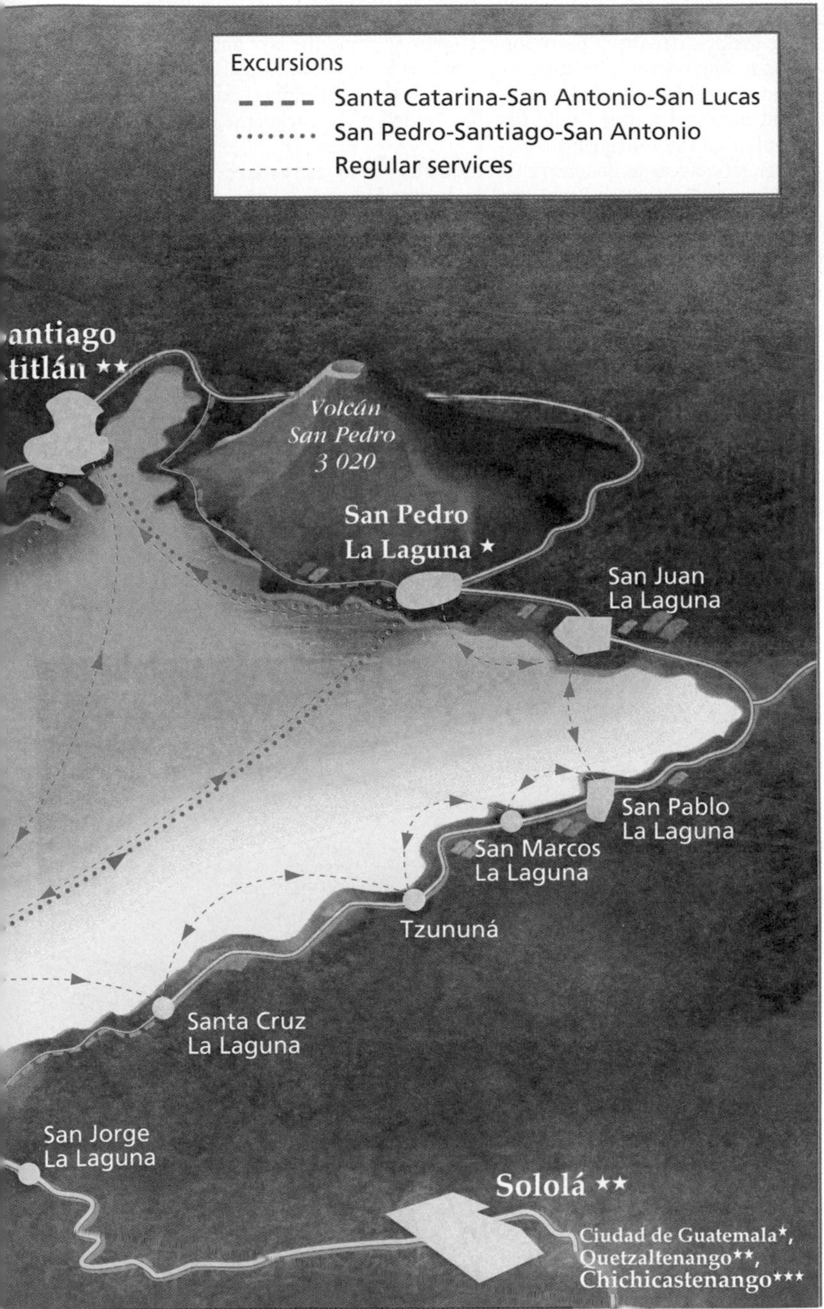

Excursions

**- - - -** Santa Catarina-San Antonio-San Lucas

**·······** San Pedro-Santiago-San Antonio

-------- Regular services

*antiago*
*titlán* ★★

*Volcán*
*San Pedro*
*3 020*

**San Pedro**
**La Laguna** ★

San Juan
La Laguna

San Pablo
La Laguna

San Marcos
La Laguna

Tzununá

Santa Cruz
La Laguna

San Jorge
La Laguna

**Sololá** ★★

**Ciudad de Guatemala**★,
**Quetzaltenango**★★,
**Chichicastenango**★★★

**■ Panajachel –** With its excellent tourist amenities and easy access, "Pana" is the best departure point for excursions around the lake and exploring the surrounding region. The appearance of this former Cakchiquel village has changed considerably with the passing years; the wave of hippies has been followed by an incessant tourist traffic that has earned it the nickname of "Gringotenango" (place of the foreigners).

Its reputation as a temple of tourism is not exaggerated. In the vicinity of **Avenida Santander** Panajachel looks just like one enormous souvenir shop, its textiles covering every millimetre of frontage and pavement. The stalls form a sort of giant patchwork, punctuated only by entrances to hotels, restaurants and travel agencies.

Further on, however, streets with a more authentic feel await discovery, and it is in fact easy to forget the agitation of Panajachel when strolling dreamily down Calle del Lago at sunset, looking out over an unforgettable **panorama★★★** of the lake girdled by its volcanoes – when the weather is clear!

*4km of track along the lakeside from Panajachel to Santa Catarina Palopó.*

**■ Santa Catarina Palopó★ –** After passing the Santa Catarina hotel above the landing-stage the road leads into a picturesque square overlooked by a church and several *comedores*. The village then climbs up the hillside, offering a lovely **viewpoint★★** over the lake. This former fishing village has suffered from the introduction of bass into the lake waters and its inhabitants now earn their living mainly from agriculture and selling textiles.

The Highlands

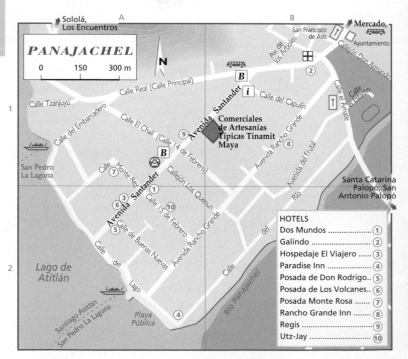

HOTELS

Dos Mundos .................... ①
Galindo ........................... ②
Hospedaje El Viajero ...... ③
Paradise Inn .................... ④
Posada de Don Rodrigo.. ⑤
Posada de Los Volcanes.. ⑥
Posada Monte Rosa ....... ⑦
Rancho Grande Inn ........ ⑧
Regis ............................... ⑨
Utz-Jay ........................... ⑩

Santa Catarina is in fact the birthplace of the **traditional costumes\*\*** of bright blue and green herringbone, their original colours distinguishing them easily from the other costumes of the region. As soon as a boat ties up, the young village girls in their local dress surround new arrivals to try and sell their woven fabrics. It is not, however, easy to take photos of the locals, as being used to tourist "generosity" they will agree to show themselves only in exchange for a few quetzals.

*The track continues for 5km after Santa Catarina Palopó.*

■ **San Antonio Palopó\*** – Seen from a distance San Antonio resembles a set of child's building bricks. Arriving by boat you will see a charming steep village of small adobe cottages

G. Bludzin

Young girls from Santa Catarina Palopó

Lake Atitlán

topped by corrugated tin roofs, clinging to a hillside cultivated in stepped terraces. Walk up to the top for a superb **panorama\*\*** over the lake. The somewhat shy inhabitants usually refuse to be photographed but the attractive setting is well worth a visit.

*Return to Panajachel and take the old road to Guatemala City (via Patzún). Go through the village of San Andrés Semetabaj (24km) and continue another 26km, ignoring all turn-offs to the left.*

■ **San Lucas Tolimán** – The village itself is of no great interest apart from its pretty **location\***, sheltering in a cove at the foot of the **Tolimán volcano**. It is from here that local guides can be found to accompany visitors wishing to climb the **Tolimán** and **Atitlán volcanoes** *(8hr climb for each)*. This is the only lakeside village, apart from Panajachel, that is linked to the rest of the country by a major road, which explains why it is a dynamic trading centre with trucks frequently passing through.

16km of unmetalled road link San Lucas Tolimán to Santiago Atitlán. Halfway along, after running alongside the lake, the track snakes between the Tolimán volcano and the **Cerro de Oro** (hill of gold). Legend recounts that this hill was formed by a volcanic eruption that buried the hidden treasure of the Tzutuhiles.

When travelling by boat you round **Poc Island**, named after a species of grebe. Lake Atitlán was the sanctuary of this web-footed water bird, which is an endangered species, but the hand of man and the drop in the water level have damaged the reeds that formed its habitat; in addition the bass introduced into the lake have not only caused some of the fish it feeds on to disappear, but are also a direct threat to the *poc's* offspring.

*Access by the unmetalled road from San Lucas Tolimán.*

■ **Santiago Atitlán**★★ – Nestling in a deep bay between the Tolimán and San Pedro volcanoes, this Tzutuhil village is the most interesting, and the most touristy, of the lakeside villages after Panajachel. Visitors are met by a crowd of souvenir sellers, a tiny tourist office and dozens of children crying "Maximón, Maximón" (pronounced "Mashimon") and offering to escort them to the house of the local divinity.

**La costumbre** (the customs) – Santiago Atitlán remains deeply attached to the "customs", the name given to the syncretism of Catholic religion and Mayan rites. Despite the threat posed by the Protestant sects that have appeared in the village, a large number of *Atitecos* (Santiago inhabitants) remain faithful to their traditional ceremonies, through the existence of **cofradías** (brotherhoods). These religious institutions, which during the colonial era formed a link between the Catholic Church and the native populations, have enabled ancestral beliefs and the cultural identity of the Mayan community to be preserved. The village's main *cofradía*, under the patronage of La Santa Cruz (the Holy Cross), makes a positive cult of **Maximón**, a saint also to be found in a few other places in Guatemala (*see p 67*).

The village children lead visitors to his sanctuary, which is usually in the home of one of the brotherhood members. A small donation is required to enter the house of Maximón and observe the rites dedicated to the saint, who is deeply revered by the people. In the middle of the room, obscured by swirling smoke from his cigar, the wooden statuette, wearing a hat and draped in layers of clothing with several thicknesses of scarves, seems to listen unmoved to the entreaties addressed to him by the shamans. The effigy is also the central figure in major processions during Holy Week.

In the centre of the village stands the **parish church**, bearing obvious witness to religious syncretism with its statues of saints wrapped in traditional fabrics and the figure of *Yum Kaax* (the Mayan maize god) carved on the priest's chair.

A plaque in the adjoining convent commemorates the assassination on 28 July 1981 of the North-American priest who officiated here. This village, so serene in appearance, has experienced many a tragedy of this sort, and the population has paid a heavy tribute to the years of war which have bloodied Guatemala. One striking event was the shooting that cost the lives of thirteen inhabitants in December 1990 and led to the closing of the military base in Santiago.

**The market**★★ – Close by the church is held one of the most important markets on the lakeside. On **Fridays** trading is positively exuberant and it is hard even to squeeze a way between the mountains of fruits and vegetables. In this vast area, protected from sun and weather by tarpaulins and corrugated tin roofing, there is only room to move in single file through a hive of activity in which each individual appears to pursue a very precise route and goal.

Serena/HOA QUI

**Lake Atitlán**

Santiago Atitlán women, their heads wrapped in "tocoyales"

Many communities from around about meet up here, but the **traditional costumes★★** of the *Atitecas* (village women) stand out. They wear a *tocoyal*, a long fabric strip up to 20m long which is wound around the head. This superb head-dress is unfortunately becoming increasingly rare. Their *huipiles* are easily recognisable with their depictions of birds and flowers on a white background, crisscrossed by horizontal mauve stripes and thinner vertical lines – with a little imagination you could believe you were looking at frames from an animal film!

*The 16km of dirt road between Santiago Atitlán and San Pedro La Laguna go around San Pedro volcano and through a pine forest.*

■ **San Pedro La Laguna★** – The silhouette of **San Pedro volcano** (*5hr climb*) looks down over this pleasant Tzutuhil village. It is now the second most popular tourist destination on the southern bank of the lake, as announced by the strains of international music floating out of the bars above the landing-stage. There is a relaxed feel about the place that has inevitably attracted backpackers and hippies weary of Panajachel. Some have settled here and opened bars and guesthouses, which occasionally upsets the tranquillity of the place.

The street which leaves from the landing-stage leads into the centre of the village, a pleasant walk but of no special interest apart from the evangelical chapels on every street corner.

■ 3km from San Pedro the village of **San Juan La Laguna** is only of interest in that it specialises in weaving reed *petates* (mats).

Continuing northwards, on foot or by boat, halfway between San Juan and the next village you come to a popular bathing spot known by the promising name of **Aguas Cristalinas★** (crystal waters).

■ 8km from San Juan La Laguna the road stops at **San Pablo La Laguna**, a modest village with little to interest tourists. On the roadside leading up to the village, however, the men will happily explain the painstaking work they are carrying out: crushing *maguey* (agave) leaves in order to extract the vegetable fibres used to make basketwork items (baskets, hammocks), a San Pablo speciality.

*San Marcos is linked to the previous villages by a track. From Panajachel it can be reached either by 50km of road via Santa Lucía Utatlán (turn off at km 148 on the Pan-American Highway) or 16km of mountain path.*

■ **San Marcos La Laguna** – Houses scattered over the hillsides look out over a pretty stretch of Lake Atitlán's shoreline. To the left of the landing-stage a narrow reed-lined track provides an attractive walk into the centre of the village. The guesthouses here offer the prospect of a peaceful stay in a delightful natural setting.

A "tienda" in San Pedro La Laguna

■ **Santa Cruz La Laguna** – *10km of mountain path from Panajachel.* Near the landing-stage the patios of a few guesthouses open out over an exquisite view. The village is reached by a steep road giving a bird's-eye **view**★★ of the lake; the main street of this Cakchiquel village finally comes into sight after a half-hour climb. The women sit weaving in the backyards of their modest cob cottages and will sometimes venture to invite passers-by to watch them working. In comparison with other townships, daily life in Santa Cruz La Laguna seems surprisingly quiet. Perhaps it is the steep walk up that protects its inhabitants from too-frequent visits by tourists.

## Away from the lake

Lake Atitlán is very fortunately located only 20km or so from an important cross-roads, from which various roads lead to fascinating places: Chichicastenango to the north, Quetzaltenango to the west and Antigua and the capital to the east. Visitors are spoilt for choice!

## Market day** in Sololá

*9km from Panajachel on the road to Los Encuentros. Allow 20min by bus. To admire the landscape, sit on the left going and on the right coming back.*

The capital of the department of the same name, Sololá is situated halfway between the Altiplano and the Pacific coast, where cold lands and hot lands meet. What with the goods on sale and the costumes of the various communities in the region, it offers a rich palette of colour.

The **Friday** morning market is a must. At the foot of the cathedral the women weavers carefully select their hanks of brightly dyed yarn; small boys elbow their way through the crowds, heads down and foreheads encircled by their *mecapales*, bearing loads far too heavy for them; old women watch over their piles of fish, shellfish, fruit, vegetables and basketwork items. Wads of quetzals, worn flimsy by excessive handling, change hands and the *tzutes* (lengths of fabric folded on the head) and baskets of the market regulars gradually fill up with rice and beans. Around the square the *camionetas* honk their horns at regular intervals, while the *ayudantes* reel off their destinations to take the laden villagers back home. In the midst of this colourful parade the **local costume***** stands out with its predominant shades of pink, red and mauve. Unlike many villages, where the men's attire is tending to become "Ladinoised", here the men still wear their traditional dress proudly. They look almost like cowboys in their wide-brimmed hats and short jackets decorated with a filigree of colours and adorned with the stylised bat motif that is the symbol of the Cakchiquel dynasty in power at the time of the conquest. Around the hips of their richly embroidered trousers they tie a *ponchito*, a strip of brown and white check fabric intended to protect them from the cold.

On Sunday mornings in Sololá processions of *cofradías* can be watched on their way to mass.

## Returning to Los Encuentros

An opportunity to relax for travellers stiff from long hours on the road, a godsend for hungry and thirsty passengers, a waiting-room for those with connections to make – Los Encuentros is one immense meeting-point and a major road traffic junction. The buses scarcely have time to stop before being surrounded by multitudes of hawkers brandishing smoking *tortillas*, packets of *jocotes* (a sort of plum) or peanuts, cans of cool drinks, ice-creams etc. After a brief halt the vehicles set off again and the vendors rush to get at the latest arrivals.

**Lake Atitlán**

B. Brillon/MICHELIN

A Sololá man in his traditional costume

*If you are heading for the capital or Antigua, drive 40km to km 87 on the Pan-American Highway and go into the town of Tecpán Guatemala.*

Tecpán is not really worth stopping in, but the **ruins of Iximché** (*9am-5pm. Fee.*), 4km to the south, are open to the public. This archeological site is located in a lovely **natural setting**★ where Guatemalans often come to picnic in the shade of the pines. They also come to consult the shamans who practise their traditional rites in the forest. The tranquillity of the place would also seem to inspire evangelists, who set up their microphones to preach in this desert of ruins to assemblies of the faithful congregating on the steps of the pre-Columbian temples.

The ancient **Cakchiquel capital**, established here in 1470 by the population that fled Chichicastenango (*see p* 174), was not to resist the army of Pedro de Alvarado half a century later. And yet the Cakchiqueles, allies of the Spanish against the Quichés and the Tzutuhiles, had in fact invited the conquistadors to set up camp near their city and it was here that **Santiago de Los Caballeros**, the colony's first capital, was officially founded in 1524. Peaceful co-existence between the two capitals was short-lived. The Cakchiqueles rapidly began refusing to supply the gold and riches demanded by their neighbour, and this rebellion marked the end of the alliance. The Cakchiquel population took flight and their city fell into the hands of the Spanish.

This **Post-Classic** site comprised four large ceremonial squares, along with two smaller ones. The platforms are still visible but the adobe temples have long since succumbed to destruction by man and time. At the site entrance, in a modest museum (*closed 12noon-2pm*), are exhibited archeological finds, photos of the excavations, some examples of contemporary handicrafts and a model of the city.

# Making the most of Lake Atitlán

## COMING AND GOING

**By bus** – Panajachel has no bus station but a *parada de buses* (bus stop) on the corner of Ave Santander and Calle Real, outside Banco Inmobiliario (B1), plus another on Calle Real near the market (towards B1). Departures approx every hour, especially mornings, from Panajachel to Guatemala City (3hr), Chichicastenango (90min) and Quetzaltenango (2hr30min). If there is no direct bus, change at Los Encuentros (1hr). This also applies for Huehuetenango (5hr) as there is no direct service. One bus daily at 10.45am for Antigua (3hr) or change at Chimaltenango. Departures every 30min for Sololá (20min) and every hour from 9.15am for Santa Catarina Palopó (30min) and San Antonio Palopó (45min).

**By private minibus** – Almost all the travel agencies run minibus services between Panajachel and the other tourist centres, including several services daily to Guatemala City, Antigua, and Chichicastenango on market days. It is, of course, possible to arrange minibus transport to any desired destination (a worthwhile solution for groups).

## GETTING AROUND

A few villages around Lake Atitlán are accessible on foot or by bus, but boats are the most practical and pleasant means of transport.

**By boat** – The boat ("lancha") timetable is posted at the entrance to INGUAT and in front of the main landing-stage on the public beach below the Barceló del Lago hotel. Some boats for San Pedro La Laguna also call at the second landing-stage at the end of Calle del Embarcadero. Frequent connections between the 3 main villages of Panajachel, San Pedro La Laguna and Santiago Atitlán. Approx 7 crossings a day between Panajachel and Santiago (1hr), 10 between Panajachel and San Pedro (90min) and 10 between San Pedro and Santiago (30min). The villages on the northern shore of the lake (including Santa Cruz La Laguna and San Marcos La Laguna) are served by the Panajachel-San Pedro boats. Connections between Panajachel and other villages are less frequent: 2 boats a day to Santa Catarina Palopó, San Antonio Palopó and San Lucas Tolimán, a single boat back in early afternoon.

A round trip of the lake leaves from Panajachel and stops off for approx 1hr each in 3 villages, San Pedro-Santiago-San Antonio or Santa Catarina-San Antonio-San Lucas. Leaves in the morning, returns early afternoon, approx US$8 per person.

To visit other villages or spend more time on the spot, a private "lancha" can be hired (US$40-50 a day). They are easy to find, as many boat owners offer their services on the public beach.

**By taxi** – Vehicles wait near San Francisco de Asís church and on the corner of Calle Real and Ave Santander, ☎ 762 1571.

**By rental bike** – *Moto Servicio Queché*, Ave de los Árboles, opposite El Chisme restaurant, rents motorbikes and bicycles. *Taller El Centro*, Calle Real opposite Banco Inmobiliario.

## ADDRESS BOOK

**Tourist information – INGUAT** (B1), ☎ 762 1392, is on the ground floor of the shopping arcade at the start of Ave Santander, near Calle Real. 8am-1pm / 2pm-5.30pm. Boat and bus timetables as well as simple maps of Lake Atitlán and Panajachel are available.

There is another tourist office at Santiago Atitlán, a few metres from the landing-stage. Very basic information.

**Bank / Currency exchange – Banco Industrial**, Ave Santander, a few metres from Calle El Chali. 9am-3pm; closed Saturday afternoons and Sundays. Cashpoint for Visa cards. *Banco Inmobiliario*, corner Ave de los Árboles and Calle Real. 9am-8pm / 6pm Saturdays; closed Sundays.

**Post Office / Telephone** – the post office is near San Francisco de Asís church, close to the market. *TELGUA* (A1), Ave Santander next to Banco Industrial. 8am-7.30pm / 9am-4pm Sundays. The souvenir shops and travel agencies on Ave Santander offer much lower tariffs for international calls and sending faxes.

**Medical service** – *Farmacia La Unión*, Ave Santander on the right of El Patio restaurant. Daily 9am-11pm. In an emergency contact the **Centro de Salud**, Calle Real, ☎ 762 1258.

## WHERE TO STAY

Panajachel has an impressive range of accommodation. Around Ave Santander there is a vast choice of dozens of very modest guesthouses and more comfortable hotels. It is nevertheless recommended to book in the high season and at weekends. To avoid the crowds some tourists prefer to stay in other villages around the lake, where accommodation for all tastes and purses is also to be found, from the rudimentary comfort of the Santa Cruz and San Pedro La Laguna guesthouses to the charming hotels in San Marcos La Laguna and the more luxurious ones in Santa Catarina Palopó.

● **Panajachel**
*Under US$15*
**Hospedaje El Viajero**, Final Ave Santander, ☎ 762 0128 ⌂ A quiet little hotel, shielded from the noise on Ave Santander and reached by elbowing through bags and fabrics at the entrance and then crossing a courtyard. Modest rooms, but offering good value for money all the same.
*Under US$25*
**Hotel Galindo**, Calle Real, ☎ 762 1168 – 12rm ⌂ The owners seem to have given up on taming their delightful garden, abandoning it to luxuriant vegetation. Basic accommodation, variable in quality, but useful if stuck. The big rooms with fireplaces are slightly more expensive but preferable.
**Hotel Utz-Jay (Casa Buena)**, Calle 15 de Febrero, ☎ 762 1358 – 6rm Sergio and Lisette offer accommodation

in either their own chalet or the main house, where 4 impeccably maintained rooms share a bathroom, a large lounge with fireplace and a terrace overlooking the garden. Nearby are 2 small bungalows with private bathrooms. The owners know the region perfectly and organise excursions round about. Sergio takes his guests to Sololá market on Fridays (returning on foot through the mountains). One of the best addresses in Panajachel.
**Hotel Posada Monte Rosa**, Calle del Monte Rey, ☎ 762 0055 – 5rm ⌂ A pity there is no greenery in the courtyard, making this little place look like a motel, but the unpretentious rooms are clean and comfortable.
**Posada de Los Volcanes**, Ave Santander 5-51, Zone 2, ☎ 762 0244 – 6rm ⌂ TV A newish building sharing a tiny garden with the Villa Martita guesthouse. The rooms are not exceptional but they are well maintained.
**Hotel Paradise Inn**, Calle del Río, ☎ 762 1021 – 12rm ⌂ TV CC At the mouth of the river, facing the lake and outside the village centre. Rooms without charm but perfectly comfortable and with fireplaces. The prices quoted for the high season are prohibitive for what is provided.
*Around US$50*
**Hotel Regis**, Ave Santander 3-47, Zone 2, ☎ 762 1149, Fax 762 1152 – 20rm ⌂ TV CC The bungalows, scattered around the park, have spacious, comfortable rooms. At the bottom of the garden is a little swimming-pool, fed by a hot spring of volcanic origin.
**Hotel Dos Mundos**, Ave Santander 4-72, Zone 2, ☎ 762 2078 – 16rm ⌂ TV ✗ ⌇ CC For a peaceful stay in a lounger by the swimming-pool, far from the hustle on Ave Santander. Pleasant, comfortable rooms, well-lit and with very new toilet facilities. The place is constantly being improved and everything is impeccable, from floor to ceiling and from rooms to garden. Breakfast included. Friendly welcome.
**Hotel Rancho Grande Inn**, Ave Rancho Grande, ☎ 762 2255, Fax 762 2247 – 14rm ⌂ ♪ ✗ CC

Bungalows in a variety of architectural styles set in an immense garden in a quiet street parallel to Ave Santander. 2 types of rooms at different prices; fireplace and TV in the bigger ones (no 7 with its mini-lounge and kitchenette is delightful). Excellent breakfast included.

*Around US$90*

*Hotel Posada de Don Rodrigo*, Final Ave Santander, ☎ 762 2326, Fax 762 1163 – 30rm ⌂ ☕ TV ✕ ⚌ CC This branch of the well-known Antigua establishment enjoys one of the best locations in Panajachel, at the end of the main street facing the lake. Luxurious colonial-type decor, tastefully decorated rooms and good quality service.

*Hotel Atitlán*, Finca San Buenaventura, ☎ 762 1441 / 1429 / 1416 – 62rm ⌂ ☕ TV ✕ ⚌ ⚘ CC On the lakeside 2km west of the town centre on the road to Sololá. One of the loveliest hotels in Guatemala in a wonderful setting. Lovely walks in the park, home to a large number of birds and multitudes of sweet-smelling flowers (butterfly farm nearby). The elegant rooms with every comfort reflect the colonial style of the building. First-class reception.

• **San Marcos La Laguna**

From the landing-stage, turn left along the lakeside for 500m then take the road to the right of Posada Schumann; the hotels mentioned are all in the vicinity.

*Under US$20*

*Hotel Paco Real*, San Marcos La Laguna, ☎ 762 1196 (Panajachel public telephone) – 9rm ✕ Rustic bungalows in a pretty garden. Charming rooms (some with a mezzanine) and a dormitory. Run by a Swiss overflowing with energy and very welcoming. Often full, but the easiest way to book is to go there!

*Posada Schumann*, San Marcos La laguna, ☎ 202 2216 or 360 4049 (Guatemala City) – sleeps 22 ✕ One of the prettiest hotels on the lake. Those seeking tranquillity and nature will be delighted by the garden with its coffee,

banana and avocado trees. Charming stone and wood cottages decorated with local handicrafts. The 3 bungalows and 4 rooms (with or without bathrooms) have balconies overlooking the lake.

*Hotel La Paz*, San Marcos La Laguna, ☎ 702 9168 – sleeps 10 ⌂ ✕ Although pleasant, the 3 bungalows do not have the character of the previous 2 establishments, but this hotel is still good at the price.

• **San Antonio Palopó**

*Around US$30*

*Hotel Terrazas del Lago*, San Antonio Palopó, ☎ 762 1288 (public telephone) – 15rm ⌂ ✕ A 5min walk to the right from the landing-stage. The hotel stands on a promontory facing the lake. Well-maintained rooms. Nos 6 and 12 have a superb view over the lake.

• **Santa Catarina Palopó**

*Around US$80*

*Hotel Villa Santa Catarina*, Santa Catarina Palopó, ☎ 334 8136-39, Fax 334 8134 – 36rm ⌂ ✕ ⚌ CC Luxury hotel looking slightly out of place in this humble village, so no difficulty in finding it on arrival at the landing-stage. All the rooms are comfortable, only the view makes the difference. Suites 51 and 40 at the end of the building facing the lake enjoy a view on two sides. Of the standard rooms nos 23 (the best) to 27 have a view of the lake; the others look out onto the swimming-pool in the middle of the garden.

• **Santiago Atitlán**

*Around US$50*

*Posada de Santiago*, Santiago Atitlán, ☎ 721 7168 or 702 8462 – 12rm ⌂ ✕ ⚘ Very pretty 20min walk to the east of the village, towards San Pedro La Laguna. Stone cottages scattered around a park overrun with vegetation. Comfortable rooms, tastefully decorated and with fireplaces. This attractive setting can be enjoyed from a hammock or the belvedere that looks out over the lake. Reservation recommended.

**Making the most of Lake Atitlán**

171

## EATING OUT

### ● Panajachel

*Under US$10*

Snacks and take-away food can be bought at modest prices from the stall holders on either side of Ave Santander.

***Restaurante Mario's***, Ave Santander, opposite TELGUA (A1). 8am-8pm. The veranda offers a strategic view down Ave Santander. Meals are good and co-pious but the place is most agreeable at breakfast or tea time. Take-away bread and pastries.

***The Last Resort / El Último Refugio***, Calle El Chali (A1), ☎ 762 2016. 🍴 7am-11pm. The terrace with its shady parasols is the ideal refuge on a hot summer afternoon. Light meals at very reasonable prices.

***Restaurante Deli 2***, Final Ave Santander (A2). 🍴 7am-10pm; closed Tuesdays. Tables set in a garden near the lake. A pleasant place for having breakfast or enjoying American pastries at any time of day, to classical music.

*Around US$10*

***Sunset Café***, Final Ave Santander (A2). 🍴 11am-10pm. From the candle-lit terrace there is an exceptional panorama over Lake Atitlán. Ideal for having a drink or enjoying good Mexican special-ities as the sun disappears behind the volcanoes. Live music at weekends.

***Restaurante El Patio***, Ave Santander (A1-B1), ☎ 762 2041. 🍴 7am-9pm. Just opposite the entrance to the hand-icrafts market, on a terrace opening onto Ave Santander. Snacks, a few dishes of international cuisine and breakfasts at reasonable prices.

***Restaurante Chinitas***, Ave Santander (A1-B1). 8.30am-10pm; closed Mon-days. Tables set out in the shopping centre gallery, to the left of El Patio restaurant. Good Chinese dishes nicely presented. Excellent value for money.

***Restaurante Descansillo***, Calle Real, opposite Calle El Amate (B1), ☎ 762 1095. 7.30am-10pm; closed Tuesdays. Artists sometimes come and hang their works on the yellow walls of this little restaurant. There are also

tables in the garden, in the shade of a multitude of exotic plants. A friendly place serving international cuisine.

***Circus Bar***, Ave de los Árboles (B1), ☎ 762 2056. 🆑 12noon-12midnight. Attractive decor of old circus posters, soft lighting, small covered patio. The bar and dining room are often very crowded. A good place to eat a pizza or have a drink, to live music.

***Restaurante El Chisme***, Ave de los Árboles (B1), ☎ 762 2063. 🍴 🆑 7.30am-10pm. Seating for all seasons, in the sun on the terrace, in the shade of the veranda or inside at the counter. A pleasant place to eat or have a drink at any hour of the day.

*AroundUS$15*

***Restaurante La Lanterna***, Ave San-tander 4-72, in the Dos Mundos hotel (A1-A2). 🆑 7am-3pm / 6pm-10.30pm. Excellent Italian pasta to be enjoyed under an immense straw roof with big bay windows opening onto the garden of the hotel. Its location, back from Ave Santander, is both an asset (very quiet) and a disadvantage (often empty). A pity it is not fre-quented more; at lunch time you can also take advantage of the swimming-pool.

***Restaurante Casablanca***, Calle Real, at the top of Ave Santander (B1), ☎ 762 1015. 🆑 12noon-10pm. A restaurant that stands out from the others, with a lovely veranda slightly above street level and more sophisti-cated international cuisine (meat, fish, seafood); this is reflected in the bill. Aperitif on the house and efficient re-ception.

## GOING OUT, HAVING A DRINK

Surprising as it may seem for such a touristy place, there is not a lot to do in Panajachel once night falls.

**Bars –** It is, of course, possible to have a drink in the places listed under "Eating out". Good atmosphere at ***Sunset Café***, ***Circus Bar*** and ***Last Resort***.

**Disco –** ***El Chapiteau***, Ave de los Árboles, opposite the Circus Bar. From 9pm; closed Sundays and Mondays.

The Highlands

## OTHER THINGS TO DO

**Excursions** – The Panajachel travel agencies organise excursions lasting one or several days to other parts of the country and in the immediate region. These intermediaries are not essential for visiting the villages around the lake by boat (see "Getting around") or taking the bus to Sololá market. Be careful if walking to the villages around about (Santa Catarina Palopó, San Antonio Palopó, Sololá). The same advice applies when climbing the volcanoes around Lake Atitlán.

**Films** – A few bars show videos in English or Spanish. *Grapevine Video Bar*, Ave Santander, 100m from INGUAT on the way down to the lake.

**Outdoor pursuits** – Diving classes organised by *La Iguana Perdida* hotel, Santa Cruz La Laguna, a few metres from the landing-stage. Horse-riding near Hotel Atitlán, Panajachel.

## SHOPPING GUIDE

**Arts and Crafts** – Panajachel is something of a big tourist market, with dozens of hawkers accosting tourists on their arrival in Ave Santander, which is in addition lined all the way down with tourist stalls. On this avenue there is also the *Tinamit Maya* handicrafts market (B1), little different from the rest, about 200m from INGUAT on the same side. Superb "huipiles" can be bought in the villages around the lake as well as in Sololá – places which are all on the way to becoming as touristy as Panajachel.

**Making the most of Lake Atitlán**

# CHICHICASTENANGO★★★
## (SANTO TOMÁS)
El Quiché department
144km from Guatemala City – Alt 2 071m
See map p 137

**Not to be missed**
Market and mass on Sundays.
A "cofradía" procession.
The festival of Santo Tomás (14-21 December).
**And remember...**
Arrive the night before market to watch the preparations.
Book your hotel for the night before market day and festivals.

Wedged between mountains and ravines, the village of "Chichi" on its steep hillside is a peaceful township like many others in the Altiplano, except on market days – Thursday and Sunday mornings – and the previous evenings. Then crowds of vendors, buyers, lookers-on and tourist coaches flood the village. When evening comes, the tide of visitors ebbs again. This perpetual movement is not the only rhythm in community life: religious ceremonies, both modest and spectacular, combining the Catholic liturgy with Mayan rites, also take place at regular, frequent intervals. Scarcely have the *pom* vapours dispersed than the shaman is already swinging the censer; fresh flowers carpet the ground replacing the rose petals blown away by the wind, and new candles light the altars with a fresh glow.

P. Cheuva/DIAF

Chichicastenango "cofrade"

### The sacred village of the Quiché
The original inhabitants of this site, then named Chaviar, were Cakchiquels. In 1470 the population was forced to move to Iximché to escape threats from its Quiché neighbours settled in K'umarkaaj *(see below)*. The Quiché, chased in turn from their capital by Pedro de Alvarado in 1524, took refuge in Siguán Tinamit (city surrounded by ravines), the present-day Chichicastenango (place of the *chichicaste*, a type of nettle that grows in the region). Despite Spanish missionaries' attempts to convert them, the Quiché managed to safeguard the beliefs of their ancestors and continue to practise their traditional rites. The social and religious Ladino structures have been superimposed on those of the Mayan community without ever fully superseding them.

The Highlands

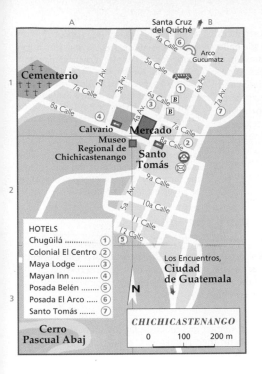

Map labels:
A | B
Santa Cruz del Quiché
4a Calle
Arco Gucumatz
5a Calle
Cementerio
2a Av.
3a Av.
7a Calle
8a Calle
6a Calle
Calvario
Mercado
7a Calle
Museo Regional de Chichicastenango
Santo Tomás
8a Calle
9a Calle
5a Av.
10a Calle
11 Calle
12 Calle
Los Encuentros, Ciudad de Guatemala
N
Cerro Pascual Abaj

HOTELS
Chugüilá .............. ①
Colonial El Centro .②
Maya Lodge .......... ③
Mayan Inn ............ ④
Posada Belén ........ ⑤
Posada El Arco ..... ⑥
Santo Tomás ....... ⑦

CHICHICASTENANGO
0     100     200 m

**Religious syncretism –** You need only walk into the church in Chichicastenango to witness the fusion between Catholicism and Mayan beliefs. Since the religious orders were expelled from the country in the 19C, syncretism has been constantly on the increase, owing to the activities of the **cofradías** (brotherhoods). Each of the fourteen *cofradías* in Chichicastenango is under the protection of a particular saint, the most important being St Thomas, patron saint of the town. Every year for the festival of St Thomas, the brotherhood designates a new team of *principales* (officers) whose leader is responsible for preparing a new sanctuary to hold the statue of the saint. These changes of residence involve big processions (*photography forbidden or only on payment*) during which the men's traditional costumes can be admired. The *cofrades* wear a fringed woollen jacket over bermuda shorts with a side vent. This black costume decorated with sun symbols is set off by a red *tzut*, a length of fabric skilfully folded on the head and falling onto the shoulders.

Although the inhabitants continue to observe certain Catholic rites – on St Thomas' day all the children born during the year are baptised –, weddings and funerals remain the responsibility of the **chuchqajaus** (literally, mother-fathers). These shamans, intermediaries between the faithful and the spirits, are called on to ward off ill fortune and to practise the arts of divination and healing. They can be seen at work in Santo Tomás church or in front of the altars in the vicinity of the village, especially at Pascual Abaj and K'umaarkaj.

**A dual municipality**
The "alcalde" (mayor) and town council are elected as in the rest of the country, but alongside these the Mayans designate their own "municipalidad indígena", a municipal authority that deals with local affairs. This doubling-up is also to be found in the religious institutions.

**Pagan festivals for a Christian calendar –** Chichicastenango remains one of the few places where the 260-day *tzolkin* calendar is still observed (*see p 27*), although in parallel with the Christian calendar. All Saints, Holy Week and the saint's day festival of each *cofradia* are all periods of great fervour, although they bear no comparison to the festivities in honour of the village's patron saint, which last until St Thomas' Day on **21 December***. During this festival of colours, firecrackers, incense and alcohol vapours, the villagers attend several performances of pre-Hispanic dances. For the **baile de la Conquista** (conquest dance) participants wear wooden masks to depict the fight between Spaniards and Mayans. The fascinating spectacle offered by the **Palo Volador** (flying pole), which originated in Mexico, is now unfortunately disappearing: held only by a rope tied to the feet, the dancers throw themselves into space and spin around a pole about twenty metres high.

**A horseman from the skies**

During the major processions, and in particular for St Thomas' Day, one dancer is responsible for bearing Tzijolaj, the protector of pyrotechnists. Although this statuette is supposed to depict Santiago, patron saint of the conquistadors, on horseback, to the Maya it represents a messenger from the gods. The horse and rider are first pulled up to the top of the church bell-tower and then, by means of a cable, pulled into the centre of the square, into the throng of villagers who welcome them as a blessing from the heavens.

## Visiting the village
*Allow 1hr.*

Visiting "Chichi" means little more than a tour of the main square. On **market\*\*** days the adjacent alleyways act as the wings from which to observe the bustle, before being carried along by the crowd out onto the main stage where religious fervour and commercial fever combine.

### The market place\*\* (B1)

It is worth arriving on the eve of market day to sit under the arcades and watch the preparations. The traders set up their stands with prodigious dexterity and rapidity. Gradually the square is covered with scaffolding, around which silhouettes dimly lit by candles busy themselves as if in a shadow puppet theatre. Once everything has been set up, the vendors curl up in their blankets and spend the night near their stalls to keep an eye on them.

As dawn breaks the bundles of merchandise reveal their treasures: shimmering textiles, wooden masks, leather goods, displayed row on row for the tourists. Unfortunately, the considerably less lucrative stalls selling fruit and vegetables are being pushed out by the souvenir merchants, which is gradually depriving this market of its authenticity. It is not easy to stroll about: the vendors vaunt their wares constantly in all languages, flocks of children rush after you endlessly selling knick-knacks and the shoe-shiners dog your steps.

On Sunday mornings and feast days there is an incredible amount of activity in the **church of Santo Tomás\*** (B2) *(mass at 8am)*. Built by the Spanish in 1540 on the site of an ancient Mayan altar, then rebuilt in the 18C, this church is of no great architectural interest, but the **rites\*\*** that take place on its steps and inside the building are fascinating *(taking photos in the church is forbidden and foreigners should use the side door to enter the building)*.

The steps are invisible under the crowds of worshippers, vendors and lookers-on, forming an incredible multi-coloured pyramid of fabrics and flowers. At the top a man swings his rudimentary censer, a pierced tin can exuding the strong fragrance of *pom*, over the parvis. Through a thick, almost palpable, cloud of incense the faithful enter the porch. In the long, plain nave everyone seems to be going about their own business under the protective eyes of the

Plumed float in the streets of Chichicastenango

saints placed on either side. A family is united in prayer at the foot of the altar while in the central aisle the **shamans** transmit the requests of the faithful to their ancestral divinities. On small platforms strewn with rose petals stand candles of various colours corresponding to different prayers: for a good harvest, a recovery, a happy marriage, success in business etc.

To the right of the church is the former monastery. This is where Father **Francisco Jimenez**, who was responsible for converting the Mayans to Christianity, discovered the sacred book of the Quiché, the *Popol Vuh*, which he translated into Spanish in the early 18C (*see p* 30).

On the other side of the square, to the west, stands the **Calvario** (A1), as white as the church of Santo Tomás. This houses a carved statue of Christ that is taken out for major religious celebrations.

On the south side of the square, the **Museo Regional de Chichicastenango** (A2-B2) (*Tuesdays and Wednesdays 8am-12noon / 2pm-4pm; Thursdays to Sundays 8am-2pm; closed Mondays. Fee*) houses a small collection of archeological items brought together by the North American priest Ildefonso Rossbach. Most of the Pre-Classic ceramics, terracotta figurines and censers and the jade jewellery on show there come from the surrounding area.

### Leaving the market

*Walk along 8a Calle, past the "calvario" (on your right).*

From the top of this street the coloured tombs in the **Cementerio General**★ (A1) (*6.30am-5.30pm*) look like brightly-coloured doll's houses. To find the entrance to the cemetery, which is perched on the hill and looks down over the entire village and its surroundings, walk down to 1a Avenida. Among the modest burial mounds and the blue, green, yellow, pink and red tombs – repainted every year for All Saints – can be seen altars where the villagers regularly practise their ancestral rites.

# Around Chichicastenango

The village ends just a few hundred metres from the main square, so in a few minutes you are out in the countryside, at the foot of the surrounding hills.

### Pascual Abaj Hill★ (A3)

*Follow 9a Calle to the bottom of the hill. Cross the courtyard of the wooden mask workshop and follow the path to the top of the hill (20min walk). Ceremonies generally take place on market days but there is no fixed timetable. Details can be had from inhabitants.*

At the top of the hill (*cerro*) stands Pascual Abaj (also known as **Turkaj**), a smoke-blackened stone idol. When the place is deserted only a few wax drippings and the occasional chicken feather scattered on the altar indicate that ceremonies have taken place here. The **view**★ over the surrounding countryside is well worth admiring before going back down to the village. Several "sorcerers" may officiate in the course of a single session, each independently and taking turns to perform their incantations, flagellations with branches, and sometimes the sacrifice of a chicken, amid the snap of firecrackers and smoke from cigars and the fire, frequently revived by *aguardiente* (distilled alcohol). The most surprising element is the capacity of the shamans and their clients to ignore the crowds of curious onlookers massed around them (*taking photos is usually tolerated but ask permission beforehand*).

Wooden masks in Chichicastenango market

## Exploring El Quiché

*Numerous buses leave from the corner of 5a Ave and 5a Calle going north. Allow 30min to Santa Cruz del Quiché.*

After 19km of hairpin bends the road reaches **Santa Cruz del Quiché**, the department capital. Its huge daily market is very different from the one in Chichicastenango, with foodstuffs and everyday utensils taking over the town centre; the few tourists to be seen are simply waiting for connections at the bus station.

*Continue on foot or take a pick-up at Quiché bus station. Leave by 10a Calle to the west of the town.*

3km of unsurfaced road to the west of Quiché lead to the **ruins of K'umarkaaj**, also called **Utatlán** *(daily 8am-5pm. Fee)*. The remains of the former Quiché capital are of limited interest, but the place is nevertheless worth a visit. Like most towns of that era, K'umarkaaj sits in a grandiose **site★★**, on a rocky promontory encircled by *barrancos* (ravines).

This **Post-Classic city,** established at the beginning of the 15C, was destroyed by **Pedro de Alvarado's** army in 1524. In fact, the conquistador came to K'umarkaaj at the invitation of its rulers. The Quiché were determined to avenge their leader, Tecún Umán, who had just perished at the hand of Pedro de Alvarado. But they failed in their project; Pedro de Alvarado succeeded in avoiding their trap and, after burning their two princes alive, set fire to the town. The survivors took refuge in Chichicastenango.

Almost nothing is left of the city other than a few remnants of the main square, much of the stone having been used to build the houses of Santa Cruz del Quiché. However, a model in the museum *(8am-4pm)* at the site entrance gives an idea of how K'umarkaaj looked before it was destroyed. The site attendants will also point out the **cueva** (cave), a long tunnel, where shamans still regularly hold ceremonies *(torch required)*.

The road from Santa Cruz del Quiché continues northwards to the **Cuchumatanes mountains** *(see p 196).*

## Making the most of Chichicastenango

### COMING AND GOING

**By bus** – Buses stop on the corner of 5a Calle and 5a Ave, 1 block from the Arco Gucumatz as you leave the town centre. Direct buses between "Chichi" and Guatemala City (4hr) every 30min, 5am-6pm, to Panajachel (90min) and Quetzaltenango (3hr30min) every hour, or change at Los Encuentros (30min). No direct connections with Antigua (3hr30min), change at Chimaltenango on the Pan-American Highway. Buses every 30min to Santa Cruz del Quiché (30min).

**By private minibus** – Most travel agencies in Guatemala City, Antigua and Panajachel run day trips to Chichicastenango on Thursdays and Sundays.

### ADDRESS BOOK

**Tourist information** – No INGUAT, so try the Mayan Inn hotel (A1).

**Bank / Currency Exchange** – Banks are open Sundays (market day). **Banco del Café**, 5a Ave 6-14, ☎ 756 1021. Closed Sunday afternoons and Mondays. **Banco del Ejército**, 6a Calle 5-40 near the Farmacia Girón. Closed Mondays.

**Post office / Telephone – Correos** (post office), 7a Ave 8-47. For urgent mail use **DHL**, 4a Calle 6-62, ☎ 756 1242. Phone calls and faxes at **TELGUA**, 7a Ave 8-21.

**Medical service – Farmacia Girón**, corner 5a Ave and 6a Calle. 7am-12noon / 2pm-9pm; closed Saturday afternoons.

### WHERE TO STAY

On the eve of market day the guesthouses are overrun and the up-market hotels generally reserve their rooms for the tour operators. It is advisable to arrive early in the day.

*Under US$10*
**Hospedaje Colonial El Centro**, 8a Calle 6-24, ☎ 756 1249 – 6rm. Very basic guesthouse. 2 small rooms, with bathrooms to be added, on the street side. The terrace has a very lovely view over the village.

*Under US$20*
**Hotel Posada Belén**, 12 Calle 5-55, ☎ 756 1244 – 16rm ✗ Family guesthouse on the edge of the village with a view of Pascual Abaj hill. The owner is a colourful character who welcomes vis-

The Highlands

itors warmly. Modest but clean rooms with or without bathrooms. TV on request and for a supplement. The tiny garden throbs with a multitude of hummingbirds.

**Posada El Arco**, 4a Calle 4-36, ☎ 756 1255 – 4rm 🛏 Climb to the top of Arco Gucumatz by the west stairway (on the left as you leave the village). The most charming guesthouse in "Chichi". As soon as you arrive the owners take you around their delightful garden and recount innumerable anecdotes about the region. Rooms full of charm with fireplaces. Unlimited hot water by solar energy.

*Around US$30*

**Hotel Chugüllá**, 5a Ave 5-21, ☎ 756 1134 – 37rm ✘ cc A welcoming building with its big paved patio overlooking a flower-filled terrace. Vast rooms (some with fireplaces) that could do with a coat of paint. Worthwhile prices for the rooms without bathrooms.

**Hotel Maya Lodge**, Parque Central, ☎ 756 1167 – 10rm 🛏✘ The hotel entrance opens onto the centre of the market. A pity the rooms have not been renovated: they are spacious but a little sinister.

*Around US$80*

🏛**Hotel Santo Tomás**, 7a Ave 5-32, ☎ 756 1061, Fax 756 1306 – 43rm 🛏 ♂ ✘ ≋ cc A hotel that has successfully recreated a colonial atmosphere with modern comforts. Big rooms with fireplaces; nos 29-37 have superb views over the "barrancos". Dormitory accommodation is possible in the big room near the swimming-pool for groups of 8-16 people. Swimming-pool on the terrace and jacuzzi.

🏛**Hotel Mayan Inn**, corner of 8a Calle and 3a Ave, ☎ 756 1176, Fax 756 1212 – 30rm 🛏 ♂ ✘ cc Chichicastenango's chic hotel, a veritable colonial museum hidden away in tropical vegetation. Over the years this lovely residence has been filled with decorative objects and furniture from all corners of Guatemala. The rooms are furnished with marquetry wardrobes, wooden chests and antique mirrors.

Nos 1-16 are in a calmer and more intimate second building on the other side of the street.

**EATING OUT, HAVING A DRINK**

Apart from the hotel restaurants, "Chichi" does not have a great choice of places to eat. To taste local cuisine, try the "comedores" in the centre of the market, but with caution.

*Under US$10*

**La Villa de los Cofrades**, corner of 7a Calle and 5a Ave, Parque Central (B1), ☎ 756 1122. 9am (7am on market days)-10pm; closed Monday afternoons and Tuesdays. A tiny dining room extended by a few tables under the arcades in front of the market. Soups, meats, vegetables and salads at low prices. Excellent expresso coffee. Customers are much solicited by the shoeshiners and souvenir sellers. A second restaurant of the same name has opened 50m further down on the corner of 5a Ave and 6a Calle. Its first floor balcony overlooks the street buzzing with activity.

**Restaurante La Fonda Tzijolaj**, Centro Comercial Santo Tomás, Parque Central (B1). 7.30am-9pm; closed Tuesdays. North of Parque Central; you can watch the market from its first floor. Acceptable cuisine at reasonable prices.

**Restaurante La Parrilla**, 10a Calle 5-08 (B2), ☎ 756 1321. 9am-11pm. Rustic decor for a restaurant specialising in grilled meats at low prices. The place is pleasant and calm but the cuisine is sometimes disappointing. Home deliveries.

**GOING OUT**

**Concerts** – Marimba concerts in the patio of the Mayan Inn hotel.

**SHOPPING GUIDE**

**Arts and crafts** – Chichicastenango market is one of the most touristy in Guatemala. Textiles, souvenirs, wooden masks, jewellery etc, at slightly higher prices than in the rest of the country. Be ready for some hard bargaining.

# QUETZALTENANGO★★
## (XELA)
Capital of Quetzaltenango department
2nd largest town in the country – Pop approx 125 000
200km from Guatemala City by CA1
Alt 2 333m – Cold at nights – See maps p 136 and p 187

**Not to be missed**
Hot chocolate and home-made pastries at La Luna café.
A day at Fuentes Georginas.
The church of San Andrés Xecul.
The Friday market at San Francisco El Alto.

**And remember...**
Take warm clothes for the evenings.
The region's markets start early.
Book a hotel in advance for the Feria Centroamericana
12-18 September.

The built-up area of Quetzaltenango spreads out over a plain surrounded by hills and mountains, guarded by the **Siete Orejas** (3 370m), **Santa María** (3 772m), **Zunil** (3 533m) and **Santo Tomás** (3 505m) volcanoes. Located in the heart of the Altiplano, it offers an infinite choice of visits and walks in a region of enchanting villages, markets and landscapes. Apart from its setting, the town itself makes a pleasant halt with its mixture of urban rhythms and good-natured provincial simplicity.

Until it was struck by natural disaster, this "city of stars", birthplace of a large number of artists, was for many years the cultural and commercial rival of Guatemala City. From this golden past Quetzaltenango has conserved some Neoclassical buildings of daring proportions, and above its now-buried dreams of grandeur other projects have arisen. Over the last few years the town has made itself an excellent reputation as a centre for Spanish language teaching, in competition with Antigua; a new challenge that the *Quetzaltecos* are ready to take up with the same energy that they have shown throughout their history.

## Under the sign of the quetzal
When it came under Quiché domination in the 14C, this former Mam city was baptised **Xelajú** ("under the ten" – probably a reference to the hills surrounding the town), a name still used in its shortened form of Xela (pronounced "Shayla"). Once conquered by the Spanish in 1524, it was renamed Quetzaltenango (place of the quetzal) by the Mexican allies of Pedro de Alvarado, apparently inspired by the head-dresses of quetzal feathers worn by the Quiché lords and their leader **Tecún Umán**. This great warrior, who lost his life in single-handed combat against Pedro de Alvarado a few kilometres from the town, is immortalised at the entrance to Xela in a bronze statue by artist Rodolfo Galeotti Torres.

**The wind of independence** – Quetzaltenango is indeed a very apt name; if the national bird symbolises autonomy and independence, in the course of its history the town has also proved it has a fierce desire for freedom.

The Highlands

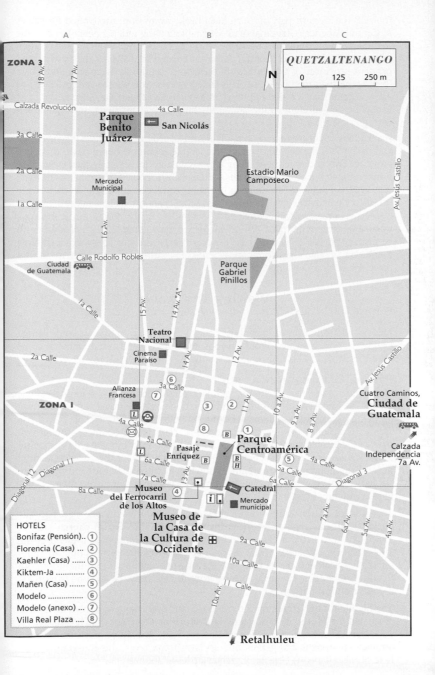

N

0    125    250 m

ZONA 3

18 Av.
17 Av.

Calzada Revolución

4a Calle

Parque
Benito
Juárez

San Nicolás

3a Calle

2a Calle

1a Calle

Mercado
Municipal

16 Av.

Estadio Mario
Camposeco

Av. Jesús Castillo

Calle Rodolfo Robles

Ciudad
de Guatemala

Parque
Gabriel
Pinillos

1a Calle

1a Calle

15 Av.

14 Av. "A"

Teatro
Nacional

2a Calle

Cinema
Paraíso

14 Av.

12 Av.

Av. Jesús Castillo

ZONA I

Alianza
Francesa

3a Calle

⑥

⑦

③

②

11 Av.

10 a Av.

9 a Av.

8 a Av.

Cuatro Caminos,
Ciudad de
Guatemala

4a
Calle

L

⑧

B

①

Parque
Centroamérica

Calzada
Independencia
7a Av.

5a Calle

L

Pasaje
Enríquez

B

B
H

⑤

4a Calle

6a Calle

13 Av.

7a Calle

Diagonal 12

Diagonal 11

8a Calle

Museo
del Ferrocarril
de los Altos

④

i

Catedral

Mercado
municipal

6a Calle

Diagonal 3

7a Av.

6a Av.

5a Av.

4a Av.

Museo de
la Casa de
la Cultura de
Occidente

9a Calle

10a Calle

10a Av.

11 Calle

HOTELS

Bonifaz (Pensión).. ①
Florencia (Casa) ... ②
Kaehler (Casa) ...... ③
Kiktem-Ja ............. ④
Mañen (Casa) ....... ⑤
Modelo ................ ⑥
Modelo (anexo) ... ⑦
Villa Real Plaza .... ⑧

Retalhuleu

In 1828 the western part of Guatemala broke away from the United Provinces of Central America (Guatemala's new name following independence) to become the independent **State of Los Altos** with Quetzaltenango as its capital. It then joined the Federation of Central America, created in 1824 by the newly independent provinces of Guatemala, El Salvador, Honduras, Nicaragua and Costa Rica, as the sixth member state. This independence was short-lived: in 1840 Los Altos became part of the Republic of Guatemala. Quetzaltenango's separatist ideas re-emerged eight years later, but the people's uprisings were put down with great severity.

**Aspirations countered by nature** – The land all around Quetzaltenango is fertile, and in the 19C the city enjoyed a considerable economic boom based on coffee growing. This dynamic, flourishing city became an increasingly dangerous rival for the capital, but on two occasions natural catastrophes were to alter its destiny. The **1902 earthquake** left nothing but ruins in its wake, putting an end to any threat to Guatemala City. The town was rebuilt, and in 1930 a railway line was opened between Quetzaltenango and Retalhuleu (Pacific coast). But following a **hurricane** three years later, President Jorge Ubico ordered this railway line to be dismantled (*see below "Museo del Ferrocarril de Los Altos"*). This was a fatal blow to Quetzaltenango's economic prosperity, relegating it henceforth to second place, far behind Guatemala City.

# Visiting the town
*Allow half a day.*

Xela is relatively spread out, but Zone 1, the town centre around Parque Centroamérica, is easily toured on foot. Most hotels and restaurants are to be found less than 500m from the main square.

## Parque Centroamérica★ (B3)
The main square bears witness to Xela's prestigious past – a long rectangle framed by Neoclassical buildings and imitation Greek temples with colonnades topped by Corinthian capitals. The public buildings – Town Hall, Casa de la Cultura and Banco de Occidente, the oldest bank in the country – are all vestiges of Quetzaltenango's former cultural and economic influence. In the centre of the square a raised **public garden★** provides benches for the population amid flower beds, columns and fountains. But when night falls the mist and cold chase strollers away, leaving the grey buildings of volcanic stone sole masters of a ghostly square.

To the right of the long Town Hotel (*Ayuntamiento*) colonnade is a Baroque **façade★★**, all that remains of the former **Espíritu Santo parish church** built in 1535. The rest of the building succumbed to an earthquake at the end of the 19C. The new **cathedral of the diocese of Los Altos** (B3-B4) was built in 1899, set slightly back and out of line with the original building. From the front both façades can be seen, but approaching from the left only the old one is visible – a perfect optical illusion!

The big building overlooking the southern part of the square houses the tourist office and the **Museo de la Casa de la Cultura de Occidente★** (B4) (*8am-12noon / 2pm-6pm; Saturdays 9am-1pm; closed Sundays. Fee*). Just like a dusty attic where remnants of epochs and genres pile up layer upon layer, this museum holds a host of miscellaneous objects of greater or lesser interest.

*The Highlands*

The cheerful façade of the church of San Andrés Xecul

The ground floor of the building houses archive documents on the history of Quetzaltenango, photos of the town and sports trophies. In the room devoted to music a marimba sits enthroned amid dance masks and wind instruments. On the first floor, cramped display cabinets exhibit finds from archeological digs, including a very lovely Late Classic **censer**. You can then examine the national flag in detail and end the visit in the small natural history section with its stuffed animals, herbaria and collection of fizzy drinks bottles!

In 7a Calle, near INGUAT, the **Museo del Ferrocarril de Los Altos** (Los Altos Railway Museum) (B3) *(8am-12noon / 2pm-6pm; closed weekends. Fee)* recounts the brief history of the railway line between Quetzaltenango and Retalhuleu. A series of photos shows the titanic work undertaken through the region's rough terrain in order to lay the tracks, the inauguration of the line on 30 March 1930 and its destruction by a hurricane three years later.

To the northwest of Parque Centroamérica, **Pasaje Enríquez**★ (B3) is no more than a shadow of the elegant shopping arcade built in 1900 in a style reminiscent of the Parisian arcades. An evocative example of Xela's past splendours, but the dilapidated metal structures and glass roof could well do with some renovation.

## Leaving Parque Centroamérica
Although the main square itself holds most of the monuments of interest, it is nevertheless pleasant to explore the whole of this city, which is considerably less hectic than the capital.

*Proceed to 14 Ave, 2 blocks west of Parque Centroamérica, and go up this street to 1a Calle.*

**The Teatro Nacional** (B3) occupies an imposing building in the same Neoclassical style as the town's other public buildings. Inaugurated in 1895, the theatre seats an audience of around 2 000 (it is presently being renovated). It is a venue for many cultural events during the annual **Feria Centroamericana de la Independencia**, 12-18 September, and it is here that the **Juegos Florales de Centroamérica** (Central American Floral Games) awards for literature, theatre and poetry are presented.

*Continue 2 blocks west on 1a Calle then turn right into 15 Ave.*

Street vendors and open-air stalls line 15 Avenida in serried ranks in the vicinity of **Parque Benito Juárez\*** (A1). Better known as **Parque La Democracia**, this tree-shaded square is one of the most pleasant in the town. Exuding provincial nonchalance, it would be an agreeable place to pause a while if it were not for the dense traffic on Calzada de la Revolución running along its north side. East of the square stands the **church of San Nicolás** (B1) with its eye-catching Neo-Gothic architecture.

2km west of Parque Benito Juárez, at the end of Calzada de la Revolución, appears, somewhat unexpectedly, the **Templo de Minerva**, a large Neoclassical temple dedicated to the Roman goddess of literature and the arts. The crossroads at the foot of this building is one of the city's nerve centres, as both a big market and the bus station are to be found here.

Returning to the city centre, Diagonal 3 leads eastwards to **Cerro El Baúl**. The **belvedere\*\*** at the top of this hill looks out over the entire city and its surroundings. *(NB, ask advice at the tourist office first, as they strongly discourage this excursion because of the risk of mugging.)*

# The villages around Quetzaltenango
*Allow 2 days using Quetzaltenango as a base.*
*See map p 187.*

A week is the ideal length of time to spend in Quetzaltenango to explore its region thoroughly. This means you can discover each village on market day *(see box)* and combine the visit with walks in the surrounding area. This tour to the northeast goes through **Cuatro Caminos**, an important road junction 13km from Quetzaltenango where the Pan-American Highway and the roads to Huehuetenango and Totonicapán meet.

---

## Market days
All the villages around Quetzaltenango have a weekly market day (some have two)

| | |
|---|---|
| Monday | **Zunil** |
| Tuesday | San Miguel Totonicapán, Salcajá |
| Wednesday | Momostenango |
| Thursday | San Andrés Xecul |
| Friday | **San Francisco El Alto** |
| Saturday | Almolonga, **San Miguel Totonicapán** |
| Sunday | **Momostenango**, San Cristóbal Totonicapán |

The Highlands

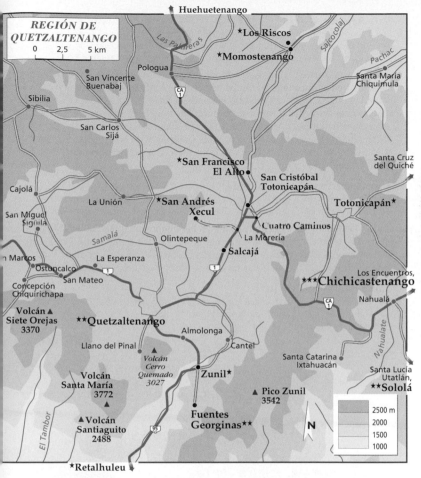

REGIÓN DE QUETZALTENANGO
0   2,5   5 km

## Salcajá

*7km from Xela on the road to Cuatro Caminos.* This is one of the major weaving centres in the region, as indicated by the numerous workshops where the men can be seen concentrated on their *telares de pie* (foot looms). It is also worth visiting the **church of San Jacinto★**, said to be the oldest in the country. Outside its opening hours *(Saturdays 6.30-9am)* the key is held at the green-painted grocery shop on the opposite side of the square.

## Jaspe

All along the roadside from Xela to Cuatro Caminos you can see cotton yarn stretched out for dozens of metres between stakes. This yarn is then tied in numerous places before being plunged into vats of dye. Once untied, the knots reveal undyed bits of yarn which, depending on how they are introduced into the loom, enable weavers to create a variety of motifs. This jaspé process – similar to Indonesian ikat – is used to make the "cortes" (skirts) that can been seen in the region.

### San Andrés Xecul★

*At La Morería crossroads, 5km from Salcajá on the way to Cuatro Caminos, a queue forms in the vicinity of the Esso petrol station; from here, buses covered in a thick crust of dirt tackle the 4km of dusty, bumpy dirt track leading to San Andrés Xecul.*

On the main square of this village stands the most unusual **church** in Guatemala, its bright yellow **façade**★★ crammed with naive motifs, both painted and carved, depicting angels, fruit, animals and garlands of flowers. The colour of the façade used to change regularly but that tradition has now been broken and the inhabitants have definitively opted for yellow. The alleyways that climb up to the top of the village lead to the **calvario**, a small building with colours and motifs that reflect those of the church. From in front there is a vast **panorama**★★ over San Andrés Xecul and its region.

### San Cristóbal Totonicapán

*Returning to the main road, continue to Cuatro Caminos crossroads and turn left towards Huehuetenango. 1km further on, San Cristóbal Totonicapán appears on the left.*

Here a gigantic 17C **church**★ rises above the adobe cottages. The nave, its generous proportions emphasised by a ceiling shaped like a ship's hull, holds some fine gilt wood altarpieces as well as a sumptuous Baroque silver altar. Walking around the village, the men can be seen working their *telares de pie* as in Salcajá.

### San Francisco El Alto★

*Further down the road to Huehuetenango, 1km beyond San Cristóbal Totonicapán, take the road on the right to San Francisco El Alto,
perched at an altitude of 2 610m.*

The Highlands

R. Marca

Momostenango,
in the heart of the Altiplano

Queues of buses and cars are reduced to a walking pace in the vicinity of the village every Friday, which is **market day★★★**; this is the largest market in the region and definitely one of the most fascinating in all Guatemala. Processions of buyers climb the steep alleys, glancing furtively at the goods spread out on the pavements, before all diving down one street into an incredible crush of people *(NB, San Francisco El Alto also has a reputation for pickpockets)*. The crowd sweeps you along into the main square, which is entirely covered with stalls. The arcades of the buildings are hung with *jaspe*, forming a predominantly blueish decor, with the white church standing out in the centre. From the roof of this building there is a bird's-eye **view★★** over the village and its surroundings. One block to the left behind the church is the access to the **livestock market★** esplanade, where buyers and sellers haggle amid a concert of mooing, bleating and cackling.

## Momostenango★

*15km north of San Francisco El Alto.* The road that climbs north reveals an exceptional **panorama★★** over San Francisco El Alto, then goes through a pine forest before descending to Momostenango (place of the altars).

On **market★** days, especially Sundays, the stalls display thick **chamarras**, the wool blankets that have given the village its reputation. Apart from the weaving of woollen fabric, the prestige of this Quiché locality resides in its profound respect for traditional rites. Mayan priests are numerous here and the surrounding hills shelter many a little altar (hence the name of the village) to which the Mayans come on the first day of the *tzolkin* (260-day Mayan calendar round). But unlike other ceremonial centres, here the rites tend to be celebrated away from curious eyes.

On the outskirts of the village, about 1km north by 2a Calle, you come to the foot of **Los Riscos★**; these stalagmite-like volcanic rock formations are now increasingly threatened by erosion.

### Totonicapán★

*Returning to Cuatro Caminos crossroads, the road east continues 12km to Totonicapán (not to be confused with San Cristóbal Totonicapán).*

The capital of Totonicapán department – also called **San Miguel Totonicapán** – is an important handicrafts centre. Most of the houses have a pottery, weaving, silversmithing or cabinet-making workshop. *(The Casa de la Cultura Totonicapense, 8a Ave 2-17, Zone 1, supplies a list of around sixty workshops in town).* To get an idea of what is produced in the area, it is best to visit "Toto" on **market★** days, especially Saturdays. On the main square a sculpture by Rodolfo Galeotti Torres pays tribute to **Atanasio Tzul**, the Mayan mayor who led an uprising against the colonial authorities in 1820. He was named king of the Quiché and ruled for 29 days before being imprisoned.

**Around Quetzaltenango**

# South of Quetzaltenango

Dotted at intervals along the road to Retalhuleu via the village of Almolonga are public baths fed by volcanic hot springs. This tour goes through a narrow valley flanked by carefully cultivated mountain slopes.

## Zunil★

*9km south of Xela.* The village nestles right at the foot of a volcano, just as its inhabitants wrap themselves in their big brightly-coloured shawls to keep out the cold. A colourful **market**★★ is held on Mondays in the church square but the immense wholesale warehouse at the entrance to the village is also worth visiting. In this building with its floor strewn with bales of flowers, cabbages and onions, the mauve splashes of the *huipiles* blend into the half-light, shrouding the place in a mysterious atmosphere in which transactions are made in hushed voices. Zunil is also one of the rare places in Guatemala where the inhabitants worship the cult of **Maximón** (*see p* 67), a saint whose "house" can be recognised by the smoke rising from it. In the centre of a room filled with offerings, alcohol fumes and incense smoke, the faithful come in droves to consult a figure dressed in European clothes, its face hidden behind sunglasses.

## Las Fuentes Georginas★★

*Pick-ups are the only means of transport to cover the 9km to the most attractive hot springs in the region; they wait in front of Zunil church.*

The road, which should soon be surfaced, goes through hills patchworked with small fields before arriving at a little health resort nestling in luxuriant tropical vegetation. A soothing landscape, sunny in the mornings, misty in the after-

Cultivated hillsides in the Totonicapán region

R. Tixador/TOP

noons and clear at night, in which bathers can swim a few lazy strokes or doze against the rocky walls, whatever the weather. The best idea is to spend the night there (*see p* 194) and enjoy the tranquillity of the place in the early morning or late evening. It is also possible to go walking along the paths that criss-cross the surrounding hills.

## Climbing the Santa María volcano

*The path starts from Llanos del Pinal, a village approximately 10km south of Xela.*

Of all the volcanoes encircling Quetzaltenango, the perfect cone of Santa María (3 772m) is the most impressive. From the top there is not only a fine view over the entire region but also a close-up of **Santiaguito** (2 488m), the second volcano that sprang from its slopes in 1902. The wreaths of smoke rising from its smoke-hole are obvious proof that it is permanently active and may therefore be dangerous, so it is advisable to hire specialist guides for this taxing excursion, which takes 5hr from **Llano del Pinal** (*see "Making the most of" section*).

**Around Quetzaltenango**

# Making the most of Quetzaltenango

**The Highlands**

## COMING AND GOING

**By bus** – At the end of Calzada Revolución (Zone 3), near the Minerva temple, lines of buses set off down a bumpy, dusty dirt road that starts on 27a Ave. To walk to **Terminal Minerva** (direction A1), cut through the market by following the sound of horns being blown. Practically all the buses also stop at **La Rotonda** (direction C3), at the intersection of 7a Ave (Calzada Independencia) and 8a Calle, Zone 2, in the east of the city. Several direct buses a day between Quetzaltenango and Guatemala City (4hr), Panajachel (3hr) and Chichicastenango (3hr30min), or change at Los Encuentros. Buses every hour for Huehuetenango (2hr), Retalhuleu (1hr), San Marcos (90min) and the Mexican border via Tecún Umán (3hr) or La Mesilla (4hr). First class buses to Guatemala City leave 4 times a day from **Transportes Autopulman Galgos** (A2), Calle Rodolfo Robles 17-43, Zone 1, ☎ 761 2248 and **Transportes Líneas América**, 7a Ave 3-33, Zone 2, ☎ 761 2063. If there are no direct buses for towns to the north and east of Quetzaltenango, change at Los Encuentros. Buses every 30min for Totonicapán (1hr), San Cristóbal Totonicapán (20min), Salcajá (15min) and Zunil (15min), every hour for San Francisco El Alto (45min) and every 2 hours for Momostenango (75min) and San Andrés Xecul (35min). Otherwise change at Cuatro Caminos, an important junction on the Pan-American Highway, 13km north-east of Quetzaltenango.

**By pick-up** – When the bus services finish, the pick-ups parked around the markets and bus stations sometimes take over to ensure transport for latecomers. Same tariffs as the buses.

## GETTING AROUND

With the exception of the bus station everything is within a radius of 500m from Parque Centroamérica. When staying in the centre there is therefore no need to use public transport.

**By bus** – The Santa Fé town buses crisscross the city. It is not easy to spot bus stops or to identify destinations but the locals are helpful. Nos 2 and 6 run between Terminal Minerva and Parque Centroamérica.

**By taxi** – Taxis wait on Parque Centroamérica, in front of the cathedral and outside Banco de Occidente. **Taxis Catedral Quetzaltenango**, ☎ 761 8472. **Taxis Unión**, ☎ 761 4747.

**By rental car** – Tabarini, 9a Calle 9-21, Zone 1, ☎ 763 0418.

**By rental bike** – Information from **Xela sin Límites** travel agency, 12a Ave C-35, Zone 1, ☎ 763 0692.

## ADDRESS BOOK

**Tourist information – INGUAT** (B4), 7a Calle 11-35, Zone 1, on the southwest corner of Parque Centroamérica. 8am-12noon / 1pm-4.30pm; closed Saturday afternoons and Sundays, ☎ 761 4931. A lot of tourist information posted at the entrance to Salon Tecún (see "Eating out") and in the language schools. Information in French at **Casa Iximulew**, corner of 15 Ave and 5a Calle, Zone 1 (headquarters of INEPAS language school).

**Bank / Currency Exchange** – Most of the banks, concentrated around Parque Centroamérica, have the same opening hours: 9am-6pm; closed Saturday afternoons and Sundays. **Banco de Occidente** (B3), 4a Calle 11-38, Zone 1, ☎ 761 2378. Changes Thomas Cook traveller's cheques. **Banco Industrial** (B3), corner of 11 Ave and 5a Calle, Palacio Municipal, Zone 1, ☎ 761 2258. Cashpoint for Visa cards. **Banco del Café** (B3), 12 Ave 5-50, Zone 1, ☎ 761 2652.

**Post office / Telephone** – The main post office (A3) is just opposite **TELGUA** (B3), on the corner of 4a Calle and 15 Ave, Zone 1 (1st floor for telephoning or sending faxes). Other firms provide identical services including Internet access at much better prices. **Maya Communications**, Parque Centroamérica, Zone 1, on the 1st floor of Salon Tecún. 9am-7pm. **C@fé.net**, 14 Ave 4-52, Zone 1, ☏ 761 2717.

**Medical service – Hospital San Rafael** (B4), 9a Calle 10-41, Zone 1, ☏ 761 4414. **Hospital Privado Quetzaltenango**, Calle Rodolfo Robles 23-51, Zone 1, ☏ 761 4381.

**Safety –** No Policía de Turismo in Quetzaltenango but INGUAT supplies last-minute information on places to avoid for safety reasons.

**Language schools –** Quetzaltenango's language schools have a good reputation. A list of them is available from IN-GUAT. **INEPAS**, corner of 15 Ave and 5a Calle, Zone 1, ☏ 765 1308 Fax 765 2584, is run by a French-Guatemalan couple. **Proyecto Lingüístico Quetzalteco de Español**, 5a Calle 2-40, Zone 1, ☏ 763 1061. **Utatlán**, 12 Ave 4-32, Pasaje Enríquez, Zone 1, ☏ 763 0446.

**Laundry – Lavandería Minimax**, 14 Ave C-47, on the right of the Teatro Nacional. 7.30am-7.30pm; closed Sundays.

### WHERE TO STAY

Quetzaltenango offers a wide range of accommodation: lots of little guesthouses in the town centre (more or less recommendable) plus some good hotels, but also accommodation with locals through homestay formulas proposed by language schools, and rental apartments (information from INEPAS, see above).

• **City centre**

*Under US$10*

**Casa Kaehler**, 13 Ave 3-33, Zone 1, ☏ 761 2091 – 7rm. About 50m from the big Elektra household appliances shop. Sunbathing on loungers outside the rooms or in the small courtyard. Modest rooms but quite large. Only n° 7 has its own bathroom. Very warm welcome.

*Around US$25*

**Hotel Kiktem-Ja**, Edificio Fuentes, 13 Ave 7-18, Zone 1, ☏ 761 4304, Fax 761 2667 – 20rm ⌂ A lovely building set around a central courtyard with car parking. Rooms are of unequal

quality: some darker than others, some with fireplaces and others without, some noisier than others. Nos 4, 6 and 11 have fireplaces and balconies on the street side (noisy). Nos 16, 17 and 18 are light and quiet.

**Anexo Hotel Modelo**, 14 Ave A 3-22, Zone 1, ☏ 765 1271 – 9rm ⌂ TV ✗ CC This small hotel gives the best value for money in town. Comfortable rooms, all very clean. Nos 31, 32 and 33 are the lightest but are on the street side. This annex shares the reception desk and restaurant of Hotel Modelo, located about 50m away in the same street (see below).

*Around US$30*

**Hotel Casa Florencia**, 12 Ave 3-61, Zone 1, ☏ 761 2326 – 9rm ⌂ TV CC Despite efforts to make the place attractive (carpeted rooms, plants in the entrance) this hotel is starting to look a bit jaded.

**Hotel Modelo**, 14 Ave A 2-31, Zone 1, ☏ 761 2529 / 763 0216, Fax 763 1376 – 20rm ⌂ ℘ TV ✗ CC Founded in 1892, this hotel has a somewhat old-fashioned colonial ambience. Rooms are more expensive but bigger than in the annex (some have fireplaces). A large business clientele.

*US$50-60*

**Hotel Villa Real Plaza**, 4a Calle 12-22, Zone 1, ☏ 761 4045, Fax 761 6780 – 59rm ⌂ ℘ TV ✗ CC A lovely hotel that has lost its former sparkle. A choice between big rooms on the street (noisy) or on the inside (dark). Rather expensive for what is provided.

**Casa Mañen**, 9a Ave 4-11, Zone 1, ☏ 765 0786 – 9rm ⌂ TV CC Although opened only recently this place already has character. Rooms furnished with considerable taste and every comfort. Delightful suite with mezzanine and fireplace at an affordable price. Very intimate and welcoming.

**Hotel Pensión Bonifaz**, 4a Calle 10-50, Zone 1, ☏ 761 2182 / 761 2279, Fax 761 2850 – 74rm ⌂ ℘ TV ✗ ⌓ CC The most illustrious hotel in town, slightly back from Parque Centroamérica. A building with colonial el-

The Highlands

egance but rooms a little disappointing for the price. On the other hand, the covered swimming-pool, jacuzzi and view over the town from the top storey are well worth it.

• **Outside the town**
*Around US$30*
**Hotel del Campo**, km 224 Carretera a Cantel, ☎ 763 1663, Fax 763 0074 – 96rm ⚑ [TV] ✕ ⚒ [cc] 4km east of Quetzaltenango on the road to Cantel stands this modern, comfortable but not particularly attractive hotel. Apartments for groups of friends or families. It is best to have transport.

• **Fuentes Georginas**
*Under US$20*
**Turicentro Las Georginas**, Zunil – 9rm ⚑ ✕ ⚒ The setting is so pleasant that you can ignore the lack of comfort for one night. Basic three-bed rooms with toilet facilities that could be improved a lot. Bring warm clothing as the nights are damp despite a log fire. The hotel is overrun at weekends so arrive early in the morning or book in advance (by going there, as it is not on the telephone).

**EATING OUT**
*Under US$10*
Take-away food from the market near Parque Centroamérica and around Parque Benito Juárez.
🍴**Panificadora La Vienesa**, 9a Ave 5-26, Zone 1 (C3). 3.30pm-7pm; closed Sundays. For afternoon tea, Guatemalans meet up on the benches of this crowded little room over which floats a delicious smell of hot bread. Choose your pastries at the counter while awaiting the hot chocolate. No smoking.
**El Rincón de los Antojitos**, corner of 15 Ave and 5a Calle, Zone 1 (A3). 8am-8pm; closed weekends. A small restaurant on the right of Casa Iximulew (see "Tourist information"). Local cuisine and vegetarian dishes in an informal atmosphere. Excellent soups.
🍴**La Luna Café y Chocolate**, 8a Ave 4-11, Zone 1 (C3), ☎ 761 2242. 9am-9pm; weekends 4pm-9pm. In this fine colonial residence, reminiscent of a museum, you could spend hours simply chatting, reading or just daydreaming over a hot chocolate and the excellent home-made pastries.
**Diego Rivera Café**, 15 Ave 5-31, zone 1 (A3-B3). 8am-8pm; closed Sundays. This little patio with its bright colours is ideal for enjoying the early rays of the day's sun. On the menu: cereals, tarts, cakes, hamburgers and... books (see "Bookshops").
**Baviera's International Coffee Shop**, 5a Calle 13-14, Zone 1 (B3), ☎ 763 1855. 7am-9pm. The walls of this café recount the city's history through photos and old press cuttings. A fountain, plants and relaxing music to accompany a light meal or a copious breakfast. A second coffee shop is to open in the premises previously occupied by the Alliance Française, 14 Ave A A-80, Zone 1.
**Blue Ángel Video Café**, 7a Calle 15-22, Zone 1 (A3). 2pm-11.30pm. A friendly cafe where students of all nationalities come to revise their lessons, read or watch videos. A pleasant place to eat a salad or a sandwich or have a drink in the evening.
**Salon Tecún**, Pasaje Enríquez, Parque Central, Zone 1 (B3). 8am-12midnight. Ideal for a little snack (not too) late at night and to meet travellers from all over the world. Wooden tables, yellowing walls decorated with traditional costumes and, most important, a big terrace on Pasaje Enríquez. Snacks, Italian specialities and very good expresso.
*Around US$15*
**Pizza Cardinali**, 14 Ave 3-41, Zone 1 (B3). 11.30am-10pm. Italian colours, tourist posters and neon lighting; an unexceptional dining room, but the lively atmosphere and warm welcome make up for it. Acceptable cuisine in generous servings.
**Royal París**, 14 Ave A 3-06, Zone 1 (B3). 10am-11pm; closed Mondays. French restaurant on the first floor of the shopping arcade. Very kitsch decor of mauve ceilings and orangey walls with gilt lacquer furniture and bar stools covered in fake fur. Very good brasserie-type cuisine. Live music on Friday evenings.

## GOING OUT, HAVING A DRINK

**Bars / Concerts** – The places under US$10 listed in the "Eating out" section are all equally pleasant places to have a drink.

**Los Chocoyos**, 7a Calle 15-20, Zone 1. 10am-12midnight. This open-air bar on the left of the Blue Ángel Video Café puts on barbecue evenings and concerts.

**Casa Verde**, 12 Ave 1-40, Zone 1, ☎ 763 0271. 4pm-12midnight; closed Sundays. A variety of cultural activities take place in this bar (concerts, plays, poetry readings).

## OTHER THINGS TO DO

**Excursions** – Thierry Roquet, the French director of **INEPAS** (see "Language schools") organises expeditions to the volcanoes and excursions around Quetzaltenango.

**Viajes SAB** agency, 1a Calle 12-35, Zone 1, ☎ 761 6402, also runs excursions in the region.

**Theatre** – The programme can be obtained direct from the **Teatro Municipal**, 1a Calle between 14 Ave A and 14 Ave, Zone 1.

**Cinema** – Videos in English or Spanish at **Cinema Paraíso**, 14 Ave A 1-04, Zone 1. Times are advertised in the language schools and at Salon Tecún. **Blue Ángel Video Café** 7a Calle 15-22, Zone 1.

**Alliance Française** (A3), 15 Ave 3-64, Zone 1, ☎ 761 4076. French films shown on Thursdays.

## SHOPPING GUIDE

**Arts and Crafts** – Quetzaltenango does not have a great choice of handicrafts in comparison with the surrounding villages. It is best to take advantage of excursions to buy textiles at Zunil cooperative or San Francisco El Alto market. The Momostenango area is a centre for the production of lovely colourful woollen blankets that can be seen all over the country.

**Bookshops – Frida Kahlo** (A3-B3), 15 Ave 5-31, Zone 1. 9am-1pm / 3pm-7pm. In the same building as the Diego Rivera Café. Books in Spanish and English.

**Vrisa** (A3), on the left of the Alliance Française. Lots of second-hand books in English.

# THE CUCHUMATANES★★
2-day tour – See map p 136

**Not to be missed**
Sunrise over the Cordillera de los Cuchumatanes.
The Saturday market in Todos Santos Cuchumatán.

**And remember...**
If you are not worried about comfort, spend the night in Todos Santos.
Hire a car to explore the Cuchumatanes region, as buses are scarce.
Take warm clothes for the mountains.
Check safety conditions in the region with your embassy.

The rugged slopes of the Cuchumatanes, Central America's highest non-volcanic mountains culminating at 3 837m, spread over the north of the department as far as the Verapaces (Cobán region) like an emerald-green cloth crumpled in anger. Discovering this vast and beautiful region is far from relaxing; access is difficult and its slopes are extremely precipitous, with a glance at the relief map in the main square of "Huehue" enough to convince anyone. But the majesty of the landscapes you pass through is ample reward for the inconveniences of the journey.

Here, closer to the heavens, far away from colonial power, the indigenous communities just about managed to preserve their pre-Columbian traditions in the face of Christianisation. However, in the 1970s the Cuchumatanes, especially around the Ixil triangle (El Quiché department), were among the most vigorous

On the way to Todos Santos

F. Dyan

The Highlands

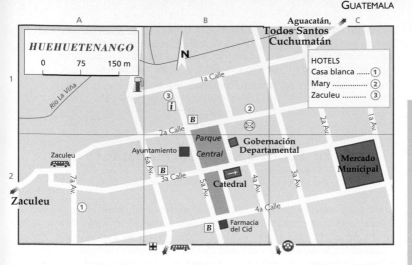

The Cuchumatanes

hotbeds of guerrilla activity, which brought savage repression by the army: torched villages, torture, kidnappings, massacres, populations displaced into "model villages", exodus to Mexico – such was the sinister daily lot of the inhabitants right up to the peace accords of 1996 (*see p 43*). This region, so severely traumatised by the war, is now relatively tranquil once again, although isolated acts of violence still take place from time to time.

# Huehuetenango
*Allow 3hr to visit, including Zaculeu.*

"Huehue", the department capital, sits 1 900m above sea-level. The last major town before the Mexican border and the link between the Cuchumatanes hamlets and the rest of the country, it is the archetypal staging post. Although it has no particular attractions apart from its lively daily **market**, its tourist facilities make it an almost compulsory gateway to the "doors of heaven": the Cordillera de los Cuchumatanes.

## The Zaculeu archeological site★ (direction A2)
*To reach this site, located 4km west of the town centre, take a taxi or a bus (bus stop on the corner of 2a Calle and 7a Ave, Zone 1).*
*8am-6pm. Fee. Allow 1hr.*

This city, founded around 600 AD, only took the name of Zaculeu (white earth) in the 14C. Capital of the Mam people, it expanded considerably during the **Post-Classic** period, although this was interrupted by a few years of Quiché occupation in the 15C. It came back under Mam rule in 1475, but with the arrival of the Spanish fifty years later it experienced the same dire fate as the other Mayan cities. Despite having defences and a site protected by *barrancos* (ravines) and a river, Zaculeu was taken by the army of **Gonzalo de Alvarado**, one of Pedro's brothers, in 1525 after a four-month siege.
In 1946 the United Fruit Company provided the funds for restoration work. With its temples now abusively cemented, the ancient Mayan city disappoints most visitors. It has several Mexican-influenced pyramids surrounding a vast

central square. Climbing the stairway up to the top of the **main temple**, a single hallway with three openings, gives an excellent view over the entire archeological complex. In the centre of the esplanade the remains of platforms can be seen, probably used for sacrifices; to the east is the **ball court**.

**The museum** at the site entrance contains a few ceramic and jade items found during the excavations. It supplies some interesting details about Mayan daily life, their ceremonial practices and funerary rites.

# From Huehuetenango
# to Todos Santos Cuchumatán★★

*43km – Allow 90min by car and 2hr30min by bus.*
*Journey times are almost twice as long by bus as by car.*

In the early morning the clear skies and first rays of sunshine bathe the countryside in an extraordinary light. Leave before daybreak to watch dawn rising on the mountains and make the most of the market in Todos Santos. Peaks wreathed in cloud, hillsides caressed by the sun, plateaux whipped by glacial winds – violent and spectacular landscapes rise out of this rugged and irregular land that alternates between coniferous forests, rocky peaks, stretches of arid soil, pasture-lands dotted with sheep and hamlets nestling in fertile, isolated valleys.

6km northeast of "Huehue" the road goes through the village of **Chiantla**, which shelters a real treasure in its church: the **Virgen de la Candelaría**, reputed for her miraculous powers of healing. This statuette of the Virgin, clothed in a long mantle of repoussé silver from the region's mines, is said to be the work of sculptor Quirio Cataño. Since the 17C it has made Chiantla a place of pilgrimage; every year on **2 February★★** the faithful arrive in crowds to give thanks to the miraculous Virgin.

*At Chiantla, take the road that climbs northward up into the Cordillera de los Cuchumatanes towards Todos Santos.*

10km north of Chiantla on the left side of the road is a **belvedere** with 9 stelae, each bearing a verse of *A Los Cuchumatanes*, the poem by Juan Diegues Olaverri in homage to this magnificent region. In clear weather the **panorama★★★** stretches as far as the volcanoes around Quetzaltenango *(stop on the way out, as the weather tends to cloud over in the afternoons).*

The road continues to climb, for about 2km, up to a high plateau swept by gusts of wind and covered in frost in winter. This arid **landscape★★** stretches for some ten kilometres, with only a few cactus hedges to break the monotony of rocks and close-cropped vegetation; but as daylight breaks, when dawn floods the countryside with its pink glints, this desolate place becomes magical.

*Halfway across this plateau the road forks (at the Acoduhe sign). Continue bearing left; the right fork leads along a difficult track to Barillas, a village about 120km away.*

On leaving the plateau, follow a bumpy track that runs for about 15km along the side of a gorge squeezed between two wooded massifs *(a 4WD is necessary during the rainy season).* Apart from some *camionetas*, few vehicles go down to Todos Santos.

R. Mattes

Marimba players in Todos Santos

**The Cuchumatanes**

■ **Todos Santos Cuchumatán**★★ – This Mam township sits in the heart of the mountains at an altitude of 2 540m. Its **market**★★ on Wednesdays and Saturdays does not claim to rival those of San Francisco El Alto or Sololá, but it is the only trading centre for a good many hamlets round about. The men of Todos Santos are easy to pick out in the crowd from the unequalled brilliance of their **traditional costume**★★★. They sport a shirt with a wide collar, richly embroidered in shades of pink, and red trousers with white stripes, over which is worn a black overgarment, a vestige of the *maxtatl* (loincloth) of pre-Columbian times. A small straw hat encircled by a band of studded fabric and a *morral* (bag) slung across the chest complete the outfit.

Faithful to their traditions, the villagers still use the *tzolkin*, the 260-day ritual calendar, and continue to practise their rites in the ruins of a pre-Hispanic ceremonial site to the south of Todos Santos. The Christian festivals of **Holy Week**★★ and **All Saints**★★★ are nevertheless not neglected.

The rest of the time this place is a haven of tranquillity – which is starting to attract increasing numbers of backpackers. The single alleyway lined with open shops can be rapidly explored, but the Cuchumatanes offer fine opportunities for horse riding or walking to isolated townships such as **San Juan Atitán** (*5hr walk*) or **Santiago Chimaltenango** (*6hr*).

**An astounding cavalcade**
All Saints' Day coincides with the patron saint's day of Todos Santos, and the resulting celebration is richly colourful and awash with alcohol. Every 1st November morning, with bodies and minds overheated from a long night of dancing, music and alcohol, the men stagger to the starting line of the great annual horse race. Arrayed in their finest clothes, the riders gallop headlong around a muddy track, stopping after each lap to swallow a few gulps of aguardiente or beer. The rare competitors who manage to stay on their mounts come out of this challenge haloed with immense social prestige.

**199**

# From Huehuetenango to the Ixil triangle★★

*80km – Approx 6hr by bus including changes.*

Travellers in a hurry and desirous of comfort should refrain from this trip across the Cuchumatanes from west to east (from "Huehue" to Cobán). Buses make very slow going along interminable dirt roads, every now and then passing a sign that proudly proclaims *"está llegando la luz"* ("electricity is coming"). From time to time the bus will stop in the middle of nowhere to let off a family weighed down with bundles, a little caravan that struggles off across the fields towards an isolated hamlet several kilometres away. *Camionetas* are rare and therefore overcrowded; moreover their timetables, and sometimes their routes, are unpredictable, so there is a real risk of getting stuck halfway!

*At Chiantla turn east along the Cuchumatanes for 18km.*

■ **Aguacatán** – Its **market**★, on Thursdays and Sundays, is known for its stalls of locally-grown garlic and onions.
Two kilometres beyond the village, in the same direction, is the **nacimiento del río San Juan**★ (source of the Río San Juan). This fast-flowing stream feeds a canal built around a little park. You could not call the place wild but it makes a refreshing halt.

*Continue east for 28km.*

■ **Sacapulas** –This Quiché village is spread out along the valley of the Río Chixoy. Since pre-Columbian times, Sacapulas has had two main livelihoods: extracting salt on the banks of its river, and silversmithing.

*At the junction of roads linking several regions, Sacapulas is of particular strategic importance. The village is located halfway between Huehuetenango and Santa Cruz del Quiché, from where it is easy to return to Chichicastenango and Lake Atitlán. Continuing east another 8km, you come to the El Entronque crossroads, from where the road to the right continues on to Cobán (122km) via Uspantán. NB, as there are no connections, it is impossible to make the journey by bus from "Huehue" to Cobán in a single day.*

*The left fork leads to Nebaj, after a slow 20km/2hr30min climb up a steep road that looks out over the entire mountain chain.*

■ **Nebaj**★ – This township has the most acceptable tourist amenities *(see "Making the most of Nebaj")* in the **Ixil triangle**, a linguistic area whose boundaries are marked by Nebaj and the villages of **San Juan Cotzal** *(17km from Nebaj)* and **Chajul** *(22km)*, both of which can be reached by bus *(timetables uncertain!)*.
Nebaj **market**★★ on Thursdays and Sundays provides an opportunity to admire the inhabitants' shimmering **traditional outfits**★★★, the most sumptuous in the region and perhaps in the whole country. Although the men's costumes are tending towards "Ladinoisation", the women are still magnificently clothed from head to toe. Over a bright garnet-red skirt they wear a *huipil* skilfully embroidered in shades of green, mauve, yellow, red and white. The distinguishing mark of the village women is above all their head-dress: a band of embroidered fabric elegantly tied around the head and terminating in voluminous tassels. It is hard to resist the women weavers' pressing invitations to take you to their homes to sell you fabrics.
Apart from its textiles, Nabaj has some lovely walks in its vicinity; the villagers are happy to point the way to the **waterfall**★, an hour's walk from the village on the road to Chajul.

# Making the most of Huehuetenango

## COMING AND GOING

**By bus** – The **Terminal de Buses** (direction B2) is located in Zone 4, 2km southwest of the town centre. Several buses a day run between Guatemala City and "Huehue" (5hr); departures every hour to Quetzaltenango (2hr) and one bus in the morning to Nebaj (5hr30min). Travelling to Cobán by the Transversal del Norte means changing several times (see p 211 "Making the most of Cobán"). For Panajachel or Chichicastenango, change at Los Encuentros (2hr). There are few buses for Todos Santos Cuchumatán, so check the timetable (the first leaves around 4.30am; 2hr30min journey) and arrive early, for they are often jam-packed. NB, buses for Zaculeu stop on the corner of 2a Calle and 7a Ave, Zone 1.

## GETTING AROUND

**By bus** – Regular town bus service between Parque Central and the bus station.

**By taxi** – Taxis wait on Parque Central, opposite the church and in front of the bus terminus. No meters; approx 10 quetzals from Parque Central to the bus station. Taxis Unidos, ☎ 764 2218.

**By rental car** – **Amigos Rent A Car**, 5a Ave 1-56, Zone 1, ☎ 764 2655. **Tabarini**, Sector Brasilia, Zone 7, ☎ 764 1951.

## ADDRESS BOOK

**Tourist information** – At the **Ixquil** handicrafts shop (B1), 5a Ave 1-56, on the left of the Hotel Zaculeu. Information given very sparingly.

**Bank / Currency Exchange** – Most of the banks are in Zone 1, near Parque Central. **Banco del Café**, 3a Calle 5-56. **Banco Agrícola Mercantil**, 4a Calle 5-70. **Banco G & T**, 2a Calle 4-66.

**Post office / Telephone** – The post office is in 2a Calle 3-54, opposite Hotel Mary. For telephone calls, **TELGUA** (direction C2), 4a Ave 6-54.

**Medical service** – **Farmacia del Cid**, 5a Ave 4-11, Zone 1, on Parque Central. 8.30am-12.30pm / 2pm-7.30pm. Acts as 24hr chemist; outside opening hours, ring at the first door to the left of the shop, on 4a Calle. In an emergency, **Hospital Nacional**, Aldea Las Lagunas, Zone 10, ☎ 764 1414.

**Consulate** – The Mexican consulate occupies the same premises as Farmacia del Cid.

## WHERE TO STAY

*Under US$15*

**Hotel Mary**, 2a Calle 3-52, Zone 1, ☎ 764 1618 – 32rm [TV] A modern building with small rooms, basic but clean; some have bathrooms. Most look onto the corridor and so suffer from lack of light.

*Around US$30*

**Hotel Zaculeu**, 5a Ave 1-14, Zone 1, ☎ 764 1086, Fax 764 1575 – 40rm 🍴 [TV] ✕ [CC] The patio is overgrown with dense vegetation. The rooms on the 1st floor have been renovated but are twice as expensive as those on the ground floor, which have a certain outdated charm. Avoid no 4 which is tiny.

**Hotel Casa Blanca**, 7a Ave 3-41, Zone 1, ☎ 764 2586 / 769 0777 – 15rm 🍴 [TV] ✕ [CC] A charming little building with spacious, comfortable rooms. This is Huehuetenango's top hotel, but it cannot be called luxurious.

## EATING OUT

*Under US$10*

**Restaurante Las Brasas**, corner of 4a Ave and 2a Calle, Zone 1 (**B1**). 9.15am-10pm. This rather dark but friendly restaurant is often crowded. Generous helpings of acceptable international and Asian cuisine.

**Restaurante Schibolet**, 5a Calle 5-60, Zone 1. 7am-10pm. Small, unpretentious eatery, but the quality of both reception and cuisine make up for its simplicity. Snacks (very good sandwiches) or meals (meat, shellfish).

**Restaurante Le Kaf**, 6a Calle 6-40, Zone 1. 11am-11pm; closed Tuesdays. Live music Thursdays to Sundays 7pm-10pm. A pizzeria with brick and wood walls and check tablecloths. Polite service, a lively atmosphere and the pizzas are good.

**La Fonda de Don Juan**, 2a Calle 5-34, Zone 1 (B1). 9.15am-10pm. The tables under the arcades on the patio are much more pleasant than those in the dining room. Italian and international specialities at reasonable prices.

### GOING OUT, HAVING A DRINK

**Bars – Mi Tierra Café**, 4a Calle 6-46, Zone 1. 7am-10pm; closed Mondays. At last, some real effort put into the decoration: brightly coloured walls, covered patio, plants, fountain. Well-off young Ladinos come to study or have a drink here. The café also serves meals (salads and international cuisine) and croissants for breakfast.

### SHOPPING GUIDE

**Arts and Crafts** –The **Ixquil** handicrafts shop (see "Tourist information") sells all sorts of fabrics and handicraft items. Wait until the villages of Todos Santos and Nebaj to buy fine traditional garments.

## Making the most of Todos Santos Cuchumatán

### ADDRESS BOOK

See "Making the most of Huehuetenango".

### WHERE TO STAY

*Under US$10*

**Casa Familiar**, 30m from Parque Central – 7rm ✕ The rooms sleep 1-6 persons. Shared showers with hot water.

Breakfast on the chalet terrace, facing the mountains, makes you forget the lack of comfort in this guest house.

### SHOPPING GUIDE

Shopping in the market or the shops in the main street: a vast choice of traditional men's costumes, new or secondhand.

## Making the most of Nebaj

### COMING AND GOING

**By bus** – The bus stop is on Parque Central opposite the church. 2 direct buses to Guatemala City (around 6am and 11pm). To get to Cobán by the Transversal del Norte means several changes and a night in Uspantán (see p 211 "Making the most of Cobán"). A few direct buses between Nebaj and Santa Cruz del Quiché (4hr30min) or Huehuetenango (6hr), otherwise change at Sacapulas. The best bet is to leave very early in the morning, as buses are not frequent in the afternoons in either direction.

### WHERE TO STAY

*Under US$10*

**Hotel Ixil**, corner of 5a Ave and 10 Calle, ☎ 755 1091 – 9rm. 4 blocks from Parque Central going towards Sacapulas. This house, set around a dilapidated patio, must have seen better days. The rooms, although basic, are very spacious and the welcome is friendly.

*Under US$15*

**Hotel Posada de Don Pablo**, 6a Ave 5-15, ☎ 755 1033 – 8rm. Opposite Comedor Irene, 1 block from Parque Central. Nebaj's most recent and most comfortable accommodation is func-

The Highlands

tional but totally lacking in charm. Very small rooms, extremely well kept, with new toilet facilities (private bathrooms in all the rooms but 2). It is presently being extended.

## EATING OUT
### Under US$10
**Restaurante Maya-Inca**, 5a Calle 1-90. 7am-9pm; 6pm on Sundays. 3 blocks from Parque Central, in the street running alongside the square (with the church on the right). Wooden benches and check table cloths in a restaurant as charming and welcoming as its Peruvian owner. He serves his country's specialities, in particular "papas rellenos" (stuffed potatoes).

**Comedor Irene**, 5a Calle. 7am-9pm. 1 block from Parque Central, this small, unpretentious restaurant serves good local cuisine in an authentic setting.

## SHOPPING GUIDE
**Arts and Crafts** – Hard to resist Nebaj's beautiful traditional costumes. "Huipiles" and skirts on sale on the stalls around Parque Central and in the neighbouring streets. The village women also invite tourists into their homes to sell them fabrics.

**Making the most of Nebaj**

Bargaining in Nebaj market

J.-L. Dugast/HOA QUI

# COBÁN★

Capital of Alta Verapaz department
214km north of Guatemala City
Alt 1 317m – humid subtropical climate
See maps (El Petén) and (Altiplano)

**Not to be missed**
The Cobán Folklore Festival.
A day at Semuc Champey.
Tasting kak-ik, a local turkey speciality.

**And remember...**
Take rainwear.
Book your hotel in advance for the Folklore Festival.
Join a guided tour to visit Semuc Champey.

Jeremiahs maintain it rains thirteen months a year in Cobán, and its very name means "cloudy place"! The *chipi chipi*, a drizzle with a name that sounds like raindrops falling on the road, is indeed an integral part of the landscape. Without it Cobán would be deprived of its verdant setting and nature would not be beating so forcefully at the gates of the town. Within this green vestment enveloped in silence, the only staccato sounds are those of the Kekchi language: Tactic, kak-ik, chipi chipi.

## War and peace

This region is unique in the history of the Conquest. After resisting Quiché incursions for a century, its population inflicted their first defeat on the Spaniards. Incapable of gaining control of Kekchi territory, in 1530 the Spanish gave up using armed force to try to conquer the area – which they baptised **Tezulutlán** (Land of War).

In 1537 the priest **Bartolomé de Las Casas**, who distinguished himself by his crusade in favour of the Amerindians *(see p 37)*, suggested a "gentle" colonisation. He obtained authorisation to Christianise the region peacefully – whence the name of *Verapaz* (true peace) that it later adopted. With the exception of Dominican missionaries, access to the region was forbidden to all Spaniards for five years. Bartolomé de Las Casas made a success of his "battle" by sending out Christianised Mayan traders to preach the Gospel in song. The local caciques let themselves be cajoled by these religious songs sung in their own language, and that is how the submission of the common people was obtained. Santo Domingo de Cobán, founded in 1543, was given the status of **Imperial City** by Charles V, a prestigious title that still greets visitors on their arrival.

## Coffee time

Cobán had its hour of glory in the second half of the 19C, thanks to major reforms carried out by **Justo Rufino Barrios**. After confiscating the clergy's property during the 1871 Revolution, the State put a call out for foreign investors and the region was colonised by Europeans, mostly **Germans**, who set about growing coffee – and cardamom – using indigenous labour on their plantations. Cut off from the rest of the country, Cobán enjoyed considerable economic prosperity at that time, sending its exports direct to Europe via the Río Polochic and the Río Dulce.

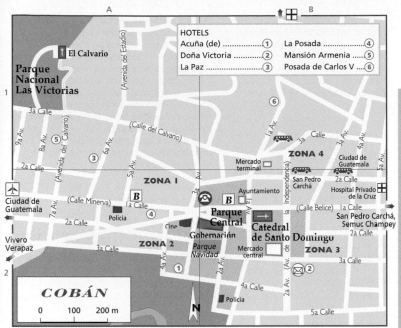

HOTELS
Acuña (de) ................①    La Posada ...................④
Doña Victoria ............②    Mansión Armenia .....⑤
La Paz ........................③    Posada de Carlos V ....⑥

*Cobán*

The Second World War dealt a severe blow to the region: support for Hitler's Germany from some of the immigrants led the United States to put pressure on Guatemala. Some were expelled, others sent as prisoners of war to the United States, and their lands were confiscated. Of their presence there now remain only a few surnames and some architectural vestiges.

*Most of the roads leading to Cobán are in a dubious state; the Cuchumatanes dirt road to the west and the one leading to El Petén to the east discourage a good number of travellers. For a fast and comfortable journey we recommend you take the surfaced road that goes through the Verapaces. Vehicles coming from the capital or Oriente should leave the Carretera al Atlántico (CA9) at El Rancho crossroads to follow this route to Cobán.*

## Visiting the town
*Allow 2hr.*

In the last week of July two elections take place: that of the *Rabin Ajau*, the most beautiful Amerindian girl in Guatemala, and that of the *Princesa Tezulutlán*, chosen from among the Kekchi women of the department. The **Festival Folklórico Nacional** follows this from 31 July to 6 August. During this fortnight of festivities, thousands of people can admire the superb traditional costumes and watch the many dance performances.

### Parque Central★ (B2)
This square is the hub of the town and the central point of the four zones that divide it up. When a ray of sunshine manages to pierce through the veil of mist, the *Cobaneros* invade the central garden, a long triangle scattered with flowerbeds,

turning it briefly into a buzzing hive of vendors and shoe-shiners. At the first drops of rain, everyone disappears into thin air, leaving the square to its bookshops sheltering under the **Gobernación** arcades along its southern side.

Behind the bandstand, a sort of kitsch flying saucer that completely blocks the view, rises the façade of the **cathedral of Santo Domingo**★ (B2) built in 1561. In

**He lost his head, a disarming experience!** To hide the signs of wear on the statue of the Virgen del Rosario, it was decided to clothe her, a delicate operation when it comes to slipping a garment over a woman holding an infant. Faced with this problem, a decision had to be made... and it was! The head and arms of the Baby Jesus were removed in order to clothe the statue, and another Infant was placed on top of the fabric. The sacrilege was only discovered several years later when the statue was being restored. The mutilated body was then given a new head and limbs.

its entrance stands a huge cracked bell *(campana rajada)*, a massive bronze piece that fell and broke when the bell-tower was struck by lightning. Among the few period remains to be seen are the main altar and, behind it, the **Virgen del Rosario**, a sculpture thought to date from the 16C.

## A walk through Zone I

Walk down the continuation of 7a Avenida to the corner of 3a Calle and climb the 131 steps up to the **calvario** (A1), following the procession of faithful who stop along the way to place offerings in the little chapels on either side of the stairway. The parvis offers an excellent **view**★★ over the town and Parque Nacional Las Victorias.

The main entrance to **Parque Nacional Las Victorias**★ (A1) *(8am-5pm. No fee)* is located near the junction of 3a Calle and 9a Avenida, but there is also access from the calvario. This small forest covering 82ha in the centre of Cobán is a pleasant place to picnic or stroll along its fern-bordered paths.

### The vivero Verapaz★ (Verapaz nursery) (direction A2)

*8am-4pm. Fee. 4km west of Parque Central via the former exit towards the capital. By bus, get off at La Garita (at the Texaco petrol station) then go 2km down the road on the left.*

This former coffee finca is now devoted to growing **orchids**, for which Cobán is famous. During the flowering season from **November to January** this 10-*manzana* (approximately 7ha) estate is submerged in flowers by the thousand, including the *Monja Blanca* (white nun), Guatemala's national flower. The rest of the year the nursery is less interesting but it is still a pleasant place to walk and a haven of tranquillity for the tourists who stay there *(see p 211 "Making the most of Cobán")*.

# The road to Semuc Champey★

*73km from Cobán to Semuc Champey. 3hr30min journey.*
*Allow a day for the excursion, to have time for a swim and a visit to the Lanquín caves.*

The humid climate of this limestone region on the border of El Petén fosters an exuberant tropical vegetation that hides innumerable rivers, waterfalls, lakes and caves, to the great delight of bathers and potholers.

*Those wishing to cool off without going on an expedition as far as Semuc Champey can stop off at San Pedro Carchá, 6km east of Cobán.*

F. Dyan

Semuc Champey: a haven of coolness and greenery

■ **San Pedro Carchá –** Take 5a Calle on the left of the church and follow the signs to **Balneario Las Islas** (fee), tucked away behind a hill 2km from the village centre. Apart from its delightful natural waterfall, this park, created around a lake dotted with sandy islets, resembles an open-air municipal swimming-pool. To be avoided at weekends because of the crowds!

Beyond San Pedro Carchá the road sheds its asphalt and changes into a narrow track that is terribly dusty in dry weather and muddy in the rainy season. Surfacing it would mean temporarily closing the only road link between the Verapaces and El Petén, so it is left as it is!

*About 50km from Cobán, turn right off the main road at Pajal onto another track that leads to the village of Lanquín.*

■ **Lanquín –** Before visiting the caves, go to the Municipalidad (Town Hall) to pay the entrance fee. It is also worth taking a look at the colonial church with its blackened façade, at the top of a rather steep flight of steps.

From the church, go back down the Cobán road to where, 2km northwest of the village, a river surges out of the **Grutas de Lanquín**★ (7.30am-12noon / 1pm-5pm. Fee. Torch and non-slip shoes advisable). In these caverns oozing damp and silence, bats flit about and the unexpected shapes sketched by stalactites and stalagmites in the glow of the light bulbs spark the imagination. On the way in, a few smoke-blackened **altars** can also be seen, vestiges of religious ceremonies which sometimes last several days. The network of galleries, even now only partially explored, has electric lighting for only a few hundred metres.

*Go back through Lanquín village and continue southeast for 10km, the worst stretch of the journey, to Semuc Champey (Fee), 200m after the suspension bridge.*

■ **Semuc Champey**★★ **–** From the car park a footpath leads 500m to an idyllic setting lost in the forest, where several natural pools are joined by a series of waterfalls, offering a well-deserved swim in the heart of a landscape bathed in total peace and quiet. These pools, fed by part of the **Río Cahabón**, are in fact on a sort of natural bridge under which the rest of the river runs. A 10min walk upstream takes you to the entrance of the underground passage into which the Río Cahabón disappears in a deafening roar (NB, the ground is slippery!); its tumultuous waters rush into this tunnel, emerging several hundred metres lower down and much calmer.

## South of Cobán

*13km south of Cobán the road forks at the village of Santa Cruz Verapaz. To the right, via San Cristóbal Verapaz, begins the long trek through the Cordillera de los Cuchumatanes to Huehuetenango. To the left, the main road continues towards Baja Verapaz department. From Santa Cruz Verapaz, make a 6km detour to San Cristóbal Verapaz.*

■ **San Cristóbal Verapaz –** From Parque Central, the road that runs along-side the Municipalidad (a green building) climbs up to the **calvario**, from which there is an excellent view over San Cristóbal and the **Laguna Chichoj**. To reach this lake, go back to Parque Central and down 1a Avenida, to the right of the church. At the end of this avenue is Parque Chichoj, a garden laid out on the water's edge – a relaxing place for the locals who come to picnic, but the water-weeds choking the bank make swimming difficult.

The Highlands

*Returning to Santa Cruz, take the main road to Tactic. After 13km, when you reach the Esso petrol station, a dirt track goes off to the right to the Pozo Vivo.*

The tiny **Pozo Vivo** (living well) pond is a curious physical phenomenon: the water starts moving whenever the sound of steps or voices is heard. But it is a real shame that a place that so well symbolises the dialogue between man and nature should be so littered with rubbish.

To the right of the petrol station, a 2km detour leads to **Tactic** with its charming colonial church. Otherwise the main road continues straight on into Baja Verapaz department.

## Through Baja Verapaz department
*Allow 1 day taking your time.*

This department, encircled by the Cuchumatanes to the northeast, the Sierra de Chuacús to the south and the Sierra de las Minas to the east, has little in the way of roads. The suggested itinerary is therefore designed for tourists who are not in a hurry and are happy to get off the beaten track. Those who prefer to go straight back to the capital should all the same stop on the way to visit the quetzal nature reserve.

■ **The Biotopo Mario Dary Riveral** (Biotopo del Quetzal) – *7am-4pm. Fee. On the main road to Guatemala City; continue about 20km beyond Tactic until you see the entrance to the reserve, on the right 4km after Purulhá (km 161 when coming from the capital). Accommodation available close by (see p 212). Take rainwear and swimwear.*

This 1 253ha biotope reserve was created by the University of San Carlos to protect the magnificent quetzal *(Pharomachrus mocinno)*. Although chances of spotting the national bird are infinitesimal even at the most likely time of the year from **April to June**, it is well worth scrutinising sky and foliage, for the reserve shelters over 80 different species of birds *(for keen bird-watchers, a list is available at the entrance)*. The trade winds blowing in from the Caribbean, down the corridor formed by Lake Izabal between the Sierra de Santa Cruz and the Sierra de Las Minas, are halted by the mountains, guaranteeing regular rainfall in this humid sub-tropical forest. The reserve, with its plethora of ferns, lichens, orchids and mosses – providing a habitat for an abundance of wildlife – can be visited either by the **Vereda de los Helechos** (fern path) or the **Vereda de los Musgos** (moss path), 1 800m and 3 600m long respectively; the moss path leads to a waterfall where you can swim.

*On leaving the biotope reserve, turn right and continue for 25km to the Santa Elena (or La Cumbre) crossroads. The main road continues straight ahead. The road to the right leads to Salamá via San Jerónimo (7km from Santa Elena crossroads).*

■ **San Jerónimo** – Near the village church is an **ingenio** (sugar mill) from the colonial era that is worth a visit.

*You can also stop off in Salamá, 10km from San Jerónimo.*

■ **Salamá** – The capital of Baja Verapaz does not offer much of interest apart from its colonial **church**. The main gardens are to be given a bandstand, hopefully with greater success than in Cobán.

*A thin, dusty ribbon of road twines around the mountain between Salamá and Rabinal (19km, 1hr by bus).*

**Around Cobán**

**A legendary bird**
Its long tail feathers, a sumptuous airborne train of shimmering blue-green, have been both the splendour and the misfortune of the quetzal. This sacred bird played a dominant role in the Mayan world, from the Mexican divinity Quetzalcoatl – the famous plumed serpent – to the head-dresses of their great warriors. As the "nahual" (animal protector equivalent to a totem) of the Quiché leader Tecún Umán, a quetzal observed the one-to-one combat between Pedro de Alvarado and the Mayan cacique. Legend has it that when the latter fell under the conquistador's sword, the bird flew down and perched on the warrior's heart. Since that day its throat feathers have been coloured blood red.

H. Choimet

The quetzal, a many-faceted symbol

■ **Rabinal** – This settlement, founded in 1537 by Bartolomé de Las Casas, owes its fame to the *Rabinal Achí*, a pre-Hispanic dance play (*see p 69*). During its **patron saint's festival**★★ from 19 to 25 January you can watch many traditional dances, including the *Patzca*, which is performed to obtain a good harvest. Apart from these ceremonies, the village comes out of its torpor on Sundays, which is **market day**★. On the central square laid out before a big colonial church, the vendors set up their stalls under the generous branches of a *ceiba* (silk cotton tree); they sell pottery and receptacles made from painted gourds.

# Making the most of Cobán

## COMING AND GOING

**By air** – Cobán airport is 3km west of the town (1km after the road to Guatemala City goes off to the left). The **INTER** company flies a service between Cobán and Guatemala City (30min flight). Departures daily from the capital at 9.50am and from Cobán at 10.30am. Tickets on sale from **W E Dieseldorff Sucs**, 3a Calle 4-12, Zone 2, ☎ 952 1286 / 952 1032.

**By bus** – Every hour from 4am to 5pm, 1st class buses to and from Guatemala City (4hr) from outside the **Transportes Escobar "Monja Blanca"** offices (B2), 2a Calle 3-77, Zone 4, ☎ 952 1536. The **Terminal de buses** (B1) is 300m from Parque Central on 1a Ave, behind 3a Calle, Zone 4 (behind the market). Five buses a day between Cobán and El Estor (8hr). Brave souls taking the Transversal del Norte through to Nebaj or Huehuetenango have to spend the night in Uspantán (one bus daily, 6hr journey), then continue on to Sacapulas (3hr) the following morning and change again for Nebaj (2hr) or "Huehue" (3hr30min). The same in the opposite direction. The journey to Flores is even longer: change at Fray Bartolomé de Las Casas (6hr) then again at Poptún (6hr from Las Casas) and through to Flores (5hr from Poptún).
Buses every 30min for San Cristóbal Verapaz (45min). NB, buses for San Pedro Carchá (15min) leave every 10min from opposite El Refugio restaurant, on the corner of 2a Ave and 2a Calle, Zone 4 (B2).

## GETTING AROUND

The town centre is not very big, so it is easy to get around on foot.

**By taxi** – Taxis wait behind the cathedral and on Parque Central. **Taxis Cobán**, ☎ 952 1490 and **Taxis Imperial**, ☎ 952 1897.

**By rental car** – **Inque Rentautos**, 3a Ave 1-18, Zone 4, ☎ 952 1994. **Tabarini**, 7a Ave 2-27, Zone 2, ☎ 952 1504.

## ADDRESS BOOK

**Tourist information** – No INGUAT, so try asking at Hostal Doña Victoria or Hostal de Acuña (the latter gives far better information).

**Bank / Currency Exchange** – **Banco de Occidente**, 1a Calle 1-11, Zone 1, ☎ 951 3651. **Banco Industrial**, 1a Calle 4-39, Zone 1, ☎ 952 1491. ATM, Cash machine for Visa cards.

**Post office / Telephone** – The post office (B2) is on the corner of 2a Ave and 3a Calle, Zone 3. To make phone calls and send faxes, **TELGUA** (B2), corner of 1a Calle and 3a Ave, Zone 1, on Parque Central.

**Medical service** – **Hospital Privado de la Cruz**, 5a Ave 1-64, Zone 4, ☎ 952 1805.

## WHERE TO STAY

### • Town centre

*Under US$10*
**Hotel La Paz**, 6a Ave 2-19, Zone 1, ☎ 952 1358 – 23rm ✗ A simple guesthouse, clean and pleasant, set around a courtyard cheerfully set with plants. Rooms with or without bathrooms. Good value for money.

*Under US$20*
**Hostal de Acuña**, 4a Calle 3-11, Zone 2, ☎ 952 1547 – 7rm ✗ CC Service worthy of a big hotel in this "youth hostel". 1 double room and 2 dormitories for 2 or 4 people (twin beds), shared according to how full the place is. The rooms and toilet facilities are spotlessly clean. Big sofas and restaurant tables around a sunny garden.

**Hostal Doña Victoria**, 3a Calle 2-38, Zone 3, ☎ 952 2213/4 – 8rm ✗ With its patio where parrots hide in the luxuriant vegetation, its tousled garden behind the restaurant, its softly-coloured walls, old tiles and wooden ceilings, this 16C residence offers the ultimate in charm. Rooms sleep 2, 3 or 4 and are all decorated differently. Lovely bathrooms, with an old zinc bathtub in room 4. A pleasant stay at a low price.

*Around US$30*

**Hotel Mansión Armenia**, Ave del Calvario 2-18, Zone 1, ☎ 952 2284 – 27rm ⚲ ✎ TV ✗ CC In a very quiet street leading to the steps up to the village calvary. The rooms have every comfort but lack charm.

**Posada de Carlos V**, 1a Ave 3-44, Zone 1, ☎ 952 1780 – 14rm ⚲ TV ✗ CC Near the bus terminus. From the reception, in a chalet at the end of a dead-end street, you would expect a hotel with more character. It is, however, nothing exceptional, just a newish building in the shadow of a hill. The rooms are well kept but a bit depressing.

⌂ **Hotel La Posada**, 1a Calle 4-12, Zone 2, ☎ 952 1495 – 14rm ⚲ ✗ CC Beautiful 18C house that has kept all its colonial cachet. Parquet flooring and wood furniture in rooms with character, some of which have fireplaces (6 and 8). For relaxation you can contemplate the big garden from the restaurant terrace or a hammock.

• **Outside town**
*Under US$30*

**Eco-Cabañas Verapaz**, on the old road out of Cobán to the capital, ☎ 952 1133 – 6rm ⚲ 4km from the town centre, right in the middle of the Vivero Verapaz (*see p 206*), 3 new bungalows with 2 rooms, lounge and fully equipped kitchen. Superb natural setting and total calm. An excellent base for visiting Cobán and its surroundings if you have your own transport. Sliding-scale tariff depending on how long you stay. Reservations at Café El Tirol (see "Eating out").

• **Lanquín**
*Around US$25*

**Hotel El Recreo Lanquín Champey**, ☎ 952 2160 – 25rm ⚲✗ Leaving Lanquín on the road to the caves. A good place to stay, to take your time visiting the region; also avoids the tiring round trip from Cobán to Semuc Champey in one day.

• **Biotopo del Quetzal**
*Under US$15*

**Hospedaje Ranchitos del Quetzal**, km 160.5 Carretera Las Verapaces, ☎ 853 9235 – 9rm ✗ Its location 200m from the reserve entrance is practical for those wishing to visit the quetzal reserve as soon as it opens. Basic accommodation. The double rooms with shower are big and well kept.

*Around US$40*

**Posada Montaña del Quetzal**, km 156.5 Carretera Las Verapaces, ☎ 335 1805/6 – 24rm ⚲ ✗ ⌿ CC 4km after the reserve on the road to Salamá. A pleasant tourist complex but of little interest without private transport. Rooms and bungalows to sleep 2 or 4.

### EATING OUT, HAVING A DRINK
*Under US$10*

**Cafetería Santa Rita**, Parque Central (B2). 7am(weekends 7.30am)-9pm. This little eatery opposite the cathedral serves good quality local dishes (eggs or meat accompanied by beans and plantain). Its two dining rooms are generally bursting at the seams.

**Café El Tirol**, 1a Calle 3-13, Parque Central, Zone 1 (A2). ☕ 7.30am-8.30pm. Serves a variety of different coffees with home-made pastries on a terrace on a dead-end street.

**Café La Posada**, 4a Ave between 1a and 2a Calle, Zone 2 (A2). 12.30pm-9pm. A room with a fireplace or a terrace with a view over the whole of Parque Central. It serves snacks only (toasted cheese, "nacho", sandwiches).

*Around US$10*

The restaurants in the La Posada, Doña Victoria and Acuña hotels are pleasant places serving good food.

**Restaurante Kam-Mun**, 1a Calle 8-12, Zone 2 (A2), ☎ 952 1109. 11.30am-10pm. A big, rather cold, dining room but the food is acceptable. Generous helpings of Asian specialities.

**Restaurante El Refugio**, corner of 2a Calle and 2a Ave, Zone 4 (B2). 10.30am-12midnight. Go up the stairs in 2a Ave to reach the restaurant above street level. Good Mexican and international specialities for all appetites (snacks or larger dishes). Fast and efficient service.

*(side tab)* **The Highlands**

## OTHER THINGS TO DO

**Excursions –** The Doña Victoria and Acuña hotels organise day trips by 4WD to Semuc Champey and the Grutas de Lanquín. Approx US$25 per person.

**Cinema –** A big cinema on Parque Central, between 3a and 4a Ave, Zone 2.

## SHOPPING GUIDE

**Bookshops –** A big new and second-hand book market is held under the Gobernación arcades on Parque Central. 8am-9pm; Saturdays until 5pm; closed Sundays.

**Making the most of Cobán**

The patio of the Doña Victoria hotel

F. Dyan

B. Brillion/MICHELIN

Mangrove tree, a paradise for egrets

THE PACIFIC COAST
 The Guatemalan

# THE PACIFIC COAST

From the foot of the volcanoes to the Pacific Ocean stretches a fertile plain bursting with sun and moisture, with endless sugar cane plantations, mango trees bearing plump sun-ripened fruits and coffee bushes growing in the shade of the trees. This mostly little-known region forming a corridor between Mexico and El Salvador reveals another facet of Guatemala. Adding to the pleasures of discovering archeological remains still scattered about the fields is the prospect of a seaside break, to enjoy the immense and virtually deserted beaches of black sand and take a peaceful boat trip through mangrove swamps populated with birds.

# THE PACIFIC COAST★
## FROM THE CHIQUIMULILLA CANAL TO CHAMPERICO

Two-day tour
Hot, humid climate
Accommodation in Monterrico and Retalhuleu

**Not to be missed**
Dawn over Monterrico nature reserve.

**And remember...**
A private vehicle makes it easier to tour this region.
Bathing in the Pacific is dangerous, so be careful.
Take effective mosquito repellent.

Parallel with the chain of volcanoes just to its north, the **Carretera del Pacífico** runs the length of the plain between Mexico and El Salvador without ever touching the coast. Only a few secondary roads go down to the sea, through cotton fields and sugar cane plantations replete with heat and humidity. There the tumultuous tides and breakers of the Pacific crash onto beaches of volcanic black sand. The Costa Sur (south coast), although disappointing to lovers of fine

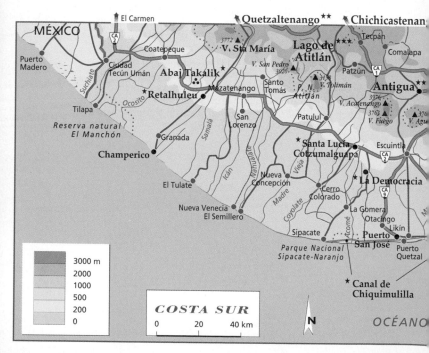

beaches and crystal waters, will delight travellers seeking solitude. For amateur archeologists, there are still interesting remains to be discovered scattered around the *fincas* (large farms) of the region.

## A cultural jigsaw

Many civilizations have travelled the corridor formed by the Pacific slope. The mystery surrounding the inhabitants of this region, and in particular the craftsmen to whom we owe the treasures unearthed in the plantations, has still not been entirely resolved. Each new archeological discovery adds another piece to the cultural jigsaw, but raises more questions about the region considered by some archeologists to be the cradle of Meso-American civilization.

Around 1500 BC the southern part was apparently occupied by primitive hunter-gatherer tribes originally from Mexico. Then from 600 BC the Pacific coast entered its golden age, influenced by the **Olmec** culture as can be seen by certain remains found in the region. Between AD 400 and 900 the **Pipil**, originally from the state of Veracruz in Mexico, settled here and down as far as El Salvador, cultivating cacao. First threatened by the advancing Quiché and Cakchiquel, they then lost their kingdom forever with the arrival of the Spaniards.

## An agricultural region

Right from the beginning of colonisation the Franciscans started clearing these lands, but the inhospitable natural environment and tropical diseases rapidly made them abandon their attempts, and the savannah, forests, marshes and

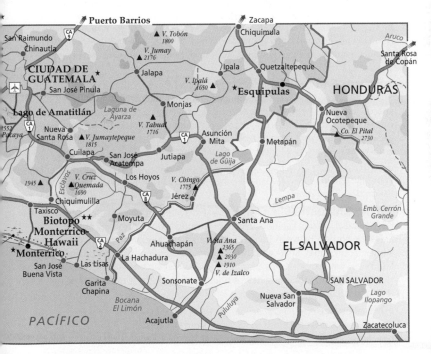

mangrove swamps reasserted their rights over the area. At the end of the 19C banana plantations were created, among them those of the powerful **United Fruit Company** *(see sidebar p 274 "The Caribbean coast")* around Tiquisate. The fruit was transported on the railway built in 1880 from Guatemala City to Puerto San José. Over the following decades crops were diversified and the Pacific plain became divided into livestock grazing areas, fields of sugar cane, banana and cotton, and coffee plantations in the foothills.

Its fertile volcanic soil and hot, humid climate make it one of the most productive farming regions of Guatemala, where retailers and big Ladino land-owners get rich. At harvest time the **fincas** call on the indigenous peasants of the Altiplano, who come down onto the Pacific plain to work for derisory salaries (on this subject, see the book by the Nobel Peace Prize-winner, *I, Rigoberta Menchú*).

## Between beach and mangrove swamps

*Allow 1 day by bus or car.*

Leaving the capital early in the morning you can easily make the return trip to the coast in a day, but spending a night there gives you the chance to combine a day lazing on the beach with a cruise on the Chiquimulilla Canal at dawn the following day. There are two routes from Guatemala City, one to Puerto San José, the other to Monterrico *(either way there is a car ferry crossing to make).*

*From Guatemala City, take the Carretera al Atlántico (CA9) to Escuintla (64km).*

*– If you are going directly to Monterrico, turn left onto the Carretera del Pacífico (CA2) to Taxisco, 48km further on. From there follow the road to the right for 19km to La Avellana, on the canal bank, then allow 20min to cross the canal to Monterrico.*

*– To reach Puerto San José, continue straight on down the Carretera del Atlántico (CA9) for 49km.*

■ **Puerto San José –** Now playing second fiddle to the modern facilities in Puerto Quetzal *(3km east)*, the country's former major port is running at half-speed. Its main street, lined with *cantinas* (taverns) whose fans scarcely stir the muggy, iodised air, leads down to the Pacific Ocean, but the closest beach to the capital offers only a wide ribbon of black sand littered with waste paper and empty cans. Wait for Monterrico to go swimming!

*From Puerto San José, follow the coast east for 13km to Iztapa. Cross the Río María Linda by boat (or ferry for cars) to Puerto Viejo. From here buses and boats go to Monterrico, 20km away.*

■ **The Chiquimulilla Canal★ –** Excavated in the 1930s, this waterway runs parallel to the Pacific Ocean for around 100km from Sipacate to the El Salvador border. Between Puerto San José and Monterrico, a driveable road runs alongside the canal, lined with flamboyant, banana, coconut and palm trees, and bamboos; you can visit this region by *lancha*, car or bus – the buses have to go slowly, using only their engines to brake, and take 2hr30min to cover the 20km to Monterrico!

■ **Monterrico★ –** *Immediately to the left of the main street are the resort's 4 hotels.* The village is nothing more than a few sandy streets that disappear into a long **beach★** of black sand. During the week only a handful of visitors share the kilometres of shoreline, with the crashing waves and a few mosquitoes the only risk of disturbance.

While staying here you can visit the **Reserva Natural Monterrico**, located in the **Biotopo Monterrico Hawaii\*\***. Before reaching the Pez de Oro hotel, a track leads off to the **tortugario**, a series of ponds in which threatened species reproduce: caymans, iguanas and turtles, including the enormous *Baule*. This centre also administers 2 800ha of reserve partially covered by **mangrove swamps**. The disappearance of this ecosystem from the Guatemalan coastline is posing a threat to many species of flora and fauna *(see p 16)*. Dawn is the best time to observe the multitudes of birds in the reserve. The *lancha* brushes past the mangroves with their aerial roots anchored in the swamps and their branches dotted with graceful herons, while pond and water lilies part as ducks swim by. From time to time a *cuatro ojos* (four eyes) fish zips past like a little motorboat; it has the unusual characteristic of seeing simultaneously both above and below water. *Although many of the lancha owners offer their services as guides, it is better to ask directly at the tortugario, since its competent staff know the mangrove swamps like the backs of their hands.*

**Turtle Derby**
The Monterrico nature reserve has set up an original way of increasing public awareness for saving the turtles. Every Saturday during August and September, the hatching season, visitors are invited to sponsor a baby turtle. At sunset the participants meet on the beach with their "protégés" in their cupped hands. When the signal is given, everyone sets their turtle down and watches excitedly, with beating heart, as it rushes frantically down to the ocean. The turtle that reaches the sea first wins its sponsor a meal in one of the resort hotels.

## The archeological tour
*Allow half a day to visit from Escuintla.*

The sites on the Pacific plain are scattered around a number of farms, some distance from each other and not easily accessible by bus. This tour is best made by car or taxi.

*From Escuintla follow the Carretera del Pacífico west for 25km to the village of Siquinalá. From there, a road to the left leads to La Democracia, 10km away.*

■ **The "big heads" of La Democracia\*** – The main square of the village has for some years been home to some bulky **statues\*\*** found at the neighbouring site of Monte Alto. Their siting was not, at the time, approved of by all the inhabitants, some of whom found the sculptures so ugly they would have preferred flowers to be planted instead! They have now become the symbol of this locality and figure on the schedule of many package tours.

Protected from the weather by awnings *(which makes photographing them awkward)*, these enormous heads and pot-bellied figures, also known as the *Barrigones* (paunchy ones) are scattered about the square around a gigantic *ceiba* (silk cotton tree).

R. Marca

Enigmatic face at La Democracia

The Pacific coast

The mystery shrouding the age and origins of these huge blocks of carved basalt has not yet been elucidated. They are thought to date from 300 BC and to be influenced by the Olmec style which flourished in the Mexican regions of Veracruz and Tabasco from 1200 to 400 BC. Some archeologists believe these statues date right back to 2000 BC. The **Museo de Arqueología** (*8am-12noon / 2pm-5pm; closed Mondays. Fee*) on the square exhibits some less imposing objects found in the region. One of the more remarkable items is a **jade mask**.

*Returning to Siquinalá, continue west down the Carretera del Pacífico for 8km to Santa Lucía Cotzumalguapa.*

■ **Around Santa Lucía Cotzumalguapa★** – This is where to leave from if bent on some field expeditions to hunt out sculptures or stelae hidden in the sugar cane plantations round about.

*1km north of Santa Lucía, go past the calvary and turn right straight away. Continue straight ahead for about 2km then turn left onto a dirt road. Ask the locals to show you the exact site of the place they call Las Piedras.*

The **Bilbao★** site is nothing more than a few stelae hidden in a sugar-cane plantation. When it was discovered at the end of the 19C, most of the monuments were transferred to a Berlin museum. Of the **stelae** still standing on the site, two are worth looking at closely. Stela 21, said to date from the 5C AD, depicts a ball player amid a profusion of zoomorphic and floral motifs; some drawings show cacao pods, a particularly important crop here at that time. Stela 19 shows an emaciated man framed by figures with the attributes of the serpent and jaguar. Since these bas-relief vestiges have been completely covered over with graffiti and paint, their delicacy cannot be appreciated until they have been restored.

*Return to the main road and continue right, to the north, for about 2.5km. After the bridge a sign shows El Baúl to the right. Take this track for 1km then fork to the right again and continue for 300m to a small hill.*

At the top of this hillock is an important ceremonial site known as **El Baúlito★**. In the shade of an *amate* tree, the gigantic head of a stone idol half-buried in the ground is hidden by clouds of incense. Drips of wax still bead the forehead of this hook-nosed divinity, and facing it a stela with Mexican-influenced glyphs likewise receives its share of offerings during ceremonies.

*Retrace your steps back to the main road and continue north for 3km to the entrance to the Finca El Baúl refinery.*

Once inside the **Ingenio El Baúl** – which you can also visit to see how a sugar refinery works – you will find the **museum★★** (*Fee*) at the end of the alley. It consists of a few sculptures found on the *finca*, dumped any old how under a thatched roof – a disappointing collection at first glance. But it does include some interesting pieces: a carving of a rampant jaguar and a stela depicting ballplayers wearing jaguar masks (copies can be seen at Finca Las Ilusiones). Near the museum there are some old locomotives on show.

*Returning to Santa Lucía Cotzumalguapa, take the Carretera del Pacífico east towards Siquinalá. After 1km, just before the Esso petrol station, take the dirt road to the left.*

At the end of the road going through **Finca Las Ilusiones** is an open-air exhibition of stelae and sculptures – reproductions and originals – next to the **Museo de la Cultura Cotzumalguapa★** (*Fee*). The caretaker, in the first house on the right of the museum, will open the building. Numerous objects found in the region are on show, along with a set of photos describing the work of reproducing the stelae using fibreglass.

*Returning to Santa Lucía Cotzumalguapa, take the Carretera del Pacífico westward via Mazatenango, for 90km. At the El Zarco crossroads, leave the road to Quetzaltenango to the right and continue 3km to the San Sebastián crossroads. Take the road left (Hotel Siboney is on the right) and drive south for 5km to Retalhuleu.*

## Retalhuleu and its area
*Allow half a day.*

■ **Retalhuleu★ –** *"Bienvenidos a Retalhuleu, Capital del Mundo"* ("Welcome to Retalhuleu, Capital of the World"), proclaims a sign at the entrance to the town. Such a small world and yet an entire universe. The warmth of both its climate and its inhabitants envelopes "Reu" (pronounced "Ray-oo") in a delightful tropical atmosphere, just 1hr by road from Quetzaltenango.

Its **Parque Central★★** (A2-B2) with its many benches shaded by pergolas is one of the most graceful in all Guatemala. The royal palms in the centre of the garden look like little green Bengal lights waving around the foot of the immense **church of San Antonio de Pádua** (A2-B2), flanked by its two bell-towers. Built initially in 1627, the church has had to be rebuilt several times as a result of frequent earthquakes.

The **Palacio Departamental** (B2), a big Neo classical building finished in 1913 under Jorge Ubico, then governor of the department, overlooks the southeast side of the square. The tower is topped by a beautiful carved quetzal.

**The Pacific coast**

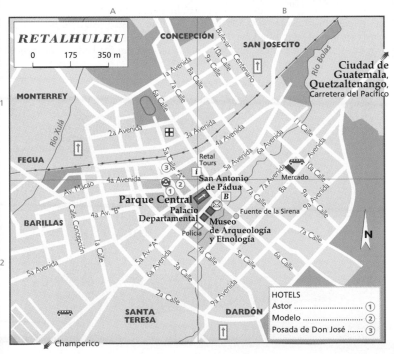

To the left of this building is the **Museo Nacional de Arqueología y Etnología de Retalhuleu** (B2) *(8am-1pm / 2pm-5pm; Sundays 8am-12noon; closed Mondays. Fee).* In the Pre-Classic room the exhibition of ritual and domestic objects found at Abaj Takalik forms a complement to the visit to the archeological site itself. The Classic room holds a big collection of ceramics and the Lithic room has a series of everyday utensils including *metates* (grinding stones) and obsidian objects. On the 1st floor a small exhibition of photos of the town and the display of a traditional Quiché costume from San Sebastián comprise the ethnological part of the museum.

*At the San Sebastián crossroads, turn left towards the Mexican border and drive 10km to the Abaj Takalik sign. Turn right to El Asintal village 4km further on. The entrance to the ruins is 4km to the north of this village. Buses stop at El Asintal, from which it is a 1hr walk to the site. You can also take a taxi there.*

■ **The Parque Arqueológico Abaj Takalik**★ – *Daily 7am-5pm. Fee. Ask for a guide at the entrance.* A bumpy track leads through the plantations of *hule* (rubber), coconut palms and coffee trees to Abaj Takalik (Quiché for "raised stone"), a major ancient city just at the meeting point between coastal plain and cold lands. The archeological site covers 6.5sqkm, spread across five private properties in a superb natural setting jammed between the Río Ixchíya to the east and the Río Xab to the west. The present excavations are limited to an area of 22 *manzanas* (roughly 15.4ha) given by the owner of the Santa Margarita *finca*.

Abaj Takalik appears to have been a cosmopolitan city with its monuments in both Olmec and Mayan styles, but relations between these two civilizations have not yet been totally elucidated. The site would seem to have been occupied from the **Middle Pre-Classic** (900-300 BC) to the Late Classic (AD 550-900). The oldest structures were of adobe, as in Kaminaljuyú *(see p 124 "Guatemala City"),* whereas the later ones were built with stones taken from the beds of the neigh-

Champerico jetty, reaching out into the Pacific

bouring rivers; one example is **Temple 12**, thought to date from 300 BC. Around this temple stand several monuments displaying Mayan and Olmec imagery alternately: figures emerging from jaguar heads on Monuments 8 and 67, whereas an enormous toad (Monument 68) and a colossal head (Monument 91) are more reminiscent of Olmec influences. **Stela 5**, in front of the main entrance to the temple, is a fine example of Mayan art: men depicted with one foot in front of the other and bearing a ceremonial bar in the form of a serpent at chest level. In the centre of the stela, glyphs indicate the year AD 126 (166 years before the first stela at Tikal). Abaj Takalik also has its ball court, but there is no point in looking for it, as it has had to be reburied to protect it from erosion.

*Leave the town by 5a Ave A. A straight road cuts through cane fields and mango plantations for 38km.*

■ **Champerico** – The third most important port in the country is now no more than a decrepit seaside resort sitting on a sad beach of black sand. It does not take long to see all there is in Champerico, particularly by *triciclo* (rickshaw), the local means of transport.

To the right as you stand facing the sea, you will notice a long jetty (*muelle*) of rusty salt-corroded iron stretching out into the ocean. At the end of this delicate lacework, pulleys creak, orders ring out and muscles brace, to heave the boats up out of the angry waves. Once the fish have been offloaded, the boats are kept on the pontoon until they next go out to sea.

# Making the most of Monterrico

## COMING AND GOING

**By bus** – Monterrico can be reached via either Puerto San José or La Avellana – the simplest route. When coming from or going to anywhere else in Guatemala, you have to change at Escuintla. Frequent services between Guatemala City and Puerto San José (2.5hr), from where you take a bus to Iztapa. Behind the bus stop *lanchas* cross the Río María Linda to the village of Puerto Viejo. From there another bus covers the 20km from Puerto Viejo to Monterrico (2hr30min journey!). The alternative is a bus from the capital to La Avellana (3hr30min), sometimes changing at Taxisco. From La Avellana "lanchas" go down the canal to Monterrico (20min).

**By private minibus** – Some travel agencies in Antigua run round trips to Monterrico (with a night there), or one-way journeys. A minibus leaves La Avellana for Antigua every Sunday at 2.30pm.

**By boat** – A more agreeable (but more expensive) way of travelling between Iztapa and Monterrico is to take the Chiquimulilla Canal (parallel to the road). Negotiate the price for the trip with the owner of a private *lancha*. Allow US$30-50. For the return trip go to the Tortugario Monterrico.

**By car** – At Iztapa or La Avellana there are car ferries across to Monterrico.

## ADDRESS BOOK

**Bank / Currency Exchange** – No bank in Monterrico, so you have to go to Puerto Barrios. **Banco del Café**, corner of 13a Calle and 7a Ave. **Banco Industrial**, 7a Ave Norte #73.

## WHERE TO STAY, EATING OUT

● **Monterrico**
The 4 hotels lined up on the beach are only a few metres apart. They all have mosquito nets in the rooms. Two advantages to coming during the week: rooms are both cheaper and easier to find.

The Pacific coast

*Under US$20*
**Hotel Playa Baule**, ☎ 473 6196 / 202 4152 – 17rm ⚲ ✗ ⊒ ✿ The rooms are basic but the atmosphere and reception are excellent. Loungers and hammocks facing the sea, just inviting you to do nothing.

*US$20-30*
**Hotel Kaimann Inn**, ☎ 202 6513 / 369 1258 – 8rm ⚲ ⊼ ✗ ⊒ ✿ The rooms are not really much different to the ones above, but this hotel is still good value for money.

**Hotel Johnny's Place**, ☎ 337 4191 (Guatemala City) – 14rm ⚲ ⊼ ✗ ✿ ᴄᴄ 7 bungalows each with 2 double bedrooms and a lounge with kitchenette. Not luxury accommodation

but may be practical for a family. Weekend tariff (based on 4 people). 🐚 **Hotel Pez de Oro**, ☎ 204 5249 / 331 2020 (Guatemala City) – 9rm ⚲ ⊼ ✗ ⊒ ✿ With its pretty bungalows painted in bright colours and topped by palm roofs, this hotel is without question the most attractive on the beach. Its rooms are simple but very pleasant. Same price for one or two people.

### OTHER THINGS TO DO

**Excursions –** The Tortugario Monterrico organises fascinating trips by *lancha* on the Chiquimulilla Canal and into the thick of the mangrove swamps.

## Making the most of Retalhuleu

### COMING AND GOING

**By bus –** The **Terminal de Bus** (A2) is 700m from Parque Central, on the continuation of 5a Ave A towards Champerico. But there is no need to go out that far, as the buses also stop at the La Galera station, 10a Calle between 7a and 8a Ave, three blocks northeast of Parque Central. Frequent services to and from Guatemala City (3hr30min) and Quetzaltenango (1hr). Buses every 30min between Retalhuleu and Champerico (45min).

### GETTING AROUND

**By taxi –** Taxis wait on Parque Central and at the bus stop on 10a Calle.

**By rental car – Tabarini**, 6a Calle 4-50, ☎ 771 1025 / 771 0646; shares premises (and director) with Retal Tours travel agency.

### ADDRESS BOOK

**Tourist information –** Ask at **Retal Tours** (same address as Tabarini above) (A1-B1). Edgar Champney, who runs the agency, communicates his passion

for the region and hands out very useful advice for finding your way around the town and its surrounding area.

**Bank / Currency Exchange –** The banks are on Parque Central. **Banco de Occidente**, 6a Calle 6-06. **Banco Industrial**, 6a Calle 5-17.

**Post office / Telephone –** The post office (B2) is on Parque Central, on the corner of 6a Calle and 6a Ave. For international calls, **TELGUA** (A2), 5a Calle 4-40.

**Medical service – Farmacia San Antonio**, 5a Ave 5-75, on Parque Central. In an emergency contact the **Hospital Nacional**, 3a Ave between 5a Calle A and 6a Calle, ☎ 771 0112/6.

### WHERE TO STAY

• **Town centre**
*Under US$15*
**Hotel Modelo**, 5a Calle 4-53, ☎ 771 0256 – 7rm ⚲ ⊼ The price is the only reason for choosing this hotel. The rooms are spartan and the service offhand.

*US$15-30*

🏨 **Hotel Astor**, 5a Calle 4-60, ☎ 771 0475, Fax 771 02562 – 15rm ⚏ 🖹 ✕ TV ✕ CC Delightful colonial-style house set around a patio with garden tables and a fountain. Extremely clean rooms with all modern comforts. The most intimate and welcoming hotel in town.

*US$30-45*

**Hotel Posada de Don José**, 5a Calle 3-67, ☎ 771 0180, Fax 771 1179 – 25rm ⚏ 🖹 ✐ TV ✕ ⚒ CC The rooms are spacious but in no way exceptional. But the swimming-pool is a definite asset in the heat of Retalhuleu.

- **Outside the town**

*Around US$40*

**Hotel Costa Real**, km 182.5 Carretera al Pacífico, ☎ 771 2141, Fax 771 2142 – 32rm ⚏ 🖹 ✐ TV ✕ ⚒ CC A superb park, long since neglected, and big rooms with bay windows that have seen better days. A pity this hotel is not better looked after, its natural setting and big swimming-pool could have made it a choice place.

**Hotel Siboney**, Cuatro Caminos San Sebastián, ☎ 771 0149, Fax 771 0711 – 25rm ⚏ 🖹 ✐ TV ✕ ⚒ CC 5km northeast of the town. The little buildings in bright colours are extremely well maintained both inside and out. Of the three hotels outside the town this offers the pleasantest accommodation. Two swimming-pools, one for hotel guests only.

*Over US$50*

**Hotel La Colonia**, km 178 Carretera al Pacífico, ☎ 771 0038, Fax 771 0191 – 42rm ⚏ ✕ TV ✕ ⚒ CC Buildings in different styles set in a beautiful park, but rooms of unequal quality. The *cabañas*, wooden maisonettes (fans, no air conditioning), are more welcoming than the 1950s buildings. A little expensive for what is provided.

**EATING OUT**

With a few exceptions, the hotel restaurants are all that is available.

*Under US$6*

**Cafetería La Luna**, corner of 5a Calle and 5a Ave. 7.30am-10.30pm. The long wooden bar, old jukebox and tired fan confer a real tropical atmosphere on this big room where the waitresses fan themselves while awaiting customers. Chinese cuisine or snacks and a good view of Parque Central.

**OTHER THINGS TO DO**

**Excursions –** Visit the ruins of Abaj Takalik. Go to **Retal Tours** (see "Rental cars" and "Tourist information") to organise other excursions in the area.

**Water park – Parque Acuático Xocomil** at San Martín Zapotitlán, km 180.5 on the Quetzaltenango road, about 10km northeast of Retalhuleu. For children and adults alike, this park has several swimming-pools, water chutes and 2 wave pools. Open Thursday-Sunday all year round.

**Making the most of Monterrico**

Detail of a Ceibal bas-relief

# EL PETÉN

Amid an ocean of emerald that has engulfed the remains of many Mayan cities, here and there grey temple roof-combs break through the treetops to capture a sliver of sky. Tikal, one of the few accessible sites in El Petén and one of the most admirable archeological sites of our entire world heritage, has retained all its magic. Beyond the ruins, a fragrance of adventure emanates from the jungle. This is Guatemala's ultimate wildlife sanctuary, where other treasures of the Mayan civilization are still held prisoner, and the jaguar, that incarnation of the night-time sun, slinks away at daybreak as the brilliant beaks of the toucans sketch furtive rainbows, and the roaring of the howler monkeys echoes throughout the forest.

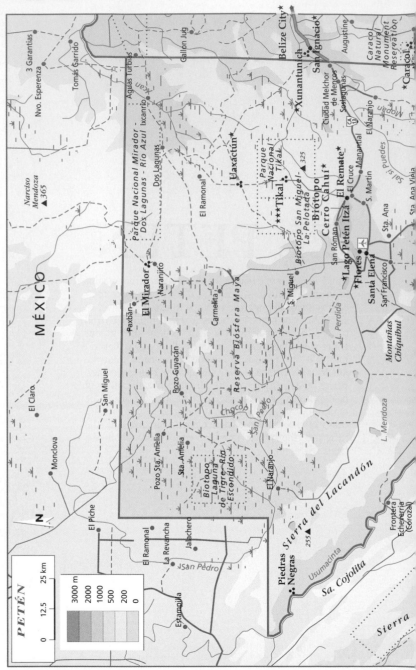

# LAKE PETÉN ITZÁ★

El Petén department
488km north of Guatemala City
45min flight – 10-20hr road journey depending on season
Warm, damp climate – See map p 228

**Not to be missed**
Sunset on the lake from El Balcón del Cielo bar.
**And remember...**
For comfortable accommodation choose Flores.
Efficient mosquito repellent is advisable.
It is better to visit El Petén's sites during the dry season (Oct-April).

Lake Petén Itzá, an oasis of civilization in the heart of the jungle, makes an excellent base for excursions to El Petén's archeological sites. Although long restricted to the Flores island, tourist facilities are now flourishing discreetly on the lakeside. It is here that travellers prepare to explore Tikal, swap advice, recount their adventures and share their wonderment.

## The last bastion

During the Post-Classic period the **Itzá** abandoned Chichén Itzá (on the Yucatán peninsula) to found **Tayasal**, on the site of present-day Flores. In 1525 Hernán Cortés made a brief halt in their capital on his way to Honduras. Of this visit, history retained only an anecdote about a wounded horse abandoned by the Spaniards: the Maya plied it with offerings but allowed it to starve to death. It was then deified and given the name *Tzimin Chac* (horse of thunder), and a statue was carved in its effigy. When the Franciscans arrived less than a hundred years later, they put an end to the Maya's worship of this idol, which now lies at the bottom of the lake. Legend maintains that the horse's silhouette can be made out when the water level drops.

For over a century and a half, the Spanish made scarcely any incursions into the region, isolated as it is from the rest of Guatemala. The army of Martín de Ursúa finally took Tayasal in 1697.

## Flores / Santa Elena

*Allow half a day.*

To the south of the lake, Flores and Santa Elena – the latter continuing to the west as San Benito – form a single conurbation. The fact that Flores stands on an island linked to the mainland by a dyke road has saved it from too much agitation.

### Flores★

Flores sits on the lake like a floating island, threatening to drown every time the waters rise. Little houses in bright colours jammed side by side, tin roofs rusting from the damp, paved alleyways tiered in concentric circles and a church at the top of the village – this department capital resembles a peaceful fishing town that has managed to keep all its charm, despite innumerable hotels, souvenir shops and Internet cafés.

El Petén

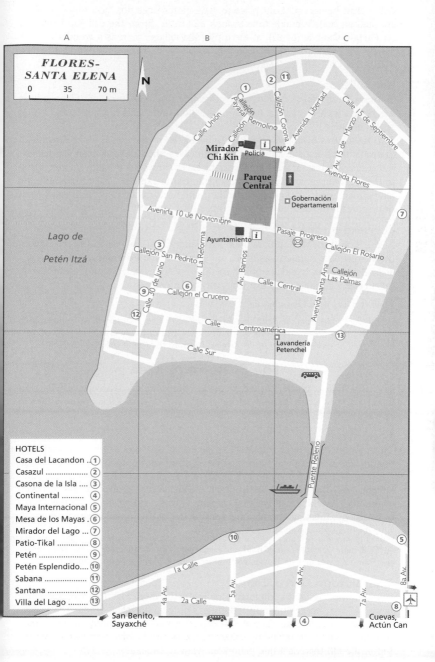

**FLORES-
SANTA ELENA**

0    35    70 m

N

Lago de
Petén Itzá

Calle Unión
Callejón Remolino
Callejón Payasa
Callejón Corona
Avenida Libertad
Calle 15 de Septiembre
Av. 15 de Marzo

**Mirador
Chi Kin**    Policía    CINCAP

**Parque
Central**

Avenida Flores

Avenida 10 de Noviembre

Gobernación
Departamental

Ayuntamiento    Pasaje Progreso

Callejón San Pedrito

Callejón El Rosario

Av. La Reforma

Av. Barrios

Calle Central

Avenida Santa Ana

Callejón
Las Palmas

Callejón el Crucero

Calle 30 de Junio

Calle

Calle Centroamérica

Calle Sur

Lavandería
Petenchel

Puente Relleno

HOTELS

la Calle

4a Av.    2a Calle    5a Av.    6a Av.    7a Av.    8a Av.

San Benito,
Sayaxché

Cuevas,
Actún Can

Other than being a pleasant place to stay, Flores does not have much to offer, and half an hour is ample time to look around it. From the Chi Kin belvedere on **Parque Central** (B1-B2), at the top of the village, there is a wonderful clear **view**★★ over the lake. *Information on the region can be obtained near the church, from INGUAT or CINCAP (see "Making the most of Flores").*

## Santa Elena

On terra firma south of the dyke road leading to Flores lies Santa Elena, a little less serene with its exhaust fumes, bus station traffic and the hustle and bustle of the market.

Two kilometres from the centre of Santa Elena, to the south of 7a Avenida, a driveable track leads to a hill pocked with caves, the **Cuevas Actún Can**★ *(8am-4.30pm. Fee).* A map at the entrance to the caves shows the evocative names given to these geological formations; it is an interesting exercise to try to identify the tall pointed hoods, the rain god, the thousand needles, the ice waterfall, the giant death's head, the marimba, the monkey's head, the stone rose etc.

## A cruise on the lake★

At the foot of the dyke linking Flores to Santa Elena, the *lancha* (motor launch) owners propose mini cruises on Lake Petén Itzá. The **Petencito** *(7am-6pm. Fee),* a small zoo on an island about half an hour away by boat, is not of great interest but makes a pleasant objective for a trip on the lake.

*Tikal is 33km from Flores by road.*

*If arriving by bus from the Belize border, get off at El Cruce crossroads, the intersection with the Santa Elena-Tikal road. Normally taxis wait at the times the buses pass, otherwise you have to walk 2km to El Remate (turning right onto the road to Tikal).*

# The El Remate area

The new "tourist centre" on the east side of Lake Petén Itzá is beautifully situated in a very lovely natural setting not far from Tikal *(30min journey from El Remate to Tikal).*

## El Remate★

This modest village on the lakeside, reputed for its wood carvings, is spreading continually as its popularity increases as a cheap and attractive place to stay in the region. It attracts a great many backpackers, drawn by the communal atmosphere and the natural environment. Time slips peacefully by between swimming, kayaking and walking, cycling or horse riding. But with the advent of electricity, this tiny international enclave lost in the jungle is rapidly going to find itself caught up in the modern world.

*At El Remate, leave the main road and continue along the lakeside by the road on the left from La Casa de Don David. Walk 2km to the El Gringo Perdido hotel.*

## The Biotopo Cerro Cahuí★

*6am-5pm. Fee.* A dozen kilometres of footpaths crisscross this tropical forest whose 650ha shelter numerous specimens of local flora and fauna. The reserve is the habitat of the *pavo petenero* (wild turkey) and a multitude of butterflies, birds and mammals, including spider monkeys and howler monkeys. From the top of the hill there is a fine panoramic view of the lake.

# Some excursions in El Petén

*Information from CINCAP in Flores (see "Making the most of Flores").*
*Excursions run by tour operators and hotels in Flores and El Remate.*

A hundred or so Mayan cities are still imprisoned in El Petén's jungles, the realm of archeologists and the *chicleros* who come to gather gum from the sapodilla tree. Most of these ruins, hidden deep in the virgin forest, are difficult to get to and are only partially excavated, but their enchant-ing natural settings alone often justify the ex-cursion. The more distant sites, such as Piedras Negras and El Mirador, are mainly for very keen archeologists and trekkers who do not much mind about comfort. If the idea of spending several days in the jungle on foot or mule-back or in a dugout canoe does not attract you, then at least visit El Ceibal, which is easily accessible from Lake Petén Itzá.

## El Ceibal★

*Allow 90min to cover the 61km from Flores to Sayaxché. From here take a "lancha" down the Río de la Pasión (90min trip) or drive 15km down a bad track. It is best to hire a guide to find your way around the site. Fee.*

The natural setting and boat trip down the Río de la Pasión alone make it worth visiting this site, which is a veritable for-est of *ceibas* (silk cotton, or kapok, trees), palm trees and stelae. A visit that can also reserve some unexpected surprises! Wan-dering along a path you are equally likely to see a petrified Mayan sovereign looming

A. Reffet/EXPLORER

Stela in Ceibal

up, or one of the enormous tarantulas which hide in the park (*avoid wearing sandals*).

El Ceibal was one of the most important ceremonial centres in El Petén during the 9C until, like many other Mayan cities, it was suddenly deserted around the year 900. An exceptional feature of the monuments at this site is the delicacy of their bas-reliefs, some of which depict figures with un-Mayan-like features, a sign that they were influenced by the **Putún**, a people who came from Mexico around 820 AD.

Group A, about a 30min walk from the landing-stage, is formed by a pyramid surrounded by some remarkable stelae sculpted around the mid-9C. **Stela 10★★**, standing to the north of the building and portraying a sovereign crowned with plumes, stands out by virtue of the very high quality carving on it.

On the way to the circular temple, at the end of a path, stands a structure unique in El Petén, the astonishing **Stela 2★**, known as the **Mascarón del Mono** (monkey mask); this grotesque mask of a monkey sticking its tongue out and surmounted by a death's head does not belong to Mayan iconography.

Lake Petén Itzá

## Piedras Negras

*Sayaxché is also the departure point for "lanchas" going on this excursion, which generally lasts about a week (about 270km to reach Piedras Negras by boat). Ask at the Flores tour operators or at the Expediciones Maya agency in Guatemala City (see p 95 "Other things to do"); this agency specialises in white-water rafting and proposes a 2-week programme combining rafting down the Río Usumacinta with visits to several archeological sites, including Piedras Negras. The more participants there are, the less it costs per person.*

A week-long excursion to the further reaches of the virgin forest offers the prospect of many a fine adventure! The *lancha*, a real little observatory for watching local flora and fauna, navigates along the **Río de la Pasión** then the **Río Usumacinta**, which forms the border between Guatemala and Mexico.

Standing on the edge of the Usumacinta, the Piedras Negras site, which is one of the great Classic centres, is not very informative for the uninitiated. However, the carvings here demonstrate an incredible artistic sophistication, as can be seen from the superb bas-reliefs on view in the archeology museum in Guatemala City! In fact most of the stelae and wooden lintels discovered on the site have been transferred to various museums.

Discovered by **Teobert Maler** in 1895, Piedras Negras was excavated on a large scale in the 1930s. This work brought to light an unbroken sequence of stelae erected at the end of each *hotun* (5-year period) from the early 7C to the early 9C, along with thirty or so stelae recounting the lives of several rulers of Piedras Negras. The city also had a large number of *temazcales* (sweat-houses), the structures of which are still visible.

## El Mirador

*The first 60km of the journey are by car along the dirt road from San Andrés (on the shore of Lake Petén Itzá, 30km west of El Remate) to Carmelita. From there you have to walk 35km through the forest. Manuel Soto, owner of the Mirador del Duende (see "Making the most of El Remate"), organises good 5-day excursions, with mules to carry the equipment.*

Located in the north of El Petén, 7km from the Mexican border, El Mirador dominated the region during the Pre-Classic period. The heart of this great ceremonial centre covers 16sqkm – like Tikal – but since this remote area is so hard to get to, the excavation work is far less advanced.

With its colossal buildings emerging above the forest to reveal fabulous **panoramas★★**, El Mirador fully deserves its name. **The Tiger Pyramid** (Pirámide del Tigre) stands 43m tall, well short of the **Tapir Pyramid** (Pirámide de la Danta), whose 70m make it the tallest Mayan temple discovered so far.

Serena/HOA QUI

Lake Petén Itzá carpeted with water lilies

**El Petén**

# Making the most of Flores / Santa Elena

**El Petén**

## COMING AND GOING

**By air** – The *Aeropuerto Internacional* (direction C4) is at Santa Elena, 2km east of the town centre. Several flights a day to and from Guatemala City (see below "Airlines"). Daily services between Flores and Belize City by Grupo TACA (which includes Aviateca) and the 2 Belizean companies, Tropic Air and Maya Island Air. US$20 airport tax on leaving the country. Take a taxi or town bus from the airport to Flores.

**By bus** – The transport companies *Fuente del Norte, La Petenera / Línea Dorada* and *Líneas Máximas del Petén* each have their own terminus in Santa Elena, on 4a Calle near the market. Several buses a day to Guatemala City via Poptún, Río Dulce, La Ruidosa. A wearing journey lasting anything from 10-20hr depending on the season. The Línea Dorada night bus that leaves every evening at 8pm from 4a Calle is preferable; seats are more expensive, but you get a luxury service (air-conditioning, toilets, reclining seats, blankets, pillows, packed meal). Change at La Ruidosa for Puerto Barrios and at Río Honda for Chiquimula.

*Transportes Rosita* runs 10 services a day, 5am-6pm, to Melchor de Mencos (border with Belize). *San Juan Travel*, corner of 6a Ave and 2a Calle, Santa Elena, ☎ 926 0041, goes right through to Belize City (6hr). Leaves at 5am.

**By private minibus** – The hotels and travel agencies run a minibus service to Tikal (1hr) via El Remate, at the halfway point. Departures every hour, 4am-10am; return at 12.30pm, 2pm, 4pm or 5pm.

## GETTING AROUND

**By bus** – A town bus service runs every 15min between Santa Elena and the Flores isthmus.

**By taxi** – In Flores taxis wait on Calle 30 de Junio, in front of Hotel Petén. In Santa Elena the taxi rank is on the corner of 4a Calle and 4a Ave.

**By boat** – The "lanchas" moored near the start of the road between Santa Elena and Flores offer trips around Lake Petén Itzá.

**By rental car** – *San Juan Travel* rents 4WDs and minibuses. So does **Hertz**, airport, ☎ 926 0332. **Koka**, airport, ☎ 926 1233 / 0526.

## ADDRESS BOOK

**Tourist information** – *INGUAT* office (B2) on Parque Central near the church (8am-5pm; closed weekends). The office at the airport is open every day. For information about the region you can also go to *CINCAP* (Centro de Información sobre la Naturaleza, Cultura y Artesanía del Petén) (B1) on Parque Central. 9am-1pm / 2pm-7pm; Sundays 1pm-5pm; closed Mondays.

**Bank / Currency Exchange** – No banks in Flores but most of the hotels and shops change traveller's cheques and dollars. In Santa Elena the banks are on 4a Calle. *Banco Continental*, 8.30am-7pm; Saturdays 10am-2pm, changes only American Express traveller's cheques and cash. *Banco del Café*, 9am-7pm; Saturdays 9am-1pm. *Banco Industrial*, 9am-4pm; Saturdays 10am-2pm. Cashpoint for Visa cards.

**Post office / Telephone** – In Flores the post office (C2) is in Pasaje Progreso, near Parque Central. In Santa Elena the post office is on the corner of 2a Calle and 7a Ave. Just next door you can send urgent letters and parcels by DHL via *Fanny's Express*, 2a Calle 6-80, Santa Elena, ☎ 926 1440.

To telephone go to the *TELGUA* offices on the corner of 5a Calle and 6a Ave, Santa Elena. 7am-10pm; Sundays 9am-4pm.

In Flores there is an e-mail and Internet service at *C@fé.net* on the corner of Ave Barrios and Calle Central. 8am-9pm. *Tikal Net*, Calle Centroamérica. 8am-8pm; closed Sundays.

**Medical service** – In Santa Elena, *Centro Médico Maya*, 4a Ave 2-35, ☎ 926 0180. *Centro de Salud*, 3a Ave 5-25, ☎ 926 0025. In Flores, *Farmacia Nueva*, Ave Santa Ana, next door to Las Puertas restaurant.

**Airline companies** – All the hotels and travel agencies in Flores and Santa Elena sell plane tickets for Guatemala City. You can also buy them at the airport from the

companies themselves: **Aerovías**,
☎ 926 0513 (the cheapest), **Aviateca**,
☎ 926 1337 /1238 or **Tikal Jets**,
☎ 926 0386.

**Travel agencies** – These have taken
over the streets of Flores and Santa
Elena. Prices and services can be compared at leisure. **San Juan Travel**, corner of 6a Ave and 2a Calle, Santa Elena,
☎ 926 0041, is reputed for its
efficiency.

**Laundry** – **Lavandería Petenchel**,
Calle Centroamérica, Flores. 8am-7pm;
closed Sundays.

## WHERE TO STAY

### • Flores

*Under US$25*

**Hotel Villa del Lago**, Calle Centroamérica, ☎ 926 0508, Fax 926 0629
– 13rm 🌊 ✘ cc This hotel offers a
friendly welcome and family ambience
above all else. The rooms without showers are quite comfortable and cheap and
those at the front of the building have
bathrooms and air conditioning (more
expensive). In the latter category choose
nos 110 or 201 with a view of the lake.
A lot of tourist information and excursions organised.

**Hotel La Casa del Lacandon**, Calle
Unión – 8rm 🔲 🌊 This new hotel has
impeccable little rooms at worthwhile
prices. The telephone had not yet been
installed when we visited.

**Hotel Mirador del Lago**, Calle 15 de
Septiembre – 22rm 🔲 🌊 The rooms in
this recent hotel are ordinary but well-
kept. If you are at the end of the building upstairs there is a fine view of the
lake. The place should soon be getting a
telephone connection.

**Hotel la Mesa de los Mayas**, Callejón
El Crucero, ☎ 926 1240 – 20rm 🔲 🌊
✘ cc Rooms that are particularly well
cared for and comfortable, with fans or
air conditioning. Warm welcome and
very reasonable prices for what is provided.

*Around US$30*

**Hotel Petén**, Calle 30 de Junio,
☎ 926 0692, Fax 926 0593,
lacasona@gua.net – 19rm 🔲 📋 🌊 📺
✘ ⟁ cc A modern building built with

a colonial feel. Big rooms, well lit in the
case of those overlooking the lake. Inside
swimming-pool. Very good value for
money.

**Hotel Sabana**, Calle Unión, ☎ 926
1248 – 28rm 🔲 📋 📺 ✘ ⟁ cc This
imposing, orange-coloured building can
be seen a long way off. The rooms have
every comfort but lack space and character. Ask for a room on the lake side.

*US$30-50*

**Hotel Casazul**, Calle Unión, ☎ 926
1138, Fax 926 0593, lacasona@gua.net
– 8rm 🔲 📋 🌊 cc This blue house
has pleasant, spacious rooms despite a
slightly impersonal atmosphere. Once
again, those looking out over the lake are
the best choice. Every comfort and impeccably clean, at a reasonable price.

**Hotel La Casona de la Isla**, Calle 30
de Junio, ☎ 926 0523, Fax 926 0593,
lacasona@gua.net – 27rm 🔲 📋 🌊 ✘
⟁ cc Amenities equivalent to the
places mentioned above. Only the
rooms on the lake side are of any interest, the others being a bit too dark.

**Hotel Santana**, Calle 30 de Junio,
☎ 926 0262, Fax 926 0492 – 32rm 🔲
📋 𝒫 📺 ✘ ⟁ cc A modern, very
comfortable hotel. The rooms are big
and very clean. Most have a balcony that
looks out over the lake.

### • Santa Elena

*Under US$10*

**Hotel Continental**, corner of Calle Ro-
dríguez Macal and 6a Ave, ☎ 926 1017
– 38rm 🌊 ✘ This hotel near the market is a favourite with backpackers.
Good atmosphere, although the owners
are not very helpful. Basic rooms, well
kept (some have private bathrooms).

*US$30-60*

**Hotel del Patio-Tikal**, corner of 2a
Calle and 8a Ave, ☎ 926 0104 /1229 –
21rm 🔲 📋 🌊 📺 ✘ cc Behind
the austere façade of the building is a delightful hotel with colonial architecture
set around a patio. The rooms are pleasant with all modern comforts. Breakfast
included. Excellent value for money.

**Hotel Maya Internacional**, corner of
1ra Calle and 8a Ave, ☎ 926 1274,
stpvillas@pronet.net.gt –28rm 🔲 🌊 ✘

**Making the most of Flores / Santa Elena**

**El Petén**

◢ cc Rustic buildings with palm roofs scattered around a garden that stretches out over the lake. All the rooms with balconies have pleasant views. A calm and attractive hotel, a pity the welcome is so lacking in warmth.

*Around US$100*

**Hotel Petén Esplendido**, 1ra Calle, ☎ 926 0880, Fax 926 0866, hpesplen@gua.net – 62rm ◢ 🍴 ✐ 📺 ✕ ◢ cc Santa Elena's luxury hotel supplies a lot of services, including a conference room for business people. The double rooms all have balconies with a view of the lake, unlike the single ones. The place is proud of possessing the only lift in El Petén, a detail that may be of some importance after visiting Tikal!

### EATING OUT

• **Flores**

*Under US$10*

**Posada del Peregrino**, Ave La Reforma (B2), ☎ 926 0477. 7am-9pm. An unpretentious restaurant serving good local cuisine. One of the few places that opens early for breakfast.

**Poch'o Restaurant & Bar**, Calle Sur (B3). ☂ 10am-11pm. On the first floor of a building facing the lake, with a big sheltered terrace that livens up to reggae in the evenings. The cuisine is not unforgettable but it is a pleasant place for a drink.

**Restaurante Gran Jaguar**, corner of Calle 30 de Junio and Callejón San Pedro (B2), ☎ 926 0844. ☂ 12noon-10pm; closed Mondays. The immense dining room leads to a terrace overlooking the lake where it is pleasant to dine in the evening. Good meat and fish dishes in generous helpings. Rustic setting, relaxed atmosphere and cheerful service.

☺ **Restaurante / Bar Las Puertas**, corner of Ave Santa Ana and Calle Central (C2), ☎ 926 1061. 8am-12midnight; closed Sundays. Its big dining-room with a high ceiling and good

ventilation is pleasant at any hour of the day. The menu offers good and varied dishes, either snacks or more substantial (hamburgers, soups, pasta, meat). For dessert, try the delicious filled pancakes. Very convivial atmosphere with live music every evening.

**Restaurante / Bar La Luna**, corner of Calle 10 de Noviembre and Calle 30 de Junio (B2). 12noon-11pm. A very cheerful place with its green ceiling and big blue doors opening onto a tiny patio. A good selection of international dishes at moderate prices.

• **Santa Elena**

*Under US$10*

**Restaurante Petenchel**, 2a Calle 4-40 (B4), ☎ 926 1125 ☂ 7.30am-10pm; Sundays 5pm-10pm. Near Parque Central, identifiable by its delightful terrace under a thatched roof. Good regional specialities and international cuisine.

### HAVING A DRINK

**Bars – Las Puertas**, **La Luna** and **Pocho'o** (see "Eating out") are very lively in the evenings. The **Coctelería El Balcón del Cielo**, Parque Central, is a world of its own. Its covered terrace looks out over Flores and the lake. Ideal for having a cocktail at sunset. 3pm-1am; closed Tuesdays.

### OTHER THINGS TO DO

**Excursions –** The travel agencies and hotels organise visits to numerous archeological sites in El Petén. Ceibal and Uaxactún are among the most accessible but, unlike the trip to Tikal, you may have to wait a day or two while they find other clients for the excursion.

**Outdoor pursuits –** Hiking in the jungle is offered by many tour operators. Manuel Soto, owner of the **Mirador del Duende** (see p 239 "Making the most of El Remate"), is an excellent guide.

# Making the most of El Remate

## COMING AND GOING

**By bus** – Buses between Flores and Belize drop you at El Cruce, a crossroads 2km south of El Remate. Taxis generally wait for passengers on arrival, otherwise you have to walk to the village.

**By private minibus** – Minibuses between Flores and Tikal go through El Remate every hour, 4.30am-10.30am, and return at 12.30pm, 2pm, 4pm and 5pm. Reserve a seat through your hotel.

## WHERE TO STAY, EATING OUT

With one exception, all the places in the village are simple and committed to protecting the environment. Increasingly, they are attracting travellers in search of peace and nature. With the arrival of electricity, El Remate is likely to lose this "authenticity" that has helped to make it a popular resort.

*Under US$12*
**Mirador del Duende**, ☎ 926 0269 (public telephone) – sleeps 40 ✕ Ecological camp site perched on a promontory above the Flores-Tikal road. The ideal place for backpackers with a penchant for communal life and ecology. You can sleep in a hammock or on a mattress in pretty whitewashed bungalows with palm roofs. No doors, few walls, all the "rooms" open to the outside. The owner, who is passionately interested in alternative medicine and Mayan culture, organises expeditions into the jungle lasting several days.

*US$15-30*
🐨 **La Casa Roja**, ☎ 926 0269 (public telephone) – 4rm ✕ Nestling in a dense garden, 500m from the main road to the Cerro Cahuí nature reserve. This place

works on the same principal as the Mirador del Duende, with its rooms almost entirely open to the outside. At the foot of each bed there is an oil lamp and a padlocked wooden chest in which to keep your valuables. Rustic setting and original decoration (especially in the communal showers). An original place with a warm welcome. They are presently building an additional bungalow.

*La Casa de Don David* – 10rm ⌐ ✕ At the intersection of the Flores-Tikal road and the turn-off for the Cerro Cahuí nature reserve. This hotel does not lack charm, although it is more conventional than the 2 above. Pleasant, well-kept rooms opening onto a peaceful garden on the edge of the lake. A generator provides 24hr electricity.

🐨 *Parador Ecológico El Gringo Perdido*, ☎ 334 1967, Fax 334 2305 – 12rm ⌐ ✕ In the Cerro Cahuí nature reserve, 2km from the Flores-Tikal road. Several wooden buildings scattered around a superb park that goes right down to the lake. All types of accommodation (hammocks under thatched roofs, 8-person bungalows or rooms) in an attractive rustic style. Impeccably clean. Very good restaurant.

*Around US$130*
**Westin Camino Real Tikal**, ☎ 333 4633, Fax 337 4313, caminor@guate. net – 72rm ⌐ ▤ ✆ TV ✕ ⌐ CC Luxury complex on the edge of the lake, 5km from the Flores-Tikal turn off on the road to the Cerro Cahuí nature reserve. The rooms have all the modern facilities of a 5-star hotel and the architecture blends discreetly into the landscape. For tour groups or travellers with their own transport.

**Making the most of El Remate**

# TIKAL ★★★

El Petén department – Alt 254m
65km from Flores and 32km from El Remate
Accommodation at the site entrance or in Flores and El Remate (see p 236)
See map p 228 and plan p 242

### Not to be missed
The view from the top of Temple IV.
Sunset from the Lost World pyramid.
The flora and fauna of Parque Nacional Tikal.

### And remember...
Allow 2 days to visit the site in full.
Dawn is the best time to observe wildlife.
Take walking shoes, a hat, water and mosquito repellent.
For the more inaccessible parts, visit during the dry season (Jan-May).

R. Marca

"Tikal"

Tikal, as magical a name for amateur archeologists as Angkor, Petra, Borobudur, Machu Picchu or the Great Wall of China; one of the wonders of the world's archeological heritage. Besides the fascination of the monuments themselves, there is the excitement of exploring them and the wonderment felt in the midst of this luxuriant wilderness just waiting for the chance to bury its treasures once more.

Discovering a pyramid still hidden under the moss and mould of tree trunks interlaced with creepers, is as strongly emotional an experience as gazing down the freshly mown lawn of Plaza Mayor, with its majestic temples soaring skyward.

## The splendours and misfortunes of a city
*(See p 19 "The ancient Maya")*

The emergence of a city as grandiose as Tikal in a natural environment as inhospitable as El Petén, with its meagre natural resources and sparsely irrigated soil, bears witness to the incredible labours of the Maya, working without the wheel and with no draught animals.

**The first stones –** It was in the 7C BC that the first occupants settled on the site, close by some big flint deposits, and it was this flint, used for making tools and arms, that gave Tikal its trading reputation in the region. The first large-scale building works were carried out

**A reminder**
Pre-Classic period (from 2000 BC to 250 AD)
– Early (from 2000 BC to 900 BC)
– Middle (from 900 BC to 300 BC)
– Late (from 300 BC to 250 AD)
Classic period (from 250 AD to 900 AD)
– Early (from 250 to 550)
– Late (from 550 to 900)
Post-Classic period (from 900 AD to the Conquest)
– Early (from 900 to 1250)
– Late (from 1250 to 1524)

around 200 BC, the date established for the oldest buildings buried beneath the North Acropolis of Plaza Mayor.

**Fluctuating influence –** By the end of the Late Pre-Classic period, Tikal was already an important ceremonial and trading centre in a region still dominated by El Mirador, the largest city-state of the period. Around the year 250, the eruption of the Ilopango volcano in El Salvador prompted a wave of migration into El Petén, causing changes in alliances that benefited two rival cities, Uaxactún and Tikal. The fall of the ruler of Uaxactún in 378 heralded the beginning of a prosperous era for Tikal, once again marked by foreign influences as can be seen in the iconography of Stela 31 (445 AD), typical of Teotihuacán, which was discovered beneath the North Acropolis.

Then it was Tikal's turn to bow down to another Mayan centre: in 556 AD it was vanquished by Lord Water, ruler of **Caracol** in Belize. Caracol's rulers were to govern several kingdoms of El Petén for over a century. This foreign domination slowed down Tikal's development, as is reflected in the almost total absence of monuments relating events in the city during this period.

**The golden age of the city** – The accession to the throne of ruler **Ah Cacao** (682-734) marked the return of a strong dynasty in Tikal and the start of an era of extraordinarily wide influence over the Mayan world that lasted two centuries. Among the major works carried out during this period are the monumental temples in Plaza Mayor. In the heart of the virgin forest, the city centre – reserved for the elite – housed around 10 000 people. Archeologists have estimated that a population at least six times that size lived in huts built of perishable materials on the outskirts of the ceremonial centre.

**A ghost town** – The last stela in Tikal dates from 869. At the end of the 9C the city was suddenly abandoned by its inhabitants. Of all the theories advanced by researchers to explain this mysterious phenomenon, that of a combination of factors seems to be unanimously accepted today: deforestation, soil erosion and drought are thought to have led to famine and conflict, and finally dislocation of the power structure. The jungle at once began to weave its web around the city of stone.

## Natural and cultural heritage

Almost ten centuries were to pass before the first archeologists forced their way through the jungle and tried to free the ruins from the all-enveloping vegetation. The Parque Nacional Tikal, an immense natural and cultural reserve listed as a **UNESCO World Heritage Site** since 1979, is spread over 576sqkm. The main archeological site, the heart of the ancient city, covers 16sqkm; over 3 000 buildings have been identified, along with around 200 stelae accompanied by altars, and no less than 100 000 objects. Most of the constructions visible date from the Late Classic period, some of them built on top of older structures.

**When the archeologists discovered Tikal** – The ruins of Tikal were officially discovered in 1848 by a government mission led by Modesto Méndez and Ambrosio Tut, accompanied by the painter Eusebio Lara. Thirty years later, the Swiss doctor Gustav Bernoulli visited the site and took away the wooden lintels of Temples I and IV – which can now be admired in Basel museum, Switzerland. The first photographs of the site were taken by the British archeologist Alfred Percival Maudslay in 1881.

Since the beginning of the 20C other archeologists have taken an interest in Tikal: Teobert Maler of Harvard University came here in 1895 and 1904, followed ten years later by Sylvanus G Morley, who was the first to try to decipher the hieroglyphs. In 1956 Pennsylvania University set up a study programme, but since 1970 the Guatemalan government has taken over responsibility for the excavations.

Tikal

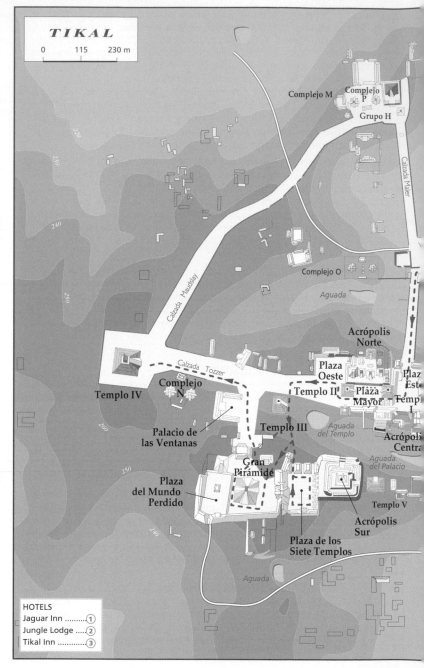

TIKAL

0    115    230 m

Complejo M
Complejo P
Grupo H
Calzada Maler
Complejo O
Aguada
Calzada Maudslay
Acrópolis Norte
Calzada Tozzer
Templo IV
Complejo N
Plaza Oeste
Plaza Este
Templo II
Plaza Mayor
Templo I
Palacio de las Ventanas
Templo III
Aguada del Templo
Acrópolis Central
Aguada del Palacio
Gran Pirámide
Plaza del Mundo Perdido
Templo V
Acrópolis Sur
Plaza de los Siete Templos
Aguada

HOTELS
Jaguar Inn ..........①
Jungle Lodge ....②
Tikal Inn ............③

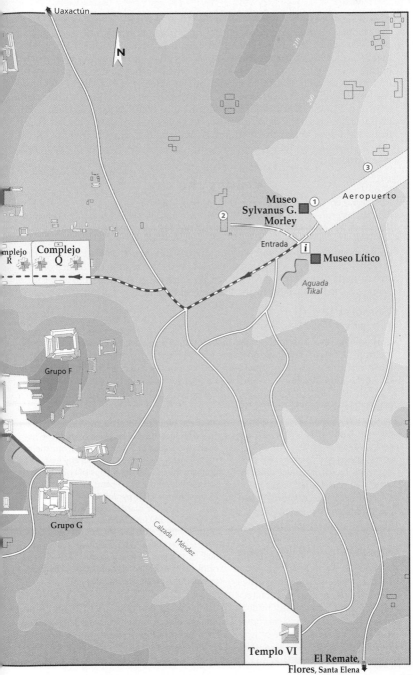

Uaxactún

N

Museo
Sylvanus G.
Morley ①

② 

Aeropuerto ③

Entrada *i*

Museo Lítico

Aguada
Tikal

mplejo
R

Complejo
Q

Grupo F

Grupo G

Calzada Méndez

Templo VI

El Remate,
Flores, Santa Elena

243

**A protected nature reserve** – Visiting Tikal also means exploring a luxuriant tropical forest, with *ceibas* (silk cotton or kapok trees), *zapotes* (sapodilla trees, the sap of which is used in the manufacture of chewing-gum), palm, breadfruit, cedar and mahogany trees rising above a tracery of creepers and bushes forming a dense jungle, through which swing spider monkeys with their strident calls. Haunt of jaguar, puma, anteater and snakes, including the formidable *barba amarilla* (fer-de-lance), the forest of Tikal is more than anything else a gigantic aviary in which more than 300 species have been identified: toucans, birds of paradise, white herons, vultures and parrots to name but a few. When the first rays of sunlight are fingering the tops of the temples, an extraordinary concert starts up – all the sounds of the jungle intermingled.

# Visiting the site

*5am-5pm. Fee. You can ask permission to stay to watch the sunset. Guides available at the entrance. Allow at least 5hr to visit the main monuments. Allow a day to complete the main tour (from Complex Q to Temple IV).*

To move around the site without getting lost in the forest, take the ancient processional causeways (*sacbeob*) used by the Maya, now bearing the names of great archeologists. The loveliest views can be admired at sunrise from the top of Temple IV and at dusk from the Lost World pyramid.

## Complex Q★

*Allow approx 15min to walk from the site entrance.*

This architectural ensemble is the first stop on the classic tour itinerary through the ruins, a sort of introduction to the site. The track opens onto a vast 2ha man-made platform known as a **twin-pyramid complex**, with a building at each of the cardinal points. To east and west stand two identical pyramids with stairways on each side, to the south is a building with nine openings, and to the north is an enclosure. Inside this enclosure stands **Stela 22★★** accompanied by **Altar 10★**, indicating the end of *Katun* 17 of *Baktun* 9, which corresponds to 771 AD. The stela depicts Chitam, the last ruler of Tikal to be identified, who came to the throne in 768; dressed in ceremonial robes and wearing a heavily plumed head-dress, the king holds his ceremonial bar in one hand while the other scatters something on the ground.

### The twin-pyramid complexes

Seven architectural ensembles of this type have been discovered at Tikal; all date from the period of intensive building that the city embarked on from the 7C. These groups of constructions are all built on the same plan: a man-made platform with identical pyramids on the east and west sides; a low construction with nine doors along the south side; and to the north, an enclosure with a stela and its altar. Archeologists believe that these "vast, open-air sanctuaries" built at the end of every "katun" (20-year period) were intended to hold large crowds, assembled for public ceremonies.

To the west of Complex Q lies **Complex R**, a similar architectural ensemble apparently built in 731 to mark the end of *Katun* 15. The absence of inscriptions on the stela, however, makes dating more difficult. The partially excavated monuments are of less interest than those in the previous group. *Cross the esplanade from east to west and turn left into Calzada Maler.*

## Plaza Este★★
*15min from Complex R.*

Its siting at the junction of ceremonial causeways and near Plaza Mayor emphasises the important role played by Plaza Este within the city. Edged by the Central Acropolis and Temple I (which can be visited from Plaza Mayor), this vast esplanade also holds other important buildings. In the centre of the square stretches an immense quadrilateral laid out around an interior courtyard which archeologists believe may have housed a **mercado** (market). On the other side of Calzada Méndez (opposite Plaza Mayor) a small structure has been discovered similar to the **temazcal** (sweat-house) still in use in the Altiplano (*see p 52 "Daily life"*); this was certainly used for the priests' purifying rites before ceremonies.

Between the market and Temple I is a **juego de pelota** (ball court) thought to date from the end of the Classic period. The frieze of hieroglyphs that ran along its walls has been worn away by time.

To the south of the ball court, at the foot of the Central Acropolis, **Structure 5D-43** consists of a platform with three stairways leading up to a temple. This Late Classic building borrows its *talud-tablero* style (tiers formed by a succession of slopes and vertical panels) from Teotihuacán architecture.

## Plaza Mayor★★★ (Great Plaza)

Two majestic temples soaring to the skies, a profusion of stelae and altars, superposed pyramids, "palaces" linked by a maze of courtyards and corridors – Tikal's main ceremonial centre is a grandiose architectural ensemble, the grey stone punctuating the clearing with fragments of history dating from 150 BC to 700 AD.

**Temple I★★** (Templo del Gran Jaguar) – To the east of Plaza Mayor, the 45m-tall Temple of the Great Jaguar looks down over the entire site. Access to the top is by a steep stairway which, with its 70-degree slope and high, narrow steps, seems to rise vertically. A vertiginous climb rewarded by a magnificent and incomparable **view★★** across the square!

Atop this limestone pyramid with its nine terraces (a number sacred to the Maya) stands a temple. As is usual in Mayan architecture, the building's imposing proportions contrast with the size of the sanctuary. The corbelled vaulting – the famous Mayan arch – that roofs the three cramped rooms seems to reduce the space inside even more. The lintels of *zapote* (sapodilla) wood that lay above the communicating doorways are today in private collections and foreign museums. On the top of the temple, the **crestería** (roofcomb), once decorated with coloured stucco, seems to point to the sky.

To continue the visit, descend into the entrails of the pyramid. Built around 700 AD, it once held a tomb; while excavating the base course, archeologists discovered a funeral chamber buried 6m below ground level. Alongside the bones of ruler Ah Cacao were laid out sumptuous offerings of jade, polychrome ceramics, shells and delicately carved bones. **Tomb 116** cannot be visited but there is a reconstitution of it in the Sylvanus G Morley museum (*see below p 249*).

At the foot of the pyramid on the southern side is a small Late Classic **ball court**.

**Temple II★★** (Templo de las Máscaras) – This temple owes its name to the two **masks** carved on either side of the stairway. With its three-platform pyramid and broader stairway, this building echoes the Temple of the Great Jaguar, which seems to be sizing it up from across the square.

**Tikal**

Built several years before its opposite number, Temple II follows a similar architectural plan: the sanctuary at the top of the stairway is composed of three corbel-vaulted rooms whose sapodilla-wood lintels met the same fate as those of the Great Jaguar temple. The **graffiti** on the inside walls are believed to date from the Classic and Post-Classic periods; the most legible depicts the death of a prisoner, killed by the lance of a masked warrior. Despite erosion, the carving on the **crestería (roofcomb)** is still visible, although it has lost its yesteryear splendour and a few metres in height – the temple now measures only 38m as opposed to its original 42m! Archeologists believe this temple was built in honour of the wife of ruler Ah Cacao, for no tomb has so far been discovered in its base course.

Near the Temple of Masks is the entrance to the **chultunob**, cavities dug in the limestone bedrock, which must have served to store food such as maize and the fruit of the *ramón* (breadfruit tree).

**The North Acropolis★** – It takes several minutes to distinguish the various buildings that make up the acropolis, a positive cascade of stone in which stairways, terraces, corridors and temples intermingle, some dozen metres above Plaza Mayor. The elevation is due to the superposition technique so dear to the Maya: something like a hundred constructions (some dating from 200 BC) are buried beneath later buildings, like a set of Russian dolls.

At the foot of this immense architectural ensemble, between the Temple of Masks and the Temple of the Great Jaguar, stands a row of stelae and altars commemorating rulers. Among these monuments, **Stela 5★** (744 AD) stands out as the most sophisticated, along with **Stela 11** *(eleven)* which bears the most recent date in Tikal (869 AD).

The central **pyramid** (Structure 5D-33) of the Acropolis is an excellent example of the Mayan way of encasing old buildings in new ones, as archeologists have uncovered three superposed structures. A gap in the most recent pyramid allows visitors to admire two **masks★**, one on each side of the stairway of the earlier temple. These huge, 3m-high masks of long-nosed divinities were until recently imprisoned in the walls. Also found beneath this structure was the famous **Stela 31★★** ( 445 AD), which can be seen in the museum; dedicated to King Stormy Sky, this delicate monument shows a strong Teotihuacán influence, as can be seen from the costume, arms and effigy of Tlaloc (the Mexican god of rain in his warrior form). To the left of the central pyramid, under **Structure 5D-34**, archeologists found **Tomb 10**, which held the bones of a ruler buried with his nine servants, turtles, a crocodile and some superb ritual vases in the Teotihuacán style. **Stela 26** (Pre-Classic), now visible in the museum, also comes from the base course of this structure.

**The Central Acropolis★** – This vast ensemble, south of Plaza Mayor and Plaza Este, is 215m long. In contrast to the vertical thrust of the temples, the buildings in the Central Acropolis are built horizontally, which is why they have been termed "palaces". Linked by a series of stairways and corridors, these buildings must have been designed for residential or administrative use. They date from between the mid-6C and the end of the 9C and are laid out on several floors around **six patios**.

Patio 2, the highest in the acropolis, has some interesting buildings. **Maler's Palace★** (or Structure 5D-65) contains two parallel rows of rooms furnished with masonry benches on which some of the graffiti are still visible. The palace was named after German archeologist Teobert Maler, who slept there during the

R. Marca

The Temple of the Great Jaguar, Tikal

excavations he led in 1895 and 1904. To the west of the patio only **Structure 5D-66**, with its cramped room at the top of a platform, might be considered a religious building. Facing this "temple" and to the east of Maler's Palace, the **Five-Storey Palace** (Palacio de los Cinco Pisos) is in fact made up of two structures (5D-50 and 5D-52), composed of two and three floors respectively. The building overlooks a ravine at the bottom of which is the immense **Palace Reservoir** (Aguada del Palacio), now dry.

## Plaza Oueste

Behind Temple II, to the west of Plaza Mayor, this square contains some stelae accompanied by their altars and the remains of a **palace** (Structure 5D-15) erected around the end of the Classic period. To the east of the square stands a **pyramid** (Structure 5D-73) which must have been topped by a temple built of perishable materials. The tomb discovered in its base course held some superb polychrome vases and jade objects.

South-west of Plaza Oueste, the slender summit of **Temple III**★ can be seen between the trees. From the top of its 55m there is a wonderful **view**★★ over the site – but the climb up is arduous! Built in 810 AD, the pyramid is surmounted by a two-room sanctuary, one of the lintels of which portrays an obese figure clad in a jaguar skin, from which it takes its other name of **Templo del Sacerdote Jaguar** (Temple of the Jaguar Priest).

## Plaza de los Siete Templos★ (Plaza of the Seven Temples)

To the south of Temple III is this square which owes its name to the seven structures along its east side, backing onto the South Acropolis. The temple (Structure 5D-95) at the centre of this ensemble is marked by a smooth stela with its altar. To the north of the square, a **triple ball court** comprising three identical playing areas dates from the Classic period.

East of the square, beyond the South Acropolis (not yet excavated), is **Temple V**, topped by an impressive **crestería**. The sanctuary stands 58m above the ground, on a base course with rounded corners.

## Plaza del Mundo Perdido★★ (Plaza of the Lost World)

To the west of Plaza de los Siete Templos is the Plaza of the Lost World, enchantingly named by the archeologists who discovered this isolated spot tucked away in the luxuriant jungle. It is a square formed of 38 structures dating from different periods, and is also called **Plaza de la Gran Pirámide**, from the 32m-high **pyramid**★ in the middle (Structure 5C-54). In fact this is five superimposed pyramids, the oldest of which is thought to date from 700 BC. This ancient astronomical observatory makes an excellent **belvedere**★★ for admiring the sunset.

To the north of this square stands the **Palacio de las Ventanas**★ (Palace of Windows) or **Palacio de los Murciélagos** (Palace of Bats). Both names are evocative enough, for at nightfall swarms of the little creatures can be seen streaming out of its windows. This is a Late Classic building with two floors of rooms.

*Continue to Calzada Tozzer and turn left.*

Two hundred metres to the left stands **Complex N**★, another example of a twin-pyramid structure, dating from 711 AD (earlier than groups Q and R). The stela and altar in the enclosure form a remarkable group: **Stela 16**★★ depicts a warrior carrying a bag on which can be seen the head of Tlaloc, an indication of Teotihuacán influence. **Altar 5**★★ bears a circle of glyphs, in the middle of which two priests stand near an altar on which a skull and bones are piled up.

At the end of Calzada Tozzer, where it meets Calzada Maudslay, stands the 64.5m-high **Temple IV**★★, also called **Templo de la Serpiente de Dos Cabezas** (Temple of the Two-Headed Serpent). Built around AD 740 AD, it is the highest building in Tikal and one of the tallest in all pre-Columbian America. Wooden steps and ladders have been put up the north-east side so that visitors can climb up its steep sides. From the top there is a stunning **panoramic view**★★★, particularly at dawn and dusk when only a few stone roofcombs, pink-tinged in the first or last rays of the sun, emerge from the sea of jungle.

*By spending a second day at the site you can visit the more distant groups.*

**North Complexes**
*From Temple IV via Calzada Maudslay or from Plaza Este via Calzada Maler, it takes about 20min to walk to the North Complexes.*

Most of the structures in **Group H** are still only mounds in the process of being excavated. The twin pyramids of **Complex M**, with its enclosure containing a stela and an altar, were built in 692 AD. In **Complex P**, which dates from 751, a **temazcal** was discovered, one of only two sweat-houses found on the Tikal site.

**South Complexes**
*From Plaza Este via Calzada Méndez, allow 25min to walk to Temple VI. Because it is some distance from the rest of the site it is advisable to go there in a group or with a guide.*

To the right, 300m from Plaza Este, is **Group G**, a large Late Classic palace whose walls still bear a few traces of mural paintings.

Calzada Méndez leads to **Temple VI**★, known as **Templo de las Inscripciones**, rising 12m high. This Temple of the Inscriptions ( 766 AD) takes its name from the hieroglyphic text running along the **crestería (roofcomb)** built atop a sanctuary of two vaulted rooms. **Stela 21**★ at the foot of the temple also bears a sequence of glyphs.

## To complete the visit of the site
*The two museums are located close to the old landing strip.*

**The Museo Sylvanus G Morley**★★ *(8am-5pm; weekends 8am-4pm. Fee)*, next to the Jaguar Inn hotel, contains numerous jade and ceramic items, some superb polychrome vases, bones engraved with scenes from the underworld, and censers, all discovered during the excavations. There is also an interesting reconstitution of **Tomb 116** found underneath Temple I in Plaza Mayor *(see above)*.

**The Museo Lítico**★ *(8am-5pm; weekends 8am-4pm. No fee)* stands next door to the visitor centre. Among the stelae from Tikal and neighbouring archeological sites, the extraordinary work on **Stela 16**★★ and **Altar 5**★★ *(see Complex N)* is particularly fascinating.

# An excursion north of Tikal
*Allow half a day including visiting the site.*

Of the many archeological sites scattered about the jungle in the vicinity of Tikal, only Uaxactún is easily accessible.

## Uaxactún★
*Entrance tickets sold at Tikal ticket office. 25km north of Tikal by a track negotiable in a 4WD vehicle, otherwise allow 6hr on foot. It is advisable to take a local guide at Tikal, through a Flores travel agent or at the El Chiclero hotel beside the old Uaxactún landing strip.*

**Tikal**

*Arriving by the Tikal road, turn right and drive alongside the landing strip for about 500m. Paths on either side of the strip lead off to different parts of the site.*

This ceremonial centre, which rivalled Tikal in the 4C, is architecturally similar to its neighbour, but its less imposing temples have not been restored. The site consists of eight distinct groups of structures scattered on either side of the former landing strip.

During excavations led by the Washington Carnegie Institute between 1926 and 1937, the archeologists unearthed a set of buildings forming an **astronomical observatory\***, part of Group E in the south eastern part of the site *(path to the right of the landing strip when coming from Tikal)*. An example of how advanced the Maya were in the study of the stars, it enabled them to determine the dates of solstices and equinoxes. Looking straight ahead from the top of Pyramid E-VII towards the platform surmounted by three temples, you will see the middle temple which marks the point on the horizon where the sun rises on the equinoxes (21 March and 21 September); the left-hand temple (to the north) marks the point at which the sun rises on the summer solstice (21 June) and the right-hand temple that of the winter solstice (21 December).

Pyramid E-VII was built on top of one of the oldest constructions so far discovered in El Petén, referred to as **Structure E-VII Sub\***. This primitive structure, dating from the end of the Pre-Classic period (approximately 200 AD), is remarkably well preserved, having been protected for several centuries by the second pyramid built over it. Stairways flanked with stucco masks of serpents and jaguars lead up to a platform on which there are sockets that once held the posts of a temple built of perishable materials.

El Petén

# Making the most of Tikal

## COMING AND GOING

**By private minibus** – See p 236 "Making the most of Flores".

## GETTING AROUND

All the hotels are at the site entrance, a 15min walk from Plaza Mayor.

## WHERE TO STAY

The electricity supply only functions for a few hours morning and evening.

*Under US$15*

You can pitch your tent or hang your hammock up in the *camp site*, not far from the old landing strip. You can also sleep in tiny wood cabins scattered around the lawns.

*US$25-60*

**Jaguar Inn**, ☎ 926 0002, solis@quetzal.net – 10rm ✕ ⅽⅽ Rooms with minimal comfort and dormitories for

groups. Somewhat unappetising accommodation but at a reasonable price.

**Hotel Jungle Lodge**, ☎ 476 8775, Fax 476 0294 – 46rm ⅹ ✕ ⅼ ⅽⅽ The cheapest rooms are basic and the toilet facilities somewhat rundown. For a not inconsiderable price difference you can have new rooms that are better maintained.

**Hotel Tikal Inn**, ☎ 594 6944, Fax 599 6212 – 26rm ⁿ ⅹ ✕ ⅼ The most pleasant of the 3 as far as efforts at reception and decoration go. The cheaper rooms in the main building are simple but clean. The 15 rustic bungalows around the swimming-pool are comfortable and prettily decked in Guatemalan fabrics. Reservations only possible for the latter category.

## EATING OUT

Apart from the hotel restaurants there are 3 "comedores" at the site entrance.

F. Dyan

Casa Rosada in Lívingston

# THE ROAD TO THE CARIBBEAN

This hot and humid region of banana plantations gravitates around the imposing Esquipulas Basilica, the Lourdes of Central America. The region is also extraordinarily rich in archeological remains. Legions of giant stelae, fifty kilometres apart as the crow flies, seem to perpetuate in art the war that once raged between the city-states of Quiriguá and Copán (Honduras). A *lancha* takes you down the Río Dulce to the Atlantic Ocean. At the river mouth, the colourful cottages of Lívingston village surprise visitors – this is a Caribbean enclave in Maya territory, more coconut bread than tortilla, more African than Amerindian, more reggae than marimba.

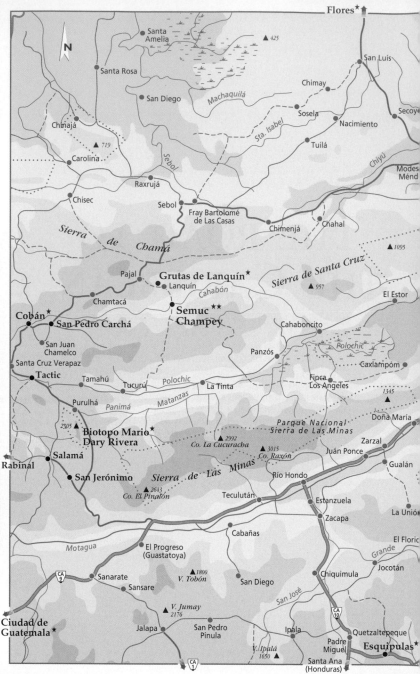

Flores ★

Santa Amelia

Santa Rosa

San Diego

▲ 425

*Machaquilá*

San Luis

Chimay

Sosela

Secoy

Nacimiento

*Sta. Isabel*

Tuilá

*Chiyú*

Modes Ménd

Chinajá

▲ 719

Carolina

*Sebol*

Raxrujá

Chisec

Sebol

Fray Bartolomé de Las Casas

Chimenjá

Chahal

*Sierra  de  Chamá*

▲ 1095

Pajal

Grutas de Lanquín ★

Lanquín

*Cahabón*

*Sierra de Santa Cruz*

▲ 957

El Estor

Chamtacá

Semuc ★★ Champey

Cobán ★

San Pedro Carchá

Cahaboncito

San Juan Chamelco

Santa Cruz Verapaz

Panzós

*Polochic*

Caxlampóm

Tactic

Tamahú

Tucurú

*Polochic*

La Tinta

Finca Los Angeles

*1345*
▲

Purulhá

*Panimá*

*Matanzas*

Doña María

*2305* ▲

Biotopo Mario ★ Dary Rivera

*Parque Nacional Sierra de Las Minas*

▲ *2992*
Co. La Cucuracha

Zarzal

Salamá

▲ *3015*
Co. Raxón

Juán Ponce

Rabinal

San Jerónimo

*Sierra  de  Las  Minas*

Río Hondo

Gualán

▲ *2643*
Co. El Pinalón

Teculután

Estanzuela

La Unión

Zacapa

Cabañas

El Floric

*Motagua*

El Progreso (Guastatoya)

*Grande*

CA 9

Sanarate

Sansare

▲ *1800*
V. Tobón

San Diego

Chiquimula

Jocotán

*San José*

CA 10

Ciudad de Guatemala ★

▲ *V. Jumay*
*2176*

Jalapa

San Pedro Pinula

Ipala

Quetzaltepeque

CA 1

*V. Ipalá*
*1650* ▲

Padre Miguel

Santa Ana (Honduras)

Esquipulas ★

254

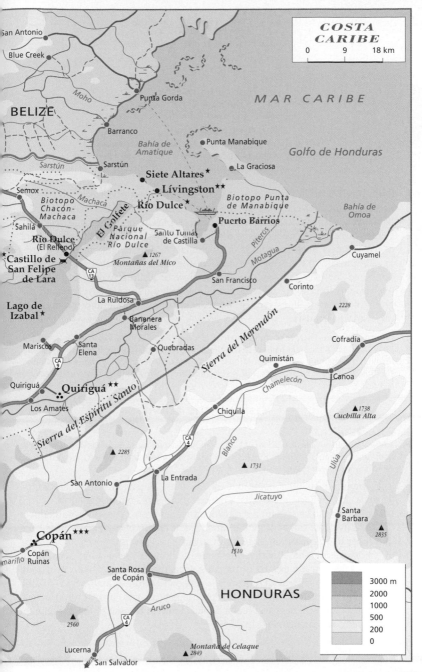

COSTA
CARIBE

0    9    18 km

San Antonio

Blue Creek

Moho

Punta Gorda

MAR CARIBE

BELIZE

Barranco

Bahía de
Amatique

Punta Manabique

Golfo de Honduras

Sarstún

Sarstún

La Graciosa

Semox

Machaca

Siete Altares ★

Lívingston ★★

Río Dulce ★

Biotopo Punta
de Manabique

Bahía de
Omoa

Biotopo
Chacón-
Machaca

El Golfete

Parque
Nacional
Río Dulce

Puerto Barrios

Sahilá

Río Dulce
(El Relleno)

★
Castillo de
San Felipe
de Lara

CA
13

▲ 1267
Montañas del Mico

Santo Tomás
de Castilla

Piteros

Motagua

Cuyamel

San Francisco

Corinto

▲ 2228

Lago de
Izabal ★

La Ruidosa

Bananera
Morales

Sierra del Merendón

Cofradía

Mariscos

Santa
Elena

Quebradas

Quimistán

Canoa

CA
9

Chamelecón

Quiriguá

Quiriguá ★★

Los Amates

Sierra del Espíritu Santo

Chiquila

CA
4

Blanco

Ulúa

▲ 1738
Cuchilla Alta

▲ 2285

▲ 1731

San Antonio

La Entrada

Jicatuyo

Santa
Barbara

▲ 2835

Copán ★★★

Copán
Ruinas

amarillo

Santa Rosa
de Copán

▲ 1510

HONDURAS

Aruco

CA
4

3000 m
2000
1000
500
200
0

▲ 2560

Lucerna

San Salvador

Montaña de Celaque
▲ 2849

# ESQUIPULAS★

Chiquimula department – Alt 954m
215km from Guatemala City
See map p 217 and p 254

**Not to be missed**
The Black Christ.
The view of the town from the Morola hill.

**And remember...**
Hotel room prices can be negotiated on weekdays.
For major pilgrimages (15 January and 9 March) and Holy Week,
reserve hotel rooms well in advance.

Rounding a bend in the road, you suddenly see Esquipulas Basilica below, its blinding whiteness eclipsing the town stretched at its feet. An eloquent vision of a town that gravitates around the most important pilgrimage centre in Central America. At weekends and during religious festivals, long processions of worshippers flock from all over Guatemala and its neighbouring countries to pay homage to the *Señor de Esquipulas*, the Black Christ that has now been honoured for over four centuries. This flow of visitors makes Esquipulas a lively town where deep devotion combines with a festive atmosphere and pilgrims of all nationalities veer between silent contemplation and the music of the mariachi bands.

*From Guatemala City, take the Carretera al Atlántico (CA9) to Río Hondo (km 131). Take the road to the right leading to the Honduras border and follow it for 70km, passing through Chiquimula. At Padre Miguel crossroads, fork left and continue 14km to Esquipulas. All the hotels, bars and restaurants are located in the town centre near the basilica.*

## Visiting the town

### The Basilica★★

*6am-8pm; daily mass at 6.30am, 11am, 5pm; additional mass Sundays and festivals at 8am and 9.30am. To see the Black Christ, enter the basilica on the left side behind the "Entrada a venerar" sign.*

This imposing building holds one of the most venerated statues in Central America. In 1595 the great artist Quirio Cataño was commissioned to carve a **Black Christ**★★ in balsam fir, a dark wood that has grown constantly darker over the years from the smoke from the candles. The choice of colour may have been due either to an apparition of a Black Christ on this precise spot, or to the hope of Christianising the Amerindians quickly through assimilation with black divinities that already existed in the Mayan pantheon. The sculpture was soon renowned for its supernatural powers. During a visit to Esquipulas in 1737, the archbishop of Guatemala, Pedro Pardo de Figueroa, was himself miraculously cured of a chronic illness and had a basilica built on the site of the old church. The basilica was inaugurated in 1759.

M. Vautier

Pilgrim souvenirs: straw hats and "toquillas"

During major pilgrimages the faithful sometimes have to wait hours to pray just a few seconds at the feet of the Christ, before backing out so as not to turn their backs on the statue.

In the **park**★ outside the basilica pilgrims move down the alleys on their knees in penitence, families buy straw hats and *toquillas* (multicoloured garlands) in souvenir of their pilgrimage and groups of nuns picnic in the shade of the trees, while a brass band walks backwards down the steps of the basilica, still facing the Christ.

## The Centro Turístico Cueva de Las Minas

*Return to the main road by taking the street that runs alongside the Pollo Campero restaurant, to the right of the basilica. Turn left towards Honduras and continue 200m to the Texaco petrol station. Access by car along a track suitable for motor vehicles but barely negotiable during the rainy season, or on foot by the path to the left (15min walk). 8am-6pm. Fee.*

Pilgrims never fail to visit this tourist centre, just a short walk from the basilica. Behind the **Río Tulapa**, renowned for its miracle-working waters, the entrance to a cave can be seen. A long passage, feebly lit by candles, leads to the suffocating heat of a chamber where shamans regularly practise purification rites dating back to pre-Columbian times.

## The Cerrito de Morola★ (Morola hill)

*Go up 2a Ave to the top of the hill, about 4km from the town centre. Come back down via 3a Ave to enjoy a bird's-eye view of the basilica.*

Climbing this hill dotted with little chapels is reminiscent of the **Via Crucis** (Way of the Cross). The **mirador de la Cruz del Milagro**★★ at the top reveals a wide panorama of the town.

The road to the Caribbean

# Making the most of Esquipulas

### COMING AND GOING

**By bus** – Departures every 30min between 1am and 6.30pm for Guatemala City (4hr), in front of the **Rutas Orientales** transport company, corner of 11 Calle and 1a Ave, 1 block from Parque Central, ☎ 943 1077. In the same street, opposite the market, a minibus leaves every 15min for Chiquimula (1hr).

### ADDRESS BOOK

**Bank / Currency Exchange** – **Banco G & T**, corner of 9a Calle and 3a Ave, opposite Hotel Legendario. 9am-6pm; Saturdays 9am-1pm. **Banco Internacional**, corner of 11 Calle and 2a Ave in front of Parque Central. 9am-5pm; Saturdays 9am-1pm. Cashpoint for Visa cards.

**Post office / Telephone** – The post office is on the corner of 6a Ave and 2a Calle. Telephone calls from **TELGUA**, corner of 9a Calle and 5a Ave, open 9am-8pm; Sundays to 4pm.

### WHERE TO STAY

The hotels are often full at weekends. It is possible to negotiate reductions during the week.

• **Town centre**

*US$15-30*

**Hotel Los Angeles**, 2a Ave 11-94, ☎ 943 0607 – 20rm 📶 ⟨ ✗ cc A shop selling religious articles and a cafeteria mark the entrance to this small hotel set around a lively inside courtyard. Modest but comfortable rooms, with toilet facilities in good repair.

**Hotel Villa Zonia**, 10a Calle 1-84, ☎ 943 1133 – 15rm ⚒ ⤢ TV CC In the street parallel to the town's main thoroughfare stands this small building with balconies. The rooms are not very light but are impeccably clean.

**Hotel Payaquí**, 2a Ave 11-56, ☎ 943 1143, Fax 943 1371 – 41rm ⚒ TV ✗ ⤢ CC This hotel in the street alongside the basilica provides numerous services. The rooms are nothing special but offer reasonable value for money for someone travelling alone.

*US$30-45*

**Hotel Internacional**, 10a Calle A 0-85, ☎ 943 1131/67 – 49rm ⚒ ⤢ TV ✗ ⤢ 2 blocks from the basilica. The building's interior is almost like a prison but the rooms are clean and comfortable.

**Hotel Legendario**, corner of 3a Ave and 9a Calle, ☎ 943 1824/5, Fax 943 1022 – 40rm ⚒ ⤢ TV ✗ ⤢ CC Big rooms with bay windows set around a swimming-pool in the middle of a flourishing garden. A perfectly maintained hotel. It is possible to negotiate a better price during the week.

• **Outside Esquipulas**

*US$60-100*

**Hotel El Gran Chortí**, km 222 Carretera a Esquipulas, ☎ 943 1148/57, Fax 943 1551 – 40rm ⚒ ☰ TV ✗ ⤢ CC The most luxurious hotel in Esquipulas is located 1km outside town on the road to Chiquimula. Big rooms with every modern comfort at corresponding prices.

**EATING OUT**

*Under US$10*

**Jimmy's**, 2a Ave 11-56. 7am-10pm. On one side of the Parque below the Payaquí hotel; this fast-food chain serves grilled chicken and hamburgers, as well as breakfasts, at competitive prices.

**La Rotonda**, corner of 11 Calle and 1a Ave, opposite the Rutas Orientales head office, ☎ 943 2038. 7am-10pm. Open-air cafeteria with seating around a semi-circular counter. Local cuisine, pizzas and hamburgers. Friendly, efficient staff.

**Restaurante El Angel**, corner of 11 Calle and 2a Ave, in front of Parque Central. 8am-9pm. A modest restaurant where the TV is never switched off. Traditional cuisine, of reasonable quality and cheap.

*From US$10*

**La Hacienda Steak House**, 2a Ave 10-20, ☎ 943 1748 CC 8am-10pm. The class of this restaurant does not really fit in with the little "comedores" around it. Good grilled meat specialities. Fish and seafood dishes at about double the price.

**OTHER THINGS TO DO**

**Excursions** – The **Centro Turístico Cueva de Las Minas** is within walking distance, see above for how to get there.

**SHOPPING GUIDE**

The **market** in front of the basilica is packed out with religious articles, holy images and crucifixes. Here you can buy "coronas" (or "toquillas"), the multi-coloured garlands with which drivers adorn their cars for every pilgrimage. On the many confectionery stands you can buy the delicious local speciality of "bocadillos de coco" – tasty bars of grated coconut.

**Making the most of Esquipulas**

# COPÁN★★★

Valley of Copán (Honduras)
13km from the Guatemalan border
Accommodation in the village of Copán Ruinas (1km from site)

**Not to be missed**
The carved stelae in Gran Plaza.
The hieroglyphic stairway.

**And remember...**
Hire a guide to get the most out of your visit to the ruins.
Spend at least one night in the village so as to have an entire day at the site.
The light is at its best in the early morning and late afternoon.

R. Marca

"Copán"

In the heart of a cheerful valley carpeted with tobacco plantations hides one of the loveliest Mayan sites, reputed for the delicacy of its stelae, the refinement of its sculptures and its profusion of glyph texts. Here the genius of the city's astronomers was matched only by that of its artists; there are no vertiginous temples as in Tikal, but the city's architecture radiates a tranquil strength that leaves a lasting impression on visitors.

## "The Athens of the New World"

Copán was occupied as early as the end of the second millennium BC, but the earliest date inscribed in stone goes back to only 435 AD – and the latest to 822 AD.

**The rise to power** – The earliest ruler identified, **Quetzal Macaw**, came to the throne in 426 AD and founded the ruling dynasty of Copán. Despite the archeological finds, the history of the city-state is not yet fully elucidated.

The ceremonial centre began to grow in importance during the reign of **Smoke Sky** (578-628) and developed further under **Smoke Jaguar** (628-695), and especially **18 Rabbit** (695-738), to whom we owe the magnificent stelae in Gran Plaza and the ball court. The capture and beheading of this great king, ordered by the ruler of Quiriguá in 738, was a serious blow to Copán's prestige (*see p 270 "Quiriguá"*). On becoming ruler in 749, **Smoke Shell** put an end to the ensuing period of uncertainty and had a superb hieroglyphic stairway built that restored Copán's image. His son **First Dawn** (763-820) was the last important ruler to head this city-state with its population of over 20 000 in an area of 24sqkm. Copán then declined mysteriously in the mid-9C; as in Tikal, soil erosion and deforestation are thought to have caused famine, a hypothesis confirmed by signs of malnutrition in the skeletons discovered on the site.

**A lawyer in the Court of the Maya**
When in 1838 John Lloyd Stephens chanced upon documents mentioning unusual architecture in Central America and Yucatán, no more was needed to arouse the curiosity of this New York lawyer with a passion for archeology. The following year he set off to hunt for this civilization lost in the jungle, accompanied by English artist Frederick Catherwood. Stunned by the ruins of Quiriguá and, more especially, those of Copán (he bought the site for US$50), Stephens intended to ship the monuments back to the United States. This project was abandoned but his description of their journey, superbly illustrated by Catherwood, revealed to the European public the sophistication of a "new" civilization.

The road to the Caribbean

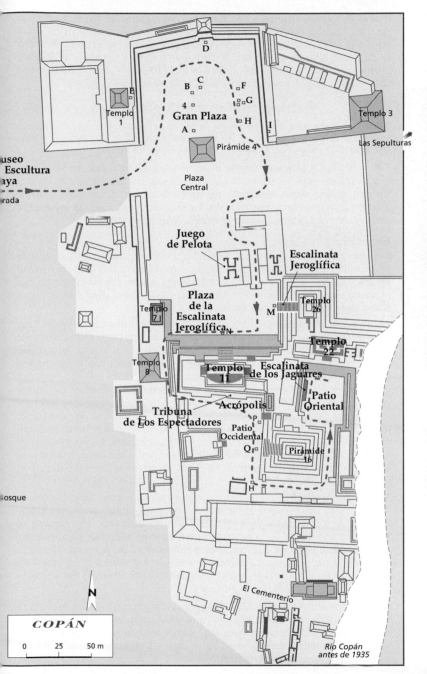

D

B  C
□  □  □ F
4  □
Gran Plaza  □ G
□ H
A  □
I

Templo
1

E
□

Templo 3

Las Sepulturas

useo
Escultura
aya

rada

Pirámide 4

Plaza
Central

Juego
de Pelota

Escalinata
Jeroglífica

Templo
26

Plaza
de la
Escalinata
Jeroglífica

Templo
7

M □

N □

Templo
22

Templo
8

Templo
11

Escalinata
de los Jaguares

Patio
Oriental

Tribuna
de Los Espectadores

Acrópolis

P
□

Patio
Occidental

Q □

Pirámide
16

H □

osque

El Cementerio

N

COPÁN

0    25    50 m

Río Copán
antes de 1935

**The rediscovery of Copán** – The ruins had been known to the Spanish since the 16C, but they were not described in writing until Colonel Juan Galindo's reports of 1834, which incited John Lloyd Stephens and Frederick Catherwood to make the journey to the site. Since the archeological missions of Alfred P Maudslay in 1885 and Sylvanus G Morley in 1910, many others have followed suit. In 1980 Copán was declared a **UNESCO World Heritage Site**.

# Visiting the archeological park

*The site is on the right, 1km beyond the bridge to the east of the village. Guides are available at the entrance or through the Aventuras Copán agency (see "Making the most of Copán"). 8am-5pm. Fee. Allow 4hr to visit, including the museum.*

The archeological park includes the main complex (political, administrative and religious centre) and two residential areas, El Bosque and Las Sepulturas. Visiting the first group, which comprises the most important monuments, may be enough for some visitors, but a full day's visit allows you to wander around the other groups of buildings, which have been excavated recently.

## Gran Plaza★★ (Great Square)

In Copán's heyday the huge crowds attending public ceremonies must have been packed like sardines in the stands lining three sides of this vast **ceremonial square**. This 3ha area of levelled ground, framed by the remains of temples and pyramids, was once entirely coated in stucco. It is now a lawn scattered with **stelae** and **altars**, a true open-air museum.

**An overview of the stelae** – The Copán sculptors are distinguished by their use of **sculpture in the round**, which attained its most advanced form during the reign of 18 Rabbit. The seven stelae in the middle of the square form a fine ensemble, a hymn to the glory of this ruler; monuments I and E date from a different period *(see below)*.

Carved from green volcanic tuff, these stelae, 3-4m high, illustrate the artistic refinement of Copán in its heyday. Often accompanied by altars, they generally stand above cavities where offerings were placed. In these works, sometimes qualified as "baroque", the Maya once again demonstrated their horror of blank spaces: every square inch has been elaborately worked until the stone resembles lace from so much chiselling. Some figures are veritable three-dimensional portraits, so realistic that they seem to be about to step away from the stone and stroll along the esplanade!

**The stelae in detail** – *The monuments are described clockwise.* Immediately on arriving in the Great Square, at the foot of a pyramid, visitors encounter a copy of **Stela A★★** depicting a figure holding a ceremonial bar, the emblem of sovereignty. Above the skilfully worked head-dress of composite plaits emerges a death's head, which actually represents the mask of the sun god. The sides and back of the monument are covered with glyphs indicating the year 731. Under the stela is a cruciform cavity designed to hold offerings; this has been uncovered so that visitors can see inside.

**Stela 4★★**, which dates from 726, also portrays the ruler 18 Rabbit in ceremonial dress. Although damaged, this monument stands out because of its exceptional carving demonstrating the Maya's total mastery of in-the-round sculpture. The stela is accompanied by an **altar** which archeologists refer to as a "sacrificial stone". Its shape is reminiscent of a *pelota* (ball), rather like a large, smooth seashell hinged by a cable twist. It is now thought that the two channels extending from the cavity on top were to allow the *pom* (copal resin) to drain away, rather than the blood of victims.

The geographical origins of the Maya have been the subject of much controversy. The theory that they came from Asia is reinforced by the iconography on **Stela B★★**, a splendid sculpture with strong Orientalist tendencies. A figure holding a finely-worked "manikin sceptre" (ceremonial bar) terminating in a two-headed serpent emerges from between the jaws of an earth monster. Above the sovereign's turban can be seen what at first glance appears to be a series of small figures sitting cross-legged and two elephants! Academics do not accept this hypothesis, however; they argue that the images in fact depict the beaks of macaws, the bird symbol of the daytime sun, although they look for all the world like elephants' trunks.

**Stela C★★**, thought to date from 782, stands out from the rest of the series by its height (3.80m) and its unusual carving. This "Janus statue" bears a human figure on both sides: an old man with a long beard, symbol of wisdom, and a smooth-chinned young man. These two sovereigns hold identical ceremonial bars, which leads us to presume they represent the same person. There are still some traces of the reddish paint that probably originally covered all the stelae. On either side of the monument stands an **altar**; one depicts a giant turtle, whereas the other was never finished.

At the base of Temple 2, **Stela D★★** depicts a masked figure that is thought to be 18 Rabbit himself. The back of this stela is exceptional for its glyphs showing full-length figures, instead of the heads that are usually used in pictograms. The symbol of Copán, a bat, can be distinguished on it, along with the date of 736, one year before the sovereign was captured by the ruler of Quiriguá. In front of this stela stands an **altar** in the form of a two-headed monster, along with the tomb of archeologist John Owens, who died of malaria during a mission in 1893.

Copán

R. Marca

Stela B in Copán

**Stela F**★★ (721) shows an intimidating figure with beard and moustache. His long coat seems to envelop the back of the stela in a remarkable series of glyphs. The accompanying **altar** is in the form of a two-headed monster.

To the south of this stela and scattered around the lawn are **Altars G**★, carved with serpents. The largest, erected around 800 in honour of First Dawn, shows a human figure emerging from the jaws of a two-headed serpent.

**Stela H**★★ (730), one of the most remarkable on the site, has given rise to much conjecture as to the sex of the figure clothed in a skirt. This would seem to be the only portrayal of a female figure in Copán, although this hypothesis is not unanimously accepted. Among the offerings left in its underground cavity was gold jewellery, the only precious metal to be found on the site and probably brought from Panama or Colombia.

In the vicinity of the esplanade two other stelae can also be seen, less sophisticated than those of the central group. Near Stela H is **Stela I**, probably dating from 800. Opposite, on the other side of the grass on the platform of Temple 1, **Stela E** is thought to be the oldest in the series since it dates back to 615.

## The Juego de Pelota★★ (Ball Court)
*See p 23 and p 34 "The ancient Maya"*

Between Plaza Central and Plaza de la Escalinata Jeroglífica stands the ball court, among the most admired of all the Mayan ball courts, despite its small size. This third version, built in 738 at the end of 18 Rabbit's reign, covers two earlier structures, one dating from the 6C and the other from the beginning of the 8C. The play area in the shape of an "I" is edged by two sloping surfaces surmounted on either side by three stone macaw heads. The play area was marked out by three **marcadores** (markers), circular stones (now in Copán's archeological museum) with sculptures depicting the various stages in the game: on the first and third, a ball hanging from a rope is thought to indicate the beginning and end of the match. The central marker portrays two players kneeling ready to hit the ball, along with glyphs referring to the Mayan god of sacrifice and to Hunahpu, hero of the *Popol Vuh* (*see p 30 and p 121*).

## Plaza de la Escalinata Jeroglífica★
(Square of the Hieroglyphic Stairway)

To the south, the ball court opens onto this square which takes its name from the monumental **hieroglyphic stairway**★★ located on its east side. Like an avalanche of glyphs relating the history of Copán between the 6C and 8C, its 63 carved steps form the longest text in the New World. On every tenth step stands the statue of a ruler, with birds and serpents ornamenting the side ramps. This stairway 10m wide and 21m high was built during the reign of Smoke Shell. With the exception of the first thirteen steps, the 1 250 stone blocks that make it up were found in a jumbled heap, the structure having collapsed. The American university in charge of restoration took away one row of stones and a statue in exchange for the work. Even without these elements, which Honduras is still claiming back, the monument has conserved most of its majesty although it cannot be appreciated to the full, protected as it is by a tarpaulin. There is a long-term project to build a replica on the site and house the original in the Museo de Escultura Maya.

At the top of the stairway stands **Temple 26**, its walls also presenting a sequence of glyphs. At the bottom, **Stela M** (756), dedicated to Smoke Shell, has a zoomorphic **altar** in front showing a head emerging from the jaws of a serpent.

To the south of the square, at the foot of the Temple of Inscriptions (*more easily accessible from the West Patio, see below*), **Stela N★★** (761) is yet another tribute to Smoke Shell. It bears a delicately carved figure on each side, one old and one young, as on Stela C.

*Access to the West Patio of the Acropolis is between the west side of Temple 11 and Structures 7 and 8.*

## The Acropolis★★

This vast ensemble of buildings rises to over 30m above a man-made terrace covering nearly 5ha, to the south of Plaza de la Escalinata Jeroglífica. It was built over a period of 400 years but, as in Tikal, only the most recent constructions are visible, almost all of which date from the reign of **First Dawn** (Yax Pac). Most of the temples in fact hide earlier structures, in accordance with the "Russian dolls" system so dear to Mayan builders. To the east the Acropolis was being eaten away by the Río Copán, so to avoid further damage an archeological mission diverted the watercourse in 1935. Time, however, has continued to take its toll and few vestiges now remain of the superb temples that once stood around the east and west courtyards.

**The West Patio** – This west courtyard is separated from Plaza de la Escalinata Jeroglífica by **Temple 11★** (*eleven*), also called **Templo de las Inscripciones** because of the panels carved with glyphs that decorate its walls. From this building, considered one of the most sacred places in all Copán, the ruler could take part in public ceremonies.

On the south side of the temple, a hieroglyphic stairway called the **Tribuna de los Espectadores★** (Tribune of the Spectators) looks down over the West Patio. At the top, two sculptures evoke the storm god in the form of torch-bearing monkeys with serpents in the corners of their mouths. This façade is the better preserved of the two, but on the other side, in the midst of the vegetation, can be seen a copy of the astounding wrinkled, toothless face of the *Viejo de Copán*; he is one of the old men known as *Bacabs* (or *Pauahtuns*), divinities holding up the world at the corners of the temple.

In the eastern part of this courtyard, **Altar Q★★** (775) is one of the most important items on the site, as much for its superb carving as for its historical interest (the original is in the museum). The 16 rulers adorning the four sides of this rectangular block of stone represent the entire dynastic line of Copán, which lasted almost four centuries. First Dawn thus receives the ceremonial bar from the preceding kings, each placed above his own glyph. Further confirming the importance of the monument, archeologists found the bones of 15 jaguars buried nearby.

Behind this altar stands **Pyramid 16**, the highest in Copán. In 1989 a magnificently preserved early temple was discovered in its base course, apparently dating from the reign of Moon Jaguar (second half of the 6C). There is a life-size model of this structure, named **Rosalila**, in the site museum.

*Behind Altar H, go around Pyramid 16 by taking the alley overlooking the residential area known as El Cementerio.*

**Copán**

P. Le Floc'h/EXPLORER

The storm god at the top of the Tribune of the Spectators

**The East Patio\*** – In the western part of this courtyard is the **Escalinata de los Jaguares\***, which owes its name to the two carved jaguars on either side of the terracing. The head emerging from between the jaws of a serpent, in the centre, represents the Sun.

To the north of this square, **Temple 22\*\***, built around 764, is considered one of the masterpieces of Classic Mayan architecture. The **door\*\*** of the sanctuary, framed by a profusion of intimidating carvings, symbolises the entrance to the underworld: surrounded by skulls, the *Bacabs (see p 265)* hold up a heavenly creature with the twin heads of the Sun and Venus. In the ruins of this temple archeologists have found fine sculptures of the **Maize God** in the form of a young man – these objects are now in various museums, including the British Museum.

## Before, during or after visiting the site

The modest size of Copán's main group makes it possible to visit the museum at any time, which makes an ideal pause during the hottest hours of the day. The **Museo de Escultura Maya\*\*** *(8am-4pm. Fee)* at the site entrance holds the **originals** of the finest of the carved items (Stela A, Altar Q), fragments of architectural decoration and reconstructions of temples in the nobles' residential quarters (scribe's palace, carved bench). The centre of the building is taken up by the copy of the Rosalila temple. The basement takes you on a journey into the underworld through the iconography generally associated with it.

The road to the Caribbean

On the main square of the village, the **Museo de Arqueología de Copán★** *(8am-4pm; closed Sundays. Fee)* makes an excellent complement to the visit. The few exhibition rooms, although a bit dated, nevertheless contain the only objects from the site that are exhibited to the general public (censer lids with effigies of kings, ball court markers etc).

Since spring 1999 several **archeological tunnels** have at last been opened to the public, allowing visitors to admire the earlier constructions, in particular the famous **Rosalila** temple *(copy in the museum)*.

# Making the most of Copán

## COMING AND GOING

**By bus and pick-up** – 8 buses a day, 6am-3pm, between Chiquimula and El Florido (3hr). If you are not going beyond Copán, there is a 10-quetzal tax to pay on leaving Guatemala, then the same sum (20 lempiras) to be paid to Honduras immigration. The frontier is open 7am-6pm.

Once in Honduras, only the pick-ups run the 12km between the frontier and Copán Ruinas. For the return journey, these pick-ups wait near the bridge east of the village on the way to the ruins. Before starting out, they go around the village several times to pick up passengers. To avoid this unnecessary detour, go directly to the bridge west of Parque Central, which all vehicles have to pass on their way to the frontier.

**By car** – To cross the frontier with a rental vehicle you must have written authorisation from the rental company.

## GETTING AROUND

The Copán archeological site is only 1km from the village and easy to reach on foot.

## FINDING YOUR WAY

The streets of Copán Ruinas do not have names, but you cannot get lost, as the hotels and restaurants are almost all located within a radius of 200m from Parque Central. The addresses indicate the number of "cuadras" (blocks of houses, about 100m) and the direction from Parque Central. The church is on the east side of the square.

## ADDRESS BOOK

**Tourist information** – As there is no official tourist office, locals will provide important information on the village and its surroundings. **Honduras Tips**, a bilingual English-Spanish guide, published by the Ministry of Tourism and available free in all the hotels, is a useful source of information.

**Bank / Currency Exchange** – **Banco de Occidente** and **Banco Atlantida**, Parque Central. Same opening hours: 8am-12noon / 2pm-5pm; closed Saturday afternoons and Sundays. Cash withdrawals on Visa cards and currency exchange (1 quetzal = approx 2 lempiras). At the border the black-market moneychangers offer lempiras, quetzals and dollars at slightly lower rates than the banks.

**Post office / Telephone** – The post office adjoins the museum. The **Hondutel** telephone company, 100m from Parque Central, is open 8am-9pm. Internet and e-mail services at the **Los Gemelos** hotel or the **Copán Net** shop, 1 block south of Parque Central.

**Laundry** – A few hotels provide laundry services, otherwise take your laundry to the **Lavandería Justo A Tiempo**, opposite Copán Net.

## WHERE TO STAY

*Under US$10*
**Hotel Los Gemelos**, 100m northeast of Parque Central, ☎ 651 4077, Fax 651 4315, maricela@hondutel.hn – 13rm ⚑ A pleasant backpacker atmosphere and a lot of services available

The road to the Caribbean

to travellers. The rooms, unexceptional but clean, are the cheapest in the village.

**Hotel California**, 150m northeast of Parque Central, ☎ 651 4314 – 4rm ⚖ ✗ Delightful bamboo cabins with palm roofs set in a garden. The little bunches of fresh flowers in each room, the fabrics on the walls and the hammocks on the veranda are all pleasant details. Relaxed atmosphere and a mainly American clientele.

*Under US$25*

**Hotel Paty**, 200m northeast of Parque Central, ☎ 651 4021 / 4473, Fax 651 4109 – 18rm ⚖ ⚖ Near the bridge on the way to the archeological site; reasonable, well-kept rooms around a courtyard. Excellent welcome. Extension work in progress.

**Hotel Bella Vista**, on the hill 400m north of Parque Central, ☎ 651 4502 – 20rm ⚖ ⚖ cc This hotel perched on the hill is pleasantly cool at nights. Only the rooms on the second floor enjoy the view over the neighbouring mountains. Not particularly attractive accommodation, but improvements are in the pipeline (hot water, TV and air-conditioning).

**Hotel Yaragua**, half a block southeast of Parque Central, ☎ 651 4464, Fax 651 4050 – 15rm ⚖ ⚖ ⚖ cc The rooms are laid out around a small inner courtyard decorated with plants. A modest but reasonable hotel.

*US$30-50*

**La Casa de Café Bed & Breakfast**, 500m southwest of Parque Central, ☎ 651 4620, Fax 651 4623 – 8rm ⚖ ✗ This hotel has pretty rooms, decorated traditionally, in a colonial setting with a superb view over Copán valley and the mountains. Communal lounge with TV and VCR and a library full of books on Central America. Breakfast included.

**Hotel Camino Maya,** Parque Central, ☎ 651 4518 / 4646, Fax 651 4517, hc-maya@david.intertel.hn – 20rm ⚖ ⚖ ⚖ ✗ cc On the southwest corner of Parque Central, a building with a veranda on the first floor. The extremely clean rooms look onto the street or a small, long patio. The music in the restaurant is a bit loud.

**Hotel Los Jaguares**, Parque Central, ☎ 651 4451, Fax 651 4075 – 10rm ⚖ ⚖ ⚖ TV cc This hotel, set around a pretty patio, looks like a top-range motel. The rooms are extremely well-kept and comfortable.

*US$50-80*

**Hotel Plaza Copán**, on Parque Central, ☎ 651 4508 / 4274, Fax 651 4039, h_copan@hondutel.hn – 21rm ⚖ ⚖ ⚖ TV ✗ ⚖ ⚖ cc The restaurant terrace opening onto Parque Central is the best sited in the village. The luxury rooms have every comfort and are irreproachably clean. Some open onto a small private terrace. A hotel that stands out through its intimate atmosphere and efficient service.

**Hotel Marina Copán**, half a block north of Parque Central, ☎ 651 4070/1/2, Fax 651 4477, hmarinac@netsy.hn – 40rm ⚖ ⚖ ⚖ ⚖ TV ✗ ⚖ cc Copán's top-class hotel stands in a pleasant natural setting around a lovely swimming-pool. Large colonial-style rooms, with terraces for nos 256-262. Top-quality service and amenities for total peace of mind.

### EATING OUT

*Under US$10*

**Restaurante Tres Locos**, in Hotel California. This little restaurant, in fact just a few tables in the middle of a garden, has a limited menu: American-style pizzas or mixed salads. Simple but tasty.

**Restaurante / Bar Tunkul**, ☎ 651 4410, 2 blocks west of Parque Central. 9am-10pm. One of the liveliest places in the evenings. You can eat here or have a drink in a delightful candlelit garden. Mexican specialities, vegetarian dishes and good grilled foods.

**Vamos A Ver**, 7am-10pm. While the Tunkul attracts the Americans, the Europeans prefer the Vamos A Ver. Relaxed atmosphere in a garden with hammocks. A varied menu, including excellent Dutch cheese sandwiches. Generous helpings of good-quality produce.

**La Llama del Bosque**, 2 blocks west of Parque Central, 6.30am-10pm. The vast dining room is ideal for groups of tourists. They serve chicken and beef dishes as well as good salads. Generous helpings, acceptable cuisine and prices, but the place lacks warmth.

## GOING OUT, HAVING A DRINK

**Bars** – The *Tunkul* and the *Vamos A Ver* are the two most popular bars in Copán. Try the *Reggae Roof* as well, behind the Marina Copán hotel, near the bridge on the way to the border; it plays hip-hop and reggae music.

**Concerts** – Marimba concerts Fridays and Saturdays at 5pm in the bar of the Marina Copán hotel.

## OTHER THINGS TO DO

**Excursions** – Apart from visiting the Copán ruins, there are several excursions to be made in the vicinity of the village (hot springs, waterfall, nature reserve). Douglas J Ramos, guide at *Aventuras Copán*, 50m from Banco de Occidente, is highly recommended for his visits to archeological sites. He knows a great deal about the flora and fauna of his country. Contact by e-mail: aventuras_copan@yahoo.com

**Cinema** – The *Café Vamos A Ver* shows a different video every evening at 7pm. Programme posted at the restaurant entrance.

**Outdoor pursuits** – Pony trekking at the Yaragua hotel and the Aventuras Copán agency. The latter also organises trips down the Río Copán on inflated inner tyres.

## SHOPPING GUIDE

**Arts and crafts** – Numerous souvenir shops sell local or Guatemalan handicrafts – fabrics, hats, basketwork – as well as Honduran and Cuban cigars.

**Making the most of Copán**

# QUIRIGUÁ ★★

Izabal department
203km from Guatemala City and 96km from Puerto Barrios
Accommodation in Quiriguá village (4km) or Los Amates (8km)

**Not to be missed**
The biggest stelae in the Mayan world.
The zoomorphs.

**And remember...**
Avoid short sleeves and shorts when night falls,
as the site is invaded by clouds of mosquitoes.

The dense jungle that haunts explorers' tales of the 19C is no longer an obstacle to visiting this site. Quiriguá's amazing stone columns, standing on the plain through which the Río Motagua flows, now look down on a vast clearing freed of its once dense vegetation; but the petrified rulers on their giant stelae and the enormous monoliths carved with fantastic animals, crouching in the shadows, still arouse untiring fascination.

## Quiriguá comes out of the shadows

Occupied from 550 to 850, this **Late Classic** site was for more than two hundred years a satellite of Copán, fifty kilometres away as the crow flies. It is therefore not surprising to see the similarities in artistic expression between the two city-states *(see p 260 "Copán")*.

**Kingdom of the "Skies"** – The first identified ruler of Quiriguá, **Cauac Sky** (Cauac Cielo), acceded to the throne around 730, opening the way for the Sky dynasty which governed until Quiriguá's decline.

The beginning of his 60-year reign was marked by a key victory over a troublesome neighbour: in 738 the ruler of Quiriguá captured **18 Rabbit** (18 Conejo), Copán's great king, and had him beheaded. This victory heralded Quiriguá's political, economic and artistic autonomy. Henceforth the city-state was able to control trade on the Río Motagua in total independence. This was when work began on the monumental stelae and the temple in the northern part of Plaza Central.

Cauac Sky's successors continued his work for another few years until the reign of **Jade Sky**, who came to the throne in 805. Five years later, the last Quiriguá date was inscribed on the Acropolis before the city-state collapsed mysteriously in the mid-9C.

**Quiriguá, a city rediscovered** – The diplomat **John Lloyd Stephens** *(see p 260 "Copán")*, accompanied by the English artist **Frederick Catherwood**, discovered the ruins of Copán and Quiriguá on his journey through Central America in the late 1830s. Awed by the stelae, Stephens conceived the idea of buying the site in order to transport it to New York by shipping its monuments down the Río Motagua. But the project had to be abandoned because of the exorbitant asking price. Later on Quiriguá attracted other explorers, including **Alfred Percival Maudslay** in 1885, who took moulds and photographs and made drawings of the sculptures held captive in the jungle. As of 1930, the University of Pennsylvania undertook the first excavations of the site, which was declared a **UNESCO World Heritage Site** in 1985.

Stela E at Quiriguá, the tallest in the Mayan world

## Original artistic expression

The sheer monumental scale of the Quiriguá **stelae** is breathtaking. Stiffer and less elegant than those of Copán, they are nevertheless superb examples of Mayan art. For a civilization that used neither the wheel nor draught animals, erecting such monuments was a positively prodigious feat. These sandstone stelae produced at the end of each *hotun* (5-year period) are decorated front and back with dignitaries in ceremonial costume. Their faces are virtually three-dimensional, in contrast to the rest of their bodies, whereas Copán artists used sculpture in the round for the whole subject. The sides of the monuments are covered in Long Count glyphs (*see p 27*), depicted here as full-length figures, whereas the traditional pictograms generally only portray the head.

Quiriguá is also outstanding for its **zoomorphs**, enormous carved monoliths portraying the king emerging from the mouth of a fantastical stone animal. Though they are often presumed to be a kind of altar, the actual purpose of these stone blocks has still not been explained.

## Visiting the archeological park

*The "camionetas" heading for Puerto Barrios drop passengers at km 200 on Carretera al Atlántico, at the Ruinas de Quiriguá stop, 1km after the village of the same name. From there, buses or pick-ups take visitors to the site entrance along 4km of track through banana plantations. There is also a short cut that involves walking along the railway line from the villages of Los Amates and Quiriguá. Ask the locals the way.*

*7.30am-5pm. Fee. Allow 2hr to visit.*

Compared with Copán or Tikal, visiting Quiriguá is a restful affair. All the altars, zoomorphs and stelae of interest are to be found in one small area, on Plaza Central or nearby. There is no risk of getting lost as the monuments are numbered in alphabetical order from north to south. Only the thatched roofs over the sculptures, to protect them from erosion, are likely to present a problem for photographers.

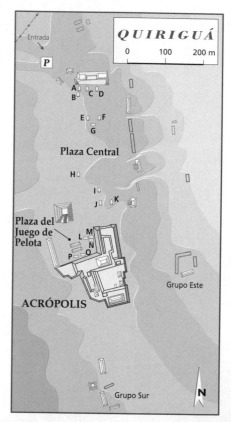

The road to the Caribbean

## Plaza Central★★

To the left on entering Plaza Central visitors find a row of three **stelae★** (**A**, **C** and **D**) characteristic of the site. At their feet sits **Zoomorph B★** (780), a frog-like creature with a ruler emerging from its jaws.

Among the ten or so monuments standing in this clearing, the proportions of **Stela E★★** (771) are particularly worth admiring: 10.5m high and weighing 65t, this is in fact the tallest stela in the Mayan world. Close by stands **Stela F★** with its superb series of glyphs, and just behind is **Zoomorph G★**, an imposing frog (or toad) with a menacing eye, seeming just about to leap at you.

Further to the south, towards the Acropolis, four stelae mark the beginning and end of artistic expression in Quiriguá: **Stela H★** (751) and **Stela J★** (756), the earliest discovered on the site, stand virtually side by side with **Stela I★** (800) and **Stela K★** (805), the most recent.

## Plaza del Juego de Pelota★★ (Square of the Ball Court)

This ceremonial square, which includes a **juego de pelota** (ball court), is the sanctuary of two impressive zoomorphs. Leaving **Altars L** (725, the earliest date in Quiriguá), **M** and **N** to the left, visitors come to the foot of the stairway in the south of the square, and the bulging silhouettes of **Zoomorph O★** (790) and **Zoomorph P★★** (795). The latter resembles a giant turtle, from which it takes its name, **Altar de la Tortuga** (Altar of the Turtle). It portrays a ruler sitting cross-legged, emerging from the jaws of a monster; the back of the monolith is covered with glyphs.

Opposite stands the **Acropolis★**, a group of buildings erected in four successive stages over the period 550 to 850. Reserved for the elite, this building must have served administrative and residential purposes.

# Making the most of Quiriguá

**WHERE TO STAY, EATING OUT**

The choice of accommodation near the Quiriguá site is extremely limited in both quantity and quality. One night here is plenty of time to have a meal after visiting Quiriguá and a rest before going on to Copán, the capital or the Caribbean coast.

• **Los Amates**

*Under US$15*

**Hotel Santa Mónica**, Los Amates, Carretera al Atlántico km 195, ☎ 947 8536 – 8rm ⌲ ✗ In the village of Los Amates, 500m from the junction with Carretera al Atlántico. Rooms with or without bathrooms in a badly sound-proofed building.

• **Quiriguá village**

*Under US$10*

**Hotel Royal**, Aldea Quiriguá, Carretera al Atlántico km 199 – 11rm ⌲ ✗ This is the closest hotel to the archeological site, 5km from Quiriguá village. Rooms with minimal comfort, with or without private bathrooms.

# THE CARIBBEAN COAST★
Izabal department
291km from the capital to Puerto Barrios
See map p 255

**Not to be missed**
The Caribbean atmosphere of Lívingston.
Tasting a *tapado* at La Casa Rosada.
A cruise on the Río Dulce.

**And remember...**
If you like nightlife,
spend a weekend in Lívingston.

*The road to the Caribbean*

Turquoise waters and beautiful sandy beaches lined with coconut palms are not on the menu! The tiny Caribbean littoral cannot claim to rival neighbouring Honduras or Belize as far as seaside resorts go, but the coast is unusual for all that, and very different from the rest of Guatemala. Arriving in Lívingston you even get the impression you have crossed the border, you will discover a Caribbean township with a Belizean feel.

## Puerto Barrios

The Carretera al Atlántico (CA9) ends at Puerto Barrios, a town submerged in a suffocating mugginess barely relieved by the trade winds. Although the town had its hour of glory as a major banana port in the golden age of the United Fruit Company, activity here has now declined in favour of the port of Santo Tomás de Castilla, 7km further south. In Puerto Barrios, the interminable sun-scorched avenues take all pleasure out of wandering. In fact, the main interest of this department capital is its jetty, from which the boats for Punta Gorda (Belize) and Lívingston leave (*see "Making the most of Puerto Barrios"*).

**The Banana Bunch**
From the late 19C the United Fruit Company reigned in solitary splendour over the Motagua valley banana plantations between Quiriguá and the Caribbean coast. Owning both the railway line and the harbour, this powerful American company shipped its banana output directly from Puerto Barrios to the United States. Nicknamed "El Pulpo" (the octopus) because of its hold over Central America's economic and political life, it intervened whenever its empire was threatened. So, in retaliation against the agrarian reform law promulgated by President Jacobo Arbenz, the CIA instigated a military coup d'état in 1954 to counter the "Communist threat" and re-establish a regime favourable to American interests; the lands confiscated were immediately handed back to the United Fruit Company. Only American anti-trust laws were finally to succeed in dismantling the "Frutera's" monopoly in the 1970s.

### While waiting for the boat
If you have a few hours to kill before sailing, consider wandering around the warehouse district. One of the liveliest streets in the harbour is 9a Calle, its wooden shacks housing a succession of dubious bars where thirsty dockers get together at the end of each day.

B. Brillon/MICHELIN

The Caribbean touch

North of the warehouses, **Hotel del Norte**★ (see "Making the most of Puerto Barrios") seems to spring from another era. This Caribbean house with its deliciously outdated atmosphere was built at the end of the 19C, at the same time as the railway line. Its veranda facing Amatique Bay provides a delightful and unexpected place to make a halt.

# Lívingston★★

The place is as unusual as its name. Lívingston sits at the mouth of the Río Dulce on the shore of Amatique Bay, just a few miles from the Belize border. As there are no roads, the only means of access being by sea or river, the village has remained isolated from the rest of the country and has been able to preserve its individuality. In a country of Mayan culture it is a surprise to come across this Caribbean ambience, with Garifunas doing dance steps outside the numerous bars from which waves of reggae float out. In this township at the end of the world you come across some very colourful characters: an American evangelical missionary who has been translating the Bible into Garifuna for decades; the owner of African Place who built this miniature Alhambra with his own hands using tin drums and milk cans to mould its multifoil arches; or the adventurers, some of them outlaws, who probably do not know that the village owes its name to Governor Edward Livingston, who codified the laws of Louisiana from which Guatemala took its inspiration in the 19C.

**The Garifunas**

These descendants of African slaves who escaped or were shipwrecked in the Caribbean Sea, speak a mixture of Creole, English and Spanish and occupy part of the coast of Belize and Honduras. The inhabitants of Lívingston are the only representatives of this ethnic group in Guatemala. Music and dance are very important aspects of the ancestral customs they still practise, and they will sometimes invite strangers to watch their ceremonies. For funerals, for example, after singing for nine days to accompany the deceased person's soul, the participants perform a trance dance that celebrates the arrival of the soul in heaven.

## A quick tour of the village

Despite its seashore location, Lívingston offers no idyllic beaches as the coconut palms reach right down to the slightly muddy waters! Apart from a few colonial houses, the streets are lined with brightly-painted wood cabins roofed with rusty corrugated iron – not very attractive at first glance, and yet this township does not lack charm. **Calle Principal**★ is the ideal place for those wishing to stroll, sit on a terrace to try a *tapado* (fish stew), watch the comings and goings of the Garifunas and Kekchis or listen to traditional music on Saturday evenings. It is well worth watching the Caribbean music and dancing if you are in Lívingston at **Christmas**★★ or for **15 May**★★; this latter date, the feast of San Isidro Labrador, also commemorates the arrival of the Garifunas in Guatemala.

## An outing to Siete Altares★

*Approximately 5km northwest of the village. Allow 90min on foot or 15min by boat. It is advisable to go in groups as thefts and attacks have been reported on the way there.*

From Lívingston jetty follow the "beach", a thin strip of grey sand interrupted by a river, which may be crossed by a ford or in a boat. At the end of the beach a path goes off into the forest, leading after another few hundred metres to **Siete**

**Altares**★ (seven altars), a series of waterfalls pouring into several natural basins shaded by superb tropical vegetation. During the dry season there is only a thin trickle of water, but it is still a pleasant place to picnic.

## A cruise on the Río Dulce★

*Allow 2hr from Livingston to the village of Río Dulce.*
*Daily departures from Livingston at 9am.*
*"Lanchas" can be hired at any time.*

A trip on the Río Dulce is the pleasantest way of reaching or leaving the Caribbean coast. Over the centuries, the river, fed by two inland lakes (El Golfete and Lake Izabal) has carved out a gorge in the limestone plateau that separates **El Golfete** from the sea.

On leaving Livingston the *lanchas* (motor launches), *cayucos* (pirogues) and yachts slip through an impressive gorge, its vertical walls hung with dense vegetation. Pelicans, cormorants and white or blue herons perch in trees and bushes while clouds of butterflies flutter from bank to bank. After ten kilometres the waterway opens out into **El Golfete**, a lake dotted with marinas where luxury yachts are anchored.

The banks close in again at the end of El Golfete and boats then pass under a modern bridge at the **village of Río Dulce** (also known as **El Relleno** or **Fronteras**). The village is strategically sited for reaching Belize, Flores, Guatemala City or Puerto Barrios by road. Most travellers simply disembark

Caribbean house in Livingston

R. Marca

and jump straight onto a bus to avoid hanging about in this dusty, noisy village. However, if you miss a connection or wish to rest up before a long journey, **Hacienda Tijax** is a choice place for relaxing (*see "Making the most of Río Dulce"*). About 3km upstream the banks of the river widen again into **Lake Izabal★**, the biggest lake in Guatemala, guarded by the **Castillo de San Felipe de Lara★** *(8am-5pm. Fee)*. This old fortress, now entirely restored, was built by the Spanish in 1652 to protect themselves from pirate incursions and to control access to the lake.

## Making the most of Puerto Barrios

### COMING AND GOING

**By bus** – The *Transportes Litegua* terminus, 6a Ave and 9a Calle, ☎ 948 1172, is the terminus for buses to and from Guatemala City . Approx 15 a day between 6.30am and 5pm. Travelling by "pullman" is more comfortable and much quicker (5hr) than by "camioneta". To get to El Petén change at La Ruidosa, and for Chiquimula change at Río Hondo. It is possible to leave luggage at the bus terminus Left Luggage (open and poorly supervised).

**By boat** – The *Muelle Municipal* (jetty) is at the western end of 12a Calle. 2 regular departures a day for Lívingston, at 10.30am and 5pm. Outside of these fixed departures, "colectivos" make the trip (1hr) with a dozen passengers. You simply put your name on the list and wait.

A boat goes to Punta Gorda (Belize) on Mondays, Tuesdays and Fridays at 8.30am – days and times are liable to change. Before leaving Guatemala you must pay the departure tax and have your passport stamped at the customs office at the end of 9a Calle, on the seafront.

### GETTING AROUND

Puerto Barrios is quite spread out. To get from one end of the town to the other you need to take a taxi. If your luggage is not too heavy you can walk to the jetty, 15min on foot from the bus station.

**By taxi** – Taxi rank on the corner of 6a Ave and 8a Calle, near the bus station. *Taxis Tívoli*, in front of Hotel del Norte, ☎ 948 0371.

### ADDRESS BOOK

**Bank / Currency Exchange** – *Banco del Café*, corner of 13a Calle and 7a Ave. 9am-8pm; Saturdays 10am-2pm. *Banco del Quetzal*, corner of 6a Ave and 9a Calle, at the bus station. 9.30am-2.30pm; closed weekends. *Banco G & T*, 7a Calle between 5a and 6a Ave. 9am-8pm; Saturdays 10am-2pm. *Lloyd's Bank*, corner of 15a Calle and 7a Ave. 9am-3pm; closed weekends.

**Post office / Telephone** – The post office is on the corner of 6a Ave and 6a Calle. For telephone calls, *TELGUA*, 13a Calle between 5a and 6a Ave.

### WHERE TO STAY

*Under US$12*

**Hotel Europa 2**, 3a Ave between 11a and 12a Calles, ☎ 948 1292 – 10rm 🖤 ⊼ This hotel has the advantage of being just 100m from the jetty. The rooms are unremarkable but quite well maintained. Cars can be parked in the courtyard.

**Hotel Miami**, 3a Ave between 11a and 12a Calles, ☎ 948 0537 – 20rm 🖤 ⊼ This hotel is right next door to Hotel Europa 2 and offers similar accommodation. For double the price you can ask for an air-conditioned room, a worthwhile expense in the damp heat of Puerto Barrios.

*US$12-30*

🏠 **Hotel del Norte**, corner of 7a Ave and 1a Calle, ☎ 948 2116 / 0087 –36rm ✕ ⊒ This lovely but rather rickety wooden residence has survived right through the 20C. The lace and sunshades have gone but the veranda caressed by the sea breeze and the charmingly colonial restaurant have conserved all their magic. The rooms are of unequal quality and prices vary according to standard (with or without bathroom, fan or air conditioning). Choose those looking out over Amatique Bay. The accommodation is far from perfect, but the real attraction of this hotel is its atmosphere.

### EATING OUT, HAVING A DRINK
Numerous little restaurants can be found around the market, near the bus station.

*Under US$6*
**Container**, at the end of 7a Calle. 7am-11pm. Opposite Hotel del Norte; this cafeteria is located in an old shipping container facing Amatique Bay. An original setting but offhand service.

*Under US$10*
**Restaurante El Fogón Porteño**, corner of 6a Calle and 9a Calle, ☏ 948 0404. 7am-9pm. You can keep an eye on your bus from the terrace as the restaurant is right opposite the bus station. Good shellfish and barbecued meat specialities.
**Hotel del Norte**, corner 7a Ave and 1a Calle. The cuisine is nothing to write home about but the setting is exquisite. At least have a drink here.

## Making the most of Lívingston

### COMING AND GOING
There are no roads to Lívingston, so access is necessarily by sea or river.
**By boat** – The **Muelle** (jetty) is at the end of Calle Principal del Comercio. Departures from Lívingston to Puerto Barrios every day at 5am and 2pm. Outside these hours, the "colectivos" make the crossing once they have gathered together a dozen passengers.
A boat leaves Lívingston for Punta Gorda (Belize) on Tuesdays and Fridays at 7am. Remember to pay the US$10 departure tax at the immigration office in the main street opposite Hotel Tucán Dugú.
Travel agents and hotels organise excursions up the Río Dulce to Lake Izabal. You can use the pleasant trip by "lancha" (motor launch) to reach Lívingston or the villages on the river banks. Departures are usually at 9am.

### ADDRESS BOOK
**Tourist information** – Tourist information and maps of Lívingston available from the **Exotic Travel** agency, at the entrance to the Bahía Azul restaurant on Calle Principal del Comercio, ☏ 947 0136.

**Bank / Currency Exchange – Banco del Café**, Calle Principal, near the Bahía Azul restaurant. 9am-5pm; Saturdays 9am-1pm. It is possible to change cash (American and Belizean dollars or Honduran lempiras) in some of the tourist shops on the main street.

**Post office / Telephone** – The post office is in Calle La Calzada, the street that turns off Calle Principal at Hotel Tucán Dugú. Just next door is the **TELGUA** office. The **Colibrí** handicrafts shop, Calle Principal del Comercio opposite Hotel Tucán Dugú, provides e-mail and Internet services.

### WHERE TO STAY
*Around US$10*
**Hotel Garifuna**, Barrio San José, ☏ 947 0183, Fax 947 0184 – 8rm ⚐ 🍴 ⚑ Go up Calle de la Iglesia towards African Place and turn right at the Tropicool bar. Continue down this street towards the beach for approx 100m. A pretty little house in a garden with basic but well-kept rooms. Balcony upstairs for cooling down.
**Hotel Waba**, Barrio Pueblo Nuevo, ☏ 947 0193 –11rm ⚑ Turn right in front of African Place and go down

towards the beach. A modest hotel run by a very welcoming Garifuna family. All the rooms have private bathrooms except two. A bit away from the centre.

**Hotel Blanco M**, Calle de la Iglesia – 5rm ⚲ ✕ On the way to African Place, 100m from the junction with Calle Principal. This red and yellow house has a few spacious but somewhat spartan rooms. The balcony is an excellent place for watching this lively Lívingston street.

*Around US$15*

⚲**African Place** – 26rm ✕ ✕ At the end of Calle de la Iglesia, before reaching the cemetery, you will see a little palace with unexpected Moorish architecture. With its whitewashed multifoil arches surrounding a delightful tropical garden, this is a little corner of Andalusia on the Caribbean coast. The rooms (with or without bathrooms) are simple but have character. Pleasant welcome. A pity it is a little distance from the jetty (15min walk).

⚲**Hotel La Casa Rosada**, Barrio Marcos Sánchez Díaz, ☎ 947 0303, Fax 947 0304, junglestudy@earthlink.net – 10rm ✕ ✕ Go up Calle Principal from the jetty, take the first street on the left for 700m until you reach a big pink house in Caribbean style, facing the bay. The little rustic bungalows on either side of it, prettily decorated with painted wood furniture, house the rooms and absolutely impeccable shared showers. Sofas on the veranda, hammocks in the garden, a minute beach and a thatched café at the end of the jetty – everything invites you to daydream in a friendly, relaxed atmosphere.

*US$15-30*

**Hospedaje Doña Alida**, Barrios Capitanía, ☎ 947 0027 – 9rm ✕ ✕ ⚲ Go up Calle Principal, turn right at Hotel Tucán Dugú and continue 500m. In a quiet district close to the centre, this hotel overlooks an uncared-for little beach. The rooms with bathrooms are quite spacious and some have a view over the bay.

**Hotel Henry Berrisford**, ☎ 947 0048, Fax 947 0471 – 36rm ⚲ ✕ ✕ ⚲ cc Go up Calle Principal from the jetty and then down the first road on the left for 100m. This unprepossessing concrete

building provides a wide range of services (fan or air conditioning, breakfast included or not). Only the rooms on the top floor and the suite are well-lit with a lovely view of the sea.

*Around US$80*

**Hotel Tucán Dugú**, ☎ 947 0078, Fax 947 0072 – 45rm ⚲ ✕ ⚲ ✕ ⚲ cc Approx 100m from the jetty on Calle Principal. The best hotel in Lívingston, with an attractive natural setting and a big swimming-pool. The rooms are extremely clean and comfortable but the price is high for what you get.

**EATING OUT**

You must taste "pan de coco" (coconut bread) and "tapado", the local stew of spiny lobster, prawns, fish, crab, coconut, plantain and coriander.

*Under US$10*

**Happy Fish**, Calle Principal ⚲ cc 6.30am-10pm. On a terrace giving onto the main street, you can enjoy excellent seafood and some fish dishes at very reasonable prices. Simple, healthy cuisine.

**McTropic**, Calle Principal, ⚲ 6.30am-10pm. Opposite the Happy Fish. This restaurant has some tables set up on the pavement, where the young people of the village come by one after another in the hope of selling you handicrafts or excursions. International and local cuisine at moderate prices.

**Bahía Azul**, Calle Principal, ⚲ cc 6.30am-11pm. The liveliest restaurant in Lívingston is in an unbeatable location for observing the main street of the village. A varied selection of light dishes and local specialities. Generous helpings.

⚲**La Casa Rosada** ⚲ 6.30am-9pm. This terrace on the seafront is a pleasant place at any hour of the day. A limited menu, with produce that is always fresh and skilfully prepared. The "tapado" is excellent (order in the morning for the same evening). For dinner the starter/main dish/dessert formula gives very good value for money. Reserve before 7pm.

**GOING OUT, HAVING A DRINK**
Lívingston wakes up at weekends.

**Bars** – The **Bahía Azul** is a pleasant place to have a drink on any day of the week. The **Tropicool** disco-bar, Calle de

The road to the Caribbean

la Iglesia, halfway between Calle Principal and the African Place hotel. Lively atmosphere at weekends.

**Concerts –** Garifuna music bands play at weekends in some of the Lívingston restaurants including the Bahía Azul.

**Discos –** *Playa Ocho*, on the seafront, on the left at the end of Calle Principal. A lot of atmosphere from midnight on Fridays and Saturdays. Also on the beach, in the vicinity of African Place, *Lugudi Barana* attracts crowds on Sunday evenings.

### OTHER THINGS TO DO

**Excursions –** Lívingston's tourist establishments propose half-day excursions on the Río Dulce to Lake Izabal, with halts at the hot springs and the manatee reserve and a visit to the Castillo de San Felipe.

### SHOPPING GUIDE

**Arts and Crafts –** *Colibrí*, Calle Principal opposite Hotel Tucán Dugú. Souvenir and handicrafts shop run by two French people. 9am-2pm / 5pm-8pm.

## Making the most of Río Dulce

### COMING AND GOING

**By bus –** The buses between Flores and Guatemala City go through Río Dulce village, the half-way point (see the "Making the most of" sections of these places). They stop in the main street opposite the market. For Puerto Barrios change at La Ruidosa.

**By boat –** "Lanchas" (motor launches) run between Río Dulce and Lívingston every day.

### ADDRESS BOOK

**Tourist information –** Available from the *Tijax Express* office near the jetty.

**Bank / Currency Exchange –** *Banco de Comercio* in the main street. 9am-5pm; Saturdays 9am-1pm.

### WHERE TO STAY

Avoid Río Dulce, an uninteresting village with only a few unappetising hotels. On the other hand, 2km away on the road to Tikal you can stop off in a superb estate. The simplest solution is to go there by boat from the main jetty near the bus station. Ask at the Tijax Express office.

*US$10-20*

🐾 *Hacienda Tijax*, ☎ 902 7825, tijax@guate.net – 14rm 🌴 ✗ 🍴 🐎 A place that charms a great number of travellers with its atmosphere and its excellent value for money. You can

camp on the site near the main entrance. There are modest rooms on the 1st floor of the restaurant and 8 little cabins, linked by footbridges, offer rustic but relatively comfortable accommodation. Lastly, there are 4 bungalows with bathrooms and kitchens for families or groups of friends. The estate covers 200ha of undulating countryside ideal for exploring. You can wander along the forest paths on foot or horseback, to a natural swimming-pool and then on to the rubber plantation. The owner has very successfully created a convivial family atmosphere.

### EATING OUT

*Under US$10*

*Restaurante Río Bravo*, near the jetty on the village side. 🍴 8am-10pm. You can eat on its waterside terrace while waiting for your "lancha". Seafood, meat and pizza specialities.

### OTHER THINGS TO DO

**Excursions –** You can of course go on a boat trip down to Lívingston or visit the village of Río Dulce and the others on Lake Izabal. Information from Tijax Express on yacht cruises on the Río Dulce (3 days) or to Belize (1 week).

# BELIZE

**Official name**: Belize
**Land area**: 22 923sqkm
**Population**: 224 000
**Capital**: Belmopan
**Currency**: the Belizean dollar

# Setting the scene

The end of the day
in Dangriga

# A VERY SMALL WORLD

Belize is easy to miss on a map of Central America, a tiny country looking out over the Caribbean, wedged between Guatemala and Mexico. In the north it is separated from the Yucatán peninsula by the Río Honda; its southern border with Guatemala follows the Sarstoon River, and to the west a perfectly straight north-south line divides its western regions from El Petén. As if to compensate for such regularity, its ragged eastern seaboard, punctuated with lagoons, blends into the Caribbean Sea.

## Geographical diversity

The smallest country in Central America after El Salvador, Belize covers 22 923sqkm (slightly larger than Wales). The longest distance from north to south is no more than 280km and it is just 109km from east to west at its widest point (*see map p 320*).

### The flat north

From the Yucatán peninsula to the northern end of the Maya Mountains stretches a vast plain flanked by two chains of low limestone hills. This northern region, only just above sea level, is partially flooded during the rainy season. It is covered by pine woods, **swamps** and **lagoons** providing a haven for an abundance of animal life, as well as immense sugar cane plantations. The north of Belize has the country's longest rivers: the Río Hondo, the New River and the Sibun River. There are fewer nature reserves here than in the south of the country; the Crooked Tree Wildlife Sanctuary (*see p 325 "Belize City"*) gives an excellent overview of the region.

### The mountainous south

The south-west of the country is the only part of Belize with a hilly relief. **Mountain Pine Ridge**, a forest of undulating pine woods, rises to almost 1 000m. Further south, the **Maya Mountains**, which culminate in Victoria Peak, at 1 120m the highest point in the country, cross the western border to join up with the Guatemalan Highlands. This region of heavy rainfall is covered by damp tropical forest. Its limestone bedrock has facilitated the formation of numerous caves and underground rivers, such as the Río Frío Cave (*see p 368 "San Ignacio"*).

### The Caribbean littoral

The Caribbean Sea is Belize's main attraction. With the exception of the Placencia peninsula, beaches are virtually non-existent as the coastline is edged with **mangrove swamps**, providing a strip of natural protection against hurricanes and erosion. The longest **coral reef** in the northern hemisphere – second only to Australia's Barrier Reef – stretches 300km, forming a line parallel to the Belizean coast. The corridor thus created between this coral ribbon and the continent is dotted with around 450 **cays**, islets that can be anything from a simple rock to an inhabited island. Further out is the scuba diving paradise around Belize's three **atolls**, rings of coral islands enclosing lagoons: Turneffe Islands, Lighthouse Reef and Glover's Reef (*see p 330 "The northern cays"*).

A very small world

# A subtropical climate

Belize revels in a subtropical climate, warm, damp, but relieved by the breath of the Trade Winds over the coast and cays and by altitude in the mountains. Temperatures vary little from one region to another.

The **dry season**, lasting approximately from February to May, alternates with the **wet season**. Annual rainfall is three times higher in the south of the country, which sometimes has only a few weeks of dry season. The wet season is characterised by tropical depressions with the risk of storms through September and October.

# From an ocean of green to a coral garden

Belize boasts an exceptionally rich flora, with 700 species of trees and over 4 000 kinds of plants. This ecotourism paradise is also extremely dynamic when it comes to environmental protection, since its natural resources are very closely linked with its history and economy (see p 292). Three-quarters of Belize is tree-covered, a real record in comparison with the rest of Central America, which has fallen victim to massive deforestation.

There are two types of **tropical forest**, depending on rainfall. In the north of the country the forests are composed of **deciduous trees**, which by losing their leaves are able to retain their moisture during the dry season. The south of Belize, which has abundant rainfall, is distinguished by its **tropical rainforest**, a luxuriant jungle where the timber that gave the country its livelihood was harvested. Side by side stand **mahogany** (the national tree), **cedar**, **silk cotton** (the sacred tree of the Maya), **sapodilla** (source of *chicle* for making chewing-gum) and **cohune palm**, a tree from which oil is extracted and the leaves of which thatch Mayan huts. This tropical vegetation is entwined with creepers and other epiphytic plants. Among Belize's 250 varieties of orchid is the **black orchid**, its national flower.

**Pine forests** (Pine Ridge) and **savannah** are to be found on the not very fertile, poorly-irrigated soils found at middle altitude, as in the northern part of the country and to the north of the Maya Mountains. This is where the **Caribbean pine** grows, the most widespread species in the country.

In the east of the country, the major part of the **littoral** and some of the **cays** are obstructed by impenetrable **mangrove swamps**. Coconut palms and other types of palm trees can also be seen along the coast.

# A sanctuary for threatened wildlife
*See also p 16 Guatemalan wildlife*

## A haven for birds

As soon as dawn glimmers, the forests and mangrove swamps ring out with birdsong and the Belizean sky is thronged with birds of every kind: eagles, falcons, ducks, hummingbirds, herons, parrots, cormorants and pelicans. Of the 520 species recorded, 370 are permanent residents in the country, the others being migratory birds from North America. Pride of place goes to the **keel-billed toucan**, Belize's national bird (see illustration p 17), recognisable by its superb multi-coloured beak and generally seen perched in the treetops. The **jabiru stork**, white with a black head and red neck, is an endangered species. With a wingspan that can reach up to 2.5m, this is the largest bird in Belize; it is found in the lagoons of Crooked Tree Wildlife Sanctuary.

The *cays* are home to colonies of sea birds. Half Moon Caye Natural Monument shelters a hundred or so species including **red-footed boobies** and **magnificent frigate birds**, which puff out their red pouches in the mating season.

## A profusion of animal life

The great stretches of forest, combined with Belize's low population density, have helped to create a favourable environment for animals. Around 150 different species of **mammal** have been recorded in the country. Like Guatemala, Belize is the realm of howler monkeys, spider monkeys, armadillos, peccaries, agoutis, coatis, opossums, honey bears and manatees. **Baird's tapir**, Central America's biggest land mammal weighing up to 200kg, has been elevated to the rank of national animal. Despite its imposing size, its nocturnal lifestyle makes it discreet. Belize is also a haven for big cats such as pumas, ocelots and above all **jaguars** (called tigers in Belize); the latter prowl peacefully around at night in their own sanctuary *(see p 348 "Cockscomb Wildlife Sanctuary")*.

**Reptiles** and **amphibians** inhabit the forests and swamps. Of the 50 species of snakes, about a dozen are poisonous including the **barba amarilla** (fer-de-lance), also known in Belize as the **yellow-jaw tommygoff**. Dozens of kinds of iguanas and lizards can be seen along the rivers, and an excursion on the New River is often an opportunity to spot a **crocodile** *(see illustration p 362)*.

**Insects** are at home here. Magnificent **butterflies** can be seen on walks along forest paths which are sometimes barred by a long column of **leaf-cutter ants** carrying chopped-up leaves.

## A giant tropical aquarium

The barrier reef forms a rainbow of sponges and wide, lace-like sea-fans behind which dart **parrot fish**, **angel fish**, **squirrel fish** and **boxfish**, all as colourful as their names. Inoffensive **nurse sharks** swim alongside **whip-tailed stingrays**, **eagle rays** and **manta rays** (or devilfish), all monstrously elegant in this underwater ballet. Dolphins and black tip reef sharks leap out of the water; marlin, barracuda and turtles come and go while **spiny lobsters**, sea urchins, prawns, crabs and **conches** litter the sea floor.

A ray, like a sail undulating in the wind

G. Bludzin

A very small world

# AN ENCLAVE IN LATIN INFLUENCE

As its archeological record shows, Belize was once an integral part of Mayan civilization (*see p 19*). Yet right from the Spanish Conquest, the country set itself apart from the rest of Central America.

## A no man's land

As opposed to neighbouring Mexico and Guatemala, we cannot really talk about conquest where Belize is concerned. Despite several attempts, the Spaniards never succeeded in gaining total possession of this land; up until the 19C only a few Spanish and British colonists occupied its territory.

### A colony without a city

The absence of any gold or other riches doubtless explains the conquistadors' disinterest in the region, but more than anything else it was its coral reef that acted as a shield, protecting the country from incursions by foreign vessels.

**Mayan resistance** – One of the first conquistadors to tread Belizean soil was most likely **Hernán Cortés**, who in 1525 travelled quickly through the southwest (now Toledo District) on his way to put down an uprising in Honduras.

**The "father of the Mestizos"**
How Gonzalo Guerrero ended up with the Chetumal Maya, no-one knows. Legend has it that he had taken a Mayan princess as his wife and also held a high rank in Mayan society. When Spanish colonists arrived in the north of Belize, he fought on the side of his adopted people and the conquistadors were driven from the city in 1532.

The first clashes on Belizean soil took place from 1528 in the north of the country, when the Spaniards under Alonso Dávila attempted to take Chetumal, where Santa Rita (*see p 356 "Corozal"*) now stands. They met with strong resistance from the Maya, led by the Spaniard **Gonzalo Guerrero**.

In 1543, **Gaspar Pacheco**, reputed for his cruelty towards the indigenous people, undertook to conquer their territory and in the following century a few missionaries tried to convert them. But all these attempts at colonisation met with hostility from the population; so much so that by the 17C the Spanish were still not firmly established in the country. Another foreign power was to take advantage of this precarious situation.

**Rivalry between European powers** – From the 17C onward, pirates and corsairs in the pay of Spain's rivals, **England**, France and Holland, scoured the seas attacking enemy vessels. In 1638 English buccaneers settled at the mouth of the Belize River and started to harvest the timber, although without abandoning their naval activities, under the leadership of the Scotsman Peter Wallace among others. The word "Belize" is said to be derived from a Spanish corruption of his name.

In 1670 the **Treaty of Madrid** between Spain and England put an end to piracy and led many of those seafarers to settle on the Belizean coast, where they took the name of **Baymen** in reference to the Gulf of Honduras. Then began the lucrative trade in **logwood**, a dye timber used in the textile industry, later replaced by the mahogany trade up until the mid-20C.

Throughout the 18C attacks by the Spanish alternated with treaties giving the Baymen concessions for logging timber. The **Treaty of Versailles** signed in 1783 ceded them a part of the territory, between the Río Hondo, the Belize River and the New River, but forbade them to build forts or to farm. Spain thus maintained a semblance of sovereignty over a region it had never really colonised, while England protected colonists that were not subjects of the Crown.

Hostilities between the two European powers reached a climax at the end of the 18C with the **Battle of St George's Caye** on 10 September 1798. Assisted by their African slaves, who made up three-quarters of the population, the *Baymen* settled on this island miraculously won the battle. But it was still not until 1862 that British Honduras officially became a **British colony**, a few years after the wave of Yucatec refugees driven from Mexico by the War of the Castes (*see p. 356*).

## Achieving independence

The problems Belize faced in achieving independence were to a great extent a result of the ill-defined colonisation of previous centuries.

**The anti-colonial movement** – The first world war opened a breach in the British Empire; Belizean soldiers returning home entertained strong feelings of revolt against the mother country, which had shown particular disregard for them during the conflict. Then the 1929 slump combined with the devastation caused by the 1931 hurricane merely accentuated Belize's social and economic difficulties.

The workers' movement born of this instability was to form the first step towards nationalist feelings. The *Labour and Unemployed Association* was formed in 1934, followed by The *People's Committee* when the currency was devalued on 31 December 1949. Economic demands gradually turned into a revolt against the colonial system.

On 29 September 1950 the Committee became the **People's United Party** (PUP); this is still today the leading political party in Belize. In 1954 the PUP was instrumental in bringing in universal suffrage and ten years later the Belizeans obtained **governmental autonomy** with George Price as Prime Minister. The country adopted a flag, an anthem and a national prayer. In 1973 British Honduras officially became **Belize**. Everything was in place for independence, but this was held up by border problems with Guatemala.

**The Guatemalan border** – In 1960 the UN voted a resolution in favour of independence for colonies, but Belize had to wait another twenty years as Guatemala's refusal to recognise its borders slowed down the British withdrawal from its territory.

The origins of this conflict go back to the 19C, at the time when the young Central American republics had decided to maintain the same borders as when they were under Spanish rule. Was Belize under the British or the Spanish crown in 1821? As far as Guatemala was concerned, there was no doubt that Belize should be part of its territory, and in 1945 it was even integrated into the Guatemalan constitution. Over the following decades several threats of invasion were checked thanks to the presence of British military forces. Despite years of negotiations the conflict has still not been resolved to this day. However, the two countries finally re-established diplomatic relations and Guatemala has recognised Belize's independence since 1992.

The historical fresco in Corozal town hall

*An enclave in Latin influence*

*G. Cozzi/ANA*

**Independence for Belize –** In 1980 the UN finally pronounced in favour of independence for Belize. On **21 September 1981** the rejoicing country hoisted its national flag and was at last able to celebrate its independence. The young republic then drafted a Constitution and created new institutions.

# The British institutional model

Belize's parliamentary democracy is based on that of Great Britain.

### Political and administrative organisation

Belize has joined the other former British colonies in the **Commonwealth**. Its head of state is the reigning **British monarch**, represented by a Belizean Governor General. Executive power resides in the Cabinet, composed of members of the ruling party under the Prime Minister.

Legislative power is in the hands of a two-chamber National Assembly elected by general election every five years maximum: the **House of Representatives**, with 29 members (ruling party and opposition), and the **Senate**, with eight senators appointed by the Governor General on proposals from the Prime Minister and the leader of the opposition.

The country is divided into **six districts**: Belize, Cayo, Corozal, Orange Walk, Stann Creek and Toledo.

### The two-party system

Since independence, the political scene in Belize has been dominated by two major parties which tend to alternate at each general election: the **People's United Party** (PUP) and the **United Democratic Party** (UDP). The other parties remain in the wings.

From 1964 to 1984 the PUP dominated the country's politics, but in 1984 the UDP led by **Manuel Esquivel** won the elections, only to lose to the PUP again five years later. In 1993 power swung back into UDP hands and at the last elections, in August 1998, the PUP won a landslide victory giving it 26 seats out of 29 in the House of Representatives. **George Price**, the PUP's historic leader, has now handed over leadership of the party to a new politician, **Said Musa**, the present Prime Minister of Belize.

# An economy built on natural resources

The country depends on imports for manufactured goods and part of its food requirements. Although the United States remains its main economic partner, Belize also trades with the European Union, Mexico and its Caribbean and Central American neighbours.

### A dominant primary sector

Until the 20C Belize's economy depended mainly on logging, but with the collapse of this market other sectors have taken over.

**Agriculture –** This is still one of the mainstays of the country's economy. **Sugar cane** plantations (particularly around Corozal and Orange Walk) are still paramount in the Belizean countryside and account for a third of exports. The country also produces **bananas** (Stann Creek and Toledo districts) and **citrus fruits** (Stann Creek). Alongside these export products, subsistence crops of **maize, rice, beans**, cacao, soya, peanuts and some vegetables are grown.

An enclave in Latin influence

**Livestock** – Orange Walk and Cayo districts are major beef, pork, poultry and egg producing regions. A large percentage of this sector is concentrated in the Mennonite communities *(see p 360 "Orange Walk")*.

**Fishing** – This accounts for around 2% of GNP but some cays have abandoned this activity in favour of tourism, which is more lucrative than selling lobster, conch and prawns.

## Bringing in foreign currency

**Tourism**, which accounts for 18% of GNP, is one of the most important sectors in Belize's economy. Development of the country's natural and cultural heritage is attracting increasing numbers of visitors – around 260 000 a year, which is about one tourist per inhabitant.

With an estimated 35 000 Belizeans living in the United States, money sent back by family members who have emigrated abroad also provides a significant input of hard currency.

## Protecting the environment

The late development of its tourist industry has enabled Belize to take advantage of the experience of neighbouring countries in order to safeguard its heritage. In the early 1980s a considerable number of environmental protection laws were passed. At the instigation of national and international organisations, the oldest of which is the **Belize Audubon Society**, an NGO based in Belize City *(see p 327 "Belize City")*, a fair number of nature **reserves** and **national parks** were created. These protected areas cover approximately one third of the country, which has provoked discontent among some farmers and loggers.

After **Half Moon Caye Natural Monument**, the first of Belize's national nature reserves, a dozen or so other national parks were created with the aim of protecting flora and fauna both on land and in the sea. Rural communities are in some cases directly involved in these programmes, as is the case for the villages around Community Baboon Sanctuary or the Kekchi, Mopán and Garifuna hamlets in Toledo District. Large-scale public awareness campaigns are also underway to educate the population in environmental matters.

Economy

# Meeting the people

Smiling Belizean
faces

# THE BELIZEAN MOSAIC

Belize is a real kaleidoscope of cultures. This little country has slightly fewer than ten inhabitants per square kilometre, the lowest population density in Central America: just 224 000 people are spread over 22 923sqkm. Half the people live in the towns, which are mostly near the coast, with Belize City accounting for a quarter of the population. In the rest of the country people live in villages separated by vast expanses of uninhabited land (vast on the scale of Belize!) covered by forest or swamp.

## A land with open doors

Perpetuating its tradition of welcoming newcomers, Belize, the only Central American country that has not experienced war in the course of the last few decades, has witnessed the arrival of large numbers of refugees, especially from Guatemala and El Salvador, who have transformed the physiognomy of the country. Despite a high level of intermarriage – over three-quarters of the inhabitants are Creole, *Mestizo* or Garifuna – the various communities appear relatively compartmentalised by language barriers, the diversity of their customs and, quite simply, geographical location.

### The Creoles

The culture of the Creoles, descended from African slaves and Europeans, has long been the main one in the country. Their language, a colourful mixture of English and African languages, is spoken throughout Belize. Although in the majority in **Belize City** and some parts of Stann Creek District such as Placencia, they now account for only **30%** of the population, a certain number having chosen to emigrate to the United States for economic reasons. Overtaken in numbers by the *Mestizos*, they now form the second largest ethnic group in Belize.

### The Mestizos

Born of intermarriage between indigenous people and Europeans, the *Mestizos* make up **44%** of the population and are in the majority in the north of the country, in Corozal, Orange Walk, Caye Caulker and Ambergris Caye. The **Hispanic** population was for a long time localised near the border with Yucatán, where refugees from the **War of the Castes** settled in the 19C.

Since the end of the 1970s, many people fleeing poverty and war in **Guatemala**, **El Salvador** and other parts of Central America have found refuge in Belize. These newcomers are estimated to number about 40 000 and are concentrated mostly in Cayo District. This unprecedented wave of immigration has considerably transformed the demography of this tiny country.

### The Garifunas

The Garifunas (also called **Garinagus**) originated on the island of St Vincent in the 17C from intermarriage between shipwrecked African slaves and Kalinagos, the indigenous Caribbean people. Because of persecution, over the following century the Garifunas scattered along the coast of Central America; a small community still lives in Lívingston, Guatemala *(see p 276)*. Since the 19C they have occupied a few seaport towns in Belize, in Toledo District and Stann Creek

District. Dangriga, which is considered their capital, is the best place to discover the original culture of this ethnic group which accounts for **7%** of the population (*see p 298 "Colourful festivities"*).

## The Maya

During the Classic period the Mayan population reached around 500 000. Victims of colonisation, the indigenous population has all but disappeared, the present-day Maya being descendants of later immigrants. Among the **11%** of indigenous people in Belize are the **Yucatec Maya**, refugees from the War of the Castes and now considered part of the *Mestizo* group in the north of the country; the **Mopán**, originally from El Petén; and the **Kekchi** from the Cobán region. The latter two groups fled Guatemala at the end of the 19C to settle in Cayo District and Toledo District respectively; both have preserved their languages and ancestral customs. When travelling in the south of Belize visitors can share in their everyday life through development aid programmes (*see p 353 "Punta Gorda"*).

## A haven for minorities

The rest of the population is split into a variety of minority groups. Some came seeking refuge at some point in the course of their history: **Chinese fleeing** the Japanese occupation, **Mennonites** keeping the modern world at bay in the heart of Orange Walk District (*see sidebar p 360 "Orange Walk"*), **Indians** who came from the subcontinent in the 19C to work in the sugarcane plantations. Others include **British** soldiers who did not return home when colonial troops were recalled, retired **Americans** having chosen Belize as their second home, and a small community originally from the **Middle East**.

# An array of religions

The many religions in Belize reflect the country's history, emphasising the diverse origins of its population.

## Vestiges of colonial Churches

Around 62% of Belizeans are **Catholic**, the religion of the original colonists from Yucatán who settled in the north of the country in the 19C. Of the 30% of Protestants, one third embraces the **Anglican** church, heir to British colonisation, and the remainder are divided among a multitude of *Protestant Christian groups*; as in the rest of the American continent, these Protestant faiths include Methodists, Pentecostalists, Presbyterians, Mennonites, Mormons and Jehovah's Witnesses. They have been gaining ground over the past twenty years or so.

The ethnic minorities remain deeply attached to their historical religious convictions, which means that alongside the Catholics and Protestants co-exist Buddhists, Hindus, Muslims, Jews, Mayan syncretists (*see p 65 "Religion"*) and adepts of the Garifuna religion.

## Garifuna worship

Although stigmatised by 19C missionaries who saw it as the works of the devil, the Garifuna religion has now established itself on a par with the others. It is characterised by ancestor worship (**aharis**: ancestors), with whom the living communicate through **buyai**, male or female shamans. Each of its rituals (*amuyadahani, chugu* or *dugu*) is accompanied by corresponding traditional dancing and singing.

An array of religions

The **dugu**, or All Souls' Day festival, is the most important to the Garifunas, sometimes requiring a year of preparation for three days of celebrations during which singing, dancing, trances (*owohani*) and animal sacrifices follow on in succession. Visitors who become friendly with Garifunas during their stay are very often invited to attend these ceremonies.

## Colourful festivities

Travelling in Belize is like turning the dial along the FM waveband. There is music all the time, everywhere, in the towns as well as on the cays. In the buses it is not uncommon to hear romantic songs crackling out of the driver's battered transistor, almost drowned out by a throbbing beat emanating from a cassette-player held by a back-seat passenger. The diversity of musical styles, be they local or imported, along with the dances that accompany them, offer yet another example of the plurality of Belizean society.

### Respecting tradition

Each community has conserved its traditional celebrations, thus ensuring the survival of its culture.

The Maya continue to play the marimba (*see p 69 "Festivals and ceremonies"*) and the *Mestizos* willingly let themselves go to the Mexican melodies of mariachi bands.

Music and dancing are the hub of Garifuna culture. During traditional ceremonies such as the *dugu* (*see above*), they enable community members to communicate with their ancestors. One of the most spectacular of their dances

Sounds inherited from Africa

H. Mattison/GAMMA

is the **wanaragua** (also called *"John Canoe"*), which can be seen in Dangriga if you are there in December. This dance, originally from Africa, is also performed in other English-speaking countries in the West Indies (e.g. Jamaica). It is the centrepiece of a very colourful festival during which dancers – costumed, masked and wearing head-dresses of pom-poms and feathers – perform to the rhythm of shells tied to the knees, which knock together with each movement, seeming to echo the beat of the drums.

The musical style always associated with Belize is of course **punta**. Musicians play a drum, a turtle shell hit with sticks, a gourd filled with seeds called a maraca, and a big shell as a wind instrument, while dancers move their feet imperceptibly and their hips considerably more suggestively. Since the early 1980s there has been a renewal of interest in punta, with the appearance of a more modern derivative.

## A wind of change

Belize is now known abroad for its **punta rock**, a modernised form of punta incorporating electric guitar and keyboards. This musical trend has earned a certain amount of international renown through the artist **Andy Palacio**, the "king of punta" from Barranco, one of Belize's Garifuna villages, who has played as far afield as Paris in the 1998 *Rythmes Caraïbes* festival.

Its geographical location at the confluence of a variety of Caribbean and Latin trends means Belize is subject to the most varied of musical influences. Its proximity to Jamaica is evident on every street corner in the **reggae** that inundates the wavebands and the Belize music scene. The few local groups have a hard time, however, competing with the emulators of Bob Marley. Alongside the Caribbean and Latin rhythms of soca, calypso and salsa, other trends have likewise emerged such as rock and rap.

# A tropical Babel

The language map of Belize follows the same contours as its population. Although most people are bilingual, the official language is **English**. A "real" Belizean, however, is distinguished by his mastery of **Creole**, a dialect which combines African languages and English, as in the other former British colonies of the West Indies. English speakers visiting the country will think they recognise certain words, but understanding this language is difficult and the pronunciation bears little resemblance to Queen's English!

Although they are **Spanish** speakers, the *Mestizos* frequently speak English, with the exception of recent immigrants from Central America. In the vicinity of the border zones with Mexico and Guatemala, the other communities generally speak Spanish as their second language.

Each community has retained its own language, thus ensuring the continuation of its culture. **Garifuna** is spoken by the Garifunas, **Mopán** and **Kekchi** by the Maya, the Mennonites speak a variety of **Low German** among themselves and there are even Belizeans who speak **Arabic** or **Chinese**.

**Practical Information**

Caye Caulker,
a tourist haven

# Before going

## • Time difference

Same time zone as Guatemala, Mexico and US Central Time. Belize is 1hr behind New York, Montreal and Toronto, 6hr behind London, 16hr behind Sydney and 18hr behind Auckland (with reference to GMT/UTC).

## • International dialling

To call Belize from abroad, dial the international service code + 501 (country code for Belize) + the area or city code (without the initial 0) + the local number.

## • When to go

Because of the subtropical climate, the best time to travel to Belize is determined by the rains, not the temperature. The dry season, from **February to May**, is the pleasantest, particularly if you intend to travel in the south of the country and explore some of the jungle. The Caracol archeological site is only accessible in this season, as the roads are scarcely practicable the rest of the year. There is also better underwater visibility for diving. NB, through September and October tropical storms are possible along the coast and on the *cays* (islets). Average sea temperatures range between 25°C in winter and 30°C in summer. If you are timing your visit to fit in with local celebrations or festivities, remember to book hotels well in advance in the towns concerned (*see p 306 "The basics"*).

## • Packing list

### Clothing

As for the Guatemalan Lowlands, take light cotton clothing that dries quickly. If staying on the cays, shorts, t-shirt, a hat, sunglasses and a swimsuit are quite enough. You do not even need shoes in the villages of San Pedro and Caye Caulker, *"no shirt, no shoes, no problem"* has become a catch-phrase on these islands! Remember, however, to take a jumper for evenings and for returning by boat after a day out at sea. Take rainwear, as well as good waterproof walking shoes with non-slip soles and high uppers to protect the ankles, for walking in the forests and visiting archeological sites.

### Accessories

220V electrical appliances (such as razors) will only work with a 220V-110V transformer and an adaptor for flat-pronged sockets. Consider taking a waterproof camera to photograph the underwater flora and fauna, and remember to take binoculars if you are a birdwatcher.

## • Travel for everyone

### Travelling with children

If you are travelling in an air-conditioned vehicle or staying only on the cays, travelling with children does not pose any problems so long as they are protected from the sun and given drinks at regular intervals.

### Single women

No reason for not travelling alone in Belize – unless you are allergic to Latino ambiences and Caribbean atmospheres. It is nevertheless advisable to follow the same general safety rules as for Guatemala.

*Senior travellers*

Belize presents no particular problems if you are staying in the main tourist areas. For exploring the country off the beaten track, an air-conditioned vehicle is essential as some trips can be hard going because of the heat and humidity.

*Disabled travellers*

There are few amenities for disabled travellers. In addition, the sandy streets on the cays are likely to make moving around difficult.

## • Address book

*Embassies and consulates*

**United Kingdom –** Belize High Commission, 22 Harcourt House, 19 Cavendish Sq, London W1M 9AD, ☎ (0171)499 9728, Fax (0171)491 4139.

**USA –** Embassy, 2535 Massachusetts Ave NW, Washington DC 20008, ☎ (202)332 9636, Fax (202)332 6888. Consulate General, 5825 Sunset Blvd, Suite 206, Hollywood, CA 90028, ☎ (213)469 7343, Fax (213)469 7346.

**Canada –** Honorary Consul, c/o Bloomfield Bellemare, 1080 Cote Beaver Hall Hill, Suite 1720, Montreal, Quebec, H2Z 1S8, ☎ (514)871 4741, Fax (514)397 0816. Honorary Consul, South Tower, Suite 3800, Royal Bank Plaza, Toronto, ON M5J 2J7, ☎ (416)865 7000, Fax (416)865 7048.

**Guatemala –** Embassy of Belize, Avenida la Reforma 1-50, Zona 9, Edificio El Reformador, Suite 803, Guatemala City, ☎ 334 5531 / 331 1137.

*Tourist information*

**USA –** Belize Tourist Board, 421 7th Ave, Suite 701, New York, NY 10001, ☎ (212)563 6011, Fax (212)563 6033.

In other countries, contact the embassies and consulates listed above or the **Belize Tourist Board**, 83 North Front St, Belize City, ☎ (02)77213 / 73255, btbb@btl.net

*Web sites*

www.belizenet.com
www.ambergriscaye.com

*International Enquiries*

To locate a Belize telephone number from abroad, dial international enquiries + 501.

## • Documents required

*ID, visas*

A **passport** valid six months after your return date and a **return ticket** (or a ticket continuing on to another country) are sufficient for a month's visit for citizens of the EU, the Commonwealth and the USA. The Belizean authorities reserve the right to check you have sufficient financial resources for your visit (BZ$100 a day). To prolong your visit go to the **Immigration Office**, Administration Building, Mahogany St, Belize City, ☎ (02)24620.

*Customs*

**Imports –** You can bring in one litre of alcohol and two cartons of cigarettes.
**Exports –** It is illegal to take items of pre-Columbian art or certain species of internationally protected animals and plants (coral, turtles) out of Belize.

*Vaccinations*

See p 82 Guatemala

*Driving licence*

An international driving licence is required to rent a car.

**Before going**

## • Local currency
### Cash
The **Belizean dollar** (BZ$) is tied to the American dollar (US$): **BZ$2 = US$1.** Almost everywhere payments can be made in either currency. In tourist places prices may be shown in either Belizean or American dollars; use of the "$" symbol for both currencies, without further precision, can lead to expensive misunderstandings. Always ask if prices quoted are in "Belize dollars" or "US dollars".

Notes: BZ$100, 50, 20, 10, 5, 2 and 1. Coins: BZ$1, and 50, 25, 10, 5 and 1 **cents** (1 dollar = 100 cents). Notes and coins bear the portrait of Queen Elizabeth II of England. Take a supply of small change when heading away from tourist centres.

### Exchange
Banks *(see the practical information in the "Making the most of" section of each town)* will only change American dollars. To buy or sell Mexican pesos or Guatemalan quetzals, you have to go to the black-market moneychangers at the border. Make sure you ask the exchange rate before agreeing to the transaction. Remember to change your Belize dollars before leaving the country, they are of no use at all outside Belize.

### Traveller's cheques
Traveller's cheques in US dollars are accepted in most tourist places. Banks will cash them for a 2% commission.

### Credit cards
Payment by Visa, MasterCard, American Express or Diner's Club cards is accepted in many shops, hotels and restaurants (some add 5% commission). Cash can also be obtained with cards over the counter at some banks. The country is starting to install **cash machines**; the one at Barclay's Bank in Belize City functions 24hr/day for holders of international Visa cards.

## • Spending money
If you are coming from Guatemala, Belize will seem very expensive. Allow around **US$30** a day to stay in a cheap hotel, eat at small local restaurants and travel by bus. The middle-range budget rapidly reaches **US$60** a day for a decent hotel and more sophisticated meals. Luxury tastes can be satisfied for around **US$250** a day, staying and eating in select establishments.

Allow an extra US$60 a day to rent a car or travel by plane on domestic flights. These budgets are for one person in a double room, excluding going out, shopping and entry fees to sites.

## • Booking in advance
It is advisable to book hotels in advance during the high season (November-May), especially for Christmas and the New Year celebrations. Prices at these periods are around 30-50% higher than during the rest of the year. Consult the calendar of local celebrations as well so as to anticipate how full a town may be. NB, hotels in Dangriga are booked up several months ahead of Garifuna Settlement Day.

## • Travel / Health Insurance
*See p 84 Guatemala.*

# GETTING THERE

## • By air

*See p 84 "Getting there" (Guatemala) and p 326 "Making the most of Belize City".*

There are no direct flights between Europe and Belize. You therefore have to fly via either the United States with **American Airlines** or **Continental Airlines**, or Central America (especially Guatemala) with the **TACA** group. The Belizean companies **Tropic Air** and **Maya Island Air** also fly daily services between Belize City and Guatemala (Flores or Guatemala City).

### Airports

The country has around forty airstrips but only one international airport. The **Philip S W Goldson International Airport**, ☎ (025)2800, is located about 15km northwest of Belize City.

### Confirmation

Remember to confirm your return flight 72hr before departure at your airline company's office (*see p 326 "Making the most of Belize City"*), and keep enough money aside to pay your taxi to the airport, airport/departure taxes, etc.

### Airport tax

On leaving the country you have to pay a BZ$30 tax, in cash.

## • By bus

Buses run daily to the Mexican border in the north of the country (*see p 358 "Making the most of Corozal"*) and the Guatemalan border in the west, on the road to Tikal (*see p 370 "Making the most of San Ignacio"*).

## • By car

As in Guatemala, car rental agencies do not allow their vehicles to cross the border.

Getting there

### • By boat

There are daily boat connections between Punta Gorda and Puerto Barrios (Guatemala) (*see p 353 "Making the most of Punta Gorda"*).

### • Crossing the borders

*See p 84.*

# THE BASICS

### • Address book

*Tourist information*

Not all towns have tourist offices but there is always a bar, association or hotel acting as a replacement. If you start your visit in Belize City, ask for general information on the country from the **Belize Tourist Board**, 83 North Front St, ☎ (02)77213 / 73255, btbb@btl.net Fuller information on the country's nature reserves is available from the **Belize Audubon Society**, 12 Fort St, PO Box 1001, ☎ (02)35004 / 34533, Fax (02)34985, base@btl.net Amateur archeologists should go to Belmopan to obtain detailed information from the **Archeology Department**, ☎ (08)22106 / 22227 (*by appointment only*).

*Embassies and consulates*

Belmopan is the administrative capital of the country but most embassies and consulates are still in Belize City.

R. Marca

**United Kingdom** – British High Commission, Embassy Square (Ring Road), PO Box 91, Belmopan, ☎ (08)22146/7, Fax (08)22761.
**USA** – American Embassy, 29 Gabourel Lane, PO Box 286, Belize City, ☎ (02)77161, Fax (02)30802.
**Canada** – Canadian Consulate, 83 North Front St, Belize City, ☎ (02)31060, Fax (02)30060
**Guatemala** – Guatemalan Embassy, 8 A St, Belize City, ☎ (02)33150 / 33314, Fax (02)35140.

## • Opening and closing times

*Banks*
Mondays to Thursdays 8am-1pm and Fridays all day to approx 5pm.
*Post offices and telephone*
Post offices are usually open 8am-5pm (Fridays 4.30pm) and closed weekends. The **BTL** telephone company is open 8am-12noon and 1pm-4pm; closed weekends. Its office in Belize City is open Mondays to Saturdays 8am-6pm.
*Shops*
Mondays to Fridays 8am-5pm (sometimes closing 12noon-1pm). In tourist places they generally close later. Shops closed on Wednesday mornings normally open Saturday mornings.
*Offices*
8am-12noon / 1pm-4pm; closed weekends.
*Restaurants*
As a general rule, meals are served 11am-2.30pm and 7pm-10pm. Restaurants are usually closed one day a week; the day may vary but many do not open on Sundays.

## • National parks and archeological sites

*Opening times*
Nature reserves and archeological sites are generally open daily 8am-5pm, but there are exceptions. It is possible to visit outside these hours if you are accompanied by a local guide (e.g. to explore the jungle by night).
*Fees*
Entrance fees vary between BZ$8 and BZ$15. NB, organised excursions do not systematically include entrance fees to sites. Go in a group to take advantage of special rates.

## • Mail

Although letters take about three weeks to reach Europe, it is worth sending mail to stamp-collecting friends as Belizean stamps are some of the most beautiful in the world. The main post office in Belize City sells a vast selection in its philately section.

## • Telephone, fax and e-mail

**BTL** (Belize Telecommunications Limited) offices, found in all major towns, provide telephone and fax services (plus Internet access in Belize City only). As in Guatemala, local and international calls can be made **"station to station"**, charged per unit as soon as anyone answers, or **"person to person"**, charged only from when the person requested answers.

The basics

Towns have a few **telephone kiosks**, often near the BTL offices, which accept coins (25 cents) and/or cards (value BZ$20/30/50).

Internet access and e-mail services are becoming more common in tourist places (Belize City, San Ignacio, San Pedro, Caye Caulker). Depending on the place, tariffs vary by a factor of up to 10: a 30min connection costs BZ$6 in Belize City and BZ$60 in San Pedro!

### International calls

**Codes –** To call out of Belize, dial 00 + the international code of the country you are calling + the national number you wish to reach (omitting any initial 0). UK: 00 + 44; USA: 00 + 1; Canada: 00 + 1; Australia: 00 + 61; New Zealand: 00 + 64.

**Tariffs –** To call abroad, BTL requires a **deposit** of BZ$40. This is reimbursed in full if the call does not connect. A call to Europe costs BZ$6 a minute (minimum 3min). 30% reduction between 10pm and 4am. It is possible to make collect calls to some countries; ask at BTL.

### Local calls

Below is a list of the codes for department capitals and the main tourist centres. These are given in brackets in the practical section of each town. To call within the town you are calling from, dial the local number without the area code; for long-distance calls, dial the area code + the local number; to call Belize from abroad, just omit the initial 0 of the area code.

| | |
|---|---|
| Belize City | 02 |
| Belmopan | 08 |
| Caye Caulker | 022 |
| Corozal | 04 |
| Dangriga | 05 |
| Orange Walk | 03 |
| Placencia | 06 |
| Punta Gorda | 07 |
| San Ignacio | 09 |
| San Pedro | 026 |

### National enquiries

Dial 113.

## • Public holidays

| | |
|---|---|
| **1 January** | New Year's Day |
| **9 March** | Baron Bliss Day |
| **March-April** | Good Friday |
| **(variable dates)** | Saturday before Easter |
| | Easter Sunday |
| | Easter Monday |
| **1 May** | Labour Day |
| **24 May** | Commonwealth Day |
| **10 September** | St George's Caye Day |
| **21 September** | Independence Day |
| **12 October** | Columbus Day (Pan American Day) |
| **19 November** | Garifuna Settlement Day |
| **25 December** | Christmas Day |
| **26 December** | Boxing Day |

**The basics**

## • Local celebrations

The national celebrations mentioned above are especially important in some towns. For Baron Bliss Day, Belize City organises a regatta near the lighthouse; the Easter processions are impressive in San Ignacio and on Ambergris Caye and Caye Caulker; carnivals are held in Orange Walk and Corozal for Columbus (Pan American) Day; and an important Garifuna festival is held in Dangriga for Garifuna Settlement Day. Apart from these celebrations, the various communities organise a multitude of local festivities (*details from tourist offices*).

# GETTING AROUND

The country is no more than 280km from north to south as the crow flies, whereas from east to west it is 109km at its widest point. Despite this modest land area, bus journeys take time – you have to allow a minimum of 8hr, in the dry season, for the 330km road trip from Belize City to Punta Gorda. Travellers in a hurry should rent a vehicle or use the domestic air routes which serve most tourist centres.

## • By car

### Rental

If you wish to explore the farthest reaches of Belize, a vehicle is an excellent, if pricey, solution. Rental agencies are concentrated in Belize City and San Ignacio. You will have to show an international driving licence and be at least 25 years old. When you sign the contract, the hirer will ask you to pay the full cost of rental and give a deposit (by credit card or in cash). Allow a minimum of US$80 a day to rent a cheap car and approx US$120 for a 4WD, unlimited mileage, insurance and taxes included. An excess of around US$750 is charged in the case of theft or accident. As in Guatemala, rental vehicles are not permitted to cross the border.

### Highway code

Belize's road network is on the same scale as the country: of its 2 250km of roadways, approx two thirds are little more than dirt tracks. The Northern Highway and Western Highway, leading to Mexico and Guatemala respectively, are both decently surfaced but the Hummingbird Highway and Southern Highway going south are only surfaced on certain stretches. Apart from these national roads, the rest of the network is made up of secondary roads that are barely practicable, or even inaccessible, during the rainy season.

Despite British colonisation, Belize drives on the right. Traffic is never very heavy, in town (with the exception of Belize City) or country. In the south very few vehicles are seen at all. Buy a good road map as road signs are virtually non-existent; the rare ones you do see show distances in miles (1 mile = 1.6km). In the absence of street-lighting, driving at night is dangerous: if problems arise it is more than likely no help will arrive before the following morning.

### Fuel

Available in all major towns. As distances are short enough not to run out of fuel, it is simply a question of filling up at every petrol station you pass. Fuel costs about BZ$1.6 a litre.

**Getting around**

*In emergencies*
Police, ☎ 911.

## • By taxi

Taxis are recognisable by their green registration plates. They do not have meters but the price of a ride, which is invariable whatever the distance, generally depends on the number of passengers. In Belize City a taxi ride for one or two passengers costs BZ$5. In other places, ask the locals what the fare is and get the driver to confirm it before setting off (make sure you are talking Belize dollars and not American).

Hiring a taxi for the day to visit sites that are difficult to get to by bus may work out to be cheaper and more convenient than renting a vehicle. Before setting off, negotiate an all-in rate per hour or per kilometre with the driver.

## • By bus

This is the most economical means of transport, with fares working out at approx BZ$6 per 100km. As in Guatemala, the buses are old and not very comfortable. However, in spite of the limited number of routes, they are rarely crowded. They serve the main towns (*see the practical section of each town*) and stop along the major highways at passengers' requests. If you intend to go off these highways, it is advisable to hire a vehicle or take a taxi.

## • Hitch-hiking

In isolated regions where public transport is unavailable, it is unwise to bank on hitch-hiking for getting around, as the roads are usually deserted!

## • By pick-up

These sometimes take over when there is no public transport. It is in fact just organised car-sharing, as the fares are about the same as bus fares.

## • Renting golf carts

Particularly fashionable on the cays, these little electric cars allow you to get about relatively quickly (20km/h), with no noise (watch out for pedestrians) or effort, along the sandy paths of San Pedro or Caye Caulker. They cost approx BZ$20 an hour – the rate goes down if you hire by the day or week. You will be asked for identity and your driving licence when you sign the rental contract.

## • By water taxi

This term covers rare collection of vessels, from old tubs through catamarans and fishing boats to powerful motor boats. Regular fast services take passengers from Belize City to some of the cays (*see p 326 "Making the most of Belize City"*). The crossing fare is the same however many passengers there are (BZ$15 to Caye Caulker and BZ$25 to Ambergris Caye). More unpredictable connections to less touristy islands may mean having to hire a boat for the crossing. Get a group together in order to pay less per person.

## • Domestic flights

For moving around the country quickly, flying remains the best bet. You thus avoid long, bumpy, muddy rides, especially in the south of the country, and can admire splendid aerial views of the cays, lagoons and jungle. The two national companies, **Tropic Air** and **Maya Island Air**, fly daily flights from the international and municipal airports in Belize City to Caye Caulker, Corozal, Dangriga, Placencia, Punta Gorda and San Pedro (*see the practical sections of these towns*). Tickets can be bought on the day of travel but it is advisable to book in advance because of the small number of seats in these little aircraft. To give an example, a Belize City-Ambergris Caye flight costs BZ$80, and a Belize City-Punta Gorda one-way flight costs twice as much.

## • Organised tours and excursions

These sometimes simplify travel when there is no reliable public transport. Ask at the reception desk of your hotel or in a travel agency to put your name down for all sorts of excursions by boat, car, on horseback, etc. *"A la carte"* tours can be arranged with a minimum number of participants but are more expensive than scheduled excursions.

# BED AND BOARD

## • Where to stay

Every district capital has at least two or three acceptable hotels making it possible to explore the surrounding area. However, the best tourist amenities are concentrated in the seaside resorts. Placencia and Caye Caulker have a vast choice of moderately-priced hotels, unlike Ambergris Caye and other islets scattered along the coral reef which tend to specialise in top-range accommodation. With the development of ecotourism, San Ignacio is attracting an increasing number of tourists; its guesthouses are aimed more at backpackers, whereas there are some very luxurious hotels nestling in the heart of Mountain Pine Ridge.

## • Price range

Accommodation costs for comparable services and amenities are higher in Belize than in other Central American countries. Prices given in this guide are calculated on the basis of a double room in high season and include **15% VAT**, **7% hotel tax** and **10% service**. To avoid nasty surprises, make sure that prices displayed include all taxes and are in Belizean dollars. During the high season (November to May) hotels in seaside resorts are generally twice as expensive as they are off-season. Nothing simpler: they just say the price per night is in Belizean dollars in the low season, and in American dollars in the high season! Off-season it is possible to negotiate reductions.

## • Various categories

The quality and cost of accommodation fluctuate considerably from one region to another.

### Hotels

It is something of a miracle to find a **budget** hotel at less than US$15 a night; they can be counted on the fingers of one hand in Belize. Rooms are spartan with no bathrooms, but you can nevertheless hope for a fan (check it works properly). The category above, US$15-30, provides a better choice; in these **cheap** hotels friendliness and hospitality are more evident than comfort. Rooms do not usually have private bathrooms. Although numerous in Placencia, on Caye Caulker and in San Ignacio, they are the exception throughout the rest of the country. For **comfortable** accommodation you will need to allow around US$60. This category covers both unexciting, functional places and hotels with character. Up to around US$130 is the **international category**, with rooms that have every modern comfort, TV, air conditioning and telephone. Over US$150 are the American-style resort hotels but also a few **luxury** hotels built on isolated cays or in the middle of the jungle. Refined decor, comfort and an exceptional natural setting generally justify the high prices.

### Camping

It is generally forbidden to camp on the beaches, but some nature reserves give visitors permission to camp on their sites and a few hotels will agree to rent space in their gardens.

### Bed & Breakfast

In Toledo District organisations have set up a programme of sleeping and eating in local people's homes, in Mayan communities and in one Garifuna village (*see p 353 "Making the most of Punta Gorda"*).

## • Eating out

### In hotels

Depending on the category of hotel, there is a choice of gourmet cuisine, international cuisine with no surprises (generally served as an as-much-as-you-like buffet) or a simple cafeteria selling local dishes. In San Pedro some hotels organise barbecues on certain evenings of the week.

### In restaurants

Apart from the traditional rice & beans, you are not likely to find much! Local dishes served in neighbourhood cafeterias and restaurants lack variety but generally constitute a means of "filling up" at a reasonable price. For a change of scenery (in your plate), you are sure to find at least one Chinese restaurant in every town. As for the tourist areas, they offer a vast choice of international menus (French, Italian, Mexican). Belize City and San Pedro have a few top-quality eating places.

# SPORTS AND PASTIMES

Belize offers a whole patchwork of activities tinged always with a hint of Caribbean blue or forest green.

## • The sea

San Pedro (Ambergris Caye) and Caye Caulker offer all sorts of water activities. Check out the practical sections of these places.

### Swimming

How can you resist the temperature and colour of the Caribbean Sea? Unfortunately, there are few beaches in Belize, except on the Placencia peninsula.

## Scuba diving

With the longest barrier reef in the northern hemisphere, three of the ten Caribbean atolls and underwater visibility at 15-30m, Belize is a diver's paradise. The best diving sites are to be found in the Turneffe Islands, on Lighthouse Reef and Glover's Reef. The shops on the main cays offer many combinations for experienced divers or beginners. Respect the coral reef: harpoonfishing is forbidden, be careful not to damage anything with your flippers, and do not pick any coral.

## Snorkelling

This is for everyone who can swim; a mask, a snorkel and flippers are all you need. Wear a t-shirt all the same, to avoid a sunburnt back. As some cays are right on the barrier reef, you only have a few metres to paddle before finding yourself surrounded by spectacular flora and fauna. In San Pedro and on Caye Caulker you will be spoilt for choice by all the diving shops in competition with each other. As the barrier reef gets farther from the coast the further south you go, excursions in the vicinity of Punta Gorda take longer but attract fewer visitors.

## Glass-bottom boats

These boats offer an original alternative for admiring the seabed without getting wet. Daily departures from San Pedro.

## Fishing

Deep-sea fishermen head out around the atolls, where the waters are alive with barracuda, tarpon, tuna and marlin. For this type of sea excursion, organised from San Pedro and Placencia, allow US$300-500 a day.

## Sailing

Even if you know something about navigation, it is not advisable to venture out alone in this region for the barrier reef is difficult to cross. Since **Hurricane Mitch** blew through in 1998 the topography of some cays has altered, making navigation even more problematic. It is therefore better to take on a skipper who knows the area perfectly. To charter a yacht or catamaran for a few days, San Pedro has, of course, the largest choice of addresses. It is also possible to organise this type of excursion from Río Dulce in Guatemala (see p 281 "Making the most of Río Dulce").

## Kayaks

Protected by the barrier reef, you can paddle from island to island (where it is possible to camp overnight). Sea kayaking is recommended during calm weather, during the dry season from February to May. The period from November to January is good for kayaking on rivers such as the Monkey River near Placencia or the Macal River in Cayo District.

### • Cross country

Inland, Cayo District takes first place for the number of outdoor activities available to visitors.

### Walking

With 75% of its land area covered in forests, Belize lends itself to innumerable walks for discovering its wealth of flora and fauna. Some of the nature reserves to be found all over the country have marked trails, but a local guide will be invaluable for your visit, teaching you to recognise birds, showing you dozens of trees with curative powers and, above all, making sure you get back safely. To watch the birds and avoid the heat, it is best to leave at dawn. Trousers, high-cut shoes and a long-sleeved t-shirt offer the best protection against insect bites.

### Mountain bikes

This sport is gaining ground in Cayo District. The roads in this undulating region are practicable from February to October; the rest of the year it is virtually impossible to get about by bike because the ground is saturated. Bicycles can be hired by the day in San Ignacio. About BZ$25 a day.

### Horse riding

Exploring Cayo District on horseback is a very popular activity and an excellent means of getting to the Caracol archeological site. Approx BZ$70 a day.

### • Night-life

Those who have still got the strength after all these outdoor pursuits can continue their exploration of Belize by night: night scuba diving, expeditions into the mangrove swamps, camping in the jungle.

For more conventional night activities, tourist centres always have bars and discos and put a few concerts on, but there is nothing particularly extraordinary in comparison with the wide range of day-time activities (*see the practical section of each town*).

# SHOPPING

### • What's on offer

### Arts and crafts

Compared with neighbouring countries, Belize is the poor cousin as far as arts and crafts go. Tourist shop shelves are filled with textiles from Guatemala, t-shirts and a few carvings in *zericote* wood (a local brown wood).

### Music

Souvenir shops generally sell a small selection of reggae and punta rock records and cassettes.

### Stamps

A corner of Belize on your envelopes. A vast range of these stamps depicting magnificent specimens of local flora and fauna are on sale in the main post office in Belize City.

### • Where to shop
*What to buy where*
The same arts and crafts items line the tourist routes from the cays to Mountain Pine Ridge. With a few exceptions the shops differ very little from each other.
*Shops*
Note the **National Handicraft Sales Center** (*see p 329 "Making the most of Belize City"*), an arts and crafts department store that is practical for buying a few things before boarding your bus or plane.

### • Duty
**VAT** (Value Added Tax) stands at 15%.

# HEALTH AND SAFETY

### • Precautions (*see p 98 "Making the most of Guatemala"*)

### • Medical kit (*see p 99 "Making the most of Guatemala"*)

### • Health
*First aid*
Ambulances, ☎ 90.
*Hospitals*
All district capitals have a hospital but it is advisable to go to Belize City or be repatriated in the case of serious health problems. The decompression chamber on Ambergris Caye treats problems resulting from scuba diving.
*Chemists / Pharmacies*
These can be found in all major towns and tourist places.
*Doctors*
Ask your consulate for a list of recommended doctors. They speak English.

### • Emergencies
Police, ☎ 911.
Fire brigade, ☎ 90 (same number as for ambulances).

# A TO Z

### • Bargaining
But what to bargain for? Opportunities to buy things are rare in Belize, unlike Guatemala. However, in the low season you can bargain down the price of hotel rooms.

### • Conversion table
Belize has maintained the Anglo-Saxon system of measurements. Distances are given in miles (1 mile = 1.6km), yards (1yd = 0.9m) and feet (1ft = 30.5cm). NB, fuel is sold by the American gallon (3.79 litres), not the imperial gallon.

**Health and safety**

### • Drinking water
Tap water is treated in major tourist centres but it is advisable to buy bottled drinks in isolated areas. Make a pleasure of necessity by trying the local *Belikin* beer.

### • Electricity
110 volts and 60 hertz, with flat-pronged plugs as in the United States and Guatemala.

### • Laundry
After a forest hike a laundry is no luxury. You will find at least one in all major towns and in the seaside resorts. Some are self-service.

### • Newspapers
The "major" national dailies are in English. The *Belize Times*, backed by the People's United Party, or the *People's Pulse*, pro-United Democratic Party, will give you a glimpse of local news and political disputes.

### • Radio and television
The two national television channels broadcast numerous programmes from the United States. Most hotels have cable TV. The few local radio stations liven up bus journeys, in English and Spanish.

### • Smoking
Most major international brands are on sale at prices somewhat lower than in the UK. A packet of cigarettes costs BZ$8 (US$4 / £2.40), three times more expensive than in Guatemala. Some places are no-smoking for safety reasons, especially in wooden houses. Smouldering cigarette ends can cause serious fires in towns or forests, so be careful.

### • Taking photographs
Take film with you, as it is more expensive in Belize than in Europe or Guatemala. Before going, consider buying a disposable waterproof camera for taking pictures of your underwater adventures.

### • Thefts
With the exception of Belize City at night, the country does not really deserve the bad reputation that has stuck to it. Just respecting a few ordinary general safety rules (*see p 101 "Making the most of Guatemala"*) is sufficient. Like anywhere else in the world, it is a bad idea to leave your belongings unattended on the beach.

### • Tipping / Gratuities
Service is normally included in the bill but you can leave a tip of 10-15 % if you are satisfied with the service.

### • Weather forecasts
Weather forecasts in the written press and on television are particularly useful during the tropical storm season as they allow people to take shelter when need be.

# USEFUL WORDS
# AND EXPRESSIONS

Depending on which part of Belize you are in, people speak either English or Spanish *(see p 103 "Useful words and expressions" (Guatemala))*. Belizean English tends towards American usages rather than British, e.g.:

| | |
|---|---|
| autumn | fall |
| petrol station | gas station |
| main road | highway |
| toilets | restroom |
| letter box | mailbox |

# Exploring Belize

A cay in its
turquoise setting

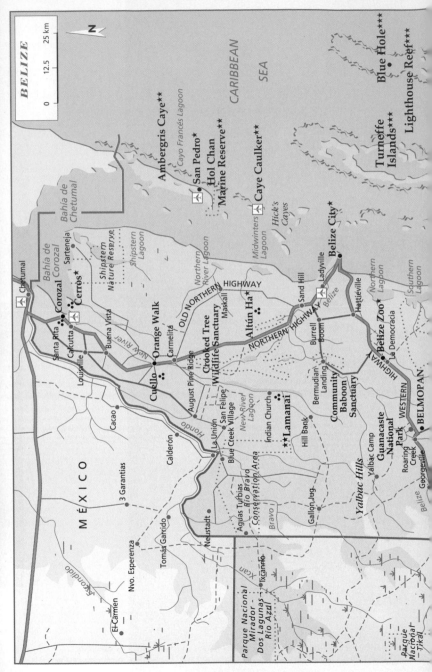

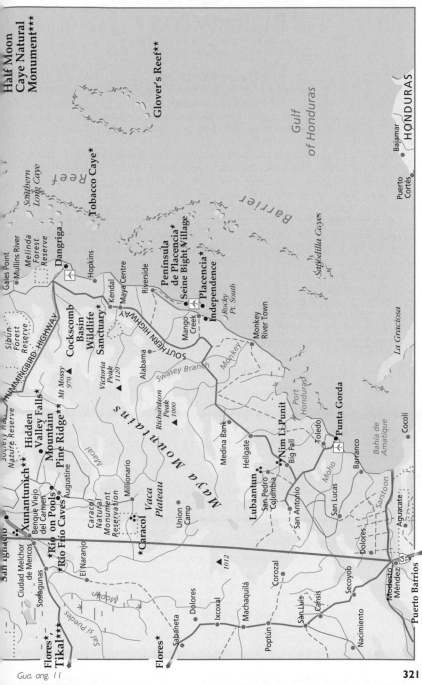

Half Moon
Caye Natural
Monument★★★

Glover's Reef★★

Gulf
of Honduras

HONDURAS

Bajamar

Puerto
Cortés

Southern Long Caye

Tobacco Caye★

Southern Reef

Barrier

Gales Point

Mullins River

Melinda
Forest
Reserve

Dangriga

Hopkins

Kendal

Maya Centre

Riverside

Peninsula
de Placencia★
Seine Bight Village

Placencia★

Independence

Mango
Creek

Rocky
Pt. South

Monkey
River Town

Sapodilla Cayes

La Graciosa

Sibun
Forest
Reserve

HUMMINGBIRD VALLEY HIGHWAY

Cockscomb
Basin
Wildlife
Sanctuary★

Mt Mossy 970 ▲

Victoria Peak
▲ 1120

Alabama

Swasey Branch

Monkey

SOUTHERN HIGHWAY

Medina Bank

Hellgate

Nim Li Punit★

Big Fall

Toledo

Punta Gorda

Barranco

Bahia de
Amatique

Cocolí

Port
Honduras

Moho

Sarstoon

Soufry Hall
Nature Reserve

Hidden
Valley Falls★

Mountain
Pine Ridge★★

Augustine

Xunantunich★

Benque Viejo
del Carmen

★Río on Pools

Río Frío Caves

Macal

Caracol
Natural
Monument
Reservation

Millonario

Vaca
Plateau

★Caracol
Río Frío Caves

Union
Camp

Richardson Peak
▲ 1000

Maya Mountains

Lubaantun★

San Pedro
Columbia

San Antonio

San Lucas

Aguacate

1012 ▲

San Ignacio

Ciudad Melchor
de Mencos

Sosfagunas

El Naranjo

Sal si puedes

Mopán

Flores★,
Tikal★★★

Flores★

Sabaneta

Dolores

Ixcoxal

Machaquilá

Poptún

San Luis

Cahsis

Nacimiento

Corozal

Secoyob

Modesto
Méndez

CA
13

Puerto Barrios

Dolores

# BELIZE CITY★
Formerly capital of British Honduras
Largest town in the country – Pop approx 53 000

**Not to be missed**
The colonial residences in Fort George District.
**And remember...**
Take taxis to get around Belize City in the evenings.
Take a group excursion or hire a vehicle to visit the surrounding area.

Belize City juts out into the Caribbean Sea as if sucking the ocean into its river and canals. The water, which is everywhere, is the only element this seaport succeeds in controlling, except when it falls from the skies. But many another peril hangs over the town. Fire threatens to reduce its Creole cottages to cinders with the slightest spark, and devastating hurricanes can hit its shores like those of 1931 and 1961; the latter swept away both a considerable part of the town and its title of capital, ceded to Belmopan *(see p 364)*. But the inhabitants remain attached to their old town, despite nature's relentlessness and the town's reputation as a seaport suffering from high unemployment, drug problems and crime. Sheltering over a quarter of Belize's population, the former capital of British Honduras has conserved the original charm of a village, in contrast with other Central American cities. Its tropical nonchalance, few remaining colonial buildings and relaxed atmosphere make it worthwhile exploring further than the bus station or jetty, to stroll around the narrow streets at a Caribbean pace.

## Visiting the town
*Allow 3hr.*

Through the middle of Belize City flows **Haulover Creek**, dotted with fishing boats, yachts, water taxis and pelicans. Spanning the river near its mouth, the **Swing Bridge★** (B2)· which is still manually operated, has been regulating the passage of boats for a century. It is an excellent landmark when exploring the town centre.

### North of Haulover Creek
Most tourists' knowledge of the town is limited to the **Belize Maritime Museum & Terminal** (B2-B3) *(7am-5pm. Fee)*. This building near the Swing Bridge houses the jetty from which water taxis leave for the cays, and a maritime museum to visit while waiting for boats. The museum takes an educational approach, showing the marine world – from mangrove swamps to high seas – through detailed plates, photos, re-creations of ecosystems and model boats.

To the east of the jetty, **Fort George District★**(C3), a residential area of plush colonial residences, juts out into the bay. At the far end of the peninsula, the **lighthouse** watches over the **Baron Bliss Memorial** (C3) in honour of an Englishman who left his fortune to Belize.

K. Amsler/EXPLORER

Haulover Creek flows through the heart of Belize

Belize City

## South of the river

The south bank of Haulover Creek, near the Swing Bridge, is the most picturesque and lively area of Belize City. Along **Albert Street** and **Regent Street** are most of the city's shops, banks and administrative buildings. After nightfall, however, this area turns into a shady district where the shadows hide all sorts of illegal dealings.

At the top of Regent Street, on the east side of Battlefield Park, the **Court House** (B3) occupies a delightful wooden building rebuilt in the 1920s after a fire.

South of Regent Street, in a seafront garden, a fine colonial villa from the early 19C houses the **Government House Museum**★ (B4) *(8am-4.30pm; closed weekends. Fee)*. This former residence of the Governors General exhibits period furniture and porcelain as well as two works dear to Belizeans, the **Sleeping Giant** – a sculpture by George Gabb depicting the diversity of the Belize peoples – and a reproduction of the **head of Kinich Ahau** discovered at Altun Ha *(see below)*.

A hundred metres from the museum, the British influence is obvious: **St John's Cathedral** (B4), the oldest Anglican church in Central America, was built by slaves between 1812 and 1824 using bricks brought from Great Britain as ships' ballast. In the 19C three kings of the Mosquito Coast (Nicaragua) were crowned in this local version of Westminster Abbey.

# Along the Northern Highway

*For the sights along the Western Highway, see p 364 "Belmopan".*

## Altun Ha★ archeological site

*55km from Belize City. 33km down the Northern Highway, fork right at the Shell petrol station. Continue along the Old Northern Highway (the old road) for 19km to Lucky Strike, then take the left-hand unsurfaced road to the site, 3km further on. 9am-5pm. Fee.*

Altun Ha was a major city-state founded around 600 BC which flourished during the Classic period. Many sacrificial rites must have taken place in this ceremonial centre, and sumptuous offerings of jade and obsidian have been discovered in the **Temple of the Green Tomb**. Overlooking a second square is the **Temple of the Masonry Altars**★, the highest building on the site, standing 18m above the forest. Here the **head of Kinich Ahau** (the Sun God) was found; weighing almost five kilos, this is the largest piece of carved jade ever found in Mesoamerica.

## The Community Baboon Sanctuary

*43km from Belize City. 23km down the Northern Highway a sign indicates Burrell Boom to the left. Drive 6km to this village and turn right at the sign indicating 9 miles (14km) to the Community Baboon Sanctuary. 8am-5pm. Fee.*

This sanctuary for **black howler monkeys** is a good introduction to the way rural communities live in Belize. Half a dozen villages got together to preserve a wooded environment for this endangered species. It is well worth taking a walk through this tropical forest, guided by the extraordinary calls of these primates – hoarse cries that sound like car engines alternating with the roar of a lion.

## Crooked Tree Wildlife Sanctuary

*57.5km from Belize City. Take the Northern Highway for 52km then turn left onto the unsurfaced road that leads 5.5km further on to the village of Crooked Tree. 8am-5pm. Fee.*

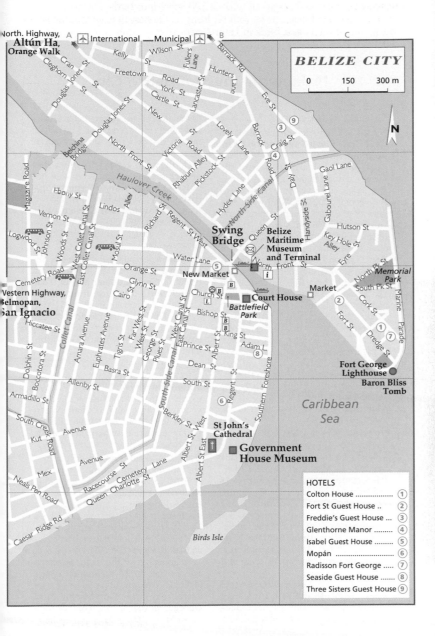

**BELIZE CITY**

0    150    300 m

N

North. Highway,
**Altún Ha,
Orange Walk**

International — Municipal

Kelly
Wilson St
Cran St
Cleghorn
Douglas Jones St
St
Freetown
Road
Fullers
Lane
Barrack Rd
Hunters
Lane
York St
Castle St
Lancaster St
Lovely Lane
New
Victoria Road
Barrack
Eve St
Craig St
⑨
⑨
④
Belchina
Bridge
Douglas Jones St
North Front St
Rhaburn Alley
Pickstock St
Hydés Lane
Barrack Road
North Side Canal
Daly St
Gaol Lane
Gabourel Lane
Haulover Creek
Ebony St
Lindos
Alley
Richard St
Regent St West
Queen
St
Handyside St
Hutson St
Key Hole Alley
Eyre
Vernon St
Johnson St
Woods St
West Collet Canal St
East Collet Canal St
Mobul St
**Swing
Bridge**
**Belize
Maritime
Museum
and Terminal**
North Front St
Memorial
Park
Logwood St
Cemetery Road
Orange St
Water Lane
⑤
**New Market**
North Pk St
Cork St
South Pk St
Marine
Western Highway,
Belmopan,
San Ignacio
Glynn St
Cairo
Church St
B
L
B
Battlefield
Park
**Court House**
Market
②
Fort St
①
⑦
Dredge St
Parade
Hiccatee St
Collet Canal
Amara Avenue
Far West St
West St
George St
Tigris St
West Canal St
East Canal St
Plues St
Bishop St
King St
Prince St
Adam L
Albert St
⑧
Dolphin St
Boccotora St
Euphrates Avenue
Basra St
Dean St
Regent St
**Fort George
Lighthouse**
**Baron Bliss
Tomb**
Allenby St
South St
Southern Foreshore
Armadillo St
South Creek Road
Avenue
Kut
Berkley St West
⑥
Caribbean
Sea
Neals Pen Road
Mex
Caesar Ridge Rd
Racecourse St
Cemetery Lane
Queen Charlotte St
Avenue
Albert St West
Albert St East
**St John's
Cathedral**
**Government
House Museum**

Birds Isle

| HOTELS | |
|---|---|
| Colton House ................. | ① |
| Fort St Guest House .. | ② |
| Freddie's Guest House ... | ③ |
| Glenthorne Manor ......... | ④ |
| Isabel Guest House ......... | ⑤ |
| Mopán ........................... | ⑥ |
| Radisson Fort George ..... | ⑦ |
| Seaside Guest House ....... | ⑧ |
| Three Sisters Guest House | ⑨ |

The swamps and lagoons of this nature reserve offer a refuge to iguanas, tortoises, crocodiles and above all to over 300 species of birds. Dawn in the dry season, when the forest echoes with birdsong, is the best time to spot the **jabiru stork**, one of the largest birds in Latin America.

## Making the most of Belize City

### COMING AND GOING

**By air** – Domestic and international flights serve **Philip S W Goldson International Airport**, ☎ (025)2800, located about 15km northwest of the town. No direct flights between Europe and Belize; change either in the USA to American Airlines or Continental Airlines, or in Central America (particularly Guatemala) to the TACA group. The national airlines Tropic Air and Maya Island Air also fly daily services between Belize City and Guatemala City or Flores. On leaving the country there is a BZ$30 airport tax payable in cash. Fixed taxi fare of BZ$30 between the airport and the town centre.

Tropic Air and Maya Island Air fly several return flights a day between Belize City and Caye Caulker, Corozal, Dangriga, Placencia, Punta Gorda and San Pedro (see the "Making the most of" sections of these towns). Most of these domestic flights land with equal frequency at the international airport and the **Municipal Airport**, 2km north of the town centre.

**By bus** – There is no real bus station as bus companies have their own termini.
– Going north: **Batty Brothers Bus Service**, 15 Mosul St, ☎ (02)72025. Buses approx every hour between 4am and 6pm to Chetumal (4hr) via Orange Walk and Corozal. **Escalante's Bus Service**, Batty Brothers terminus, has departures every 30min in late afternoon for Orange Walk. **Venus Bus Line**, Magazine Rd, ☎ (02)77390. Buses to Chetumal every hour between 11.30am and 7pm.
– Going south: **Z-line Bus Service**, Magazine Rd, ☎ (02)73937, uses the same terminus as Venus Line. Departures every hour between 8am and 5pm

to Dangriga via the Hummingbird Highway (3hr) or the coast road (2hr). Four buses a day between 6am and 3pm to Punta Gorda (8hr).
– Going west: **Batty Brothers Bus Service** runs departures every hour between 4am and 10am to Benque Viejo del Carmen (3hr) via Belmopan and San Ignacio. **Novelo's Bus Service**, West Collet Canal, ☎ (02)77372. Buses to Benque Viejo del Carmen every 30min between 11am and 9pm.

**By boat** – Several regular services a day to Caye Caulker (45min) and San Pedro (90min). **Caye Caulker Water Taxi Association** boats leave from Marine Terminal, North Front St, ☎ (02)31969 / 22992. **Triple J Boat Service**, ☎ (02) 44375, and **Andrea**, ☎ (02)48204, boats tie up at Court House Wharf, behind the Court House.

### GETTING AROUND

The tourist amenities and sights are mostly in the town centre or close by, and easily accessible on foot. When night falls it is prudent to take taxis for getting around, as some parts of Belize City have a reputation for street crime.

**By taxi** – Vehicles do not have meters but the fare for any ride in town is fixed at BZ$5 for 1-2 passengers, including to/from the municipal airport. This fare applies for a single journey to a single destination. Each halt requested by a passenger is considered a separate journey, even if you continue on afterwards without changing taxis. There are lots of taxis crisscrossing the town, recognisable by their green registration plates. Main taxi rank on Albert St, in front of Battlefield Park. **Caribbean Taxi Garage**, ☎ (02)72888, **Taxi Garage Services**, ☎ (02)73031.

Taxi drivers are willing to negotiate rates by the hour or the km, which may be more advantageous than hiring a car for the day, to visit some of the places round about that do not have good bus services (Altun Ha, Community Baboon Sanctuary). Contact *Edgar August*, ☎ 014 7393 (cell phone), who owns a roomy, comfortable, air-conditioned 4WD that is often parked in front of the Radisson Fort George Hotel.

**By rental car – Avis**, International Airport, ☎ (025)2385 or Municipal Airport, ☎ (02)34619. *Budget*, 771 Bella Vista, Northern Highway, ☎ (02)32435 / 33986. *Hertz*, 11A Cork St, ☎ (02) 35395. *National*, 4.5Mls Western Highway, ☎ (02)31650 / 31587.

## ADDRESS BOOK

**Tourist information – Belize Tourist Board** (B3), 83 North Front St, ☎ (02)77213 / 73255, btbb@btl.net 8am-12noon / 1pm-5pm; closed weekends. Helpful, professional staff, very thorough documentation on the country. *Belize Audubon Society*, 12 Fort St, PO Box 1001, ☎ (02)35004 / 34533, Fax (02)34985, base@btl.net Non-profit environmental protection association. This NGO is responsible for most of Belize's nature reserves and is a mine of information on the country's natural amenities.

**Bank / Currency Exchange – Atlantic Bank**, 6 Albert St, 8am-1pm (Fridays 4.30pm). *Belize Bank*, 60 Market Square, 8am-1pm (Fridays 5pm), has a branch at Goldson International Airport, 8.30am-10.30am / 12noon-4pm. *Barclay's Bank*, 21 Albert St, 8am-2.30pm (Fridays 4.30pm). 24hr cash machine for Visa cards. *The Bank of Nova Scotia*, corner of Albert St and Bishop St, 8am-1pm (Fridays 6pm).

**Post office / Telephone –** The main post office (B2) is on North Front St opposite Marine Terminal, 8am-5pm (Fridays 4.30pm); closed weekends. On one side of the building, in Queen St, the philately department sells superb collector stamps.

To send urgent mail or parcels, *DHL*, 38 New Rd, ☎ (02)34350, and *Trans-Express*, 31 Freetown Rd, ☎ (02)32929. The *BTL* telephone company (B3), 1 Church St, 8am-6pm; closed Sundays. Local and international calls, faxes sent, e-mail and Internet service.
*Speaking clock* (Time Clock), ☎ 121.

**Medical service – Karl Heusner Memorial Hospital**, Princess Margaret Drive, north of the town centre, ☎ (02)31548. *Ambulance*, ☎ 90.

**Embassies and Consulates – American Embassy**, 29 Gabourel Lane, PO Box 28, ☎ (02)77161, Fax (02)30802, embbelize@state.gov 8am-12noon / 1pm-4pm; closed weekends.
*Canadian Consulate*, 83 North Front St, ☎ (02)31060, Fax (02) 30060.
*Guatemalan Embassy*, 8 A St, ☎ (02)33150 / 33314, Fax (02)35140.

**Airline companies – Air France**, 95 Albert St, ☎ (02)72112.
*American Airlines*, corner of New Rd and Queen St, ☎ (02)32522.
*British Airways*, 41 Albert St, ☎ (02)77363.
*Continental Airlines*, 32 Albert St, ☎ (02)78309 / 78227 / 78463.
*Maya Island Air*, Municipal Airport, ☎ (02)35794.
*TACA International Airline*, 41 Albert St, ☎ (02)77363/4 and at the international airport, ☎ (025)2163.
*Tropic Air*, Municipal Airport, ☎ (02)45671.

**Useful numbers – Police**, ☎ 911.
*Fire Brigade*, ☎ 90.

**Other –** You can leave luggage at Marine Terminal left luggage office.

**Safety –** The *Tourist Police* responsible for visitor safety patrol certain parts of the town. It is easy to spot them in their khaki uniforms.

**Laundry – CA Coin Laundromat**, corner of Barrack Rd and Victoria St, 9am-9pm.

## WHERE TO STAY

• **South of the Swing Bridge**
*Under US$40*

**Seaside Guest House**, 3 Prince St, ☎ (02)78339, friends@btl.net – 5rm. A wooden house set in a small orchid garden, close by the sea. This guesthouse with its relaxed atmosphere, run by a Quaker organisation, is halfway between bed & breakfast and youth hostel. Its little rooms with bunk beds (including 1 dormitory) are snapped up by backpackers who gather in the evenings in a friendly shared lounge, or on the veranda. Ask for a room with a sea view.

**Isabel Guest House**, 3 Albert St, ☎ (02)73139, Fax (02)71582 – 3rm 📶 ⌧ This family guesthouse is tucked away in a dead end off Albert St, between the drugstore and Swing Bridge Café. Here you feel perfectly safe despite the area, which is not very inviting at night. The upper floor has an immense shared lounge with 3 bedrooms opening onto it, including a sort of big attic furnished to sleep up to 6. All the rooms are impeccably clean, pleasant and comfortable, at a very reasonable price.

*Around US$50*
**Hotel Mopán**, 55 Regent St, ☎ (02)77351, Fax (02)75383 – 12rm 📶 ⌧ ✗ cc This delightful colonial house has a friendly restaurant but disappointing accommodation. Its unprepossessing rooms (some with air conditioning) unfortunately do not have the same cachet as the building.

● **North of the Swing Bridge**
*Under US$40*
**Three Sisters Guest House**, 55 Eve St, ☎ (02)35729 – 4rm ⌧ A large wooden house in a quiet, pleasant district. Light, well-kept rooms with somewhat outdated but clean toilet facilities. Same price with or without private bathroom. A good address.

**Freddie's Guest House**, 86 Eve St, ☎ (02)33851 – 3rm ⌧ This guesthouse offers accommodation equivalent to that of the neighbouring Three Sisters. Small rooms, impeccably clean, share the ground floor with garden.

*Around US$50*
**Glenthorne Manor**, 27 Barrack Rd, ☎ (02)44212 – 9rm 📶 ⌧ The first chapter of Alain Dugrand's book "Belize" opens in this colonial residence tinged with old-fashioned charm. The accumulation of furniture and miscellaneous

objects, plus the way each room is decorated differently, create the pleasantest of jumbles. Even so, this bed & breakfast is relatively expensive for what it offers.

● **Fort George District**
*Around US$70*
🐌 **Colton House**, 9 Cork St, ☎ (02)44666, Fax (02)30451, coltonhse@btl.net – 5rm 📶 ⌧ In the heart of Belize City's residential district, this superb wooden house stands out from neighbouring establishments on account of its elegance, its family atmosphere and its reasonable prices. Rooms with parquet flooring and fine high ceilings, plus comfortable bedrooms decorated with a lot of taste. It is strongly recommended to book in advance.

**Fort Street Guest House**, 4 Fort St, ☎ (02)30116, Fax (02)78808, fortst@btl.net – 6rm ⌧ ✗ cc An imposing colonial building with a cachet that comes mostly from its façade. The rooms have every comfort but no private bathrooms. The interior decoration is surprisingly ordinary and impersonal.

*Around US$150*
**Radisson Fort George Hotel**, 2 Marine Parade, PO Box 321, ☎ (02)33333, Fax (02)73820, rdfgh@btl.net – 102rm 📶 🗏 ♪ 📺 ✗ ⤢ ◊ cc A hotel complex with no surprises, good or bad. Worthy of the major international chains, it provides high-class accommodation, quality service and numerous facilities for business travellers. Its capacity makes it a favourite choice for international conferences and major receptions.

## EATING OUT

Most places are closed on Sundays.
*Under US$10*
**Dit's Restaurant & Saloon**, 50 King St (B3), ☎ (02)73330. 9am-9pm; Sundays 8am-4pm. A small local restaurant where the regulars take refuge under enormous fans to tuck into a plate of rice & beans with chicken, beef or pork. Generous helpings at competitive prices. At the counter in the entrance they sell delicious take-away fruit tarts, cakes and pastries.

**Big Daddy's Diner**, Commercial Center, Market Sq (B3), ☎ (02)70932. 7am-4pm; closed Sundays. On the 1st floor of the market (marked 2nd floor). Overlooking the river opposite the Marine Terminal, this cafeteria offers one of the best views of the town. Local cuisine at reasonable prices. A pleasant place to have breakfast and watch the morning ballet of fishermen and pelicans.

**Macy's Café**, 18 Bishop St (B3), ☎ (02)73419. 11am-9.30pm; closed Sundays. This restaurant is very popular with local people. It looks like a tavern and serves a good dish-of-the-day of meat or fish, in the purest of Belizean traditions. Moderate prices but dour service.

*US$20-50*

**Sea Rock**, 190 New Town Barracks, ☎ (02)30370, 11am-11pm; Sundays 6pm-10pm. For a change from rice & beans, come and try their excellent Indian cooking. A very useful address for Sunday evenings.

**Fort Street Restaurant**, 4 Fort St (C3), ☎ (02)30116 CC 7am-10pm. This restaurant offers a very romantic evening decor on a pleasant candlelit veranda. An original menu with a selection of meat and fish dishes combining Belizean and American flavours. Cuisine and service are both meticulous but patience is required.

**Mango's**, 164 New Town Barracks, ☎ (02)34201 CC 11.30am-2pm / 6pm-10pm; closed Sundays. On the seafront, a colourful dining room and patio house Belize City's trendy restaurant. The best seafood and grilled fish in town at prices to match.

## GOING OUT, HAVING A DRINK

**Bars** – For safety reasons it is advisable to avoid the bistros in the town centre in favour of hotel bars. Less picturesque but worth it to avoid problems.

**Discos** – The disco at the **Bellevue Hotel**, 5 Southern Foreshore, is very popular.

## OTHER THINGS TO DO

**Excursions – Belize City Tour**, 5 Eyre St, ☎ (02)73897, runs a bus tour through the town. Departures twice a day (9am and 3pm) from in front of Maritime Terminal.

**S & L Travel and Tours**, 91 North Front St, ☎ (02)77593, Fax (02)75115, sltravel@btl.net Excursions outside the town and to the rest of the country.

**Cultural centre – The Bliss Institute** (B3), Bliss Promenade, ☎ (02)72110 / 72458, is the headquarters of the National Arts Council. 8.30am-12noon / 2pm-8pm; closed Saturday afternoons and Sundays. Organises a variety of cultural events (concerts, plays, exhibitions).

## SHOPPING GUIDE

**Arts and Crafts** – The **National Handicraft Sales Center** (C3), Fort St, opposite Fort Street Guest House, displays an overview of national products: basketwork, sculpture, furniture, t-shirts, post-cards, CDs and tapes of traditional music. It also sells palm or cashew wine and banana honey.

**Bookshops – Angelus Press** stationers and bookshop, 10 Queen St. **The Book Centre**, 4 Church St. New and second-hand books.

**Making the most of Belize City**

# THE NORTHERN CAYS ★★
Access to Caye Caulker and Ambergris Caye by plane or boat

### Not to be missed
Caye Caulker's laid-back ambience.
Swimming with the sharks and rays at Shark-Ray Village.
Scuba diving at the Blue Hole.

### And remember...
For a cheap visit opt for Caye Caulker.
Underwater visibility is better during the dry season.
Take a waterproof camera.

Take a map of Belize and hop from island to island – the place names are a poem in themselves. All along the longest barrier reef in the northern hemisphere, a myriad of islets dot the turquoise waters of the Caribbean Sea. From uninhabited humps through floating mangrove swamps to small corners of paradise, Belize's cays (pronounced "keys") offer superb seascapes and a vast range of water sports – diving, fishing, swimming – or just lazing around. The most popular are Ambergris Caye and Caye Caulker, which have managed to preserve their Caribbean soul despite an increasing influx of tourists.

## Caye Caulker ★★
*32km from Belize City and 24km from San Pedro.*

This little island, 7km long and 800m wide, is mainly marsh and mangrove swamp. Its only village, originally inhabited by conch and lobster fishermen, has experienced an incredible tourist boom over the last few years. Its relaxed atmosphere and reasonably priced accommodation have made Caye Caulker a favourite destination for backpackers and an ideal departure point for the coral reef.

### The village ★
Its main street – a small sandy alleyway – is pure Caribbean. From the rasta fisherman with his palm-leaf hat over dreadlocks, eating his ritual breakfast, to the hotel-keeper in his golf cart, his eyes riveted on the passengers off the last water taxi, all Caye Caulker can be found on **Front Street** ★ at some moment of the day or other. Spicy cocktails, swaying rhythms – the boat will be leaving without you. Sand creeps into every corner of the village, even covering the floors of the shops, but there is no point in looking for the beach, the cay does not have one. It is nevertheless possible to swim, north of the village around the **Split** (or **Cut**), where the island was chopped in two by Hurricane Hattie in 1961. Be careful when swimming, as the boats using this channel can be dangerous for bathers.

### Off Caye Caulker
*Allow a half-day excursion.* At **Shark-Ray Village** ★★, an area of shallow, crystal-clear waters, snorkelling fans can get close to the dozens of inoffensive **nurse sharks** that swarm around the tourist boats in the hope of a handout. The stars of this aquatic ballet are the **whip-tailed stingrays** and especially the **eagle rays**, the most graceful of them all. These generally keep divers waiting and then, suddenly appearing from nowhere, a floating silhouette passes to and fro in front of them like a sail undulating in the breeze.

Also worth visiting is the **Coral Garden** ★ with its wide variety of underwater flora and fauna.

# Ambergris Caye★★
*56km from Belize City and 16km from Caye Caulker.*
*See map p 333.*

The name of this cay, derived from the French *ambre gris* (grey amber), refers to the waxy substance that once made the fortunes of whale hunters and perfume makers. Lying between Caye Caulker and Yucatán, from which it is separated by a channel, this long, thin island (40km long) is the largest of Belize's cays. Its inhabitants – Garifunas, Creoles and Mestizos, the latter being descendants of the Yucatec refugees from the War of the Castes *(see p 356 "Corozal")* – share this island with its mix of Anglo-Saxon and Latin cultures.

## The village of San Pedro★
*Maps of the village are available from golf cart rental agencies, hotels and the tourist office.*

This fishing village has become the jewel in Belize's tourist crown, thanks to the charm and quality of its amenities. All year round, waves of divers from all over the world visit here, although rarely spending the day in it. Which means it is a haven of peace when they disappear out to sea, leaving the inhabitants a free run of the two main

The Split,
Caye Caulker's bathing place

streets that cut through the village from north to south. Front and Back Street, now rechristened with the more evocative names of **Barrier Reef Drive** and **Pescador Drive** respectively, are sandy – or, in the wet season, extremely muddy – and lined with Caribbean houses converted into souvenir shops, diving shops, hotels and restaurants.

Those not keen on diving can take advantage of the best part of San Pedro's **beach**, in front of the Ramon's Village hotel *(even if not staying there)*. North of the village, beyond the river, the coast is also dotted with some enticing beaches, stretching out at the feet of the luxury hotels that have sprung up in this part of the island.

F. Dyan

The Northern Cays

## South of Ambergris Caye

A few hundred yards off the cay are two protected areas where interesting specimens of marine flora and fauna are to be found.

The **Hol Chan Marine Reserve**★★ *(10min by boat from San Pedro)* embraces three ecosystems: the coral barrier reef, the underwater Boca Ciega cave and some mangrove swamps. This marine reserve covering 8sqkm to the south of Ambergris Caye will delight night diving fans.

Beyond the Hol Chan Marine Reserve, you can swim among **nurse sharks** and **whip-tailed stingrays** in the clear waters of **Shark Ray Alley**★★ *(20min by boat from San Pedro)*.

# The atolls★★

*Access by boat from Caye Caulker and Ambergris Caye.*
*Allow at least 1 day for each atoll.*

The atolls beyond the barrier reef offer the best diving sites in the country. These are rings of mostly uninhabited coral islands, encircling lagoons. Altogether there are ten in the Caribbean, three of them off Belize. To explore their superbly beautiful sea depths you need to spend at least one whole day, or even several, staying on board a boat or in one of the rare hotels on these islands. *To choose the best individual combination, information is available from the diving shops in San Pedro or on Caye Caulker.*

### The Turneffe Islands★★★

*40km south of Ambergris Caye (90min journey). Full day excursion.* Located about 30km from Belize City, the largest of the country's three atolls consists of 200 islets encircling three turquoise lagoons. The Turneffe Islands are equally interesting for divers and fishermen. Its limpid waters are simply crowded out with mackerel, tuna, ray, shark and dolphin, as well as lobster and conch.

### Lighthouse Reef★★★

*80km south-east of Ambergris Caye (3hr journey). Full day excursion minimum.* In the centre of the atoll, the **Blue Hole**★★★ is one of the most amazing sights in all Belize, made famous by Jacques Cousteau's expedition here in the 1970s. This ancient cavern, which filled up with water after its roof caved in when the sea level rose during the Ice Age, forms a vast cobalt-blue circle edged with turquoise, more than 400m across and 145m deep. Diving into the dizzying depths of this "gothic cathedral" is an incomparable thrill.

At the south-east end of the atoll, **Half Moon Caye Natural Monument**★★★ is easy to spot because of the **lighthouse** that gave the reef its name. This nature reserve with its idyllic beaches and exceptional sea bed flora and fauna is home to almost a hundred different bird species, including colonies of **red-footed boobies** and **magnificent frigate birds**. Turtles also come in droves to lay their eggs on the islet's beaches.

### Glover's Reef★★

*50km east of Dangriga. To get there see p 343 "Making the best of Dangriga".* This atoll is an excellent place for observing underwater flora and fauna, using either snorkel or scuba. Because Glover's Reef is further from the northern cays, the diving shops on Caye Caulker and Ambergris Caye do not programme this excursion so often.

The Northern Cays

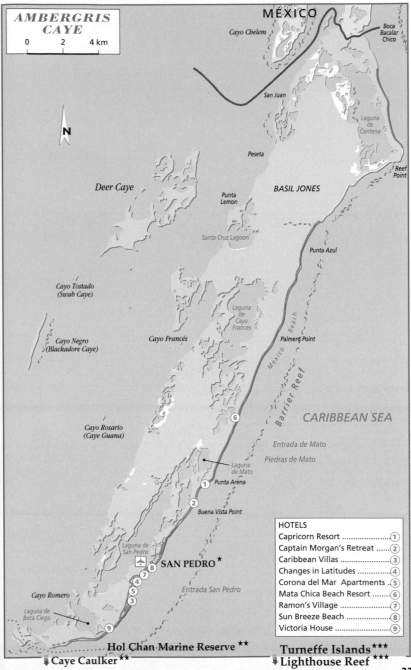

## AMBERGRIS CAYE

0     2     4 km

MÉXICO

Cayo Chelem

Boca Bacalar Chico

San Juan

Laguna de Cantena

Peseta

Deer Caye

BASIL JONES

Punta Lemon

Reef Point

Santa Cruz Lagoon

Punta Azul

Cayo Tostado (Swab Caye)

Laguna de Cayo Francés

Cayo Negro (Blackadore Caye)

Cayo Francés

Palmero Point

México Beach

Barrier Reef

CARIBBEAN SEA

Cayo Rosario (Caye Guana)

Entrada de Mato
Piedras de Mato

⑥

Laguna de Mato

① Punta Arena

② Buena Vista Point

Laguna de San Pedro

SAN PEDRO ★

⑦ ⑧

Entrada San Pedro

④
⑤
③

Cayo Romero

Laguna de Boca Ciega

⑨

HOTELS

| | |
|---|---|
| Capricorn Resort | ① |
| Captain Morgan's Retreat | ② |
| Caribbean Villas | ③ |
| Changes in Latitudes | ④ |
| Corona del Mar Apartments | ⑤ |
| Mata Chica Beach Resort | ⑥ |
| Ramon's Village | ⑦ |
| Sun Breeze Beach | ⑧ |
| Victoria House | ⑨ |

Hol Chan Marine Reserve ★★

Turneffe Islands ★★★

Caye Caulker ★★

Lighthouse Reef ★★★

# Making the most of Caye Caulker

## COMING AND GOING

**By plane** – The airstrip is at the southern end of the village. Planes on the Belize City-San Pedro route (see the practical sections of these towns) stop over on Caye Caulker. *Maya Island Air*, ☎ (022)2012 and *Tropic Air*, ☎ (022)2040.

**By boat** – Several boat companies run between Caye Caulker and Belize City (45min) and San Pedro (30min). Timetables are posted in front of the office of *Caye Caulker Water Taxi Association*, Front St, near Main Front Pier, ☎ (022)2992. *Triple J* and *Andrea* boats leave from Back Pier, on the west side following on from the main jetty.

## GETTING AROUND

Caye Caulker is a pedestrian's paradise. Vehicles of any kind are superfluous except between the village centre and the airstrip.

**By taxi** – *Island Rentals* runs a taxi service, ☎ (022)2229.

**Golf cart rentals** – *Island Rentals* hires out electric golf carts by the hour or the day.

## ADDRESS BOOK

**Tourist information** – As there is no tourist office, ask Caye Caulker inhabitants and in the tourist places.

**Bank / Currency Exchange** – *Atlantic Bank*, Back St, 8am-2pm; Saturdays 9am-12noon; closed Sundays.

**Post office / Telephone** – The post office is on South Back St. *BTL* telephone company, Front St, near the jetty, 8am-12noon / 1pm-4pm; closed Saturday afternoons and Sundays. Internet and e-mail services at *Island Girl Productions*, in a wooden cabana north of Front St, 10am-2pm / 6pm-9pm; closed Sundays.

**Medical Service** – *Caye Caulker Health Centre*, South Front St, ☎ (022)2166. Nearby is a chemist open until 10pm.

**Laundry** – *The Laundromat*, in the street leading to the jetty, almost on the corner of Front St, 7am-9pm.

## WHERE TO STAY

*Under US$30*

**Daisy's Hotel**, Front St, ☎ (022)2150 – 13rm ⌘ A small, modest hotel in the centre; the prices are more attractive than the rooms themselves.

**Johnny's Rooms**, Front St, ☎ (022)2149 – 7rm ⌘ Just a step from the main jetty; an unpretentious but quite well-kept place with 3 cabanas with private bathrooms (now a little tired) and 4 very simple rooms.

**Miramar Hotel**, Front St, ☎ (022)2157 – 19rm ⌘ cc This wooden house with its old-fashioned charm provides the absolute minimum at a low price. The rooms with shared showers are among the cheapest on Caye Caulker.

**Trends Hotel**, Front St, ☎ (022)2094 / 2307, Fax (022)2138, trendsbze@aol.com – 8rm ⌘ ⌘ cc This hotel in the centre of the village is run by a pleasant, energetic owner. The parquet-floored rooms are very pleasant, with large bathrooms. Ask for a room at one end of the building so as to look out on two sides and have better air circulation. This hotel is excellent value for money.

**Tropical Star Hotel**, Front St, ☎ (022)2347/75, Fax (022)2376 – 24rm ⌘ ⌘ cc A big wooden house north of the village, near the Split. Unexciting accommodation but moderately priced, especially for air-conditioned rooms.

**Island Sun Guest House**, PO Box 38, Front St, ☎ (022)2215, islandsun@btl.net – 2rm ⌘ ✗ cc This big house at the north end of the village has 2 simple, quiet rooms on the ground floor. The 1st floor terrace is great for relaxing over breakfast.

**Jimenez's Cabañas**, ☎ (022)2175 – 6rm ⌘ ⌘ Set back at the west end of the street that starts from the cemetery.

G. Simeone/DIAF

The Blue Hole, an inkspot in the turquoise

The 6 wooden bungalows scattered around a disorganised garden give this place a rustic feel that contrasts with the rest of Caye Caulker's hotels. Pleasant, well-kept rooms at a reasonable price.

*US$30-60*

**Tree Tops Hotel**, PO Box 29, ☎ (022)2008, Fax (022)2115, treetops@btl.net – 5rm ⛴ TV ✿ CC This pretty Caribbean-style house looks out over a peaceful garden on the seafront – access via the beach or Front St south of the cemetery. The spacious, comfortable rooms are impeccably clean and well-decorated. Most have private bathrooms and every one has a fridge. A warm family atmosphere.

**Tropical Paradise Resort**, Front St, PO Box 1573, ☎ (022)2124, Fax (022)2225 – 26rm ⛴ ⛴ ✖ ✿ CC At the south end of the main street, this hotel complex offers a varied range of rooms and bungalows at different prices. A pleasant place but without the charm of the family guesthouses.

**Rainbow Hotel**, Front St, ☎ (022) 2123, Fax (022)2172 – 17rm ⛴ ⛴ ✖ CC This long blue and green building has two categories of rooms. Those on the upper floor have television and are relatively cheerful despite a lack of natural light. The ground floor, on the other hand, is of little interest at the price charged.

**Vega Inn and Gardens**, PO Box 701, Front St, ☎ (022)2142, Fax (022)2269, lifestyles@VEGA.com.bz – 10rm ⛴ CC This wooden house with its yesteryear charm opens onto a lovely garden facing the sea in which you can camp. The rooms, with or without bathrooms, are impeccable but the prices are too high.

## EATING OUT

*Under US$10*

**The Bakery**, Back St, 7.30am-12noon / 2pm-7pm; closed Sundays. Fresh bread and delicious pastries on sale in this baker's.

**Cindy's Café**, Front St ⛴ 7am-11.30am. This little house on stilts on the village's main street is one of the most charming places on Caye Caulker. Every morning the owner prepares

excellent breakfasts served on the terrace or in her minuscule breakfast-room-cum-library. Fresh produce and very good espresso coffee.

**Glenda's**, 7am-10am / 12noon-3pm; closed weekends. Go to the end of the street perpendicular to Front St (level with Trends Hotel). The 3 dining rooms in this wooden house are packed out as soon as it opens. The cinnamon rolls and fresh pressed orange juice are famous throughout the village. No smoking.

**Happy Lobster**, Front St, south of the football field ⛴ 7am-10pm. Informal decor and relaxed atmosphere. A menu of fish and seafood specialities and pasta dishes. The cuisine is acceptable, the cost reasonable and the service amiable. To be avoided in bad weather as the terrace dining room is open to the elements.

*US$10-20*

**Sand Box Restaurant**, Front St, ☎ (022)2200 ⛴ CC 7am-10pm (the bar closes later). Caye Caulker's fashionable eatery, opposite the main jetty. The regulars – and they are numerous in this sandy-floored restaurant – have their names carved on the backs of their chairs. The dining room is welcoming and carefully decorated, the recipes inventive and beautifully presented. Efficient service and a lively atmosphere all day long.

**Popeye's**, Front St, ☎ (022)2032 ⛴ 6am-10pm. On the seafront south of the main jetty; a plethora of birds have taken up residence in the mangrove swamp in front of the terrace. Original decor with all sorts of objects imprisoned in fishing nets. This restaurant serves good pizzas in a very Americanised atmosphere. A pleasant place for a drink during the day.

## GOING OUT, HAVING A DRINK

**Bars** – The **Sand Box** (see "Eating out") is lively from morning to night.

**I & I Reggae Bar**, at the south end of Front St, turn right and continue another 50m. Reggae beat throbs out from the 1st floor bar of this little house from 6pm on.

## OTHER THINGS TO DO

**Excursions** – The sea around Caye Caulker is absolutely full of underwater flora and fauna. There are many agencies running very similar outings but the quality varies widely. It is a good idea to quiz other tourists. *Chocolate*, ☏ (022)2151 is unanimously recommended by Caye Caulker inhabitants for its excursion to the manatee reserve. Ras Creek (see below) sometimes takes groups out to observe the crocodiles at night.

**Diving** – For an unforgettable day snorkelling among the sharks and rays go to *Ras Creek*. The meeting-place is the Sand Box every morning around 11am. The *Big Fish Little Fish* agency, ☏ (022)2250, runs night-time snorkelling expeditions.

Of the various scuba diving clubs, *Anwar Tours*, ☏ (022)2327 has a good, reliable reputation. Excursions as far as the Hol Chan Marine Reserve (south of Ambergris Caye) and the Turneffe Islands.

**Cinema** – Films screened every Tuesday and Friday at 8pm at *Mike's Movie House*, the green house opposite the Health Centre.

# Making the most of San Pedro

## COMING AND GOING

**By air** – The airstrip is on Coconut Drive south of San Pedro, a 10min walk from the centre. *Tropic Air*, ☏ (026)2012, and *Maya Island Air*, ☏ (026)2435 / 2945 fly to Belize City (20min) every hour with a stopover at Caye Caulker, plus 3 flights a day to and from Corozal (20min). Taxis await passengers arriving on every flight and some hotels run shuttle services for their guests.

**By boat** – Various boat companies run services between San Pedro and Belize City (90min) with a stop at Caye Caulker. The *Caye Caulker Water Taxi Association* boats leave from Municipal Dock near Town Park. *Triple J* and *Andrea* boats tie up at the jetty at the end of Caribeña St.

## GETTING AROUND

A vehicle is not essential unless you stay in one of the hotels in the south of the peninsula. Barrier Reef Drive, San Pedro's main street, is closed to traffic 6pm-6am on Fridays, Saturdays and Sundays.

**By taxi** – Taxis are always to be found on San Pedro's streets, you just have to spot the green registration plates. Fixed price of BZ$5 for a fare in town.

**By water taxi** – The places in the north of the peninsula can only be reached by boat. *Wendy's*, tied up near Rock's Inn in the north of San Pedro (at the end of Sand Piper St), runs this service.

**By rental golf cart** – *Island Auto*, Coconut Drive, near the airstrip, ☏ (026)2790. *Polo's Ezgo Golf Cart Rental*, north end of Barrier Reef Drive, ☏ (026)3542. Around BZ$20 an hour.

**By rental bike** – Most hotels outside of the centre have bicycles to lend to their guests.

## ADDRESS BOOK

**Tourist information** – The *Tourist Information* kiosk is in the middle of Barrier Reef Drive, opposite Fido's Courtyard. The building also houses a little museum that explains the history of Ambergris Caye. 10am-12noon / 2pm-8pm; Sundays 1pm-6pm.

**Bank / Currency Exchange** – *Atlantic Bank*, Barrier Reef Drive, opposite the Alijua building, 8am-2pm; Saturdays 8.30am-12noon; closed Sundays. *Belize Bank*, 49 Barrier Reef Drive, 8am-1pm (Fridays 4.30pm); closed weekends. Most bars, restaurants and hotels change American dollars (cash and traveller's cheques).

Making the most of San Pedro

**Post office / Telephone** – The post office is on Buccaneer St, behind the Alijua building. 8am-12noon / 1pm-5pm (Fridays 4.30pm); closed weekends. **DHL** in premises on the ground floor of the Spindrift Hotel, ☎ (026)3140. The **BTL** telephone company is in the northern part of Pescador Drive. Internet and e-mail services at **Gecko Graphics**, Barrier Reef Drive, near San Carlos Pharmacy. **Belize Business Development**, Bucaneer St, on the right of the post office, charges the same BZ$20 tariff for 10min use.

**Medical Service** – **R&L Pharmacy**, Coconut Drive, near the airstrip. Daily to 10pm. **Lopez Pharmacy**, Barrier Reef Drive, behind the tourist office. Daily to 9pm. **San Carlos Medical Clinic & Laboratory**, ☎ (026)2918, 24hr emergencies ☎ 14-9251, in north Pescador Drive. Chemist open to 9pm (Sundays 7pm) and Dr Solórzano's surgery. **Ambergris Caye's Hyperbaric Chamber**, near the airstrip, opposite the Maya Island Air offices. Decompression chamber and treatment for problems arising from scuba diving.

**Airline companies** – You can book airline tickets in the major hotels or at the airline companies' offices at the airstrip (see "Coming and going").

**Laundry** – Many laundrettes in the centre. **Nellie's Laundromat**, in the southern part of of Pescador Drive. 7am-8pm; Sundays 8am-2pm.

## WHERE TO STAY

San Pedro has considerable tourist amenities. The lower-range hotels are in the town centre, American-style resort hotels line the south of the peninsula and a few luxury hotels are to be found in the wild, isolated area north of the San Pedro river. Prices given are for the high season (beginning November to end May), around 30-50% higher than the rest of the year.

### • Town centre
US$25-50

**Ruby's Hotel**, south end of Barrier Reef Drive, ☎ (026)2063, rubys@btl.net – 26rm ⤢ Right in the town centre, this modest but clean hotel is aimed at budget travellers. Its basic rooms, with or without bathrooms, are some of the cheapest on Ambergris Caye.

**Hotel San Pedrano**, north end of Barrier Reef Drive, on the corner of Caribeña St, ☎ (026)2054, Fax (026)2093 – 6rm ⌂ ⤢ ◐ cc The rooms on the 1st floor open onto a pleasant veranda above the main street. Comfortable rooms, impeccably clean. The best hotel in its class.

**Tomás Hotel**, north end of Barrier Reef Drive, ☎ (026)2061 – 7rm ⌂ ⤢ Small, very clean hotel on the seafront. Still reasonably priced for San Pedro.

Around US$70$

**Lily's Hotel**, PO Box 48, north end of Barrier Reef Drive, ☎ (026)2059, lilies@btl.net – 12rm ⌂ ⤢ ✕ ◐ cc A family atmosphere in this well-kept hotel. The best rooms open onto a veranda with a view of the ocean. Some are air-conditioned.

**The Barrier Reef Hotel**, PO Box 34, Barrier Reef Drive, ☎ (026)2075, Fax (02)2719, barriereef@btl.net – 12rm ⌂ ⤢ ▤ ✕ ⚊ ◐ cc It is easy to spot this lovely Victorian house overlooking the main street. Its big rooms are to be renovated soon. Good value for money right now but prices may well go up.

Around US$100

**San Pedro Holiday Hotel**, PO Box 61, Barrier Reef Drive, ☎ (026)2014, Fax (026)2295, holiday@btl.net – 17rm ⌂ ⤢ ▤ ✕ ◐ cc Right in the middle of town, facing the sea. A pretty Victorian-style house with every comfort but it is a pity the rooms are so impersonal!

### • South of San Pedro
Around US$75

☺ **Changes in Latitudes Bed & Breakfast**, Coconut Drive, ☎ (026)2986, latitudes@btl.net – 6rm ⌂ ⤢ ▤ ◐ cc Just behind the Belize Yacht Club, this bed and breakfast run by a Canadian woman is one of the most welcoming places in San Pedro. The day starts with an excellent breakfast served in a pleasant communal room where you can cook or simply relax. The rooms, although small, are extremely comfortable and prettily decorated. As soon as you arrive the owner goes out of her way to give you a whole lot of useful information for your stay on Ambergris Caye. It is advisable to telephone to let her know you are coming.

### US$120-140

**Corona del Mar Apartments / Hotel**, Coconut Drive, ☎ (026)2055, Fax (026)2461, corona@btl.net – 4rm ⌂ ⤬ ▤ ♪ TV ♨ ♪ CC 1km from the town centre; apartments with bedroom, living-room and fully-equipped kitchen. Stands out from the similar places that are gradually taking over the south of the peninsula because of its small size and family atmosphere. Breakfast included.

**Sun Breeze Beach Hotel**, PO Box 14, south end of Barrier Reef Drive, ☎ (026)2191, Fax (026)2346, sun-breeze@btl.net – 39rm ⌂ ⤬ ▤ ♪ TV ⤬ ⤢ ♨ ♪ CC A few minutes' walk from the town centre; a modern hotel complex in colonial style facing the sea. In its deluxe category (more spacious and more expensive than the standard category), rooms 116 and 225 have the best views. Avoid the economy category, which means dark little rooms at the end of a corridor.

### US$140-200

**Ramon's Village**, PO Box 51, Coconut Drive, ☎ (026)2071, Fax (026)2214, ramons@btl.net – 60rm ⌂ ⤬ ⤬ ⤢ ♨ ♪ CC Nestling in a forest of coconut palms, this village of palm-roofed bungalows combines chic with rustic charm. The big, impeccable rooms give onto either the garden or the sea. This place has the best-kept bit of beach in San Pedro.

**Caribbean Villas Hotel**, Coconut Drive, PO Box 71, ☎ (026)2715, Fax (026)2885, c-v-hotel@btl.net – 10rm ⌂ ⤬ ▤ ♨ ♪ CC This hotel 1.5km from the town centre stands in an attractive setting on the seafront. Its owners have limited the number of rooms so as to preserve a patch of tropical forest that shelters a multitude of birds; and there is a belvedere to watch them from. A very warm welcome with a guided tour of San Pedro when you

arrive. The rooms or apartments with fully-equipped kitchens naturally have every comfort.

**Victoria House**, PO Box 22, Coconut Drive, ☎ (026)2067, Fax (026)3280, victoria@bze.com – 31rm ⌂ ⤬ ⤬ ⤢ ♨ ♪ CC The Victorian style of the main building confers a certain cachet on this luxury hotel 3km south of San Pedro. In addition it has individual palm-roofed bungalows, two small buildings framed by palm trees, a suite (for honeymooners) on a very lovely beach and two villas facing the sea. Some rooms are air-conditioned.

### • North of San Pedro

Access by boat to the hotels north of the San Pedro river is usually provided by the places themselves. It is also possible to reach them by water taxi.

### US$100-130

**Capricorn Resort**, PO Box 65, ☎ (026)2809, Fax (02)12091, capricorn@btl.net – 4rm ⌂ ⤬ ⤬ ⤢ ♨ ♪ CC 4km north of San Pedro, this small hotel nestling in a garden facing the sea is reputed for its restaurant. The quality of the accommodation matches its renowned cuisine. The air-conditioned suite and 3 delightful bungalows have every possible comfort. Intimate atmosphere and very warm reception.

### US$160-280

**Captain Morgan's Retreat**, PO Box, ☎ (026)2567 – 18rm ⌂ ⤬ ⤬ ⤢ ♨ ♪ CC The ideal place to retire to a rustic palm-roofed bungalow, relax on a veranda facing the sea or stroll along the beach to San Pedro, just 3km away. The rooms are pleasant and enjoy a delicious sea breeze in the evenings. A new building will soon be increasing the hotel's capacity.

**Mata Chica Beach Resort**, 5 Miles North, ☎ 21-3010, Fax (02)13012, matachica@btl.net – 11rm ⌂ ⤬ ▤ ⤬ ♨ ♪ CC A corner of paradise on an isolated beach 8km north of San Pedro. The individual bungalows painted in warm colours have sophisticatedly luxurious rooms. A different decor for each, original wall frescoes and particularly attractive bathrooms. The owners (a French-Italian couple) offer their guests the

**Making the most of San Pedro**

perfect, individualised welcome. Excellent restaurant serving Mediterranean specialities (home-made pasta).

### EATING OUT

Some hotels (Holiday Hotel, Ramon's Village etc) organise barbecue evenings once a week.

*Under US$20*

**Reef Restaurant**, Pescador Drive, ☎ (026)3213. 11am-2pm / 5.30pm-9.30pm. The most popular restaurant in town serves local cuisine and good seafood specialities. A lively atmosphere in this sailors' bar with its sand floor. Good value for money.

**Estel's Dine by the Sea,** Buccaneer St ☂ 6am-8pm; closed Tuesdays. Tables on a terrace facing the sea, shaded by palm-leaf parasols. The menu offers a varied choice of snacks, Mexican specialities and seafood of all sorts. A pleasant place for a nibble, a full meal or simply a drink with your toes in the sand.

*US$20-30*

**Jade Garden Restaurant**, Coconut Drive, ☎ (026)2506. 11am-2pm / 6pm-10pm. This restaurant serving good Cantonese cuisine is near the Changes in Latitudes Bed & Breakfast. Take-away and home delivery service.

**Little Italy**, Barrier Reef Drive, ☎ (026)2866. CC 11am-2pm / 5.30pm-10pm. On the ground floor of the Spindrift Hotel; the veranda is more welcoming than the dining room. Delicious Italian pasta specialities but the pizzas are disappointing.

**Elvi's Kitchen**, Pescador Drive, ☎ (026)2176. CC 11.30am-2pm / 6.30pm-10pm; closed Sundays. A sand floor and a flamboyant tree growing up through the roof create an original setting for one of the best-known restaurants in San Pedro. The lunch-time set menu offers a selection of light dishes including some appetising mixed salads. The evening menu offers mainly fish and various seafood dishes. The service is on a par with the cuisine. Live music Thursday and Saturday evenings.

**El Patio**, Coconut Drive, ☎ (026)3063. CC 11am-2.30pm / 5.30pm-9.30pm; closed Tuesday lunch-times. This restaurant 800m south of the airstrip offers a total change of scenery with its Spanish-style patio a-tinkle with fountains (the dining room is astonishingly ordinary). Good seafood specialities and a mariachi band in the evenings.

**Mambo Cuisine**, the restaurant of the Mata Chica Beach Resort, and **Capricorn Resort** are two renowned restaurants. Both serve refined cuisine in a superb setting (see "Where to stay").

### GOING OUT, HAVING A DRINK

The "in" places for going out change constantly; talk to the locals and other tourists to find out the best places and the best times to go to them.

**Bars –** Among the most popular hotel bars is the **Pier Lounge**, on the ground floor of the Spindrift Hotel. A very lively pub in the evenings, particularly Wednesdays from 6pm when betting opens on the famous Chicken Drop held on the beach.

**Bananas Bar**, Pescador Drive. This bar perched on a terrace is the ideal place for admiring the sunset at cocktail time.

**Fido's Courtyard**, Barrier Reef Drive. Under an immense straw roof facing the sea; a very popular bar and restaurant at weekends.

**Concerts –** Not an evening goes by without a group playing in some hotel, restaurant or bar. The programme can be obtained from any of San Pedro's tourist places.

**Discos – Big Daddy's Disco**, Barrier Reef Drive, on the seafront. A disco and bar where the atmosphere is hot every night of the week. **Tarzan's Night Club**, Barrier Reef Drive, opposite Town Park.

### OTHER THINGS TO DO

Diving clubs and travel agencies are legion on Ambergris Caye. Here are just a few addresses as an example.

**Excursions –** The travel agencies on Barrier Reef Drive and the hotels run excursions of a day or more throughout Belize and even to Tikal in Guatemala.

**Share di Bread**, ☎ (026)2986 provides a team of qualified guides for both cultural visits and jungle expeditions.

**Cruises – Hustler Tours**, ☎ (026) 2538, runs catamaran trips off Ambergris Caye. **Island Guides**, ☎ (026)3474 runs an original excursion on board an old all-timber yacht. Several agencies also organise day trips in glass-bottomed boats to admire the marine flora and fauna.

**Diving** – San Pedro is just a few miles from one of the biggest coral reefs in the world – a good reason for taking diving lessons. Among the many diving clubs on Ambergris Caye, **Reef Divers** ☎ (026)3134 has a good, reliable reputation. Sea trips of one to several days are organised by **Coral Beach Dive Club**, ☎ (026)2013, or **Amigos del Mar**, ☎ (026)2706, to the Blue Hole, Lighthouse Reef or the Turneffe Islands. Snorkelling fans can discover the sea floor in Hol Chan Marine Reserve and swim with rays and sharks in Shark-Ray Alley. Ask for the excellent guide, Alfonso Graniel, ☎ (026)2584.

**Fishing – Sea Boots Sports Fishing**, ☎ (026)2911, is the specialist in deep-sea fishing. For fishing along the coral reef contact **Pedro Graniel**, ☎ (026) 2584.

## SHOPPING GUIDE

**Arts and Crafts –** Shop after shop of unexciting handicrafts line Barrier Reef Drive. Only **Belizean Arts**, in Fido's Courtyard, stands out from the others through the originality and quality of its items. At the end of the day small craftsmen lay out their wood carvings on the pavements of Barrier Reef Drive.

**Supermarkets –** If spending a day out at sea, buy provisions from **Rocks Store** in the southern part of Pescador Drive or **San Pedro Supermarket**, at the north end of Pescador Drive.

**Making the most of San Pedro**

# DANGRIGA

Capital of Stann Creek District – Pop approx 10 000
170km from Belize City and 90km from Belmopan

**Not to be missed**
The peace and quiet of Tobacco Caye.
**And remember...**
Book hotel rooms well in advance for Garifuna Settlement Day and Christmas.
Take waterproofs and protect belongings
on the rough crossing between Dangriga and Tobacco Caye.

In the early 1980s Stann Creek, capital of Garifuna culture and the main town in southern Belize, abandoned its English name in favour of Dangriga, meaning "stagnant waters" in the Garifuna language. An excellent base for excursions along the barrier reef or to the Jaguar Sanctuary (*see p 346 "Placencia"*), Dangriga is also famous for its **19 November** celebrations commemorating the Garifunas' arrival in Belize, as well as its **December** festivities, when throughout the month the town vibrates to the beat of drums and the rhythm of the *wanaragua*, a traditional masked and costumed dance (*see p 299*).

**Garifuna Settlement Day**
It is Dangriga that celebrates this national holiday with the greatest enthusiasm, with music and dancing taking over the whole town for three days. On 19 November a procession of canoes sails from Pelican Beach to the river in a reconstitution of the Garifunas' landing from Honduras in 1832.

## A walk around town
*Allow 2hr.*

The main administrative buildings along with the banks, restaurants and shop stalls line the main street, named **Commerce Street** north of the river and **St Vincent Street** south of it. Linking its two halves is the bridge that spans North Stann Creek and serves as a meeting-place in the absence of a main square. People sit on its parapet watching the comings and goings of strollers and boats alike.

Once out of the centre, Dangriga starts to look like a port village; under its wooden houses on stilts neighbours play interminable games of cards and old radios set on windowsills give out reggae or punta. At nightfall a few crabs cross the roads, brandishing their claws at passers-by and bicycles.

Two kilometres north of the town centre, Pelican Beach Resort occupies Dangriga's only **beach**, but you have to go a further 89km south to the seaside resort of Placencia before you can enjoy long stretches of sand (*see p 246 "Placencia"*).

## Off the Dangriga coast

Basking in the Caribbean Sea off Dangriga are Glover's Reef, one of Belize's three atolls (*see p 330 "The Northern Cays"*), and several idyllic islets. Tobacco Caye, the most easily accessible of these, offers a choice of accommodation facilities.

J.-P. Courau/EXPLORER

Dangriga, the Garifuna capital

## Tobacco Caye★

*20km from Dangriga. For access and accommodation see "Making the most of Tobacco Caye".* This cay is so small that you are rarely more than 100m from the sea. Out of season just half a dozen families share the 2ha islet. Tourists lucky enough to visit at that period can appreciate a delicious feeling of solitude, despite the increasing number of cabanas that are springing up in the coconut forest; the temptation is great to put off your departure date indefinitely in order to savour further moments of happiness lazing, siesta-ing, reading, swimming, snorkelling and diving.

## Making the most of Dangriga

### COMING AND GOING

**By plane** – The airstrip is at the north end of town, 2km from the centre. **Maya Island Air**, ☎ (05)22659 and **Tropic Air** ☎ (05)22129 each make 4 return trips a day between Dangriga and Belize City (30min), Placencia (15min) and Punta Gorda (15min).

**By bus** – 2 morning buses to Belize City (3hr) from **Ritchie's Bus Service** terminus, 58 St Vincent St, ☎ (05)22130. Buses return to Dangriga in the afternoon. One morning and one afternoon bus to Placencia (2hr30min). **Z-Line**, 3 Havana St, ☎ (05)22160, runs buses to Belize City about every hour between 5am and 5pm. During the dry season the coast route is faster (2hr) than the Hummingbird Highway (3hr), which involves a detour via Belmopan. 4 buses a day between 10am and 7pm run from Dangriga to Punta Gorda (5hr) via Independence.

**By boat** – Motor launches run between Dangriga and Tobacco Caye. Ask for Captain Buck at the **New River Café**

(see "Eating out"). Allow approx BZ$30 per person on a regular service, but if there are no other passengers you are obliged to hire the boat for BZ$150. Take a waterproof for the crossing and protect your belongings.

### GETTING AROUND

**By taxi** – A lot of taxis around town. *South Pride Taxi*, ☎ (05)22664. *Tino & Marie's Taxi Services*, ☎ (05)22438.

### ADDRESS BOOK

**Tourist information** – There is no tourist office in Dangriga but the owner of the Bluefield Lodge has a good stock of printed matter on the area and on the rest of Belize (see "Where to stay").

**Bank / Currency Exchange** – *Barclay's Bank*, Commerce St, next to the court house. 8am-2.30pm (Fridays 4.30pm); closed weekends. *Bank of Nova Scotia*, 10 St Vincent St, and *Belize Bank*, 24 St Vincent St, have the same opening hours: 8am-1pm (Fridays 4.30pm); closed weekends.

**Post office / Telephone** – The post office is on Mahogany Rd, next door to the Bonefish Hotel. The *BTL* telephone company, Commerce St, is opposite the police station.

**Medical service** – *Dangriga Hospital*, Court House Rd, ☎ (05)22078.

**Laundry** – *Val's Laundry*, 1 Sharp St, opposite the post office.

### WHERE TO STAY

● **Dangriga**
*Under US$20*
🦞 **Bluefield Lodge**, 6 Bluefield Rd, south of North Stann Creek, ☎ (05)22742 – 6rm ⌇ Without a doubt the best value for money in Dangriga. At the end of the street stands a plush building with a terrace on the town side. It has 2 small rooms which share a remarkably clean bathroom and 4 others with private showers and TV. Louise Belisle, the owner of this family guesthouse, devotes all her time and energy to her guests' well-being and safety.

*US$20-40*
**Pal's Guest House**, 868 A Magoon St, ☎ (05)22095 / 22365, Fax (05)22095, palbze@btl.net – 19rm ⌇ cc In the south of the town, near the Z-Line terminus; this guesthouse stands at the mouth of Havana Creek and every evening around 6pm a crocodile takes its ease on the bank opposite reception! The accommodation is in 2 buildings: the old wing houses some not very attractive rooms without private bathrooms; the newer building provides more comfort (private showers, TV and balcony overlooking the sea) at a higher price.

**Riverside Hotel**, 5 Commerce St, ☎ (05)22168 – 16rm. Choose a room on the river side staircase. The building does not lack charm, with its upstairs patio and slightly kitsch communal lounge furnished in red velvet, but the rooms are ordinary and lack ventilation.

*US$60-100*
**The Bonefish Hotel**, PO Box 21, 15 Mahogany St, ☎ (05)22165, Fax (05)22296 – 10rm ⌇ ⌇ cc This hotel is trying to be the best in town. The least expensive rooms are unfortunately on the dark ground floor. For more space and light plus air conditioning you have to pay double the price of the standard category. Despite the comfort of the place, it is poor value for money.

**Pelican Beach Resort**, PO Box 14, Scotchman Town, ☎ (05)22044, Fax (05)22570, pelicanbeach@alt.net – 20rm ⌇ ⌇ ✗ ⌇ ⌇ cc Dangriga's most chic hotel, near the airstrip, has the only beach in town. The seafront wing built in Caribbean style has attractive, spacious rooms and a lovely view. The building at the back is not as pleasant but has cheaper rooms on the garden side. A convivial atmosphere and welcoming staff.

### EATING OUT, HAVING A DRINK

● **Dangriga**
*Under US$20*
**The Exquisite Kitchen**, 12 Ramos Rd, 100m north of North Stann Creek bridge, ☎ (05)23415. 10am-10pm; closed Sundays. In a plain room lit by

green neon, this neighbourhood restaurant serves simple local cuisine at reasonable prices. A choice of ice-creams for dessert.

**The New River Café**, Riverside Drive, opposite North Stann Creek. 7am-10pm. The bar is open on Sundays but not the restaurant. This sailors' bistro gives a glimpse of local Dangriga life, although things get a bit heated as the evening wears on. Good fish specialities at moderate prices.

**Silver Garden Restaurant**, 101 Commerce St, ☎ (05)22413. 8.30am-2.30pm / 5.30pm-10pm. The menu seems endless: apart from a few traditional Belizean dishes, it offers dozens of Asian specialities. Servings are generous and the service efficient. A place to remember, particularly on Sundays when most restaurants are closed.

**OTHER THINGS TO DO**

**Excursions** – Dangriga is an excellent departure point for the islets off the coast, such as Tobacco Caye. **Pelican Beach Resort** organises stays in its South Water Caye hotel. **International Zoological Expeditions**, 35 Lemon St, ☎ (05)22119, runs excursions to Glover's Reef.

**Outdoor pursuits** – The hotels on the cays organise outings to the coral reef for scuba diving and snorkelling fans.

# Making the most of Tobacco Caye

**WHERE TO STAY, EATING OUT**
It is advisable to opt for full board as the island has no restaurants. Prices given are for accommodation and meals for 2 people in a double room. Prices drop 20-30% in low season (end May to beginning November).

*US$50-80*
**Lana's Hotel on the Reef**, ☎ (05)22571/2 – 3rm 丞 ✗ 沼 ◑ The charming couple who run it go to a lot of trouble to create a relaxed, family atmosphere. Meals are taken in a dining room where lace mats, family photos and ornaments put the finishing touches to this guesthouse's yesteryear charm. The rooms are extremely simple and clean.
**Gaviota Coral Reef Resort**, ☎ (05)12032 – 12rm ✗ 沼 ◑ A simple place where the 1st-floor rooms are the largest and best ventilated. Individual bungalows 11 and 12, on stilts and with a sublime view over the sea, are the best choice; they have no fans (unlike the other rooms) but enjoy a delicious sea breeze.
**Island Camps Caye Resort**, ☎ (02)72109, Fax (05)12033 – 9rm ✗ 沼 ◑ Of the 9 rustic cabanas laid out in an arc, only 1 room has a private bathroom.
**Reef's End Lodge**, ☎ (05)22419, Fax (05)22828 – 6rm 🗪 丞 ✗ 沼 ◑ A wooden house with 4 rooms plus 2 bungalows, all well kept and with a family atmosphere. The dining room is at the end of the jetty in a delightful cabana giving directly onto the coral reef.

*US$80-100*
**Ocean Edge Lodge**, ☎ (05)12004, Fax (05)22746 – 5rm 🗪 ✗ 沼 ◑ 5 raised cabanas linked by footbridges. This hotel has made a real effort with the decoration of its rooms, which are the most comfortable and attractive on Tobacco Caye (the only place on the island with hot water).

# PLACENCIA★
Stann Creek District
89km from Dangriga by the Southern Highway

**Not to be missed**
The beach in front of Kitty's Place hotel.
The jaguar sanctuary.
**And remember...**
In the low season you will have the beach to yourself.
Book hotel rooms in advance for Christmas and Easter.
Most restaurants are closed between 2pm and 7pm,
so take a picnic if intending to stay late on the beach.

The Placencia peninsula, squeezed between the Caribbean Sea and a lagoon sheltering multitudes of birds, was a pirate hide-out from the 17C, as witness the shipwrecks discovered out to sea. In a country that has few fine beaches except on the cays, this 20km tongue of land is the exception. Along this sand-edged littoral the palm trees are rarely more than a hammock's length apart.

## The Placencia peninsula★
*The best means of transport is golf carts.*
*There is a very pleasant beach walk between Seine Bight Village and Placencia.*

A surfaced road goes right down the peninsula from Riverside, 13km from the Southern Highway, to Placencia village sitting in splendid isolation at the southern end. The very infrequent bus service has preserved the charm of this little seaside resort; the luxury hotels lining the littoral also seem to watch jealously over the peace and quiet of the place.

### Seine Bight Village
Thirteen kilometres south of Riverside is Seine Bight Village, one of Belize's four Garifuna villages – the other three being Barranco, Hopkins and Georgetown (*see p 296 "The Belizean mosaic"*). The place derives its name from French fishermen who emigrated from Canada in the mid-18C; a century later the Garifunas settled here and have maintained their own culture every since. Traditional music and dances are sometimes performed in the village bars.

### Placencia★
Eight kilometres south of Seine Bight Village, at the tip of the peninsula, is Placencia, made up of just a few wooden houses scattered around a **beach★** with palm trees. This Creole village has the nonchalant look so characteristic of the Caribbean. Despite constantly developing tourist amenities the place has managed to preserve its warm, simple atmosphere - amply demonstrated by a visit to the post office shack!
From north to south of Placencia runs a **sidewalk** 1m wide and 1km long that ends up disappearing into the sand. On either side of this "street", supposed to be the narrowest in the world, the inhabitants perched on the steps of their cabanas on stilts chat peacefully to their neighbours, without forgetting to greet passers-by – several times a day!

G. Simeone/DIAF

The beach at Placencia

# Around Placencia
*Excursions run by diving shops and hotels.*

Despite its isolation, the Placencia peninsula occupies an ideal location enabling visitors to explore the surrounding area easily by land, sea or river.

## Off the coast★★
The coral reef sits about 20km off the coast. Although the diving sites can make no claim to rival the atolls (*see p 330 "The Northern Cays"*), they have the advantage of being less popular with tourists. Which means you can enjoy the beach on a paradise island or spend the day among the fish and coral, all in glorious solitude.

## An excursion up the Monkey River★★
*A 30min boat trip from Placencia to the mouth of the river. This excursion may be made by kayak or motor launch. Allow 1 day.*

About 20km south-west of Placencia is the mouth of the Monkey River, named after the howler monkeys living in the jungle around about. The tropical forest covering the banks of the Monkey River hosts a multitude of colourful birds including parrots and toucans, as well as hundreds of lizards and iguanas.

## The Jaguar Sanctuary★ (Cockscomb Basin Wildlife Sanctuary)
*65km from Placencia. Return to the Southern Highway, 39km from Placencia, and turn right. Continue 16km to Maya Centre then take the dirt road on the left. The reserve entrance is 10km further on. Maps are available to the public at reception. 8am-5pm. Fee.*

Be prepared for disappointment if you come to this nature reserve hoping to spot a jaguar, for these night hunters avoid humans. Only their prints along the park's marked trails indicate their passing. But the jaguar sanctuary is well worth visiting for its wealth of fauna and flora. Its 40 000ha of land cover the eastern slopes of the Maya Mountains, overlooked by Victoria Peak, the highest point in the country at 1 120m. This humid tropical jungle shelters almost 300 different species of birds – toucans, macaws, hummingbirds, king vultures –, numerous mammals such as honey bears, agoutis, anteaters, peccaries, **Baird's tapirs** (Belize's national animal, nicknamed the "mountain cow"), as well as reptiles including the fearsome fer-de-lance. Except for the birds, this abundant fauna is difficult to spot in the heart of the dense forest of palm trees, giant ferns, silk cotton trees, mahogany and orchids. Some paths lead to pleasant **waterfalls★**, so it is a good idea to take swimwear.

H. Choimet

The mysterious jaguar

# Making the most of Placencia

## COMING AND GOING

**By plane** – The landing strip is north of Placencia, 2km from the centre of the village. **Maya Island Air**, ☎ (06)23475, and **Tropic Air**, ☎ (06)23410, run several flights a day to/from Punta Gorda (20min), Dangriga (20min) and Belize City (45min). Taxis await passengers off all flights, and hotels in the north of the peninsula run shuttle services for their guests.

**By bus** – The bus stop is at the south end of the main road, opposite the petrol station. Two **Ritchie's** buses leave Placencia early in the morning for Belize City (5hr) and **Z-Line** runs a daily service between Placencia and Dangriga (90min). Travellers wishing to get to Placencia from Punta Gorda (see "Coming and going" section of that town) must get off at the junction on the Southern Highway to catch a bus coming from Dangriga. It is also possible to avoid long hours waiting at this crossroads by getting off at Mango Creek (also called Independence) then crossing the Placencia lagoon by boat.

**By boat** – From Mango Creek bus terminus walk about 500m to the jetty. The water taxi captain tries to make his timetable coincide with the buses. Outside of scheduled crossing times between Placencia and Mango Creek, you can hire a boat for about the same price. NB, it is exceedingly difficult to find a boat after 3pm. The return trip from Placencia leaves from the main jetty in the south of the village. Allow approx BZ$10 per person (20min-1hr journey depending on the type of boat).

## GETTING AROUND

Placencia can be explored on foot along the beach or the sidewalk, a sort of narrow alley parallel to the main road and which goes from north to south of the village. A vehicle may prove useful for those staying in hotels in the north of the peninsula.

**By taxi** – **Brad's Taxi Service**, ☎ (06)23326.

**By rental golf cart** – A practical and amusing means of transport, ideal for getting about the peninsula between Placencia and Seine Bight Village. The **Kul's Karts** rental agency is at the Cozy Corner Hotel.

## ADDRESS BOOK

**Tourist information** – No official tourist office, so ask for information in the village's various tourist places.

**Bank / Currency Exchange** – Placencia's first bank opened in 1998. **Atlantic Bank** is in the south of the village, at the end of the main road opposite the bus stop. At the time of writing it is open Wednesdays to Fridays 9am-2pm.

**Post office / Telephone** – The post office is in a little wooden shack on the main road, at the last crossroads before the southern end of the village. 9am-11am / 3pm-5pm; closed weekends. The **BTL** telephone company is in the central alley, near Cozy Corner Hotel. 8am-12noon / 1pm-4pm; closed weekends.

**Laundry** – There are several laundries on either side of the central alley. **The Laundromat**, in the north of the village, daily 8am-6pm.

## WHERE TO STAY

Prices can double from one time of the year to another. Those given here are for the high season (beginning November to end May).

● **Centre of Placencia**

*Under US$20*

**Conrad & Lydia's Guest House**, ☎ (06)23117, Fax (06)23354 – 8rm 🛏 🌿 ⬗ cc This modest guesthouse at the north end of the main alley has a reputation for excellent breakfasts and a friendly welcome. Both rooms and shared bathrooms are impeccably clean. Very good value for money for both categories of accommodation provided (large and small rooms).

US$25-50

**Cozy Corner Hotel**, ☎ (06)23280 – 5rm 🛏 🏖 🐾 🄰 cc This house is in an ideal location, on the beach in the centre of the village. The building is surrounded by a veranda with hammocks just inviting you to laze around. The wooden walls and furniture brightened up by a white tiled floor really do give its 5 rooms a holiday feel (2 of them have a view of the sea). Its sober, tasteful decoration, extreme cleanliness and reasonable prices make it one of the best addresses in Placencia.

**Sun Rider Guest House**, ☎ (06)23486 – 8rm 🛏 🏖 🐾 cc This wooden house next to the Cozy Corner Hotel must have known better days. The building suffers from lack of maintenance but the somewhat old-fashioned rooms are still acceptable at the price.

US$50-80

**Serenade Guest House**, ☎ (06)23163, Fax (06)23164 – 9rm 🛏 🏖 🐾 🄰 cc This recently opened hotel in the centre of the village occupies a smart house. Simple, careful decor for lovely parquet-floored rooms. An excellent address if the owners maintain the prices they have opened with.

**Cunche's Villa**, ☎ (06)23277, Fax (06)23166, lgodfrey@btl.net – 4rm 🛏 🏖 cc All the rooms in this pretty yellow house on the beach are on the 1st floor facing the sea. They are well maintained and each has two big comfortable beds.

**Westwind Hotel**, ☎ (06)23255 – 12rm 🛏 🏖 🐾 🄰 cc This hotel is in a big Caribbean style villa. 8 spacious, well-ventilated rooms open onto the sea. The four others on the side of the house do not have such a fabulous view but are considerably cheaper. All have fridges. Breakfast served on request.

• **North of Placencia (around the airstrip)**

US$100-150

**Turtle Inn**, ☎ (06)23244, Fax (06) 23245, turtleinn@btl.net – 9rm 🛏 🏖 ✕ 🐾 🄰 cc This quiet, secluded hotel is only 15min on foot from the village. Its 7 palm-thatched cabanas and 2 houses,

set right on the beach, are rustic but comfortable. The owner's personality contributes considerably to the relaxed family atmosphere.

**Kitty's Place**, ☎ (06)23227, Fax (06)23226, kittys@btl.net – 11rm 🛏 🏖 ✕ 🐾 🄰 cc 2.5km from the village on the loveliest part of Placencia's beach. This hotel composed of several buildings in different architectural styles has 3 bungalows facing the sea, plus a superb tropical garden hiding colonial- and Caribbean-style cottages. The rooms and apartments are prettily decorated and have every comfort. Two small rooms with shared showers for budget travellers.

Around US$200

**Rum Point Inn**, ☎ (06)23239, Fax (06)23240 – 22rm 🛏 🏖 ✕ 🛌 🐾 🄰 cc 300m north of the airstrip, the bungalows stand out on account of their unusual architecture in a superb natural setting. These white concrete "mushrooms" with window slits look particularly austere at first glance, but inside they give a surprising feeling of space: the walls seem to dissolve as if by magic, leaving the impression you are sleeping on the beach in the midst of the coconut palms! Luxury rooms with sophisticated decoration and pure, elegant lines. If you prefer more conventional accommodation, a building set back (with no view of the sea) offers immense rooms with air conditioning. The main building houses a restaurant, bar, pleasant terrace facing the sea and a very extensive library.

• **South of Seine Bight Village**

US$130-200

**Luba Hati**, ☎ (06)23402, Fax (06)23403, lubahati@btl.net – 7rm 🛏 🏖 ✕ 🐾 🄰 cc With neither television nor air conditioning, here peace and nature are a real philosophy. The discreetly sophisticated rooms are decorated with items of Garifuna art. They all have private terraces, ideal for relaxing in the shade, fanned by the sea breeze. The belvedere on the roof looks down onto a thick carpet of vegetation that blends into the Caribbean Sea.

**The Inn at Robert's Grove**, ☏ (06) 23565, Fax (06)23567 – 13rm 🗚📺 ✕ ♨ ♫ ♨ This large, colonial-style residence bathes in luxury and elegance. Its vast rooms decorated with furniture from all over the world open onto a veranda facing the sea. Guests are invited to relax in a superb lounge with videos and games at their disposal.

### WHERE TO EAT

*Under US$10*

**Daisy's Ice Cream Parlour**, 8am-9.30pm; closed Tuesdays. Coming from the jetty, the alley to the left just before the Flamboyant leads to a cafetaria with leatherette benches. An unpretentious place to cool down with an ice-cream under the enormous fans. One of the few places in Placencia where you can lunch after 2pm.

**The Galley Restaurant & Bar**, in front of the football pitch ☕ 8am-2.30pm / 5pm-10pm. In a relaxed atmosphere this family restaurant serves good quality local cuisine (fried chicken, chowmein and a few Garifuna dishes). Generous helpings at moderate prices.

**Flamboyant Restaurant**, ☕ 7am-10pm, kitchen closed 2pm-7pm. This pleasant bar and restaurant is on the central alley in the middle of the village. Its terrace, in the shade of a flamboyant tree, is a strategic location for observing the comings and goings of Placencia. The cuisine is not unforgettable but the breakfasts are excellent. A charming place to have a drink at any time of day.

*US$10-20*

**Kitty's Place**, in the hotel of the same name ☕ 🆑 This restaurant is one of the best places in Placencia. The lunch-time menu offers a selection of quality dishes at unbeatable prices. Ideal

for lunch or having a drink on the terrace between swims. Original cuisine and very attentive staff.

**Tentacles Restaurant**, ☏ (06) 23156 ☕ 🆑 10am-2pm / 6pm-10pm; closed Thursdays. When coming from the village and facing the jetty, turn right and walk 500m along the seafront. This pub with its Caribbean architecture has one of the best restaurants in Placencia. The menu serves fresh produce beautifully prepared, including a varied choice of shellfish and fish. The terrace jutting out over the water is a very romantic setting in the evening.

### GOING OUT, HAVING A DRINK

**Bars – The Cozy Corner Beach Bar**, in front of the hotel of the same name, has a lovely wooden terrace on the beach. Enjoy the evening sea breeze under the straw roof of the **Dockside Bar**, at the end of the Tentacles Restaurant pier. Lively atmosphere and clientele of regulars at the **Flamboyant** (see "Eating out").

### OTHER THINGS TO DO

**Excursions** – The excursion programme varies little from one place to another: hiking in Cockscomb Basin Wildlife Sanctuary (the jaguar reserve), visits to Lubaantun and Nim Li Punit archeological sites (near Punta Gorda) or expeditions up the Monkey River by kayak or motor launch.

**Outdoor pursuits** – The hotels and specialist shops propose all sorts of sea outings off the peninsula. A choice of snorkelling, scuba diving or fishing. Ask at **Placencia Dive Shop**, ☏ (06)23313, in front of the jetty. Kitty's Place and Luba Hati organise excursions to French Louie Caye, a private islet.

**Making the most of Placencia**

# PUNTA GORDA

Capital of Toledo District – Pop approx 3 000
160km from Dangriga by the Southern Highway
Hot, humid climate

**Not to be missed**
The luxuriant vegetation of Toledo District.
**And remember...**
Allow time and patience to explore the area
if you do not have your own transport.

Aldous Huxley wrote of Belize that if the ends of the earth existed, British Honduras would most certainly be one of them. And at the very end of the end of the earth sits Punta Gorda. Long accessible by sea alone, this isolated seaport in the far south of the country is now linked to the rest of the country by the **Southern Highway**. This fine road of red earth runs alongside the wooded slopes of the Maya Mountains to end at "PG", a gateway to Guatemala just the other side of Amatique Bay. It is worth spending a bit of time in this region where a tradition of hospitality going back to the 19C has created a rich mosaic of cultures with Garifunas, Chinese, East Indians (from the subcontinent) and Maya.

## A walk around town
*Allow 1hr.*

On Wednesdays and Sundays the **market** held near Punta Gorda's main square livens up with the arrival of villagers, mainly Mopán and Kekchi, from the surrounding hamlets, in an atmosphere reminiscent of a Guatemalan village. The rest of the time "PG" is a nonchalant place with two assets: a delightful sea breeze and a few terraces for having a drink. The hours slide peacefully by: a dawn stroll down **Front Street**, the seafront, breakfast at the Morning Glory Café facing the ocean, savouring an ice-cream at Marenco's with its terrace on **Main Street**.

## Around Punta Gorda
*Allow 2 days.*

Toledo District with its high percentage of indigenous people provides an opportunity to discover the Mayan world of yesterday and today through its villages and the archeological sites tucked away in luxuriant natural surroundings.

### A tour of the villages*
*An organised excursion solves the problem of inadequate public transport. Take walking shoes, a long-sleeved t-shirt, a swimsuit, a waterproof, mosquito repellent and a torch. English/Spanish guides.*

Two associations *(see "Making the most of Punta Gorda")* have set up development aid programmes for the region's communities, providing accommodation and meals with local inhabitants; a unique opportunity to share in the daily life of a Mayan or Garifuna community, discover local dances and music, listen to traditional tales, go out with fishermen, discover medicinal plants in the tropical forest, explore caves, visit archeological sites or swim in waterfall pools.

Punta Gorda

*The little Garifuna port of Barranco and a dozen Mopán and Kekchi communities around San Antonio take part in this programme. Since visitors' financial contributions go almost entirely to the village where they stay, a rotating system has been set up to share revenue out equitably among all the communities taking part. Visitors therefore have no choice as to where they stay but are of course free to choose their activities and the length of their stay.*

## Lubaantun

*30km north-west of Punta Gorda. Not accessible by public transport. Buses on the way to Belize City drop passengers at the Shell petrol station, 21km from Punta Gorda on the Southern Highway. Leave the main road to your right and continue straight on for 2.5km. The right-hand track leads to San Pedro Columbia, approximately 4km further on, from which a path leads 2.5km to the site. 8am-4pm. Fee.*

### The crystal skull

Anna, the adopted daughter of archeologist F A Mitchell-Hedges, who came on a British Museum assignment in 1926, discovered a crystal skull on the Lubaantum site on her 17th birthday. The origin of this artefact is still unknown, but the coincidence in dates has made the specialists doubt – archeological treasure or simple birthday present? The head is still in the possession of Anna Mitchell-Hedges, in Canada.

The "place of the fallen stones" lives up to its name since these ruins have not yet been fully restored. The site, which was the region's most important during the **Late Classic period** (730-890 AD), is still imprisoned by vegetation in a natural setting that increases the pleasure of the trip. From the top of **Pyramid 12** there is a fabulous view of the Maya Mountains. A major feature of Lubaantum is that no mortar was used in its construction, the stones being cut to fit into each other. Excavations have brought to light five squares and religious, ceremonial and residential buildings arrayed in concentric order.

## Nim Li Punit

*30km northwest of Punta Gorda. On the Southern Highway, 1km after the village of Big Fall, a track goes off to the west. The site entrance is 1km from the main road. To get there, take a bus going to Belize City. Start early enough in the morning to continue by the next service, if you are heading north. Otherwise, if returning to Punta Gorda, you will have to hitch-hike or wait for the afternoon bus from Belize City to get back. Take a picnic for the wait. 8am-4pm. Fee.*

This city-state, which also flourished during the **Late Classic period**, was apparently connected with neighbouring Lubaantun. Nim Li Punit was discovered in 1976; of the 25 **stelae** found here, no less than 8 are carved in bas-relief. Unfortunately the site has been extensively looted.

## Making the most of Punta Gorda

### COMING AND GOING

**By plane** – The airstrip is at the end of Prince St, a 5min walk from the town centre. The two national airline companies are both here. **Maya Island Air**, ☎ (07)22856 flies four times a day both ways between Punta Gorda and Belize City (55min) with stopovers in Dangriga and Placencia. The same goes for **Tropic Air**, ☎ (07)22008.

**By bus – James Bus Service**, 7 King St, ☎ (07)22049, runs just one daily service between "PG" and Belize City (8hr) via Mango Creek (3hr), Dangriga (5hr) and

Belmopan (6hr30min). The **Z-Line** offices, José María Nuñez St, ☎ (07) 22165, are in the reception area of the Traveller's Inn hotel. Four departures a day for Belize City between 5am and 3.30pm.

**By boat – Requena's Charter Service**, 12 Front St, ☎ (07)22070, runs a daily service leaving at 9am for Puerto Barrios (Guatemala). The jetty is near the Toledo Visitors' Information Centre. Customs formalities and departure tax payment at the Customs Department, Front St, ☎ (07)22023.

## GETTING AROUND

**By rental bike** – The Mangrove Inn restaurant and Nature's Way hotel rent out bicycles.

## ADDRESS BOOK

**Tourist information** – The town has a **Tourist Information Centre**, Front St, opposite the market. 8.30am-12noon / 1pm-6pm; closed Saturday afternoons and Sundays. There is also the **Toledo Visitors' Information Centre**, Front St, opposite the police station, ☎ (07)22470. 7am-12noon; closed Sundays.

**Bank / Currency Exchange – Belize Bank**, 30 Main St, on Central Park. 8am-1pm (Fridays 4.30pm); closed weekends.

**Post office / Telephone** – Post office on Front St, opposite the jetty; closed weekends. The **BTL** telephone company is on the corner of King St and Main St.

**Medical service – Punta Gorda Hospital**, south end of Main St, ☎ (07)22026.

**Laundry – Punta Gorda Laundry Services**, 2 Prince St.

## WHERE TO STAY

*Under US$15*

**Nature's Way Guest House**, 65 Front St, ☎ (07)22119, Fax (07)22199, thfec@btl.net – 5rm ⌖ ✗ This small house on the seafront, hidden by an untidy garden, is much appreciated by backpackers and foreign volunteers come to take part in aid programmes for the region's communities. Its veranda is a convivial place where guests like to meet up to exchange travel experiences and information on the region. The all-wood rooms with their bunk beds give this guesthouse the look of a pleasant country hostel. Spartan accommodation at a low price.

*US$20-30*

**Saint Charles Inn**, 23 King St, ☎ (07)22149 – 13rm ⌖ TV A very central hotel offering rooms (with or without private bathroom) that are quite acceptable for the prices asked. Somewhat nonchalant reception.

**Charlton's Inn**, 9 Main St, ☎ (07)22197, Fax (07)22471 – 19rm ⌖ ⌖ TV This functional, well-kept hotel has 2 prices depending on room category. The larger rooms have air conditioning. Reasonable prices for Belize.

**Punta Caliente Hotel**, 108 José María Nuñez St, ☎ (07)22561 – 8rm ⌖ ⌖ TV ✗ This hotel near the bus station is run by a Garifuna who is passionately interested in his ancestors' culture. He will certainly explain to you his collection of traditional objects on display in the dining room. The rooms are unremarkable but comfortable (2 prices depending on bedding). From the flat roof there is a panoramic view over sea and mountains.

*Around US$70*

**Traveller's Inn**, José María Nuñez St, ☎ (07)22568, Fax (07)22814 – 8rm ⌖ ⌖ TV CC The best hotel in Punta Gorda overlooks the bus station. Despite the comfort of the rooms and the pleasantness of the staff, the place has an impersonal atmosphere. The price includes breakfast.

## EATING OUT, HAVING A DRINK

*Under US$10*

**Cafeteria El Café**, North St, almost on the corner of Main St, 6am-2pm / 6pm-10pm; Sundays 7am-2pm / 7pm-10pm. This local cafeteria is worth a special mention for its irreproachable cleanliness and courteous service. Early in the morning they serve a good breakfast at the counter or in the dining room. The lunch-time and dinner menu includes traditional dishes (fried chicken or rice and beans) that are excellent value for money.

**Morning Glory Café**, corner of Front St and Prince St, ☎ 7am-3pm / 6.30pm-10pm; closed Sundays from noon. Flexible opening hours depending on the owner's schedule! Sitting at 1 of the 2 tables that only just fit on the tiny terrace, you have the best view in Punta Gorda, with the Caribbean Sea stretching to infinity. A good place for breakfast.

**Marenco's Ice Cream Parlour & Restaurant**, 57 Main St, almost on the junction with Clement St, ☎ 10am-12noon / 5.30pm-10pm; closed Sunday mornings. This terrace on the main street is as popular with locals as it is with tourists. The limited menu (fried chicken or chow-mein) is well compensated for by the varied selection of milk-shakes and ice-creams. Cheap, generously-portioned dishes.

*US$10-20*

**Mangrove Inn**, Front St, north of the Texaco filling station, ☎ (07)39910 ☎ 11am-11pm (Fridays and Saturdays to 1am); closed Mondays. Punta Gorda's fashionable restaurant has a pleasant seafront terrace (the dining room is horribly austere). Fish specialities and international cuisine at reasonable prices. Customers are mainly foreigners.

## OTHER THINGS TO DO

**Excursions** – Two agencies organise stays in Mayan or Garifuna villages. Go to Nature's Way Guest House to contact the **Toledo Tourism Association**, 65 Front St, ☎ (07)22680, Fax (07)22199, ttea@btl.net. This programme includes a variety of activities in and around a village, accommodation in a guest house and meals taken with different families. **Dem Dats Doin** (same contact details as the Toledo Visitors' Information Centre) offers total immersion in the daily life of a village, with food and accommodation with locals in basic conditions. Contact Nature's Way to organise sea outings, in particular to the islets off Punta Gorda.

The Morning Glory Café terrace in Punta Gorda

F Dyan

**Making the most of Punta Gorda**

# COROZAL
Capital of Corozal District – Pop approx 9 000
140km from Belize City and 14km from the Mexican border

**Not to be missed**
Sunrise over the bay.
**And remember...**
Mosquito repellent and long sleeves are essential for visiting
the archeological sites – the mosquitoes are voracious.

Fourteen kilometres south of the border, Corozal bathes in an atmosphere that is more Mexican than Caribbean. The mariachi guitars cover the beat of the punta, there are more Mestizos than Creoles and you hear more Spanish than English spoken; a gentle transition for travellers coming from or going on to Yucatán.

## Between Belize and Mexico
Almost 4 000 years have gone by since the founding of **Santa Rita**, formerly Chetumal *(not to be confused with the modern Mexican town of the same name on the other side of the border)*. Apart from its role as trading centre for commerce between the Highlands and Lowlands in pre-Columbian times, the Corozal region was also a meeting point between Belizean and Mexican history in the days of colonisation. During the **War of the Castes**, which in the mid-19C set Mayas against whites in the Yucatán peninsula, the town took in a large number of Yucatecan refugees. This sudden flood of immigrants accelerated British domination *(see p 290)* and transformed the physiognomy of the region, which developed a prosperous economy based on sugar cane. In 1955, however, **Hurricane Janet** devastated crops and swept away a fair part of Corozal. Despite the recent reconstruction, which has deprived it of the charm of the older towns, Corozal is still an attractive spot, mainly thanks to its bay surrounded by the waving cohune palm trees (*corozo* in Spanish) that have given the region its name.

## Visiting the town
*Allow at least half a day including a visit to the Mayan sites.*

A look around Corozal takes no longer than an hour or two, and the ruins of Santa Rita are even within walking distance, not far from the town centre. Unlike a good number of other places in Belize, here it seems a real effort is being made to highlight the local heritage.

## The centre of Corozal
Its main square holds the church and administrative buildings, including the **town hall** (Palacio Municipal) on 1st Street. An immense **fresco★** *(see photo p 291)* painted by the artist Manuel Villamor Reyes covers an entire wall of the main hall. Council employees are more than happy to comment on the work in detail. This second version, dating from 1986 and restored in 1994, relates the history of Corozal from the War of the Castes to the present day. The green whirlwind in the centre represents Hurricane Janet, which destroyed the town in 1955. By way of a signature, the artist has painted a self-portrait in the bottom right-hand corner.

*Go down 1st St to the sea leaving the town hall on the right, then turn right and walk along the bay for about 100m.*

G. Cozzi/ANA

Caribbean houses on Corozal bay

On the edge of the bay, the former **Customs House**, newly repainted in orange and green and a symbol of the place, houses the **Corozal Cultural Centre** (*9am-12noon / 1pm-4.30pm; closed Sundays and Mondays. Fee*). Temporary exhibitions and a permanent collection share the premises. Everyday utensils, a model of a Mayan hut and a section devoted to sugar evoke the history of the region. The town is also hoping to be able to exhibit archeological artefacts discovered at nearby sites. In the centre of the building, a fine cast iron **staircase★** imported from England in the 19C leads up to a belvedere.

### The Santa Rita archeological site
*1.5km northeast of the town centre on the road to the Mexican border. 9am-5pm. Fee.*

This site was inhabited from sometime in the 2nd millennium BC until the Late Post-Classic period. Situated near the ocean, the Río Hondo and the New River, the former **Chetumal** acted as a trading centre for commerce between the Yucatán and the rest of the Mayan sphere of influence. Such a strategic location could not fail to arouse the cupidity of the conquistadors, who made an unsuccessful attempt to take control of the city in 1531. Having failed, they settled at Bacalar, barring the route between Yucatán and Chetumal/Santa Rita. Deprived of this vital communication link, the city's population started to decline in the middle of the 16C.

Despite its long history, this Mayan site has only a few structures left, as the stone was used to build the town of Corozal in the 19C. One restored **temple**, however, dating from the Classic period, still offers a grand panoramic view over the bay.

## Across the bay

A second archeological site, easily accessible from Corozal, is of greater interest than Santa Rita because it is on the other side of the bay; visitors have the additional pleasure of crossing the mouth of the **New River** (*see "Making the most of Corozal"*).

**Corozal**

## Los Cerros (hills)★

*Site accessible via a long track through Progresso and Copper Bank during the dry season only. The 15min boat trip is much pleasanter and considerably quicker. 9am-5pm. Fee.*

A crossroads for sea trading in jade and obsidian, Los Cerros was occupied during the **Late Pre-Classic period** (400 BC-250 AD). This archeological site is based around several ceremonial squares but most of the structures have not yet been excavated. The tallest of these "hills", 22m high, overlooks the whole bay; an exceptional situation which has unfortunately caused some of the monuments to deteriorate, as they are flooded each time the water level rises and are subject to intense erosion. The giant stucco masks discovered by archeologists on the façades of two temples have had to be walled up again to protect them.

# Making the most of Corozal

## COMING AND GOING

**By air** – The landing strip is 5km south of Corozal. *Tropic Air* and *Maya Island Air* each fly three times a day between San Pedro and Corozal (20min). For Belize City change at San Pedro. Taxis await passengers getting off the planes (BZ$5 to the town centre).

**By bus** – Both the companies that run between Belize City and Chetumal (Mexico) stop at Orange Walk and Corozal. *Venus Bus Line*, ☎ (04)22132, 7th Ave, on the corner of 1st St South: buses going to Belize City (3hr) stop about every hour between 4am and 11.30am. They then go back to Chetumal (1hr) between 2.30pm and 8.30pm. *Batty Brothers Bus Service*, ☎ (04)23034, 13 4th Ave, on the corner of 4th St North: frequent buses 7am-2pm and two departures in the afternoon to Chetumal. For Belize City, three buses only in the mornings, then every hour between 12noon and 7.30pm.

## GETTING AROUND

**By taxi** – Taxis wait on the main square. *Corozal Taxi Association*, ☎ (04)22035. Allow BZ$3 for a town fare.

**By rental car** – Vehicles for hire from *Tony's Inn & Resort* (see "Where to stay").

## ADDRESS BOOK

**Tourist information** – Stéphane Moerman, owner of Café Kela, runs the Belize Tourism Industry Association's Corozal office. A Frenchman who has lived here for many years, he knows the area like the back of his hand. Information is also available from the *Corozal Cultural Centre*, near the market.

**Bank / Currency Exchange** – *Atlantic Bank*, Park St South. *Belize Bank*, on the corner of 5th Ave and 1st St North, on the main square. *Bank of Nova Scotia*, 4th Ave. All three have the same opening hours: 8am-1pm and Fridays 3pm-6pm; closed weekends.

**Post office / Telephone** – The post office is on the main square. *BTL* is on 2nd St South.

**Airline companies** – The Maya hotel is the official representative of *Maya Island Air* in Corozal. *Tropic Air*, South End, ☎ (04)22725.

**Laundry** – Laundry service at Nestor's Hotel.

## WHERE TO STAY

*Under US$25*

**Nestor's Hotel**, 123 5th Ave, ☎ (04)22354 – 23rm 🛏️ 🍴 The rooms in this hotel are spartan but clean. Light sleepers beware, at night the bar on the ground floor gets particularly lively during karaoke evenings and weekend concerts.

**Hotel Maya**, South End, PO Box 112, ☎ (04)22082, Fax (04)22827 – 19rm 🛏️ 🍴 ✗ cc This place is starting to look a bit worn. Simple accommodation of no special interest, but it has a warm family atmosphere. Ask for a room upstairs with a view of the sea.

*US$30-50*

🛏️ **Hok'ol K'in Guest House**, PO Box 145, corner of 4th Ave and 3rd St South, ☎ (04)23329 / 22967, Fax (04)23569, maya@btl.net – 9rm 🛏️ 🍴 ✗ cc The architecture of the building gives all the guestrooms a view of the sea. Do not miss sunrise ("Hok'ol K'in" in Maya) over the ocean. The rooms are comfortable, soberly decorated and impeccably maintained, and all have a balcony. Each has two double beds and can sleep up to four (the price is the same for 2, 3 or 4 people). There is also a kitchen and shared lounge with TV for the use of guests.

*US$50-80*

**Tony's Inn & Resort**, South End, PO Box 12, ☎ (04)22055 / 23555, Fax (04)22829, tonys@btl.net – 24rm 🛏️ 🍴 ✗ 🌿 🅿️ cc Corozal's classiest hotel is 2km south of the town. Pleasant setting facing the sea. The rooms are spacious and have every comfort (air conditioning, TV and telephone for the deluxe category).

## EATING OUT, HAVING A DRINK

Not a lot of choice apart from Chinese cuisine or the hotel restaurants.

*Under US$10*

**Gongora's Pastry & Pizza**, corner of 5th Ave and 1st St. 8am-9pm; Sundays 9am-12noon / 4pm-8pm. On Corozal's central square, a very simple cafeteria much appreciated by the locals. You can satisfy your appetite for sweet (excellent pastries) or savoury (pizzas) at any hour of the day.

🍴 **Le Café Kela**, 37 1st Ave, ☎ (04)22833. 11am-2.30pm / 5.30pm-9pm; closed Sundays. The most charming of places to make a halt, under a thatched roof in a garden facing the sea. The owner of this friendly restaurant is Stéphane Moerman, a Frenchman who is also a nurseryman and Corozal's tourist office representative and guide. He and his Belizean wife make the most of their cultural mix in the kitchen: Caribbean flavours rub shoulders with crêpes suzette, "croque-monsieur" and "cassoulet", all washed down with a glass of Perrier.

## OTHER THINGS TO DO

**Excursions –** The Cerros archeological site across the bay is easily reached by motor launch (BZ$70 for 2 people) or dinghy (BZ$40 for 2). Interesting excursions on the New River with its wealth of flora and fauna.

**Making the most of Corozal**

# ORANGE WALK
Capital of Orange Walk District – Pop approx 12 000
90km from Belize City on the Northern Highway

**Not to be missed**
The New River excursion to Lamanai.
**And remember...**
Avoid visiting Lamanai on Thursdays,
the day the cruise operators take their groups to the site.

Under its sleepy exterior, Orange Walk is in fact the most populated place in northern Belize. This stopover town on the Northern Highway, halfway between Belize City and Mexico, does not itself hold a lot of interest for tourists, but its location on the west bank of the New River makes it the best base from which to travel up-river in the wake of the ancient Maya.

## A quick look around town
*Allow 1hr.*

Orange Walk has no tourist sights but most of the places useful to visitors are to be found on **Queen Victoria Avenue** (also referred to as the **Belize-Corozal Road**), the main thoroughfare running north-south through the town. For many years the place had a bad reputation because of the cannabis plantations in this region of sugar cane and citrus fruits. The United States successfully put pressure on the Belize authorities to clamp down on this activity, and since then, apart from the music being slightly louder than in the rest of the country, its streets have settled back into their provincial calm.

Like Corozal, Orange Walk is a real mosaic of ethnic groups. Alongside the *Mestizos*, descendants of the Yucatecan refugees from the War of the Castes (*see p 356 "Corozal"*), can be found Creoles, Chinese - and Mennonites, living in rural communities along the New River.

**The Mennonites**
Adepts of an Anabaptist sect founded in Switzerland in 1536 by the cleric Menno Simonsz, the Mennonites of Orange Walk and Cayo District settled here from the late 1950s. Their ancestors emigrated to Canada in the 17C. Headscarves and long skirts for the women, cowboy hats and dungarees for the men, blue eyes, blond hair and a dialect that reminds us of their Swiss and Dutch origins – they certainly stand out from the rest of the population. The members of these isolated rural communities reject the modern world and interpret the Bible very strictly, devoting themselves to their farmwork, going into town only to sell their produce and reducing their contacts with other inhabitants to the absolute minimum.

## The archeological sites in the area

The sites discovered around Orange Walk are some of the most important in the Mayan world. Still buried beneath thick vegetation, these ruins are unfortunately not very evocative. However, Lamanai is worth having a look at, if just for the boat trip to get there.

### Cuello
*6km west of Orange Walk on Yo Creek Road. The site is on private property so visitors must obtain permission to visit from the Cuello Brothers Distillery, ☎ (03)22141. 8am-5pm; closed weekends. No fee.*

The provincial calm of Orange Walk

For the layman Cuello is nothing spectacular, but amateur archeologists should definitely have a look. The oldest Mayan ceramic, apparently dating from 1200 BC, was found on this site inhabited from the Early Pre-Classic to the Classic period.

## Lamanai★★

*Approximately 35km south of Orange Walk by river. During the dry season the site can be reached by 60km of dirt road via San Felipe. Allow one day, including 3hr for the boat journey there and back (see "Making the most of Orange Walk"). It is advisable to hire a guide to fully appreciate the site and its natural setting. 8am-5pm. Fee.*

A trip up the **New River★** from Orange Walk to Lamanai is a journey through time, back to the era when the ancient Maya used this essential waterway for trading. On the way you will discover the region's abundant flora and fauna. The river is dotted with water lilies and its banks overgrown with a tangle of water plants, a haven for numerous birds and iguanas. If the boat's engine is stopped, you are sometimes lucky enough to spot a manatee or a crocodile. On reaching New River Lagoon boats can at last tie up, close by one of the most important archeological sites in Belize.

Lamanai (meaning "submerged crocodile") was probably inhabited from sometime during the first millennium BC, reaching its peak of civilization in the **Late Pre-Classic period**. In contrast to many Mayan cities, which were suddenly deserted around the 10C AD, Lamanai was still inhabited when the conquistadors arrived and remained so until the 17C. Over 700 structures have been

H. Cholmet

Lamanai's sacred animal

counted, of which barely a tenth have been excavated up until now. The major part of this ceremonial centre therefore remains buried under dense jungle, guarded by silk cotton trees, *guanacastes* (South American walnut or tobroos) and breadfruit trees.

Entrance to the site is from the north, where the **Mask Temple** stands, its façade adorned by a **mask★★** 4m high.

Further south stands the massive outline of **Temple N10-43★**. Built in the 1C BC, this is the tallest Pre-Classic structure yet identified. Sporty types can climb its 33m to enjoy a **panoramic view★★** over the New River to the Maya Mountains. At the foot of this temple is a small ball court and, nearby, a superb **stela★** portraying a ruler emerging from the jaws of a crocodile, Lamanai's sacred animal.

## Making the most of Orange Walk

### COMING AND GOING

**By bus** – **Escalante's Bus Services** and **Batty Brothers** share the same terminus on the corner of Queen Victoria Ave and St Peter St, ☎ (03)22858. Departures every hour between 6am and 1.30pm plus 2 buses in the afternoon for Chetumal (2hr). 2 buses in the morning then approx every hour between 1pm and 8.30pm for Belize City (90min). **Venus** buses, Queen Victoria Ave, leave for Belize City every hour 5am-12.30pm, then stop by on their way back to Chetumal between 1.30pm and 8.30pm. 4 buses for Belize City leave **Urbina's Bus Service**, Main St, ☎ (03)22048, between 6.30am and 8am.

### GETTING AROUND

**By bus** – Drivers on the Orange Walk-Belize City route let passengers off at Toll Bridge, from where the excursions to Lamanai leave.

**By taxi** – Taxis wait on the right of the Town Hall, on Queen Victoria Ave (continuation of the Belize-Corozal Rd). **Taxi Association**, ☎ (03)22560. **Taxi Union**, ☎ (03)22050.

### ADDRESS BOOK

**Tourist information** – The **Tourist Information Centre** kiosk is on the bank of the New River, near the church. Its opening hours being somewhat irregular, contact the Jungle River Tours agency (see "Other things to do").

**Bank / Currency Exchange** – **Belize Bank** and **Bank of Nova Scotia**, on the corner of Main St and Park St, on Central Park. Traveller's cheques can be cashed at the New River Park Hotel.

**Post office / Telephone** – The post office is on Hospital Crescent St, near the market. **BTL** is on the corner of Park St and Lovers' Lane, on Central Park.

Making the most of Orange Walk

## WHERE TO STAY

### • Town centre

*US$25-40*

**St Christopher's Hotel**, 10 Main St, ☎ (03)21064 – 11rm ⚹ ⤬ TV In a quiet street near the Batty Brothers bus station, this is the most acceptable hotel in Orange Walk. All the rooms are big, comfortable and well-kept, but on the ground floor they are dark. Opt for those on the 1st floor, slightly more expensive, with a view over the New River at the bottom of the garden (some have air conditioning).

**Mi Amor Hotel**, PO Box 117, 19 Belize-Corozal Rd, ☎ (03)22031, Fax (03)23462 – 12rm ⚹ ⤬ TV CC An uninspiring building on Orange Walk's main street. Its functional rooms can be useful if in a spot. The disco on the ground floor is noisy.

*US$40-60*

**D*Victoria Hotel**, PO Box 74, 40 Belize-Corozal Rd, ☎ (03)22518, Fax (03)22847 – 31rm ⚹ ▤ ⤬ ⤫ CC Apart from the air conditioning, nothing really justifies choosing this hotel, even though it was long considered the best hotel in town. Like the Mi Amor Hotel, the noise of the disco is likely to keep you awake until very late.

### • Tower Hill

*US$25-40*

**New River Park Hotel**, PO Box 34, Belize-Corozal Rd, ☎ (03)23987, Fax (03)23789 – 6rm ⚹ ⤬ ✗ CC 7km south of Orange Walk, just before reaching Toll Bridge; the hotel stands beside the New River. Two types of accommodation at different prices in a pleasant rustic setting: the economy rooms (with rather tatty bathrooms) are not as comfortable as the superior category (with TV and air conditioning).

## EATING OUT

Snacks are to be had in the little eateries in the market, on the corner of Main St and Hospital Crescent St.

*Under US$10*

**Juanita's Restaurant**, 8 Santa Ana St, ☎ (03)22677. 6am-2pm / 6pm-9pm; closed public holidays. A friendly little neighbourhood restaurant serving cheap local cuisine. Where the early risers meet for breakfast.

**Park Plaza Restaurant**, Central Park. 10am-10pm; Fridays and Saturdays to 12midnight; Sundays 2pm-10pm. Blue neon marks the entrance to this cafeteria with its unprepossessing exterior. Inside there are hamburgers, sandwiches, rice & beans, chow-mein, chicken curry – simple, acceptable dishes. No smoking.

*US$10-20*

**The Diner**, 37 Clarke St, ☎ (03)23753. 8am-9pm; Fridays and Saturdays 11.30am-11pm; Sundays 7am-8.30pm. This restaurant outside the centre is difficult to get to so it is better to take a taxi. The friendly surroundings make it feel more like a table d'hôte. Despite a limited menu it serves the most refined Belizean specialities and international dishes in town. The staff is particularly pleasant. The Diner II, a branch right in the centre of town, would seem to be closed for good.

## GOING OUT, HAVING A DRINK

**Discos –** The discos in the **Mi Amor** and **D*Victoria** hotels are packed out every weekend.

## OTHER THINGS TO DO

**Excursions –** Orange Walk is an excellent base for excursions on the New River to Lamanai archeological site. Boats tie up at Toll Bridge, 7km south of Orange Walk. To benefit fully from the visit, take a professional guide. Information from **Jungle River Tours**, 20 Lovers' Lane, Central Park, ☎ (03) 22293 / 20348, Fax (03)22201. Avoid Thursdays, the day the cruise organisers take their groups to the site. **Reyes & Sons River Tours**, ☎ (03)23327, is at Toll Bridge.

**Making the most of Orange Walk**

# BELMOPAN
Capital of Belize
Cayo District – Pop approx 6 000
82km from Belize City and 38km from San Ignacio

**Not to be missed**
Your bus.
Belize Zoo.

**And remember...**
It is pleasanter to stay in San Ignacio than in Belmopan,
and to do the round trip in a day.
NB most embassies and consulates are in Belize City.

Belmopan, Belize's Brasilia. Sitting at the intersection of the Western Highway and the Hummingbird Highway, the country's new capital (since 1971) was built from scratch ten years after Belize City was destroyed by Hurricane Hattie. This artificial creation is reflected in the location chosen – the geographical centre of the country – and the choice of name, a combination of the words *Belize* and *Mopán* (the largest Mayan ethnic group in the country). With barely 10 % of the number of inhabitants planned, this underpopulated "modern" town remains a ghost town, for Belmopan's civil servants prefer to return to Belize City every evening. Only another devastating tropical storm along the coast might convince them to leave their old capital.

## Going through the capital

Travellers in a hurry can make do with just driving through Belmopan. The district jokingly known as the "town centre" is laid out around the **bus station** and the **market**, a piece of land surrounded by austere concrete administrative buildings. As for the other districts, they are of very limited interest. The wide avenues on which sun and rain beat down are hardly an invitation to stroll around, and the distances make taxis necessary.

Amateur archeologists can pay a visit to the administrative district behind the bus station. Most of Belize's national treasures are shut away in the **vault** of the **Archeology Department** (*Mondays, Wednesdays, Fridays 1.30pm-4.30pm, by appointment only,* ☎ *(08)22106 / 22227*).

History enthusiasts can take a look at the period documents and old photos in the **Belize Archives Department** (*8am-12noon / 1pm-4.30pm; closed weekends,* ☎ *(08)22097 / 22247*).

## On the way to Belize City
*These sites are easily reached from Belize City or San Ignacio.*

### Guanacaste National Park
*2km north of Belmopan, at the intersection of the Western Highway with the Hummingbird Highway. 8am-5pm. Fee.*

This national park through which Belize River and Roaring Creek flow owes its name to a *guanacaste* (South American walnut or tobroos) tree over 150 years old that stands near the park entrance. Along the trails that have been laid out, visitors can try to recognise some of the hundred species of birds that nest in this forest. Luggage should include a picnic and swimsuit.

Belmopan

## Belize Zoo★★

*Half-way between Belmopan (34km) and Belize City (48km) on the Western Highway. Buses running between the 2 towns drop visitors at the zoo entrance. 9am-4.30pm. Fee.*

This place may well reconcile you to zoos. Founded twenty-odd years ago to house retired "stars" of animal films, it now has around a hundred permanent guests including several endangered species. Among others can be seen Belize's national emblems: the **Baird's tapir**, nicknamed the "mountain cow", and the **toucan**. The natural habitat of each animal has been scrupulously respected, so visitors need to be patient in order to spot a jaguar or puma hidden away in its mini-forest, an eagle perched in the top of a tree, a group of howler monkeys invisible among the branches – a real game of hide-and-seek that adds to the enjoyment of the visit.

# Making the most of Belmopan

### COMING AND GOING

**By bus** – The capital is in the centre of the country, at the intersection of the major north-south and east-west road routes. Most buses coming from and going to Belize City (see the practical section of that town) stop at Belmopan bus terminus, on Market Square.

### GETTING AROUND

**By taxi** – *Taxi Service*, ☎ (08)23025, vehicles wait on Market Square.

### ADDRESS BOOK

**Bank / Currency Exchange** – *Belize Bank* and *Barclay's Bank* are on Market Square. 8am-1pm, plus Fridays 3pm-6pm; closed weekends.

**Post office / Telephone** – Post office and *BTL* telephone company near Market Square.

**Consulates / Embassies** – *The British High Commission*, Embassy Square (Ring Road), PO Box 91, ☎ (08)22146/7, Fax (08)22761, brithicom@btl.net Mondays-Thursdays 8am-12noon / 1pm-4pm; Fridays 8am-2pm; closed weekends.

### WHERE TO STAY, EATING OUT

The capital offers little of tourist interest and the hotels are relatively expensive for what they offer.

*Around US$50*

**Circle A Hotel**, 35-37 Halfmoon Ave, ☎ (08)20679, Fax (08)22309 – 10rm ⁴ 🛏 ✕ cc East of the town centre, this modest hotel run by a Chinese family provides rooms with basic comfort. Air conditioning on payment of a supplement. Karaoke evenings organised in the dining room.

*Around US$60*

**Belmopan Hotel**, intersection of Bliss Parade and Constitution Drive, ☎ (08)22327, Fax (08)23066 – 20rm ⁴ 🗐 🛏 📺 ✕ 🏊 cc This hotel is opposite Market Square, near the bus stop and the administrative district. Acceptable rooms but not very enticing.

**Bull Frog Inn**, PO Box 28, 25 Halfmoon Ave, ☎ (08)22111 – 14rm ⁴ 🗐 🛏 📺 ✕ cc This hotel in pleasant surroundings has two categories of accommodation. The more expensive rooms, with telephone and balcony, open onto a lawn. Good restaurant.

# SAN IGNACIO★
## (CAYO)
Capital of Cayo District – Pop 8 000
116km west of Belize City
16km from the border post of Benque Viejo del Carmen

**Not to be missed**
Exploring Mountain Pine Ridge.
**And remember...**
Plan on two nights in San Ignacio to visit the area.
Join a guided tour to visit Mountain Pine Ridge.

Just 16km from the border, San Ignacio is a dream oasis for travellers coming from or going to Guatemala. With its head in the hills and its feet washed by the Macal River, this town in its attractive setting at the entrance to one the loveliest regions in Belize, is a meeting-point for lovers of archeology and nature.

## Visiting the town
*Allow half a day including a visit to Cahal Pech.*

The capital of Cayo District is a favourite place for backpackers. Beneath its Far West village veneer, San Ignacio offers not only cheap hotels but also a lively atmosphere on **Burns Avenue** and **West Street**, its two main streets lined with slightly lopsided wooden houses. Apart from travellers, this land-locked *cayo* (cay = islet) has an incalculable number of communities which at some time or another in their history have ended up here. Sri Lankans, Cubans, Britons, Americans and Guatemalans have all gradually merged into the population.

East of San Ignacio, the metal **Hawkesworth Bridge** spans the Macal River on its way to **Santa Elena**. Those looking for peace and quiet may well be tempted by this "twin", less touristy but also less picturesque.

### The Cahal Pech site
*South of the town centre, turn right at the police station and go up Buena Vista Rd for about 800m. Go 100m past the Piache hotel and take the road left for another 800m to the site entrance. The attendant at the entrance will lend you a map of the site. 5.30am-6.30pm. Fee.*

Sitting in splendid isolation on a wooded hill overlooking the town, the other-worldly Cahal Pech is a strange place for a stroll: you have to fight your way up stone stairways and along corridors imprisoned in a tangle of plant life. This city, occupied from the Pre-Classic era (around 1000 BC) to the Late Classic (about 800 AD), has over thirty ruined palaces and temples set around seven ceremonial squares.

The **museum** at the entrance to the site houses an interesting collection of ceramic, jade and obsidian items, including a fine **mask** in a mosaic of jade and shells, the central decoration from some dignitary's belt.

San Ignacio

# Towards the Guatemalan border

*Buses every 30min between San Ignacio and the border.*

## Xunantunich★★

*11km west of San Ignacio. Ask the bus driver to drop you at the Xunantunich ruins, level with the village of San José Succotz. Cross the Mopán River by ferry then walk 1.5km up the road to the site entrance. 8am-5pm (4pm at weekends). Fee.*

This big **Classic** city, abandoned in 900 AD following an earthquake, was built around three ceremonial squares. Its ruins now stand on a lawn that seems to keep the surrounding jungle at bay. The entire site is dominated by the **Castillo**★ (castle), a 40m pyramid. This temple, recognisable by the **crenellated roofcomb** resembling the ramparts of some fortress, bore a superb stucco **frieze**★★ near the top. A fragment remains on the east side and there is a reproduction on the west side (on top of the walled-in original) depicting the Sun, the Moon, Venus and a severed head. From the top of this sanctuary there is an incomparable **panoramic view**★★ over the Maya Mountains and El Petén.

Some of the **stelae** discovered on the site are housed in a building near the entrance. You can just make out their much-deteriorated bas-reliefs.

# Mountain Pine Ridge Forest Reserve★★

*Approximately 145km round trip. Allow 1 day.*
*A 4WD is necessary in the wet season.*

Located to the northwest of the Maya Mountains, this 59 000ha nature reserve alternates between pine-clad hills and low-altitude tropical vegetation. Streams, waterfalls, cataracts and underground rivers are legion in this area of dirt tracks. A visit to explore Mountain Pine Ridge is indispensable.

## ■ Hidden Valley Falls★

*44km from San Ignacio. Go south from Santa Elena and drive 21km via San Antonio until you reach a junction. Take the dirt road to the right and after 7km fork left (the right-hand track goes to Río On) and continue for 11km. Turn left again and drive 5km to the belvedere. Fee.*

The Castillo at Xunantunich

F. Dyan

It is better to start at these falls, also known as the **Thousand Foot Falls**, so as to take advantage of the clear morning skies. From the belvedere, this impressive cataract (during the wet season, at least) can be seen in the distance, cascading 480m down to disappear into the valley below.

### ■ The Río On Pools★

*From Hidden Valley Falls, go back 16km to where the road forks and take the road left (right when coming from San Ignacio). Continue 13km to a right turn leading to the Río On 500m further on.*

During the dry season a refreshing halt at this series of shimmering blue natural pools formed by the Río On is much appreciated. The place is somewhat less enchanting during the rainy season when its waters are cloudy.

### ■ The Río Frío Caves★

*From the Río On go back to the main road and drive south for 5km to Augustine (known as the Douglas D'Silva Forestry Station). Take the track on the right for 2km to the car park in front of the entrance to the caves.*

The Río Frío flows through the biggest cave, a vast tunnel almost a kilometre long. It is possible to swim here and in some parts there are even sand banks forming little beaches. Near the car park, a nature trail goes off through the jungle *(the names of the trees are shown on signs).*

## The Caracol★ archeological site

*Allow 1 day – Access by 4WD or on horseback.*
*It is advisable to visit between January and May.*

*82km from San Ignacio. From Augustine (see above itinerary) continue south for 20km via San Luis to a turnoff 3km after the Macal River. Take the right-hand dirt road and continue 16km to the site entrance. If going there under your own steam, you must obtain a visiting permit from the Forest Office in San Antonio, ☎ (09)23280, or through the Archeology Department in Belmopan, ☎ (08)22106 /22227. 8am-5pm. Fee.*

At the end of a bumpy drive deep into the jungle beyond Mountain Pine Ridge, you come to one of the largest Mayan sites of the **Classic** period.

Discovered in 1936 by *chicleros*, these ruins buried under ten centuries of vegetation are gradually unveiling their mysteries and the grandeur of a city whose population must have reached around 150 000 at the height of its power. A sequence of glyphs inscribed on a stela in the ball court has supplied information about Caracol's influence during the reign of **Lord Water**; 562 AD marked his victory at the end of a six-year war with Tikal, and the beginning of over a century of domination of El Petén.

The ceremonial centre includes the **Caana Temple★**, the tallest pyramid in Belize, standing 42m high; close by is an immense **reservoir** still used by the archeologists during the dry season. Three of the **stelae** discovered on this site can be seen on the ground floor of the Bliss Institute in Belize City *(see p 329* "Making the most of Belize City").

# Making the most of San Ignacio

## COMING AND GOING

**By bus** – The bus station is right in the town centre opposite the market. **Batty Brothers** buses, ☎ (09)22508, leave San Ignacio every 30min between 6.30am and 1pm for Benque Viejo del Carmen (30min). From 12noon to 5pm they return to Belize City (2hr30min) via Belmopan (1hr). The schedule is reversed for **Novelo's Bus Service**, ☎ (09) 22115: buses every 30min between 4am and 11.30am for Belize City, then from 1pm to 11.30pm to Benque Viejo del Carmen.

National public transport does not cross the border. You have to get off at Benque Viejo del Carmen (BZ$7.50 departure tax) and cross the no man's land on foot to the Melchor de Mencos immigration office (30Q border tax for entry to Guatemalan territory). Taxis offer to take travellers to the bus station in the town centre, which is not necessary since the buses make a detour via the border before going on to Flores.

## GETTING AROUND

A vehicle is necessary for exploring the area around the village.

**By bus** – With the exception of the Xunantunich ruins on the San Ignacio-Benque Viejo del Carmen road, few sites can be reached by public transport.

**By private minibus** – A practical means of transport for visiting the region if you get a group together (see "Excursions").

**By taxi** – **Cayo Taxi Association** vehicles, ☎ (09)22196, wait on King St opposite the police station.

**By rental car** – **International Archeological Tours**, ☎ (09)23991, West St, near Martha's Kitchen, hires out 4WDs. The **San Ignacio Resort Hotel** is another possibility.

**By rental bike** – Mountain bikes can be hired at **Pacz Hotel** for BZ$25 a day. **Eva's Restaurant** also hires out bikes.

## ADDRESS BOOK

**Tourist information** – **Eva's Restaurant** acts as a tourist office.

**Bank / Currency Exchange** – **Atlantic Bank**, Columbus Park, opposite the police station, 8am-2pm; Saturdays 8.30am-12noon. **Belize Bank**, 16 Burns Ave, 8am-1pm (Fridays 5pm); Saturdays 9am-12noon. At the bus terminus black-market moneychangers sell quetzals, which may be useful for surviving until you find a bank in Guatemala.

**Post office / Telephone** – The post office is on the corner of Hudson St and Waight's Ave, 8am-12noon / 1pm-5pm; closed weekends. The **BTL** telephone company is on the 1st floor of the building on the corner of Church St and Eve St, near the church. 8am-12noon / 1pm-4pm; closed Saturday afternoons and Sundays.

**Top Cat Copy Centre**, 8 Hudson St, on the ground floor of the Upstairs Pollito restaurant: fax, e-mail and Internet services, daily 8.30am-9pm (Sundays 7pm). Same services available at **Eva's Restaurant**, 3pm-11pm.

**Medical service** – Near the town centre, **San Ignacio Hospital**, Hospital St, ☎ (09)22066. The **chemist** is at the north end of West St. 8am-12noon / 1pm-5pm / 7pm-9pm; closed Sunday afternoons. In an emergency, ☎ (09) 22510. **Dr Armando Betancourt** consults in West St, on the ground floor of the Hi-Et Hotel. Daily 8am-9.30am / 5pm-7pm; closed Sundays.

**Laundry** – **Martha's Laundromat**, 10 West St, at the side of the restaurant of the same name. 7am-8pm; Sundays 8.30am-2pm.

## WHERE TO STAY

• **Town centre**

*UnderUS$20*

**Tropicool Hotel**, 30 Burns Ave, ☎ (09)23052 – 12rm ⚏ A neat, well-organised hotel at the bottom of a garden. The renovated rooms on the 1st floor offer more attractive accommodation than those on the ground floor, for a minimal price difference.

**Martha's Guest House**, 10 West St, ☎ (09)23647 – 3rm ⚏ ✗ ▣ A family guesthouse with 3 rooms set around a cosy lounge. Clean, well-lit rooms and a pleasant terrace above Martha's Kitchen. This is one of the most agreeable places in San Ignacio but is often full because of its limited number of rooms.

**Hi-Et Hotel**, 12 West St, ☎ (09)22828 – 5rm ✕ A typical wooden house with a pretty veranda on the street side. Clean rooms that nevertheless look a little tired.

**Pacz Hotel**, 4 Far West St, ☎ (09)22110, pacz@btl.net – 5rm ✕ Impeccably kept rooms around a TV lounge. This guesthouse is one of the most comfortable in its category. If no-one answers the door, go to the owners' house across the alley, on the same side of the street.

● **Above San Ignacio**
Take the road to the Cahal Pech archeological site, along Buena Vista Rd to the right of the police station.

*Around US$25*
**Piache Hotel**, Buena Vista Rd, ☎ (09)22032 – 9rm ✱ ✕ ✗ CC Halfway between the village and the Cahal Pech ruins, this hotel in its quiet garden offers simple, well-kept rooms.

**Cahal Pech Cabins**, ☎ (09)23380 – 9rm ✱ ✕ TV CC Little wooden cabins close to the Cahal Pech site, overlooking the valley. Pleasant, rustic accommodation for those looking for peace and quiet.

*Around US$40*
**Rose's Guest House**, 1178 Lamanai St, ☎ (09)22282 – 5rm ✱ ✕ A white and green building perched on the hill before you reach the Cahal Pech ruins. This friendly bed & breakfast has spacious, well-cared for rooms. The owner, a former primary teacher passionately fond of cooking, serves excellent traditional breakfasts in the family dining room or on the terrace. She is planning to open a tea-room soon.

*US$60-100*
**San Ignacio Resort Hotel**, Buena Vista Rd, ☎ (09)22034 / 22125, Fax (09)22134, sanighot@btl.net – 25rm ✱ ✕ ✗ ⤓ CC On the road between the village and the Cahal Pech site. San Ignacio's top-range hotel has

three categories of rooms (only the deluxe ones have air conditioning). Despite its acceptable services and delightful setting, the prices are a bit steep for the accommodation offered.

● **Santa Elena**
The village is linked to San Ignacio by the Hawkesworth Bridge.

*US$20-35*
**The Snooty Fox Guest House**, 64 George Price Ave, ☎ (09)22150, Fax (09)23556 – 6rm ✕ TV ✗ A 15min walk along the road on the left behind the suspension bridge. The bar/restaurant (open in high season) is in a wonderful site above the Macal River but unfortunately the hotel, slightly set back, does not enjoy the same view. This functional hotel consists of 2 bungalows, each with 2 rooms and a bathroom, for budget travellers. The apartment with 2 bedrooms, a lounge and a fully equipped kitchen provides the ideal formula for families.

**EATING OUT, HAVING A DRINK**
*Under US$10*
**Popular Bakery**, Burns Ave, opposite the Venus Hotel. 8am-12noon / 1pm-7pm; closed Sundays. Bread and pastries to take away for your excursions.

🍴**Martha's Kitchen**, 10 West St, at the intersection with Waight's Ave, ☎ (09)23647 ⤓ CC 7am-10.30pm. San Ignacio's most convivial restaurant. You never tire of its delightful terrace, shady during the day and prettily lit by candles in the evenings. The menu offers a varied selection of pizzas and traditional Belizean dishes accompanied in inventive ways (a simple accompaniment of rice with coconut milk becomes an absolute delight). Charming, efficient staff.

**Yesteryear Café**, corner of Waight's Ave and Burns Ave, ☎ (09)23209. 6.30am-9.30pm. Two separate entrances lead to two interconnecting dining rooms in different styles. The choice is between the little café on Waight's Ave and the cafeteria on Burns Ave with photos recounting the history of Belize on its walls. This place serves good Mexican specialities as well as local cuisine.

**Making the most of San Ignacio**

*Eva's Restaurant*, 22 Burns Ave, ☎ (09)22267 / 23325, evas@btl.net 🏠 6.30am-11pm. A victim of its own success, this place has lost its sense of hospitality. It nevertheless remains a "must" for travellers on the look-out to meet people and glean information. Sandwiches and traditional Belizean cuisine at worthwhile prices.

*Serendib Restaurant*, 27 Burns Ave, ☎ (09)22302 🏠 [CC] 10am-3pm / 6.30pm-10pm. This Sri Lankan couple who have lived in Belize for many years now successfully combines the culinary traditions of both countries. The varied, spicy dishes offer a special treat for curry lovers. The dining room leads to a charming terrace below. A warm welcome.

## OTHER THINGS TO DO

*Eva's Restaurant* offers an infinite range of things to do in the area. Enquire also at your hotel, then compare programmes and prices.

**Excursions** – Most tour operators run a now classic excursion to the Mountain Pine Ridge area, with a halt at Thousand Foot Falls, swimming in the Río On's natural pools and a visit to the Río Frío caves. If travelling during the wet season, the type of vehicle provided – a 4WD is strongly recommended – is a criterion for deciding between two agencies.

**Archeological sites** – There are guided tours to the Cahal Pech and Xunantunich ruins, but they are easy to get to by independent means. Excursions to distant archeological sites such as Caracol (access difficult during the rainy season), Altun Ha, Lamanai and Tikal (Guatemala).

**Outdoor pursuits** – The region lends itself to all sorts of outdoor pursuits. The owner of *Pacz Hotel and Tours* organises excursions of a day or more combining potholing, climbing, river trips and jungle walks. You can also rent mountain bikes here.

Kayaking down the Macal River organised by the *Snooty Fox Guest House*. Half-day or full-day pony trekking with the *Easy Rider agency* (details from Eva's Restaurant).

## SHOPPING GUIDE

**Arts and Crafts** – The souvenir and handicrafts shops line Burns Ave.

**Book shops** – The *Bakers* book shop and stationers, Burns Ave, on the right of the Tropicool Hotel, sells interesting books on Belize history and culture.

# Notes

# NOTES

# NOTES

# NOTES

# INDEX

**Chichicastenango** (Gua): place or sight described
*Arbenz (Jacobo)*: person
Ball game: explanation of term used
Health and safety (Gua): practical section

# Maps

*Manufacture Française des Pneumatiques Michelin*
Société en commandite par actions au capital de 2 000 000 000 de francs
Place des Carmes-Déchaux – 63000 Clermont-Ferrand (France)
R.C.S. Clermont-Fd B 855 200 507

© Michelin et Cie, Propriétaires-éditeurs, 2000
Dépôt légal avril 2000 – ISBN 2-06-855801-7 – ISSN 0763-1383
No part of this publication may be reproduced in any form without
the prior permission of the publisher.

**Printed in the EU 04-00/1**
Compograveur: Nord Compo – Villeneuve d'Ascq
Imprimeur: IME – Baume-les-Dames

**Cover photography:**
Guatemalan Fabrics. B. Brillion/MICHELIN
A Belizean scene. P. Duchier/EXPLORER
Tikal temple. F. Gohier/EXPLORER

# Your opinion matters!

In order to make sure that this collection satisfies the needs of our readers, please help us by completing the following questionnaire with your comments and suggestions and return to:

| **Michelin Travel Publications** | or | **Michelin Travel Publications** |
|---|---|---|
| The Edward Hyde Building | | P.O. Box 19008 |
| 38 Clarendon Road | | Greenville, SC  29602-9008 |
| Watford, UK | | USA |

## ■ YOUR HOLIDAYS/VACATIONS:

### 1. In general, when you go on holiday or vacation, do you tend to travel... (Choose one)

☐ Independently, on your own    ☐ With your family
☐ Independently, as a couple    ☐ With a group of friends
☐ With 1 or 2 friends    ☐ On organised trips

### 2. How many international holidays or vacations of 1 week or more have you taken in the last 3 years? _____

Last 3 destinations:      Month/Year:

_____      _____
_____      _____
_____      _____

### 3. What do you look for most when planning a holiday or vacation?

|  | *Not at all* | *Sometimes* | *Essential* |
|---|---|---|---|
| Somewhere new and exotic | ☐ | ☐ | ☐ |
| Real experience/meeting people | ☐ | ☐ | ☐ |
| Experiencing the wildlife/scenery | ☐ | ☐ | ☐ |
| Cultural insight | ☐ | ☐ | ☐ |
| Rest & relaxation | ☐ | ☐ | ☐ |
| Comfort & well-being | ☐ | ☐ | ☐ |
| Adventure & the unexpected | ☐ | ☐ | ☐ |

### 4. When travelling, do you take a travel guide with you?

☐ Always      ☐ Usually      ☐ Sometimes      ☐ Never

## ■ You and the Michelin NEOS guides

### 5. About your purchase of a NEOS Guide

How long was your holiday where you used the NEOS guide?
How many days? _____
For which country or countries? _____
How long before your departure did you buy it? How many days? _____

### 6. What made you choose a NEOS Guide?

*Highlight everything that applies.*

☐ Something new and interesting    ☐ Quality of the text
☐ The layout    ☐ Quality of the mapping
☐ Easy to read format    ☐ Practical Information
☐ Cultural details    ☐ Michelin quality

**7. Which sections did you use most during your holiday or vacation?**
*Score 1-4*                 *(1 = least used)*                          *(4 = most used)*

| | 1 | 2 | 3 | 4 |
|---|---|---|---|---|
| "Setting the Scene" | ☐ | ☐ | ☐ | ☐ |
| "Meeting the People" | ☐ | ☐ | ☐ | ☐ |
| "Practical Information" | ☐ | ☐ | ☐ | ☐ |
| "Exploring …" | ☐ | ☐ | ☐ | ☐ |

**8. How would you rate the following aspects of your NEOS guide?**
*Score 1-4*              *(1 = Poor)*                         *(4 = Excellent)*

| | 1 | 2 | 3 | 4 |
|---|---|---|---|---|
| Cover design | ☐ | ☐ | ☐ | ☐ |
| Chapter Order | ☐ | ☐ | ☐ | ☐ |
| Layout (photos, diagrams) | ☐ | ☐ | ☐ | ☐ |
| Ease of reading (typeface) | ☐ | ☐ | ☐ | ☐ |
| Style of writing | ☐ | ☐ | ☐ | ☐ |
| Text boxes and stories | ☐ | ☐ | ☐ | ☐ |
| Plans & Maps | ☐ | ☐ | ☐ | ☐ |
| Star ratings system | ☐ | ☐ | ☐ | ☐ |
| Format | ☐ | ☐ | ☐ | ☐ |
| Weight | ☐ | ☐ | ☐ | ☐ |
| Durability | ☐ | ☐ | ☐ | ☐ |
| Price | ☐ | ☐ | ☐ | ☐ |

**9. Did you use other travel guides during your trip?**      ☐ Yes    ☐ No
If yes, which ones? _____

**10. Please give your NEOS guide a rating out of 20:** ____/20 (with 20 as top rating)
Would you use a NEOS guide for your next trip?      ☐ Yes     ☐ No
If no, why not? _____
Which other destinations would you like NEOS to cover? _____

**11. Any other comments or suggestions:**     _____

_____

_____

_____

_____

_____

_____

---

Surname/Last Name: _____    First Name: _____

Address: _____

Age: _____    Sex: ☐ M   ☐ F

Profession: _____

Where did you purchase your NEOS Guide: What type of store?
                                          Which country?